Undiscovered owls

Title: Undiscovered owls
Subtitle: A Sound Approach guide

Text: Magnus Robb & The Sound Approach

Artwork: Håkan Delin
Artwork covers: Killian Mullarney
Sounds: Magnus Robb (MR), Arnoud B van den Berg (AB), Dick Forsman (DF), Mark Constantine (MC), Killian Mullarney (KM) and others as indicated with names in full in captions
Sonagrams: Magnus Robb, Cecilia Bosman & Mientje Petrus
Maps: Arnoud B van den Berg & Cecilia Bosman
Photographs: Arnoud B van den Berg, Dick Forsman, René Pop and others as indicated in captions

Sound editing: Magnus Robb
Photo editing & lithography: René Pop
Text editing: Arnoud B van den Berg & Mark Constantine
Graphic designers: Cecilia Bosman & Mientje Petrus

The Sound Approach: Arnoud B van den Berg, Mark Constantine & Magnus Robb

© text, design, maps, sound and sonagrams: The Sound Approach
© artwork: Håkan Delin & Killian Mullarney
© photographs: the photographers as indicated

Published by The Sound Approach, 12 Market Street, Pocle Dorset BH15 1NF, UK © 2015
Printed by Tienkamp, Groningen, the Netherlands

ISBN: 978-90-810933-7-8
NUR-code: 435

CD labels and cover: Cucumiau, Short-eared Owl, Turkish Fish Owl and Omani Owl (*Killian Mullarney*)
Fly-leaf front and back: full moon at Al Jabal Al Akhdar, A Hajar mountains, Oman, 22/23 July 2013 (*Arnoud B van den Berg*)

You can order this book by phone: +44(0)1202-641004 or online: www.soundapproach.co.uk

Undiscovered owls

A Sound Approach guide

MAGNUS ROBB & THE SOUND APPROACH

Contents

Acknowledgements   6

Introduction   9

Chapter 1: *Tyto*   12
- Common Barn Owl *T alba*   CD1-01 to CD1-12   12
- Slender-billed Barn Owl *T gracilirostris*   CD1-13 to CD1-15   25
- Madeira Barn Owl *T schmitzi*   CD1-16 to CD1-21   29
- Cape Verde Barn Owl *T detorta*   CD1-22 to CD1-28   33

Chapter 2: *Aegolius*   38
- Tengmalm's Owl *A funereus*   CD1-29 to CD1-42   38

Chapter 3: *Athene*   50
- Little Owl *A vidalii*   CD1-43 to CD1-57   50
- Cucumiau *A noctua*   CD1-58 to CD1-72   62

Chapter 4: *Surnia*   70
- Northern Hawk-Owl *S ulula*   CD1-73 to CD1-83   70

Chapter 5: *Glaucidium*   82
- Eurasian Pygmy Owl *G passerinum*   CD2-01 to CD2-11   82

Chapter 6: *Otus*   92
- Eurasian Scops Owl *O scops*   CD2-12 to CD2-24   92
- Cyprus Scops Owl *O cyprius*   CD2-25 to CD2-36   106
- Pallid Scops Owl *O brucei*   CD2-37 to CD2-48   115
- Arabian Scops Owl *O pamelae*   CD2-49 to CD2-56   125

Chapter 7: *Asio* — 132

Long-eared Owl *A otus*	CD2-57 to CD2-76	132
Short-eared Owl *A flammeus*	CD2-77 to CD2-90	146
Marsh Owl *A capensis*	CD3-01 to CD3-11	157

Chapter 8: *Bubo* — 164

Arabian Eagle-Owl *B milesi*	CD3-12 to CD3-18	164
Pharaoh Eagle-Owl *B ascalaphus*	CD3-19 to CD3-26	170
Eurasian Eagle-Owl *B bubo*	CD3-27 to CD3-46	178
Snowy Owl *B scandiacus*	CD3-47 to CD3-53	189
Turkish Fish Owl *B semenowi*	CD3-54 to CD3-70	200

Chapter 9: *Strix* — 214

Lapland Owl *S lapponica*	CD3-71 to CD3-84	214
Ural Owl *S uralensis*	CD4-01 to CD4-15	228
Tawny Owl *S aluco*	CD4-16 to CD4-31	239
Maghreb Wood Owl *S mauritanica*	CD4-32 to CD4-38	250
Hume's Owl *S butleri*	CD4-39 to CD4-56	256
Omani Owl *S omanensis*	CD4-57 to CD4-70	266

Håkan Delin's artwork — 284

Species guide to the accompanying CDs — 286

References — 287

Index — 297

Acknowledgements

The Sound Approach is a complex organism that once began as a team of three birders: Arnoud van den Berg, Mark Constantine and myself, Magnus Robb. Three more - Dick Forsman, Killian Mullarney and René Pop - have become key members over the years, and all played an important role in the preparation of this work. When the time came, our design duo - Cecilia Bosman and Mientje Petrus – converted the raw materials into book form. Cecilia also supported Arnoud on many of his recording trips, and Mo did the same for Mark. I wrote the text in the first person, borrowing extensively from the thoughts and experiences of other team members. Any mistakes are, however, my own.

Killian provided the Omani Owl and Turkish Fish Owl for the cover, as well as the Cucumiau and Short-eared Owl used on the CDs. He and Dick both recommended Håkan Delin to be the illustrator for this book. Håkan has been watching and listening to owls with meticulous attention to detail for most of his life, and his collected owl wisdom was an invaluable bonus to this project.

Three sound recordists – Johannes Honold, João Nunes and Peter Nuyten – went out and made additional sound recordings at our request. Several others had very special sounds in their collections, which they allowed us to use: Fabio Cherchi, Roland Eve, Patrick Franke, Hannu 'Honey' Jännes, Jelmer Poelstra, Davide De Rosa and Ove Stefansson. Saydisc Records gave us permission to use a recording by Ian Strange, and The Macaulay Library at the Cornell Lab of Ornithology allowed us to use recordings by Richard J Clark, William W H Gunn, David Herr, David Moyer, Leonard J Peyton, Philip Taylor and Gerrit Vyn. We have many friends at the Lab, but would like to thank Greg Budney and Matthew Young in particular for their assistance.

It would have been impossible to record and photograph owls in so many locations without a great deal of local help. We would like to thank the following people for information about where to search, assistance in the field and/or hospitality: Kari Ahola/KBP, Per Alström, Vasil Ananian, Soner Bekir, Letizia Campioni, Carlos Carrapato, Giusi De Castro, Carlos & Claudia Cruz, Hassan Dalil, Piotr Debowski, Hampus Delin, Hugues Dufourny, Isabel Fagundes, Pedro Fernandes, Inki Forsman, Sandeep Gaonkar, Dimiter Georgiev, Hamida Hammouradia & family, Heikki Henttonen, Juha Honkala, Mike Jennings, Tomasz Jezierczuk, Özcan Kilic, Erkki Korpimäki, Olli Lamminsalo, Alexandre Leitão, Lorenzo Di Lisio, Heikki Lokki, Matilde Londner, Rui Lourenço, Pedro Marques, Mireia Martín, Teresa Massarella, Łukasz Mazurek, Dave McAdams, John McLoughlin aka *Johnny Mac*, Istvan Moldovan, Colm Moore, Antonio-Roman Munoz, Seppo Niiranen, Paulo Oliveira (Parque Natural da Madeira), Lahcen Ouacha & friends, Carlos Pacheco, Nino Patti, Fabian Pekus, Vincenzo Penteriani, Antti Peuna, Geoff Phillipson, Kari Pihlajamäki, Benjam Pöntinen, Pekka Pouttu, Vladimir Pozdnyakov, Torsten Pröhl, Beneharo Rodríguez, Luis Roma, Pertti Saurola, Georg Schreier, Sebastian Siebold, Roy Slaterus, Yuri Sofronov, Qupeleio & Jennifer De Souza, Matti Suopajärvi, Ibrahim Tuncer, Aarto Tuominen, Andrew Upton, Hannu Velmala, Sten Vikström, Noam Weiss, Dick Woets and Emin Yoğurtcuoğlu. Amanda Taylor of Lush organised the

Håkan Delin at cliff of Pharaoh Eagle-Owl *Bubo ascalaphus*, Jebel Lamdouar, Rissani, Tafilalt, Morocco, 11 March 2012 (*Arnoud B van den Berg*). Same site as in CD3-20 and CD3-24.

logistics of several of our trips. Paul Morton and Kerry Fletcher took care of me, no matter how pathetic my requests.

My understanding of owl sounds was considerably enriched by those who allowed access to reference recordings. These included Vaughan & Svetlana Ashby, Raffael Ayé, Jan-Erik Bruun, José Luis Copete, Andrea Corso, Pierre-André Crochet, Peter Flint, Karl-Heinz Frommolt (Tierstimmenarchiv.org), Bernard Geling (Birdsounds.nl), Lauri Hallikainen (personal.inet.fi/yritys/kultasointu), Micha Heiss, John Keane, Sander Lagerveld,

Harry Lehto, Antero Lindholm, Ralph Martin, Les McPherson (archivebirdsnz.com), Joseph Medley & the United States Forest Service, Manuel Schweizer, Pratap Singh, Martyn Stewart (naturesound.org), Cheryl Tipp (bl.uk/soundarchive), Deepal Warakagoda and Mike Watson. I also referred extensively to: Avian Vocalizations Center (avocet.zoology.msu.edu), the Internet Bird Collection (ibc.lynxeds.com), the Borror Library of Bioacoustics (blb.biosci.ohio-state.edu) and of course, Xeno-canto (xeno-canto.org). For the maps, we consulted various publications (eg, Hagemeijer & Blair 1992, König et al 2008, Jennings 2010, del Hoyo & Collar 2014 and various field guides). These books showed quite a lot of differences in their maps, reflecting both the dynamics of some species' distribution and a lack of knowledge; the choices we made for this book are our own, partly based on personal experience. We are also very grateful to the following photographers who contributed their work: Eric Didner, Jo Latham, 'Dirty' James Lidster, Bruce Mactavish, Eric Meek, Paulo hiro, Artur Oliveira, Torsten Pröhl, Chris van Rijswijk, Domingo Trujillo and Mike Watson. We also thank Shaun Robson for making a book like this necessary.

Luis Gordinho and Ricardo Tomé gave valuable suggestions after reading sections of the manuscript. Nick Hopper helped to popularise the sonagram annotations. André van Loon, the Cornell Lab of Ornithology and Thor Veen enabled me to obtain access to a wide range of scientific literature, which enriched this book immeasurably. Many others kindly replied to requests for literature or to specific questions. They included David Armitage, Patrick Bergier, Keith Betton, Ruud van Beusekom, Karla Bloem, Leo Boon, Oscar Campbell, Robin Campbell, Geoff Carey, Yüksel Coşkun, Edward Dickinson, Harvey van Diek, Paul Doherty, Marc Duquet, Mark Eising, Javier Elorriaga, Janneke Eppinga, Jens & Hanne Eriksen, Rainer Ertel, Michael Exo, Rob Felix, Yuzo Fujimaki, Paolo Galeotti, Kai Gauger, Barak Granit, Hein van Grouw, Ricard Gutiérrez, Kees Hazevoet, Paul Holt, Wulf Ingham, David Insall, Sureyya Isfendiyaroğlu, Justin Jansen, Alan Kemp, Abolghasem Khaleghizadeh, Roy Kleukers, Peter de Knijff, Claus König, Michael Leven, Ian Lewis, Andreas Lindén, Antero Lindholm, Alex Masterson, Rafael Matias, Matthew Medler, Ugo Mellone, John Mendelsohn, Jonathan Meyrav, Nial Moores, Nick Moran, Babak Musavi, The Natural History Museum at Muscat, The Natural History Museum at Tring, Lajos Nemeth, János Oláh, Gert Ottens, Marco Pavia, Yoav Perlman, Shaun Peters, Matt Pretorius, Marius Puttmann, Ian Riddell, Kees Roselaar, Forrest Rowland, George Sangster, Wolfgang Scherzinger, Yevgeni Shergalin, Raquel Silva, Jonathan Slaght, James Smith, Stephen Smith, David Stanton, Elchin Sultanov, Lars Svensson, Warwick Tarboton, Michel Thévenot, Mohammad Tohidifar, Magnus Ullmann, Raju Vyas, Derek Whiteley, Rombout de Wijs, Frank Willems, Duncan Wilson, Pim Wolf, Yusuke Umegaki and Christoph Zockler. To anybody that I have omitted please understand that it's my memory, not ingratitude.

For inspiration and infecting him with his fanatical interest in owls, Arnoud would like to thank Karel H Voous. For constant encouragement, we would like to thank Ian Wallace.

Manuela Nunes and our two boys Félix and Finn gave me a huge amount of support and patience as I worked on this book. I dedicate my work to all three, with love and gratitude.

Introduction

Like a crescent moon in a bright blue sky, an owl can evade discovery without even trying. Take away the daylight, the scattered clouds, the landscape and the face of a companion, the moon will be no brighter than before, but because there are fewer distractions it will be hard to miss. With an owl, the distraction is noise. Machinery and traffic, talking and barking, turbulent wind and water, it need not be deafening. Just enough to clutter our minds. Clear it away and a distant owl may resonate with the very core of our being.

Under a full moon we can see forests and rocks, creatures and almost any decent sized objects in our surroundings. Arguably, we are just seeing moonlight reflected off those objects, reaching us along myriad pathways and after all, the moon itself is only reflecting the sun. When a distant owl hoots, its sound 'illuminates' the surroundings. We never think of it this way, but countless owl-echoes allow us to 'hear' trees, fields and cliffs. We may not perceive each item separately but when blurred together, they form an integral component of an owl's sound.

On a recent trip to Sweden, Håkan and I spent several nights listening for Tengmalm's Owls *Aegolius funereus*. We would stop the car and listen outside for a couple of minutes, until either we heard an owl or the cold forced us back inside. In some areas we would find a new Tengmalm's every two kilometres or so, usually sounding incredibly distant in snowy, dense coniferous forest. On that far horizon where sound grades into imagination, the hooting sometimes disappeared, then reappeared. Slight changes in the breeze can cause this, but I believe the sound was so faint that it was moving in and out of consciousness. The more repetitive and continuous a sound, the more easily it slips away. Irregular patterns grab our attention more easily, even at the edge of perceptibility.

In reality, true silence is as rare as a Snowy Owl *Bubo scandiacus* in a hot, sandy desert. There is always audible habitat or 'atmos'. Like us, owls filter out what is constant and concentrate on irregular movements. Their filters are infinitely more refined. In our ears a rustle or a scamper, a nibble or a squeak will usually fail to register. For an owl these are exactly the sounds that matter, these and the voices of other owls much further away.

In trying to identify owls to species, I find that it helps to know which kind of calls I am likely to hear when. The simplest solution is to divide an owl's year into three main periods. First there is courtship, usually early in the year. From incubation until after the young fledge a new set of sounds gradually emerges. Finally, territorial sounds predominate after the young leave their parents, at least in those owls that are year-round residents.

At the start of courtship, male and female are usually aggressive towards one another, before they gradually settle into very different roles. The male must demonstrate his ability to catch enough prey or the female will not lay eggs. He does this through courtship feeding, a ritual accompanied by music. The male's contribution is his 'song'. In barn owls Tytonidae this

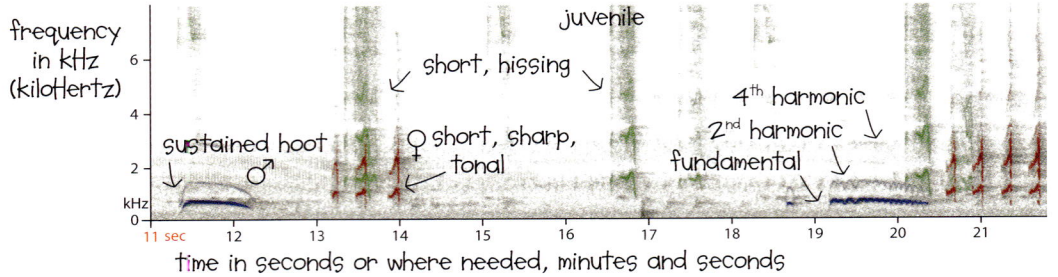

The sonagram above is derived from CD4-28 (Tawny Owl *Strix aluco*) and is repeated with different annotations later in the book. Owl sounds make thankful subjects for sonagrams, because they produce simple patterns. The vertical axis of a sonagram represents the pitch, while the horizontal axis represents time. We recommend paying particular attention to the lowest trace, the one nearest to the horizontal axis. This is the fundamental, the component that usually determines how we hear the pitch of the sound. The higher bands, when present, are harmonics and other features that determine the timbre or 'colour' of the sound. They tend to disappear with distance, leaving only the fundamental. The rhythm of an owl call can be deduced from the horizontal spacing. On a very basic level, a long, sustained, tonal sound will show as a horizontal line whereas a very short, harsh one will show as a vertical line. Likewise, a long horizontal space corresponds to a long time interval between sounds and vice versa. Within each genus, I have made sonagrams at only one or two different frequency scales to facilitate comparison. The colour coding is as shown here. Where there is significant doubt about the sex, I have used purple, with magenta indicating a second unsexed individual. Where there is only minor doubt, I sex them as I believe correct and add the annotation 'presumed male' or 'presumed female'.

is a repetitive, modulated screeching (at least in the Western Palearctic), and in the Strigidae it is hooting. The female responds with simple calls telling the male where she is and reminding him of his obligation to feed her. It would be tempting to name these 'begging calls' or even 'demanding calls' but males often produce an almost identical sound without asking anything from females except their cooperation. So I prefer to call these 'soliciting calls'. Several other sounds are characteristic of the courtship period. These include simple, rapidly repeated nest-showing calls and high-pitched copulation calls.

After laying their clutch, most owls become very quiet. We still hear the male's song and the female's soliciting calls, but only during the male's brief visits to the nest. After the young hatch, there is much more to listen to. The female's staccato 'feeding calls' are often the first sign that young have hatched, before their begging calls gradually become the dominant sound around the nest. Meanwhile, the male visits more frequently, and both adults become more nervous about intruders, especially as fledging time approaches. This is when we hear excitement calls and sometimes even weird displays designed to lure us away. We could be lazy and call these 'alarm calls', but birds do not call just for the sake of expressing emotions. When threatened they adopt a strategy, which may be to warn their loved ones ('hide!'), to call for reinforcements ('help!'), or even to threaten their enemy ('you're dead meat!').

Owls that are year-round residents usually have a secondary peak of calling in autumn. Some simply draw a few calls from the repertoire they use all year round. Others have special autumn sounds, or calls heard rarely at other times. In a few partially migratory or nomadic species, autumn calling is rare but still well worth listening for. There are one or two that we have never heard during this season, although other listeners have.

Our species taxonomy does not follow any existing authority, nor does it pretend to be one. Taxonomy is in constant flux, and in this book we based ourselves upon what was known and published on the 1st of January 2015. Subdividing the natural diversity around us is a basic human need and birthright (Shepard 1978), and we have identified what we believe to be the owl species of the Western Palearctic to the best of our abilities. Our species limits are hypotheses and we do not pretend that they are facts. The approach is integrative, considering multiple strands of evidence to decide whether a particular taxon represents a separate branch on the tree of life. Although sounds are of prime importance when defining nocturnal bird species, we have also considered genetics (monophyly), morphology (distinct appearance), geography (degree of isolation) and ecology (differences in niche), whenever possible.

When lineages diverge, different characters and 'species properties' evolve at their own pace, depending on which pressures are operating. In integrative taxonomy the absence of one such property, such as a distinct plumage, does not invalidate species rank if there is other strong evidence supporting it (Sangster 2013). Sometimes, sounds may differ between two populations when the genetic difference between them is tiny. Other times, different conditions in isolation can bring about changes in plumage and body proportions while sounds hardly change at all.

Owls often force us out of our comfort zone. At a basic level, we usually have to endure cold and darkness. In Portugal where I live, cold is not a problem and I am not afraid of the dark, but I still have to be prepared for the unexpected. Other people's fears pose the most serious threat. Once I drove through an open gate near a road, but with no inhabited houses anywhere in sight. Leaving my car in view of the road, I walked over the top of a hill to investigate a ruin that looked good for Common Barn Owl *Tyto alba* and proved to be full of pellets. When I went back over the hill I was blinded by searchlights from a police car, and walked as calmly as I could to meet them and explain myself. So far, I have not met a gun in the dark but it could happen at any time.

One of the good things about owling in Portugal is that I am allowed to be responsible for my own safety. Many sites are accessible that would be fenced off in Scotland, where I was born. Even an old mine complex with vertical shafts, pools of colourful, strange-smelling liquids and buildings on the point of collapse is open to anyone curious enough to go there. And curiosity usually gets the better of me.

Chapter 1: *Tyto*

Common Barn Owl

One night in April, at the mines of São Domingos in Portugal, I listened to a pair of Common Barn Owls *Tyto alba* making display flights around two ramshackle old mine heads, one of which contained their nest. At the start of **CD1-01**, the high-pitched screech overhead comes from the female. I call it a 'perennial screech', a sound I hear all year round from both sexes. Immediately afterwards her mate starts 'courtship screeching' at a distance, gradually coming closer. This male-only sound belongs firmly in the breeding season. If Common Barn Owl has a 'song' then courtship screeching is it. Eventually the male arrives back at the nest, followed by the silent female. We hear a little thump as she lands, slightly to the right of the male.

CD1-01   **Common Barn Owl** *Tyto alba* Minas de São Domingos, Mértola, Portugal, 23:47, 13 April 2013. Courtship flight of a pair. The more isolated, high-pitched screeches are the female while the near-continuous, harsher screeching is the male. Background: Red-necked Nightjar *Caprimulgus ruficollis*, Little Owl *Athene vidalii*, Eurasian Eagle-Owl *Bubo bubo* and Common Nightingale *Luscinia megarhynchos*. 130413.MR.234752.00

For years, most of our encounters with barn owls took place by chance. While out recording other species, we would hear a few screeches in the distance which I now know to have been perennial screeches. I for one imagined that I was hearing mostly males, although I had no clear idea of how to tell them apart from females. I only really got to know courtship screeching when I started to target Common Barn Owls specifically.

Courtship screeching peaks during the weeks leading up to egg-laying. It has a hoarse timbre caused by modulations in the frequency of the sound at a rate of about 50-60 per second. Individual screeches rise smoothly in pitch but end fairly abruptly. Gaps between them may be of just a few seconds, making long series with hardly a break. Sometimes a male takes off on a 'song flight' and his stiff, shallow wingbeats make further ripples in the sound: five little surges per second in **CD1-01**. At other times the male stays perched. In **CD1-02**, we are at a nest on the edge of Rosmaninhal ('the village of lavender') in Portugal. After the third screech, the male takes off and screeches in flight for another minute.

Lone males are among the most fanatical courtship screechers; they screech to attract females (Bühler & Epple 1980). After mating, they use the same sound to defend the female from rivals. Neighbours sometimes courtship screech in long-distance duels. Although predominantly a male sound, Mebs & Scherzinger (2004) claim that either sex can advertise availability with screeching if necessary.

Common Barn Owl *Tyto alba*, juveniles, Pancas, Benavente, Portugal, 2 July 2014 (*Artur Vaz Oliveira*). Same nest as in CD1-11.

CD1-02   **Common Barn Owl** *Tyto alba* Rosmaninhal, Idanha-a-Nova, Portugal, 21:45, 4 March 2010. Courtship screeches while perched near the nest, and then in flight. Background: Southern Tree Frog *Hyla meridionalis* and Little Owl *Athene vidalii*. 100304.MR.214545.01

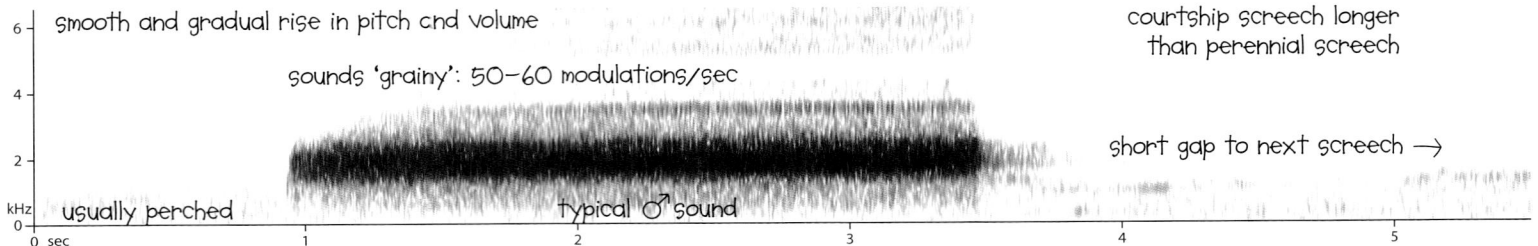

In **CD1-03**, we are in traditional montado near Lisbon, again in Portugal, with Cork Oaks *Quercus suber* and Holm Oaks *Q ilex* scattered through meadows reserved for fighting bulls. It is late March and a thunderstorm has just taken two hours to pass. Finally, the scattered trees and lush meadow grass stop rustling and the air loses its turbulence. Bit by bit as the acoustic opens up, various creatures reoccupy their niches. Crickets take possession of higher frequencies. In the lower range, fast croaks of European Tree Frogs *Hyla arborea* and a few slower ones of Southern Tree Frogs *H meridionalis* catch my attention. At centre stage, two Common Barn Owls exchange perennial screeches, one near and one far, for reasons known only to themselves.

Perennial screeching is the Common Barn Owl sound we hear most often throughout the year. Rising slowly in pitch, the screech grows in volume for one to two seconds and typically ends abruptly with a pronounced upward inflection. The timbre is a concentrated hissing, like an espresso machine with the steam on. Individual barn owls often seem to have a fairly distinctive signature based on the amount of hiss versus whistle, how strongly their screech rises in pitch, and how abruptly it ends. Barn owls give perennial screeches one at a time at long but fairly regular intervals. They may fly quite far during the gaps, so when a loud screech at close range catches our attention, the next one may seem surprisingly faint and distant. Less often, either sex may also produce perennial screeches when perched at the nest.

In **CD1-04**, a male of the subspecies *erlangeri* is flying along a flat-bottomed valley in the Jabal Samhan range in southern Oman, giving a perennial screech about once every 40-50 seconds. This

CD1-03   **Common Barn Owl** *Tyto alba* Pancas, Benavente, Portugal, 31 March 2012. Perennial screeches of two different individuals. Background: European Tree Frog *Hyla arborea* and Southern Tree Frog *H meridionalis*. 120331.MR.231814.31

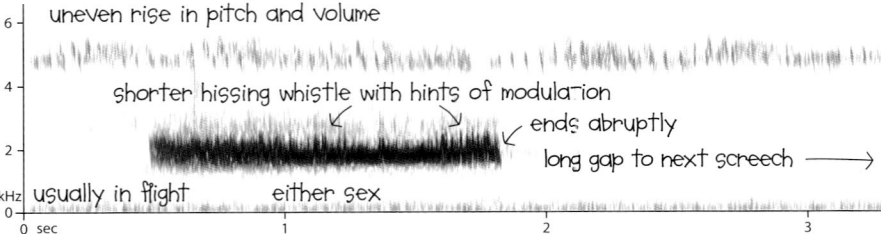

CD1-04   **Common Barn Owl** *Tyto alba* Wadi Darbat, Dhofar, Oman, 21:30, 18 April 2010. Perennial screeches in flight. The barn owls of Arabia belong to subspecies *erlangeri*. Background: Arabian Wolf *Canis lupus arabs*, Arabian Scops Owl *Otus pamelae* and Arabian Eagle-Owl *Bubo milesi*. 100418.MR.213018.12

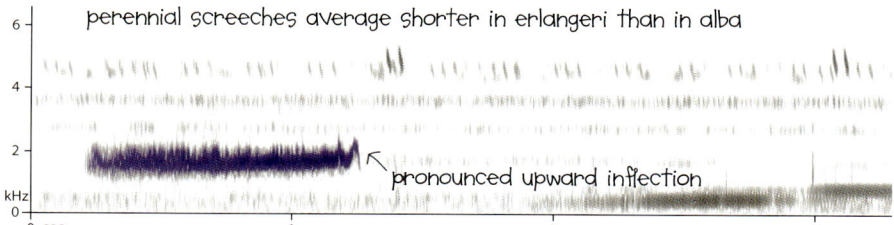

well-vegetated wadi is a popular picnic spot during the day. In April, the grass is dry but three months later it will catch the north end of the Indian Ocean monsoon. Although this is Arabia, the habitat is not so dramatically different from that of the bird's European relatives, containing grassland, a few trees and some water. The neighbours, however, could hardly be more different. Every few seconds, an Arabian Scops Owl *Otus pamelae* goes *prrr* and an Arabian Eagle-Owl *Bubo milesi* moans languidly in the distance. An Arabian Wolf *Canis lupus arabs* begins to howl. Other members of its pack join in, eventually making such a din that we are hardly able to hear the barn owl's second screech. The scratchy sounds at close range are footsteps of a scrawny cow on gravel, curious about me and apparently oblivious to the wolves.

Perennial screeching is virtually the only barn owl sound that I hear during the autumn. At my home near Sintra in Portugal, I like to record nocturnal migration of passerines on suitable nights, leaving my microphones out for the quieter hours from midnight to dawn. Barely a session goes by without me recording a couple of perennial screeches.

Despite hearing perennial screeching so often, I still have no clear idea what it 'means'. All I can say is that it is some kind of long-distance advertisement, perhaps with an aggressive or at least assertive tone. For a long time I believed this was a territorial call (Sorace 1987, Siverio et al 1999), but barn owls are not territorial in the usual sense. Instead, they occupy a huge 'home range', only defending a small area around the nest or perhaps just their mate (Barn Owl Trust 2012).

Occasionally, it can be more difficult to distinguish between perennial and courtship screeching, especially in males. Perhaps during the breeding season, male perennial screeches become more like courtship screeches. **CD1-05** is an example of such ambiguity, recorded in the Netherlands. A slightly gargling screech on my right sounds long and modulated, but more concentrated than a typical courtship screech. The owl is in no hurry and passes invisibly in front of me; 38 seconds later it screeches a little further away on my left. The third screech is surprisingly distant.

Common Barn Owl *Tyto alba* De Weerribben, Overijssel, Netherlands, 26 April 2008. Ambiguous screeches of a male. The breeding population in the Netherlands belongs to subspecies *guttata*. Background: Marsh Frog *Pelophylax ridibundus*, Common Snipe *Gallinago gallinago* and Sedge Warbler *Acrocephalus schoenobaenus*. 080426.MR.005550.11   **CD1-05**

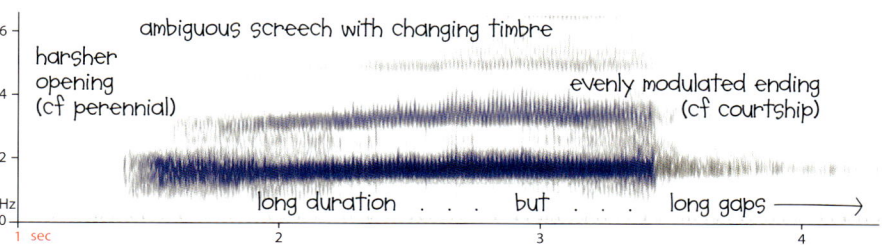

The ghost of long extinct barn owls lingers on in these ancient screeches. Several contemporary species seem to share very similar calls, so their shared ancestors probably sounded little different. Barn owls belong to the oldest surviving lineage of owls, the Tytonidae. They diverged from the Strigidae, including all the other owls in this book, in the late Eocene. The oldest known barn owl is *Necrobyas rossignoli,* dating from around 37 Ma or million years ago (Mourer-Chauviré 1987, Escarguel et al 1997). The first of the genus *Tyto* appeared more than 20 million years later, possibly in Southeast Asia and New Guinea where the highest diversity of *Tyto* occurs today (Wink et al 2009). Originally, these were birds of humid, tropical forest, and although several have subsequently evolved to live in open habitats, they are still absent from the coldest and most arid places. Like most tropical birds, barn owls are basically sedentary.

During the 20th century, '*the* barn owl' was seen as a classic example of a cosmopolitan species, having a wide range of subspecies on six continents and an array of oceanic islands. Variation in appearance is indeed extensive, expressed in overall size, the relative proportions of bill, tarsus and toes, the amount of feathering on the tarsus, the degree of darkredness and the number and size of black spots. With DNA studies showing that there are in fact quite ancient divisions within the complex (eg, Wink et al 2009, Nijman & Aliabadian 2013), the taxonomic arrangement has started to change. A deep divide separates Common Barn Owl on the one hand, including birds from Europe, Africa and most populations in Asia, from another branch that includes Eastern Barn Owls *T delicatula* from southern Asia, Australasia, parts of Indonesia and some Pacific Islands. During a warmer period in the past,

an early representative of this eastern branch made it to Alaska and founded a lineage that spread all the way to Patagonia. It includes American Barn Owl *T furcata* and Ashy-faced Owl *T glaucops,* an endemic of Hispaniola (Wink & Heidrich 1999).

In the Western Palearctic, taxonomists usually recognise five continental and three oceanic barn owl taxa. The five traditional continental taxa are nominate *alba* of the Mediterranean and western Europe, *guttata* from central and eastern Europe, *ernesti* from Corsica and Sardinia, *erlangeri* of the Arabian peninsula and adjacent areas (populations in North Africa have been variously assigned to *alba*, *erlangeri* or *ernesti*) and, at the southern border of the WP, *affinis* of sub-Saharan Africa. The three Atlantic island taxa are *gracilirostris* of the Eastern Canary Islands ('Slender-billed Barn Owl'), *schmitzi* of Madeira, the Desertas and Porto Santo ('Madeira Barn Owl'), and *detorta* from the Cape Verde Islands ('Cape Verde Barn Owl'). Up to now, only the continental taxa have been included in phylogenetic studies. Of those, the most genetically distinct is *affinis* (eg, Aliabadian et al 2012). The oceanic taxa differ in many ways from the continental ones, and I have chosen to treat each one separately.

Recognising two basic types of screeches makes it much easier to compare the sounds of different barn owl taxa. Screeches of *alba* and *guttata* are to all intents and purposes identical, while *erlangeri* differs only very slightly if at all. By contrast, there are dramatic differences between Common and American Barn Owls. American has much shorter perennial screeches, typically less than a second long, and in a wide range of recordings, I have never heard American giving anything remotely like a courtship screech. Gerrit Vyn is the author of an excellent CD on North American owls (2006). When I sent him an example of Common Barn Owl courtship screeches, he confirmed he knew nothing similar from American. This not only supports separating the two species but also the two kinds of screeches.

At the same time, American Barn Owl has a prominent flight call that is completely absent in Common Barn Owl. It was Gerrit who recorded the metallic clicking sound in **CD1-06**, which he calls the '*kleak-kleak* call' (Vyn 2006). Unpaired males use it most often (Gerrit Vyn pers comm), so it must have an important role in mate attraction. Marti et al (2005) reported that males *kleak* in the vicinity of the nest, soon after leaving the daytime roost, and when approaching with food deliveries. Several other *Tyto* species have similar calls (eg, African Grass Owl *T capensis*, Eastern Grass Owl *T longimembris* and Australian Masked Owl *T novaehollandiae*). So rather than being an American invention, it seems that Common stopped using this call and replaced it with courtship screeching.

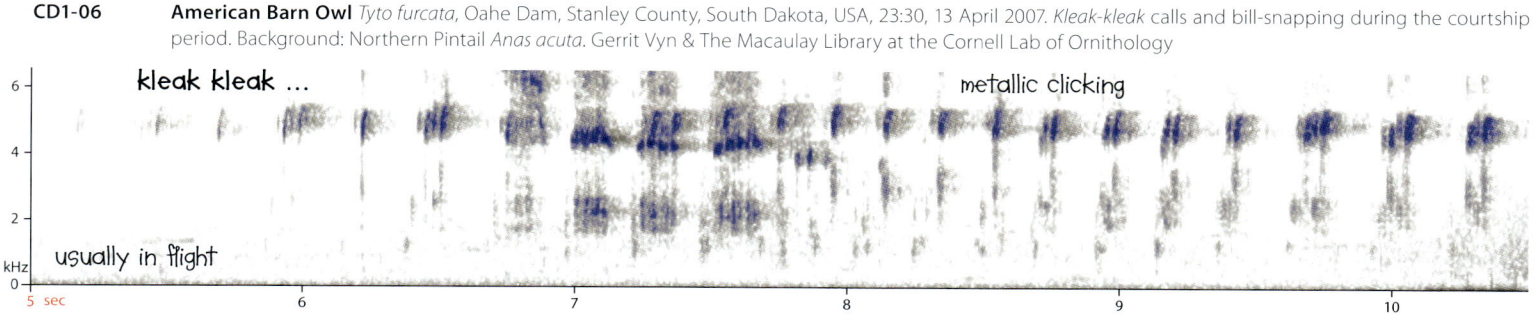

CD1-06 **American Barn Owl** *Tyto furcata*, Oahe Dam, Stanley County, South Dakota, USA, 23:30, 13 April 2007. *Kleak-kleak* calls and bill-snapping during the courtship period. Background: Northern Pintail *Anas acuta*. Gerrit Vyn & The Macaulay Library at the Cornell Lab of Ornithology

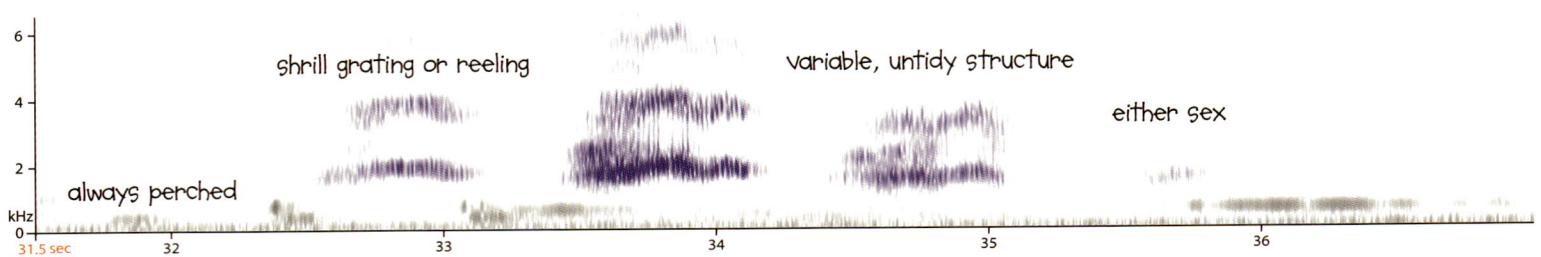

Common Barn Owl *Tyto alba* Minas de São Domingos, Mértola, Portugal, 22:58, 11 March 2012. Purring of a male and a female. Background: Southern Tree Frog *Hyla meridionalis* and Iberian Green Frog *Pelophylax perezi*. 120311.MR.225842.01

Purring is a sound related to courtship screeching but used by both sexes. A shrill grating or reeling, it is usually delivered from a perch. Sequences of purring typically lack a tidy structure and often sound rather chaotic. I like to think of purring as an excited, unisex modification of courtship screeching, reserved for close male-female interactions. In **CD1-07**, we are back at the mines of São Domingos. Peals of *Nossa Senhora de Fátima* ring out from a church in the neighbouring village, followed by several short bursts of purring. Bühler & Epple (1980) described purring in a variety of contexts, some involving aggression, while in others it seemed to be a contact call between pair members. Like courtship screeching, purring is a call that belongs to the breeding season. I have never heard it at any other time.

The rivalry scream is a particularly impressive call possibly derived from the perennial screech. A descending scream in a high, often pure-sounding voice, it is usually delivered without modulations. To those of a fertile imagination, the rivalry scream can be a heart-stopper, even at a distance. If the example in **CD1-08** fails to impress, fast forward and listen to a much closer example from a Slender-billed Barn Owl (**CD1-15**). To other male barn owls, the rivalry scream is provocative rather than scary. On a few occasions, I have been listening to courtship screeching of a male perched at close range when a distant male screamed. The nearer bird would immediately increase its screech rate, and sometimes take off to make itself more audible.

Although our priority has been to illustrate sounds that anyone may hear from a distance, occasionally we have captured more

Common Barn Owl *Tyto alba* Azrou, Western Middle Atlas, Morocco, 00:07, 24 June 2010. Rivalry screams at a distance. 100624.AB.000700.32

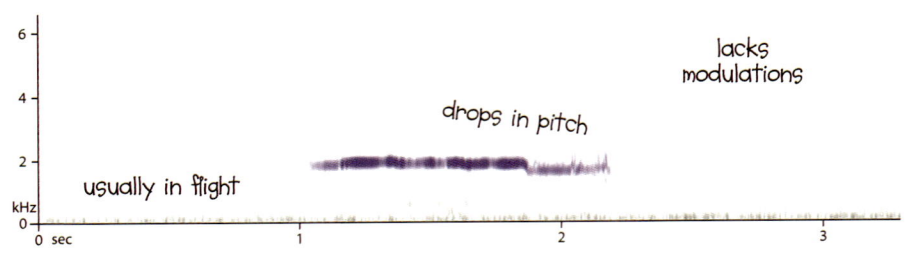

Common Barn Owl *Tyto alba*, presumed male, Rosmaninhal, Idanha-a-Nova, Portugal, 21 April 2012 (*Dick Forsman*). Possibly same bird as in CD1-02 & CD1-09 to 10.

intimate, close-range sounds. In **CD1-09** a male is giving a long sequence of subdued courtship screeches; he started nearly 40 minutes earlier. Every now and then the female purrs quietly, or gives a louder call that seems to combine purring with a perennial screech. In between louder calls she makes a very quiet, high-pitched purring (eg, at 0:06 and 0:17). This is her

CD1-09   **Common Barn Owl** *Tyto alba* Rosmaninhal, Idanha-a-Nova, Portugal, 22:21, 3 March 2010. Male courtship screeching with louder purring and extremely quiet copulation calls of a female. Background: Little Owl *Athene vidalii*. 100303.MR.222124.30

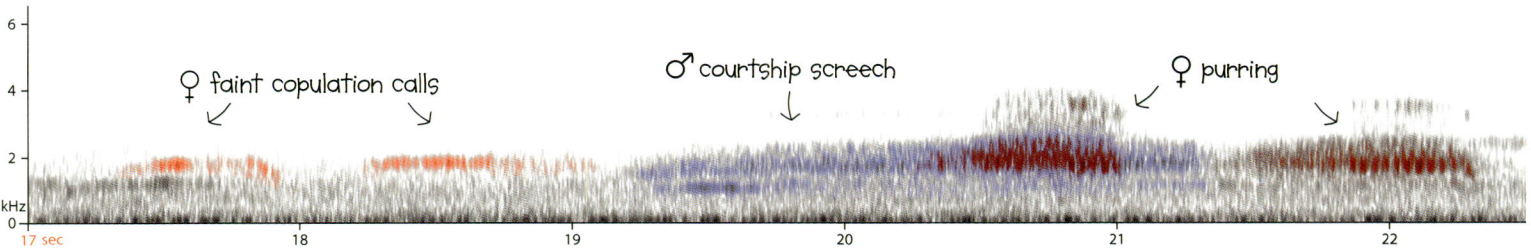

copulation call. She uses it both to solicit sex and during the act (Bühler & Epple 1980). A microphone inside the nest would probably record this call often, but from a respectful distance I have rarely heard it.

Once a pair of barn owls has fertilised and laid their clutch, all goes quiet, and you could easily spend an hour or two in the vicinity of a nest without noticing them. The female incubates her clutch for a month, during which time she is entirely dependent on her mate. As he flies towards the nest to deliver food to her, he typically gives a few short, quiet 'chirrups', often with a rising, questioning intonation. He also chirrups at the nest when he wants to start an interaction. Perhaps chirruping helps to pacify the female. In **CD1-10** there are five chirrups at the start of the recording. The male switches to food-offering calls immediately after he arrives at the nest. These are fast chattering or clucking sounds, which the female will also use a few weeks later when feeding the young. The female purrs quietly when he arrives, but soon begs for more food with a series of very quiet soliciting calls.

From about five weeks before egg-laying until the young are large enough not to be brooded, the female uses soliciting calls whenever the male is at the nest. In **CD1-11**, she is easy to

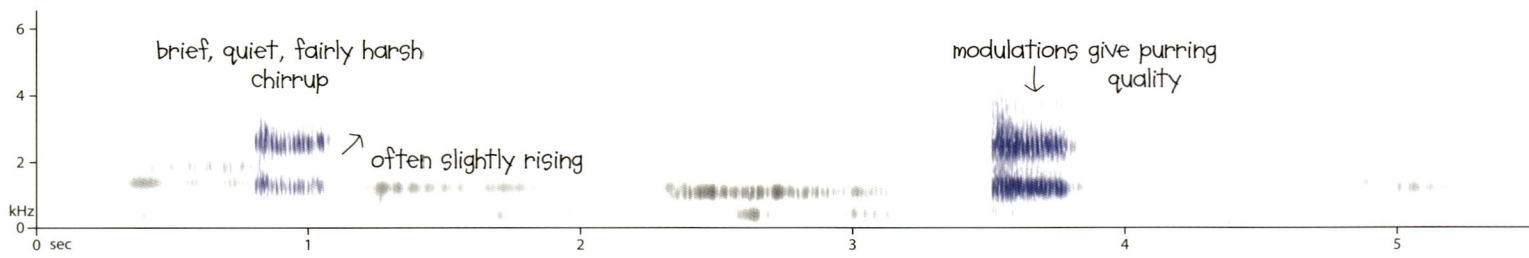

CD1-10   **Common Barn Owl** *Tyto alba* Rosmaninhal, Idanha-a-Nova, Portugal, 23:51, 6 April 2010. Chirrup and food-offering calls of male, with purring and soliciting calls of a female. Background: Little Owl *Athene vidalii*. 100406.MR.235125.01

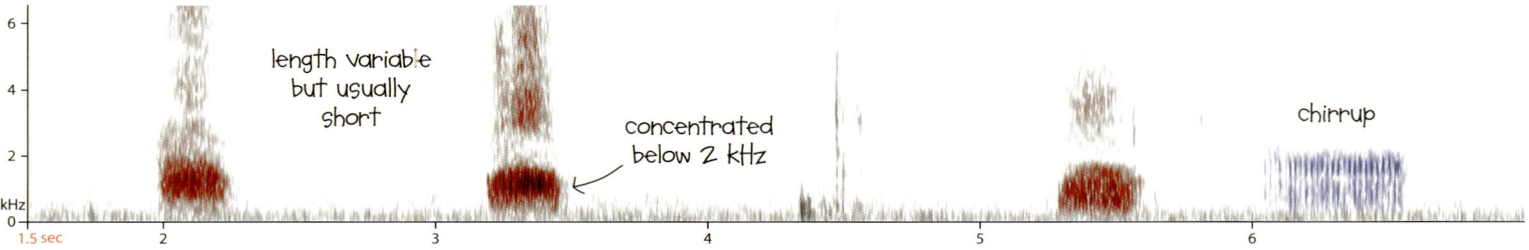

CD1-11   **Common Barn Owl** *Tyto alba* Pancas, Benavente, Portugal, 00:29, 1 March 2013. Chirrup calls of a male, soliciting calls and possibly copulation calls of a female, and very quiet begging calls of a tiny juvenile. Background: Tawny Owl *Strix aluco*. 130301.MR.002948.01

hear because the nest is a tree cavity with a large opening. The microphone is on the ground, only 3 m below. The recording starts with a male chirrup, the first of several. This immediately triggers some loud soliciting calls (as well as one or two very quiet begging calls of a tiny juvenile). The male enters the cavity at 0:27, at which point his chirrups turn into purring. The female's soliciting calls change too, becoming more like copulation calls. By the end of the recording, they revert to the way they were at the start.

Vocal activity at the nest increases gradually as the young grow up. At first their chirping calls are too faint to attract much attention. The adult female responds by offering more comfort while the male ignores them completely (Bühler & Epple 1980). From the very first day, however, the owlets also use a begging call, which both adults respond to. The begging call becomes much more noticeable after the female stops brooding and starts hunting along with the male, typically when the youngest owlet is about 10 days old (Bunn et al 1982). I often find nests thanks to begging calls, since they carry a long distance. Imagine how well the adult barn owls must be able to hear them. Evolution did not leave this to chance. The frequency of the sound fits neatly into the barn owl's most sensitive hearing range (Konishi 1973).

Roulin et al (2000) found that in the absence of adults, siblings negotiate who will get the next food item, signalling levels of hunger to one another to avoid having to fight. In **CD1-12**, several fledglings are begging under a bridge. The hungriest two are calling at the start, then at 0:12 an adult arrives with food and they all call. The young start to negotiate who's next and the calling begins to calm down, until just two are calling. Then the adult sees me and flies out from under the bridge, perching on a post just 2 m away. It gives a series of mobbing screams that intimidate me, silence the young for a little while, and probably also warn the other parent some distance away. The last scream is right above my head, strongly modulated by hovering wingbeats. Time for me to leave. Fledged owlets can also give mobbing screams when threatened, similar to the adult version but harsher.

The hardiest of all Common Barn Owls are those belonging to the dark-plumaged subspecies *guttata* that now live in central and eastern Europe. According to Voous (1950) their ancestors

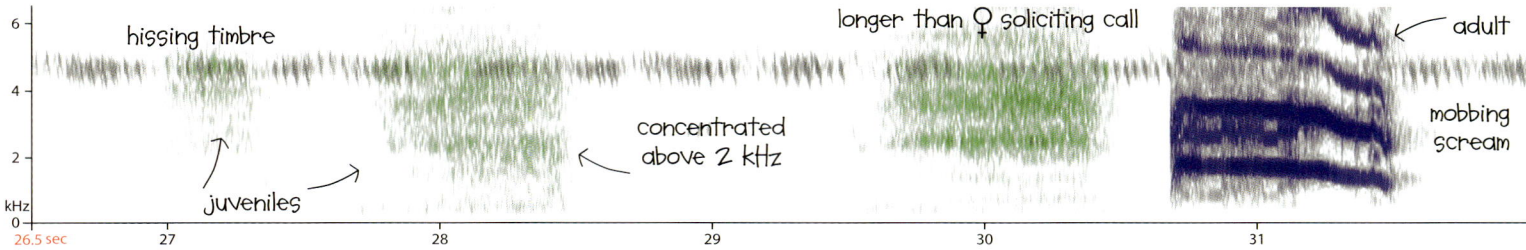

CD1-12 **Common Barn Owl** *Tyto alba* Rosmaninhal, Idanha-a-Nova, Portugal, 00:56, 14 May 2012. Juvenile begging calls and adult mobbing screams. Background: Long-eared Owl *Asio otus* (juveniles) and Common Nightingale *Luscinia megarhynchos*. 120514.MR.005632.10

survived the last ice age in a refuge somewhere near the Black Sea, while the ancestors of pale-plumaged nominate *alba* retreated to a refuge in the Iberian peninsula. When the continent began to warm up again, the owls moved north with their small mammal prey. Barn owls normally occupy lower altitudes, up to 250-300 m in Britain and 1300 m in Spain (Alegre et al 1989), corresponding to about 40 days of winter snow (Taylor 1994). Those *guttata* breeding north of the Balkan mountains and the eastern Alps are unlikely to have got there by spreading across high ground. Instead, the valleys of the Danube and other rivers must have been the corridors along which they arrived. Meanwhile, *alba* spread from Spain into France and on into Britain and Ireland, which were not yet islands. If Voous was right, *alba* and *guttata* eventually met somewhere in central Europe. Apparently lacking strong enough 'isolating mechanisms', they started to interbreed over a wide area.

The difference between the subspecies *alba* and *guttata* is essentially one of plumage with two independent features accounting for the variation, dark redness being one and black spots on the underparts being the other. From Portugal in the southwest to the Baltic states in the northeast, there is a gradual or clinal increase in plumage redness (Roulin 2004, Antoniazza et al 2011). While mixing of previously separate populations may partly account for this, there is also a striking link between redness and diet.

According to Roulin (2004), plumage redness increases from southwest to northeast across Europe because it favours the barn owls' ability to catch certain important prey species, which vary in their relative abundance. Redder barn owls in the north eat more Common Voles *Microtus arvalis*, harvest mice *Micromys*, long-tailed shrews *Sorex* and water shrews *Neomys*, while paler ones in the south eat more Wood Mice *Apodemus sylvaticus*, house mice *Mus* and white-toothed shrews *Crocidura*. This also applies at a local scale. In Switzerland, where dark red and pale individuals occur sympatrically, plumage is linked to prey choice. More recently, Dreiss et al (2011) found that this only holds for females, and noted a link with habitat. Redder females prefer to breed in habitats with more arable fields, while paler ones prefer to breed in territories with more trees.

If the subspecies *alba* and *guttata* were once clearly distinguishable, geographically separate populations, now they may be just two extremes of appearance. Any subspecies border that we draw will be arbitrary. In Israel, Charter et al

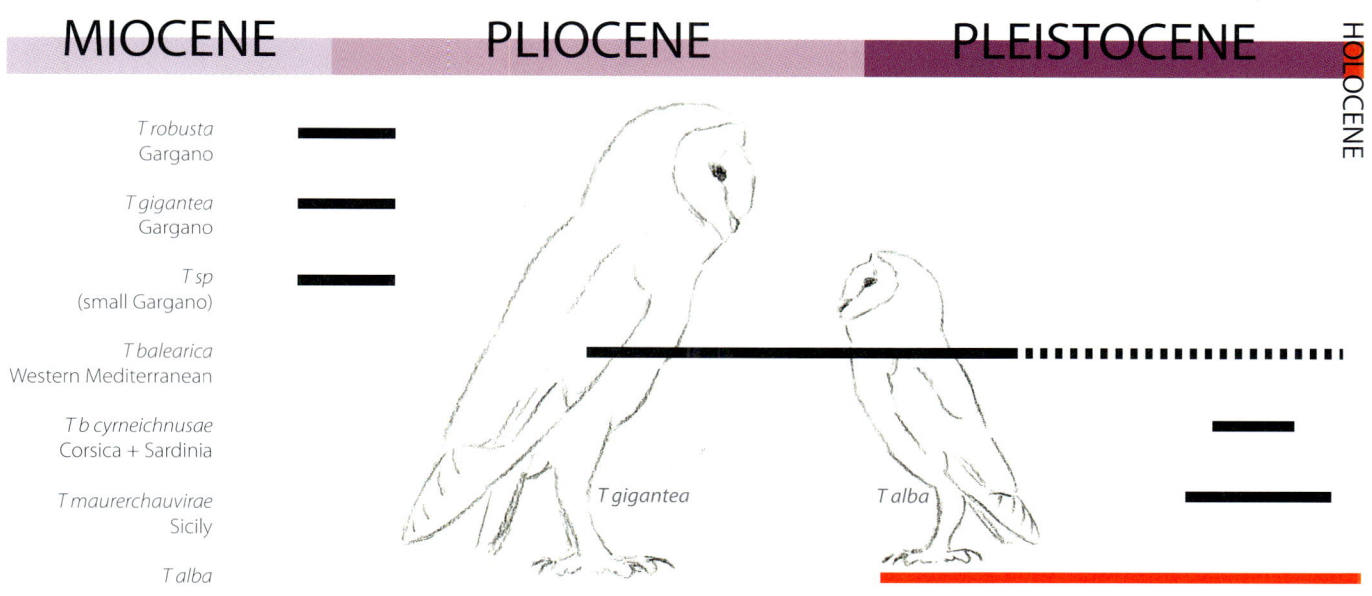

(2012) found the same relationship between redness and prey species in subspecies *erlangeri*. In this case no geographical cline was involved. So the merging of different populations is not necessary for significant local adaptations of this nature to evolve. Beyond the Middle East, no two authors seem to agree where *erlangeri* ends and *alba* begins. Genetically, there appears to be little if any difference between *alba*, *erlangeri* and *guttata* (Aliabadian et al 2013). My analysis of their sounds also failed to find any clear differences between these three. Arguably, then, *erlangeri* and *guttata* are meaningless names, which can be chucked into the taxonomic dustbin.

As for *ernesti*, some treat it as a Corso-Sardinian endemic subspecies while others include similar barn owls from North Africa and elsewhere in the Mediterranean region (eg, König et al 2008). Pellegrino et al (2014) recently discovered that little owls *Athene* from Sardinia are genetically distinct, begging the question whether this is also true of Corso-Sardinian barn owls. Several endemic barn owls did live on Mediterranean islands in the past, especially on islands around Italy, and some were very distinctive indeed.

Gargano currently forms the spur on Italy's boot, a peninsula embedded in its southeast coast. When the Miocene ended 5.33 million years ago and the Mediterranean basin suddenly filled up after a dry period, Gargano became an island. Of the mammals that found themselves trapped there, only one - an otter – was carnivorous. With reduced predation the evolution of smaller mammals went into overdrive, the most obvious result of which was that many grew larger. There were giant dormice, huge pikas, monster hamsters and supersized hairy hedgehogs. During the day, two endemic species of *Garganoaetus* eagles preyed on them. At night it was the turn of the barn owls, of which there were three on Gargano (Ballman 1973). Compared to Common Barn Owl occurring there now, the smallest, still inadequately described species was only slightly larger, the medium sized *T robusta* was about 60% larger, while *T gigantea* was more than twice its size. In fact, *gigantea* was larger and much heavier than a Eurasian Eagle-Owl *B bubo*.

Another giant barn owl lived on Sicily during the Mid-Pleistocene, *T mourerchauvineae*, and it was as large as *robusta*. Sicily also lacked mammalian predators at the time. The Sicilian Barn Owl fed primarily on a dormouse the size of a rabbit but also on other endemic dormice and shrews, and a variety of birds (Pavia 2004). It was contemporary with a dwarf elephant called *Elephas falconeri* that stood only 90 cm high. Conceivably, a large female owl might have killed the occasional runt elephant calf, although this is pure speculation on my part!

In the western Mediterranean, *T balearica*, about one and a half times the size of Common Barn Owl, preyed on large rodents (Mourer-Chauviré et al 1980). The oldest currently accepted finds are from the continent, while later ones come from islands such as Mallorca and Menorca (Mourer-Chauviré & Sanchez Marco 1988, Mourer-Chauviré & Geraads 2010). On Corsica and Sardinia, the endemic subspecies *cyrneichnusae* survived until at least 350,000 years ago. Florit & Alcover (1987) detected signs of *balearica*'s continued presence on Mallorca in the Late Pleistocene, and it may have survived until humans arrived in the Balearic Islands less than 2000 years ago.

In Macaronesia, three endemic, insular barn owls survive to this day. None is especially large, but all hunt rather unusual prey, or did until humans arrived a few centuries ago. For the sake of argument we will treat each one as a species, but let's be clear; their sounds differ only subtly and none has been the subject of a thorough genetic study.

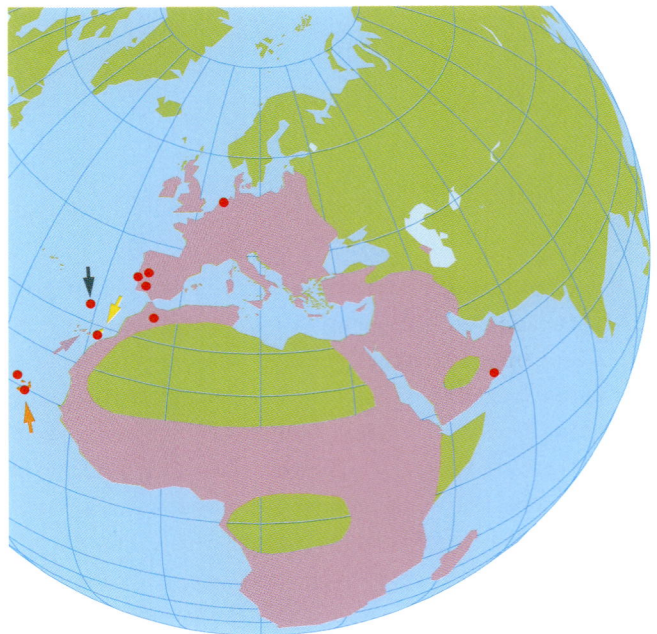

Approximate breeding distribution of Common Barn Owl *Tyto alba* ■ and breeding islands of Slender-billed Barn Owl *T gracilirostris* ■ arrow, Madeira Barn Owl *T schmitzi* ■ arrow and Cape Verde Barn Owl *T detorta* ■ arrow. Recording locations indicated by ● dots.

Slender-billed Barn Owl

Slender-billed Barn Owl *Tyto gracilirostris* is endemic to the Eastern Canary Islands: Fuerteventura, Lanzarote and associated islets. It has short wings and tail (12% and 14% shorter than *alba*: Cramp 1985) and a 'gracile' bill, combined with the strong tarsus and claws typical of an insular owl. Bannerman (1963) noted the dark grey colour of the upperparts and described the underparts as "mainly cinnamon-brown or deep rusty-buff (rarely light buff), the whole more or less heavily and regularly spotted with dark brown from the breast to the thighs, as well as the under wing-coverts." A lucky observer might see broad irregular bars of grey-brown across both webs of the primaries, or three well-marked bars on the tail.

Two discoveries from the Western Canary Islands suggest a wider distribution in the past. Jaume et al (1993) reported remains on La Gomera, more than 250 km west of the current breeding range, commenting that Slender-billed Owl is osteologically distinct enough to be regarded as a separate species. The layer containing the remains was dated to the Upper Pleistocene, ie, somewhere between about 126,000 and 12,000 years ago. On Gran Canaria in the centre of the archipelago, Alcover & Florit (1989) reported Slender-billed bones at an archaeological site approximately 2000 years old. This suggests that it became confined to the eastern isles only quite recently.

In the Western Canary Islands today there are only Common Barn Owls *T alba*, the same white birds as in Western Europe and North Africa. How they came to be there is a mystery waiting to be solved. Felipe Siverio has surveyed barn owls throughout the archipelago. I asked him whether he thought Common Barn might have arrived in prehistoric times, given that they breed in cliffs and not in buildings. Felipe replied that barn owls elsewhere started to use human structures only because of a lack of natural ones. In the Canary Islands there is no such problem, so cliff nesting tell us nothing about when they arrived. Felipe suggested that in ancient times, any larger Common Barn arriving from the continent would have had trouble surviving without suitable mammals to prey on. Perhaps with the introduction of non-native rodents, their moment arrived.

Slender-billed Barn Owl *Tyto gracilirostris*, La Oliva, Fuerteventura, Canary Islands, 7 June 2000 (*Domingo Trujillo*)

Barn owls make great collaborators for palaeontologists investigating the past distribution of small mammals (Rando et al 2011, Rando et al 2012). In the Eastern Canary Islands, Slender-billed Barn Owls have been using the same roosts and nesting sites for millennia, often volcanic tubes where the extinct Lava Shearwater *Puffinus olsoni* once bred. Some contain huge accumulations of owl pellets, broken down into layer upon layer of bones and dust. With carbon dating, we can learn the approximate age of the bones.

From one layer to the next, House Mouse *Mus musculus* becomes an important prey item, having been completely absent before. The oldest House Mouse remains come from Lanzarote, and have been dated to 128-333 AD. Pellets dated to 756 BC are House Mouse free, so they must have arrived in the intervening time. Before their arrival, the commonest prey in fossil owl pellets was the endemic Lava Mouse *Malpaisomys insularis*. The two mice species coexisted for about 1000 years, until Lava disappeared around 1271-1394 AD, roughly the same time as the Lava Shearwater. From then onwards, Black Rats *Rattus rattus* appear in the pellets. What happened? House Mice probably arrived with the Guanche, the first human inhabitants of the Canary Islands, somewhere between 1000 and 100 BC. Lava Mice and Lava Shearwaters disappeared shortly after the arrival of Europeans who brought with them their nemesis, the Black Rat.

Genetic studies currently underway may help to answer several questions. Is there any gene flow between Common and Slender-billed Barn Owl? How long have they been evolving separately? Which continental population gave rise to each? I hope we find out sooner rather than later, as Slender-billed Barn Owl is critically endangered. Felipe estimates the minimum population at between 53 and 105 pairs (Siverio 2008), putting it in the same league as Zino's Petrel *Pterodroma madeira*.

I first heard Slender-billed Barn Owl in March 2001. Having made my way towards the mountainous interior of Fuerteventura in the late afternoon, I decided to stay there for the night. When I first heard a perennial screech ringing out, I was surprised and delighted. I had not known where to start looking for this rare taxon. Further screeches rang out at a rate of about three per minute, all of them in flight (**CD1-13**). The caller remained unseen, but hearing it in that resonant valley was an experience I will never forget.

Slender-billed Barn Owl *Tyto gracilirostris* Vega de Rio Palmas, Fuerteventura, Canary Islands, 16 April 2001. Perennial screeches in flight. Background: Cory's Shearwater *Calonectris borealis*. 01.012.MR.05200.31   CD1-13

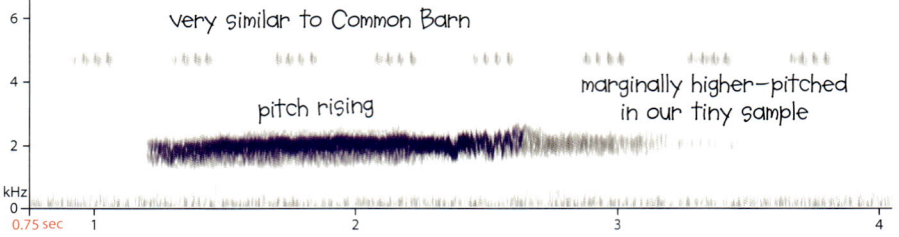

In January 2010, René Pop and I visited several sites on Fuerteventura, recommended by Felipe, to try to record more Slender-billed Barn Owls. At most sites we were unlucky. I did hear one in a volcanic crater in the north of the island which had wonderful acoustics but it was distant, high up on the crater walls. So I ended up making most of my recordings at exactly the site I discovered by accident in 2001. Nine years on, there were two nests about 650 m apart on the same rocky slope.

Slender-billed Barn Owl *Tyto gracilirostris*, Fuerteventura, Canary Islands, 29 January 2010 (*René Pop*). Possibly same bird as in CD1-14 & 15.

Our visit coincided with the peak of courtship behaviour, so there was a great deal of activity. In **CD1-14**, a male is perched on a cliff top just above his nest in a tall vertical crevice. He gives courtship screeches about once every seven seconds

CD1-14   **Slender-billed Barn Owl** *Tyto gracilirostris* Vega de Rio Palmas, Fuerteventura, Canary Islands, 20:40, 21 January 2010. Courtship screeching, at first perched above nest entrance then, after rivalry scream of neighbour, in flight. This male appeared to be unmated. 100121.MR.204033.01

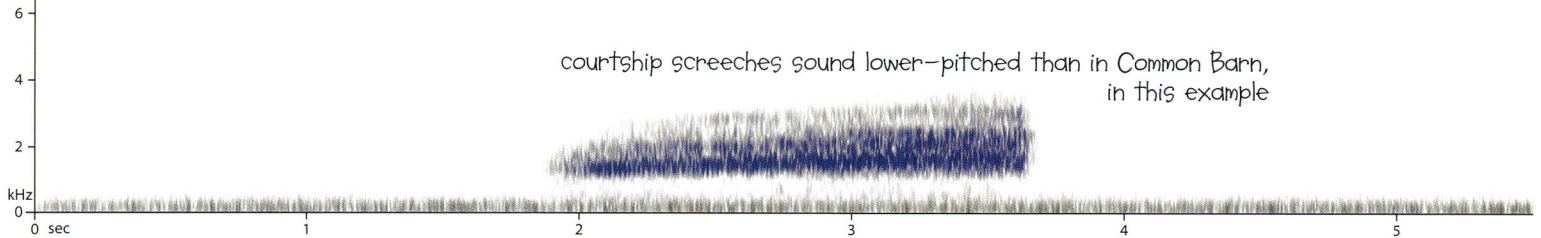

until 0:51 when his distant neighbour, who has been courtship screeching faintly in the background, gives a rivalry scream. At this he becomes livid, taking off and calling more frequently while flying around the nest area. His calls are shriller and higher-pitched than before. In the meantime, his neighbour flies closer and utters another rivalry scream. In **CD1-15**, one of these males, perhaps the neighbour, gives three rivalry screams in a solo performance, echoing off the steep rocky slope where they have their nests. At the end of the recording, René is talking to me in the distance, complaining about the futility of photographing barn owls on cliffs in the dark.

Calls evolve slowly in barn owls despite dramatic differences in ecology. The world's barn owls sound much less diverse than the world's scops owls *Otus*, for example. Isolated from Common Barn by the sea, Slender-billed may not have needed to evolve different calls. As a parallel case, Tawny Pipit *Anthus campestris* and the 20% smaller Berthelot's Pipit *A berthelotii* of Macaronesia (including Fuerteventura) also sound virtually identical.

With its much smaller size, different structure and plumage, and its isolation, Slender-billed Barn Owl may well be a species. Without the genetic part of the story we are left in suspense. At the very least, it is a unique and very rare taxon, finely tuned to life in a rather special environment. How tragic it would be if it went the way of the Lava Mouse and the Lava Shearwater, which were only missed centuries after their demise.

CD1-15 **Slender-billed Barn Owl** *Tyto gracilirostris* Vega de Rio Palmas, Fuerteventura, Canary Islands, 21:57, 28 January 2010. Rivalry screams in flight, becoming more distant each time. 100128.MR.215700.31

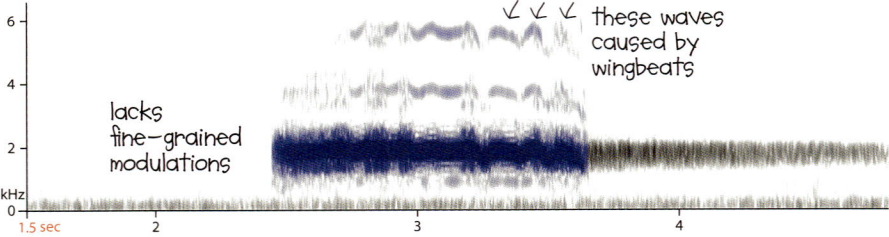

Calls of the few Slender-billed Barn Owls that we have studied differed only slightly from those of Common Barn Owl, if at all. We have only three or four males to go by, not enough to draw hard conclusions. The perennial screeches may be slightly higher-pitched than in Common Barn from Portugal and elsewhere, but the courtship screeches seem to be *lower*-pitched, a surprise considering the smaller size of Slender-billed.

Madeira Barn Owl

Here in the clouds a faint rumbling is all I sense of the sea. A moonbeam penetrates, illuminating distant crests of waves. The island of Bugio in the Desertas near Madeira is one long, sharp ridge, the top trimmed off at this end. Just 50 m wide, the grassy southern plateau is 300 m high or a 90 minute hand-and-foot climb above the sea. I sit in on the leeward side, listening among the crickets. All around me, Desertas Petrels *Pterodroma deserta* hurtle past, tying the wind in knots. Moaning like the ghosts they threaten to become, they display over their last colony in the world. A few Cory's Shearwaters *Calonectris borealis* cry in the distance, and every now and then a Madeiran Storm Petrel *Oceanodroma castro* circuits the plateau, squeaky chatters marking its path.

Every few minutes, a Madeira Barn Owl *Tyto schmitzi* screeches in flight, passes quickly and disappears over the edge. Once it passes so close that the LCD of my recorder lights it up. Its

Habitat of Madeira Barn Owl *Tyto schmitzi* on Bugio, Desertas, Madeira, 9 July 2011 (*Magnus Robb*). Same site as CD1-16. Madeira Barn Owl occurs throughout the Madeira archipelago: the main island of Madeira, the smaller inhabited Porto Santo and the uninhabited Desertas. Most nests are in the walls of gorges in cultivated areas, but they also live in towns. Despite this, very few nests on Madeira are in human constructions.

perennial screeches have an unfamiliar shape, a descending overall contour. The ending is weak, less abrupt than in Common Barn Owl *T alba*. **CD1-16** is a medley of five recordings from Bugio, the first ever published of this species. In all but one the call is descending. On Deserta Grande, 14 km to the north, I recorded a neighbour on two successive nights. Its perennial screeches also descended in pitch.

CD1-16 **Madeira Barn Owl** *Tyto schmitzi* Bugio, Desertas, Madeira archipelago, 7-9 July 2011. Five recordings of perennial screeches, probably all from the same individual. Background: Cory's Shearwater *Calonectris borealis*, Desertas Petrel *Pterodroma deserta* and Madeiran Storm Petrel *Oceanodroma castro*. 110708.MR.015751.01, 110708.MR.033742.01, 110709.MR.011026.01, 110709.MR.014455.01 & 110707.MR.031040.01

A few months before visiting Bugio, João Nunes and I recorded Madeira Barn Owls on the north side of the main island of Madeira. Lameiros is a small village up the side of a valley where few foreigners venture. So when we visited a pinnacle above two local bars, we attracted quite a bit of attention. João's colleague Liliano owns one of the bars, and that's how word got out. Every now and then we heard a rather inappropriate *tu-whit, tu-who* from down below.

It was thanks to Liliano that we came to hear about this pair, which he had been hearing most evenings from his home. João is a mountaineer and Liliano had been up the

pinnacle years before. The two of them climbed up in no time, tying a rope to make subsequent visits easier. I followed carefully, putting some microphones up top where we hoped they would have a panoramic 'view'. Unfortunately the owls proved to be rather quiet that night. The few calls that I did record were perennial screeches of the presumed male and soliciting calls of the female, which must have been on eggs or brooding small young. The first perennial screech in **CD1-17** is delivered at the nest, the second is in flight and the third is already distant. All three descend in pitch just as on Bugio.

In fact, three out of the five Madeira Barn Owls I have heard gave only descending or uninflected calls. The fourth gave both descending and ascending variants, and the fifth gave just one, which happened to be ascending. In Common Barn Owl descending screeches are much less common, occurring in roughly 10% of individuals, and I have not heard them in Slender-billed Barn Owl *T gracilirostris* at all so far.

Considering how slowly vocalisations seem to evolve in barn owls, it is remarkable that an important, long distance signal of Madeira Barn Owl sounds different. Although a descending perennial screech occasionally occurs in Common Barn Owl too, on Madeira this is the most typical variant. It suggests that Madeira Barn has been evolving along its own path, in isolation, for quite some time.

Even after visiting them in five different months, João and I have never been lucky enough to catch this or any other pair at the height of courtship. We have only recorded a few courtship screeche**s** and never long, intense sequences. Based on the few examples we have, these seem to be higher-pitched than in Common or Slender-billed Barn Owl. **CD1-18** is a sequence of

CD1-17   **Madeira Barn Owl** *Tyto schmitzi* Lameiras, Madeira, 22:44, 31 March 2011. Perennial screeches of a probable male leaving the nest. Background: Iberian Green Frog *Pelophylax perezi*. 110331.MR.224440.30

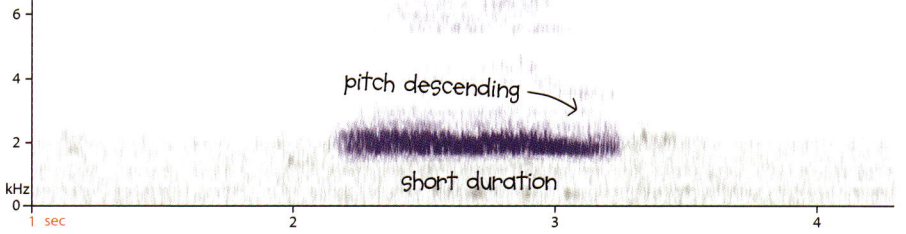

CD1-18   **Madeira Barn Owl** *Tyto schmitzi* Lameiras, Madeira, 27 February 2013. Courtship screeching of a male. 130227.JN.01440.12 João Nunes

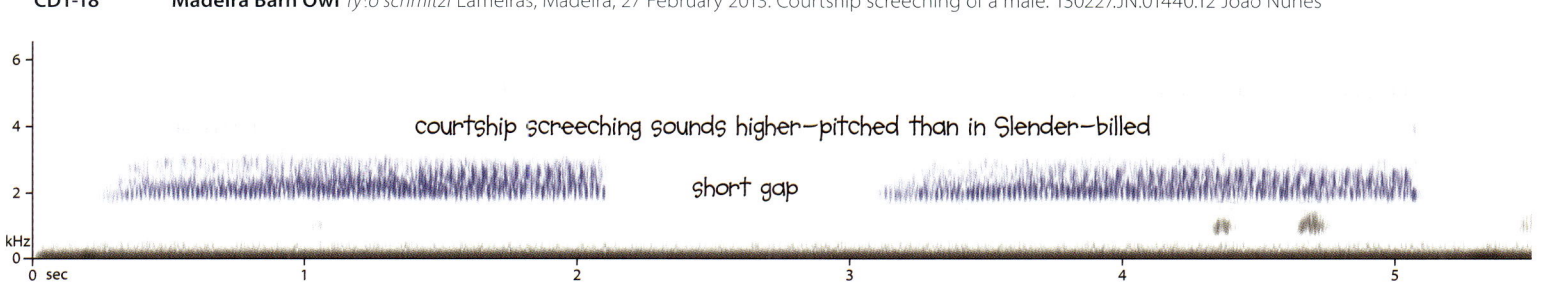

just two from Lameiras, and **CD1-19** is the longest that we have, recorded at a cliff near the sea.

Madeira Barn Owl *Tyto schmitzi* Ponta do Garajau, Madeira, 20:00, 5 April 2002. Courtship screeching of a male. Background: the sea. 02.014.MR.02200.22 **CD1-19**

Most calls of Madeira Barn Owl are easily matched with their equivalents in Common Barn Owl. I recorded the soliciting calls in **CD1-20** on April Fool's Day 2011 when the female was probably incubating. João recorded the mobbing scream in **CD1-21** during their next breeding attempt, on 11 January 2012.

Madeira Barn Owl *Tyto schmitzi* Lameiras, Madeira, 00:17, 1 April 2011. Soliciting calls of a female. Background: Iberian Green Frog *Pelophylax perezi*. 110401.MR.001737.00 **CD1-20**

Madeira Barn Owl *Tyto schmitzi* Lameiras, Madeira, 11 January 2012. Mobbing screams of an adult. 120111.JN.02324.10 João Nunes **CD1-21**

It would be fascinating to know which mainland population gave rise to Madeira Barn Owl. Intriguingly, Madagascar Red Owl *T soumagnei*, a close relative of Common Barn Owl living on an island off the other side of Africa, also has descending screeches (Thorstrom et al 2007, Huguet & Chappuis 2002). Cape Verde Barn Owl *T detorta* produces them too. Might all these barn owls have descended from a similar-sounding African population? And is it one that still exists?

If you go to Madeira to look for Zino's Petrel *P madeira* and other endemics, don't miss the chance to hear and perhaps see this fascinating barn owl, which survived for thousands of years on a diet of crickets, wall lizards and birds.

Madeira Barn Owl *Tyto schmitzi*, juvenile, Calhâu, Porto Santo, Madeira, September 1997 (*Domingo Trujillo*)

Cape Verde Barn Owl

Cape Verde Barn Owl *Tyto detorta* has a dark face, always. It is among the darkest of all barn owls. Compared to the darkest Common Barn Owls from Europe *T alba guttata*, its upperparts have larger white double spots and its flight feathers have more prominent dark bars (König et al 2008). Cape Verde is much darker than its nearest neighbour, African Barn Owl *T alba affinis*, which has a whitish facial disk. They do share other features, however, such as a large overall size with robust hunting and landing gear, and both have long and partly bare tarsi with heavy, bare toes (Cramp 1985).

Having such a distinctive appearance, Cape Verde Barn Owl has sometimes been treated as a separate species (eg, Hazevoet 1995) whereas the other two Macaronesian barn owls have barely received any attention. Other than plumage, there is actually nothing to suggest that Cape Verde has been isolated longer than the other two. All three differ morphologically from their mainland relatives, and two evolved in the complete absence of small mammals. The one furthest from any continent is actually Madeira Barn Owl *T schmitzi*, beating Cape Verde by a narrow margin.

Cape Verde Barn Owl's perennial screeches can be either descending as in **CD1-22** or ascending as in the first of **CD1-23**. I recorded both in the same valley, the focal point of a short expedition with René Pop. In 2007 I had found two cliff nests there while listening for shearwaters high on the steep slopes above. In November 2012 when I returned with René, the same two cliffs were hotspots of activity once again, but the owls were at a much earlier stage of breeding.

Fontainhas is well known as the first of several villages along Santo Antão's most popular walking route. Europeans attract little attention unless they come at night, which I recommend. The valley is a good place to listen to some of Cape Verde's nocturnal specialities, and I don't just mean owls. A few Boyd's Shearwaters *Puffinus boydi* breed there, and we heard Cape Verde Storm Petrels *Oceanodroma jabejabe* flying around the same cliffs as the barn owls (**CD1-24**). In the appropriate season, there are even a few Cape Verde Shearwaters *Calonectris edwardsii*.

Cape Verde Barn Owl *Tyto detorta* Fontainhas, Santo Antão, Cape Verde Islands, 00:50, 28 November 2012. A single, downward-inflected perennial screech. 121128.MR.005055.01   CD1-22

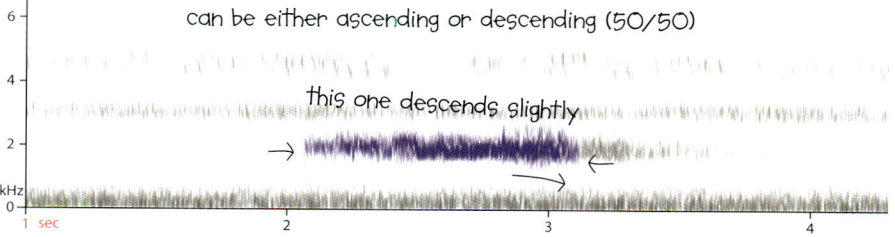

Cape Verde Barn Owl *Tyto detorta* Fontainhas, Santo Antão, Cape Verde Islands, 23:36, 27 November 2012. Two upward-inflected perennial screeches. Background: African Common Toad *Amietophrynus regularis*. 121127.MR.233636.01   CD1-23

Cape Verde Barn Owl *Tyto detorta* Fontainhas, Santo Antão, Cape Verde Islands, 18:36, 28 November 2012. A single, downward-inflected perennial screech. Background: Cape Verde Storm Petrel *Oceanodroma jabejabe*. 121128.MR.183626 & 121128.MR.204520.21   CD1-24

The storm petrels gave us our first clue about the owls' menu. Another came from Emerson and Pedro, two young brothers who delivered hay to their goats every day, underneath one of the suspected nest sites. They told me an owl often perched on wires in the village from where it would swoop down on cockroaches. Ancient pellet accumulations on the island of Santa Luzia, once inhabited but now abandoned, parallel those of Slender-billed Barn Owl *T gracilirostris*. Older prey remains consist largely of endemic vertebrates – giant geckos *Tarantola gigas* but also a few of the now extinct giant skink *Macroscincus coctei* – until the owls switched their focus to a smaller gecko *T caboverdiana* and the introduced House Mouse *Mus musculus* (Siverio et al 2007).

Habitat of Cape Verde Barn Owl *Tyto detorta*, Fontainhas, Santo Antão, Cape Verde Islands, 27 November 2012 (*René Pop*). Same location as CD1-22 to 24 & CD1-27 to 28.

I have been privileged to make several visits to the Cape Verde Islands, and my first took place in February 2004. Arnoud and I first heard and saw Cape Verde Barn Owl while recording Fea's Petrels *Pterodroma feae* on São Nicolau. A few days later I recorded one giving a perennial screech on Santiago (**CD1-25**). In late March 2007 there were several fledged young in the same area, but I also heard courtship screeching of an adult male and soliciting calls of an adult female (**CD1-26**). The pair had already raised one brood and were apparently preparing to raise a second.

CD1-25   **Cape Verde Barn Owl** *Tyto detorta* São Jorge de Orgãos, Santiago, Cape Verde Islands, 25 February 2004. A single rising, modulated perennial screech. Background: cockerels. 04.007.MR.01055.03

Santo Antão is the lushest of the Cape Verde Islands, and perhaps the most laid-back. It is also my favourite, so the barn owls were a great excuse to go back. They did not give us an easy time. Although we found them in several locations we never managed to get a decent view, not even at Fontainhas. With two pairs present, there was often something to listen to.

Cape Verde Barn Owl *Tyto detorta*, Barragem de Poilão, Santiago, Cape Verde Islands, 4 March 2012 (*Eric Didner*)

CD1-26   **Cape Verde Barn Owl** *Tyto detorta* São Jorge de Orgãos, Santiago, Cape Verde Islands, 18:55, 26 March 2007. Courtship screeching of a male and soliciting calls of a female. Background: Grey-headed Kingfisher *Halcyon leucocephala*. 070326.MR.185540.30

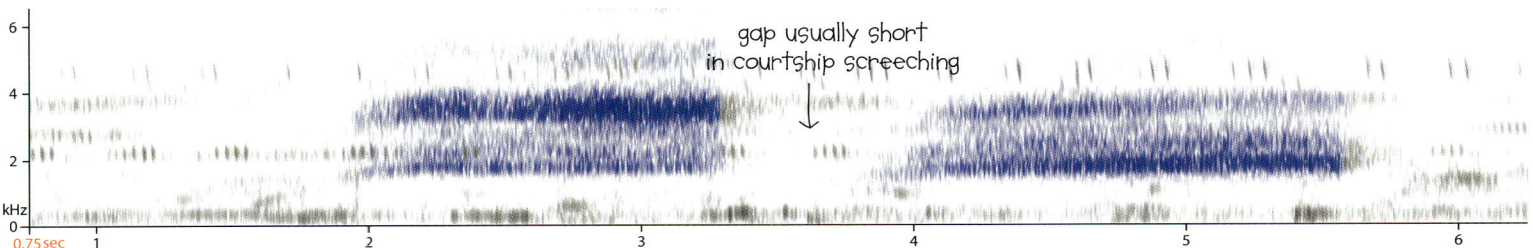

CD1-27 has rivalry screams near and far, and some faint purring. We were too early for begging calls during that trip, so here are some juveniles from February 2007 (**CD1-28**). Working back in time, their mothers must have laid eggs no earlier than November the previous autumn.

CD1-27 **Cape Verde Barn Owl** *Tyto detorta* São Jorge de Orgãos, Santiago, Cape Verde Islands, 18:55, 26 March 2007. Courtship screeching of a male and soliciting calls of a female. Background: Grey-headed Kingfisher *Halcyon leucocephala*. 070326.MR.185540.30

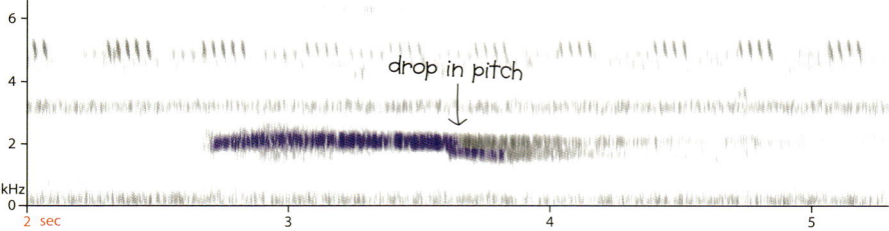

CD1-28 **Cape Verde Barn Owl** *Tyto detorta* Fontainhas, Santo Antão, Cape Verde Islands, 21:33, 23 February 2007. Begging of a juvenile in the nest. 070223.MR.213321.11

Cape Verde Barn Owl's breeding phenology is different from that of other Western Palearctic barn owls. Rainfall and ocean productivity, not temperature, determine when the owls breed. The Southwest Monsoon brings most of the year's rainfall, if any, between August and October, so plants and animals that depend on it regenerate during the last few months of the year. On the largest island, Santiago, most females lay their clutch in mid to late October (de Naurois 1982). By contrast, pairs living on seabird islets breed when storm petrels are most abundant, which coincides with a peak in marine upwelling in early spring.

On Branco, De Naurois found three freshly laid eggs on 8 March 1965, and on Ilhéu Grande, Geniez & López-Jurado (1998) found a recently vacated nest in mid-July.

Cape Verde Barn Owl is one of the least studied owls in the world. Ours are the first published recordings and only a handful of photographs exist. We could assume that Common Barn Owl is its closest relative, but the truth is that we don't know. The even darker São Tomé Barn Owl *T thomensis*, an islander living virtually on the equator, is arguably the taxon it resembles the most. I'd love to travel another 3500 km southeast to investigate, but first I must head north. From the Tropic of Cancer to the boreal forests, from a virtual unknown to a species virtually squeezed dry by science, and from eerie screeches to far-carrying hoots.

Cape Verde Barn Owl *Tyto detorta*, Boavista, Cape Verde Islands, 25 May 2004 (*Pedro Lopez Suarez*)

Common Barn Owl *Tyto alba*

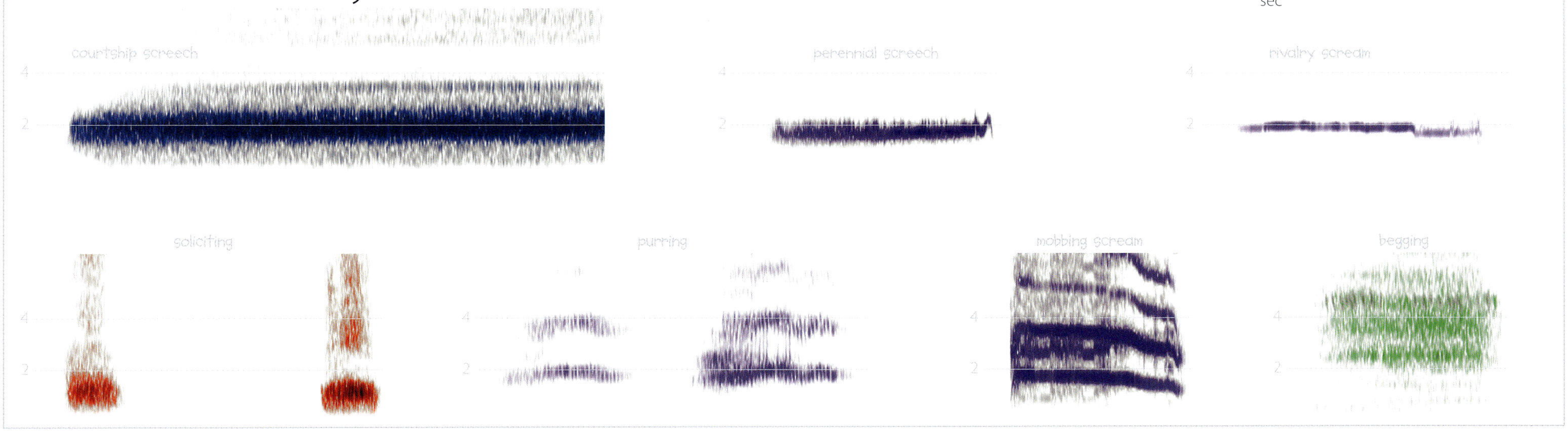

Slender-billed Owl *T gracilirostris*

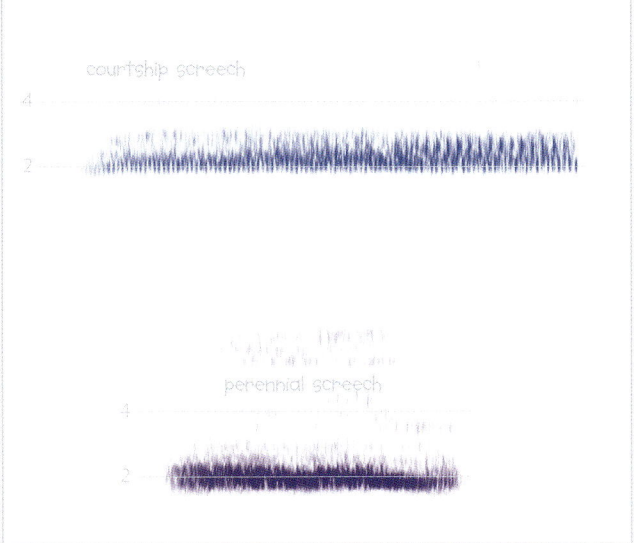
Madeira Barn Owl *T schmitzii*

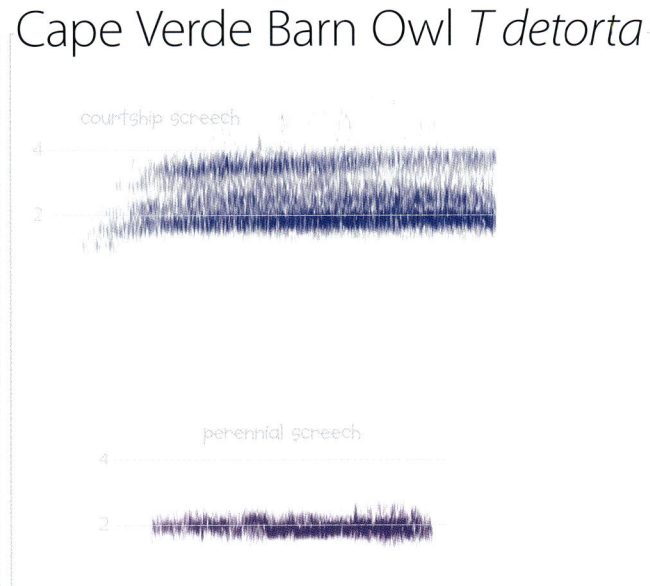
Cape Verde Barn Owl *T detorta*

Chapter 2: *Aegolius*

Tengmalm's Owl

An almost subliminal throbbing is often the first I hear of a Tengmalm's Owl *Aegolius funereus*. It can carry up to 2 km or more. Dense growth and thigh-deep snow thwart many an attempt to get closer. I eventually found the male in **CD1-29** on top of a small mountain in Sweden, but only after half an hour of hand and foot work. He promptly flew away. I felt like an idiot, sweating and panting as I stood with inappropriate shoes in the wet snow. So I tried hooting him back again. Fortunately, it worked.

Not all owls hoot. Barn owls *Tyto* don't. Their vocal anatomy forbids it (Miller 1934). Those that do belong to the Strigidae. All 'hooting owls' I can think of repeat their main territorial signal at regular intervals within a limited pitch range. In mature forests, songs with sustained pitches attract more attention. Owls hoot partly because this kind of sound works there so well.

In a dripping wet pine forest in northern Germany, a Tengmalm's Owl resonates beautifully as echoes from trunks and branches blend together in the misty air (**CD1-30**). Tengmalm's hooting varies dramatically from one individual to the next, most noticeably in the number of hoots in a series. This one averages just over 12, delivered at a rather fast pace. Another one, recorded on a windy night in a Swedish spruce forest, has

CD1-29   **Tengmalm's Owl** *Aegolius funereus* Bollnäs, Hälsingland, Sweden, 20:10, 24 March 2014. Hooting of a male, starting typically with a longer strophe or two. 140324.MR.201022.11

CD1-30   **Tengmalm's Owl** *Aegolius funereus* Lüneburger Heide, Niedersachsen, Germany, 03:58, 30 April 2008. Hooting of a male. 080430.MR.035809.11

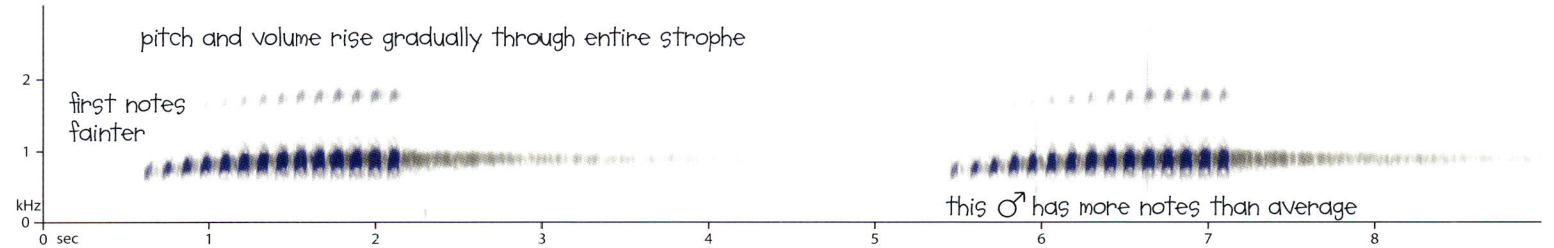

Tengmalm's Owl *Aegolius funereus*, Tornio, Lapland, Finland, 6 June 2010 (*Dick Forsman*). Note the blood-smeared face from feeding freshly killed prey to the chicks.

around seven (**CD1-31**). There can be so much variation in a single forest that larger scale geographical differences only become clear after listening to many examples.

Boreal Owl *A richardsoni* of North America sounds identifiably different from Tengmalm's Owl. Boreal generally delivers more hoots more quickly, reaching maximum pitch before the middle of the series, whereas Tengmalm's delivers a smaller number of hoots more slowly in a series that usually rises more gradually in pitch. **CD1-32** is a typical Boreal Owl. No single difference is fully diagnostic, but when all are combined, Boreal is a different sounding owl.

Tengmalm's Owl and Boreal Owl are so similar in appearance and ecology that they have always been regarded as the same species. So I was surprised to learn that their mtDNA differs by a substantial 3.69% (Johnsen et al 2010). If we apply the standard mutation rate of roughly 2.1% change per million years (Weir & Schluter 2008), Tengmalm's and Boreal went their separate ways around 1.8 million years ago. The Bering Strait has closed many

CD1-31 **Tengmalm's Owl** *Aegolius funereus* Älgsjön, Värmland, Sweden, 21:39, 26 March 2014. Hooting of a male, perhaps hesitant because of recordist's presence. Background: a strong gust of wind. 140326.MR.213944.01

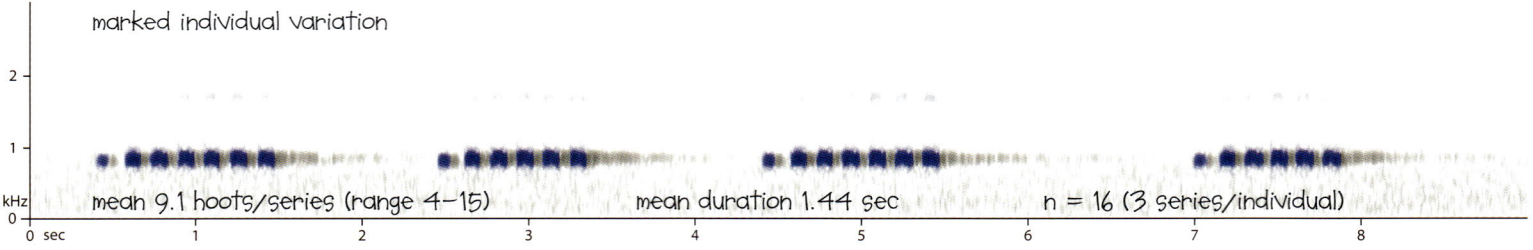

CD1-32 **Boreal Owl** *Aegolius richardsoni* Alberta, Canada, 21:00, 2 March 1977. Hooting of a male. Background: Great Horned Owl *Bubo virginianus*. William W H Gunn & The Macaulay Library at the Cornell Lab of Ornithology

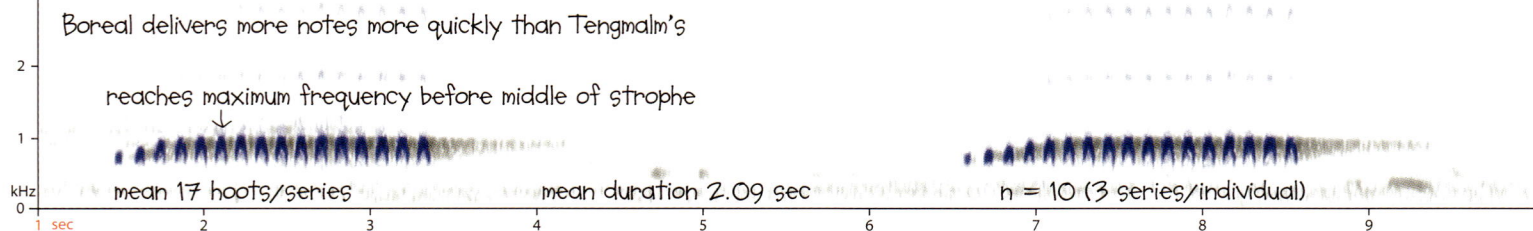

times since then, but apparently *Aegolius* genes never crossed it again. We can only guess which continent is the ancestral home of Tengmalm's and Boreal, but there are three more *Aegolius* owls in the Americas, and an extinct one used to live on Bermuda (Olson 2012).

Since Tengmalm's Owl separated from Boreal Owl, its geographical range has been in a state of flux. During colder periods, Tengmalm's occurred well to the south of where it breeds now. From east to west, remains have been found in southern Turkey, Crete, Italy and south-eastern Spain (Tyrberg 1998, 2008, Sánchez Marco 2004). In the west, it also reached Britain (Yalden & Albarella 2009). A different *Aegolius* species probably very similar to Tengmalm's lived on densely forested Sicily in the Mid-Pleistocene. Like the extinct Sicilian Barn Owl, *A martae* grew larger than its presumed ancestor (Pavia 2008) and was roughly the size of a Hume's Owl *Strix butleri*. In the Caucasus, Tengmalm's subspecies *A f caucasicus* is another southern taxon thought to have become isolated during the Pleistocene. Individuals of *caucasicus* are smaller than those of other populations of Tengmalm's.

My only encounter with a presumed *caucasicus* took place near Sivrikaya, a tiny village c 1800 m above sea level, set in a steep-sided valley in the Pontic Alps of north-eastern Turkey. Roy Slaterus and I left in the late afternoon, hoping to climb through the forests of Caucasian Spruce *Picea orientalis* and camp above the tree line some 300 m higher. At some ungodly hour in the morning we would climb another 350 m and place microphones in just the right spot, to capture sounds of the notoriously silent Caucasian Black Grouse *Tetrao mlokosiewiczi*. Or so we hoped.

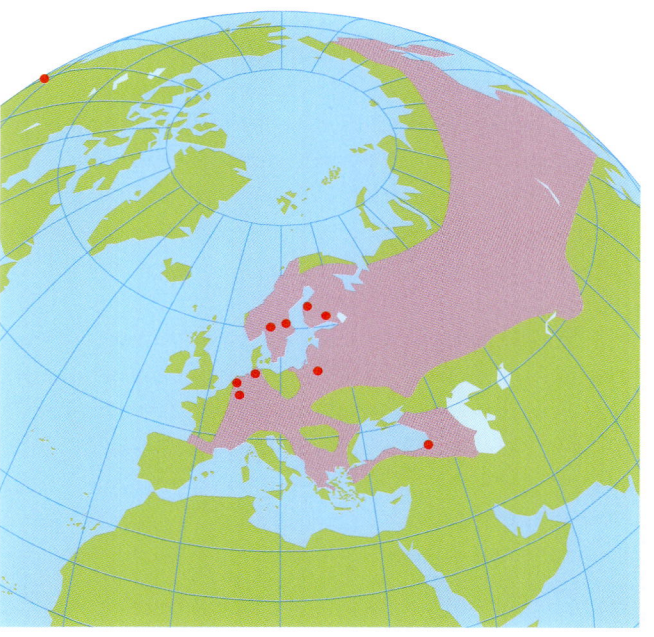

Approximate breeding distribution of Tengmalm's Owl *Aegolius funereus*. Recording locations of Tengmalm's and Boreal Owl *A richardsoni* (in North America) indicated by ● dots.

Carrying a large transparent parabolic dish, a telescope and camping gear, we astonished one Turk that we met. He warned us about bears, and we scanned the slopes in vain hope of finding one, before it found us. When we could no longer see, we kept listening. It was Roy, sitting upright in our tent, who heard the Tengmalm's Owl first. Lying down, I could hear nothing at all. Roy is razor sharp, so I had no doubt that he was right. Finally, when I sat up too, I could hear the owl faintly in the distance.

Despite being exhausted, we were determined to find it. At first while we descended into the dark spruces, the sound became louder. Then below a certain point it gradually became fainter again. Finally, we found ourselves at the lower edge of the forest, standing on the edge of a small stream. It could only be up beyond the next ridge, at least 200 m higher, and had become fainter when we descended below it. Defeated, we trudged back up to our tent.

We finally caught up with it four weeks later when we returned through the area in mid-June. Heading straight up the correct slope, we recorded it with little difficulty. Even this late in the spring, it was still singing like a mad thing, clearly an unpaired male (**CD1-33**). We know of no confirmed recordings of *caucasicus*, and one male is insufficient to judge whether it sounds any different from nominate *funereus*.

CD1-33   **Tengmalm's Owl** *Aegolius funereus* Sivrikaya, Rize, Turkey, 13 June 2002. Hooting of an unpaired male. 02.035.MR.05020.01

Voles are subject to cycles of abundance over periods of three or four years. Growth of vegetation, seed crops, the duration and thickness of snow protection in winter, and the health of predator populations all influence the timing and severity of the fluctuations (Hansson & Henttonen 1985). The extremes are greatest in the far north, where peak vole numbers can be hundreds of times greater than the minimum level, over a vast area. In temperate Europe, vole cycles show roughly 10-fold fluctuations (Korpimäki & Hakkarainen 2012), and in southern Europe they are merely local.

Tengmalm's Owls breed earlier and lay more eggs in times of plenty, when males may even mate with more than one female. In famine years, such promiscuity is unthinkable, and males face a conflict of interests. Although they might find more voles elsewhere, a thorough knowledge of their territory helps them to find the last ones as well as a few birds. So if possible they stay and defend their territories and the all-important nest holes. Meanwhile, females and juveniles disperse widely in all directions, looking for the best supplies of food.

In Finland, females move an average of 20 times further than males between successive breeding attempts (Korpimäki & Hakkarainen 2012). Northern populations are the most volatile, adult males being nomadic there to a limited extent as well as females (Hipkiss et al 2002). In central Europe, the owls travel shorter distances, although movements over 100 km are not uncommon. Even the small, apparently isolated Pyrenean population is only viable because new birds frequently arrive from elsewhere. Tengmalm's Owls from the Pyrenees, Fennoscandia and Far Eastern Siberia are very closely related (Koopman et al 2005, Broggi et al 2013). Given their mobility, birds from opposite ends of Eurasia could be maternal cousins just a few times removed.

In a vole year, male Tengmalm's Owls start singing during the coldest part of the winter and gradually increase their efforts until early spring. Sometimes it may be weeks later when a male finally detects a female in his territory. An aggressive *tsyuck* is the first sign of her presence, as well as her initial hostility. This is a call that, as we will see, has many variants and uses. On hearing it, the male immediately changes strategy from long-distance advertisement to 'warming up' his potential mate

with engagement hooting, usually from a perch close to a nest hole. The change is immediate, like flicking a switch (**CD1-34**). Engagement hooting is quieter than territorial hooting, with a stuttering rhythm (König 1968). It may last just a single evening or several, depending on the weather and how quickly the hostility thaws.

CD1-34   **Tengmalm's Owl** *Aegolius funereus* Logbermé, Liège, Belgium, 23:14, 9 April 2003. After three series of 'normal' hooting, a female's *tsyuck* immediately elicits a change to engagement hooting in the male. 03.006.AB.10153.11

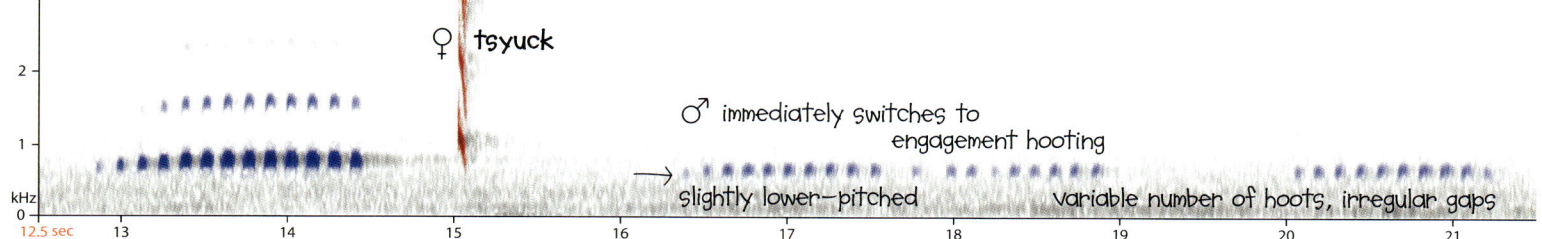

Next, the male progresses to his most excited form of hooting. He sits in the actual nest entrance and delivers an unbroken series of hoots, quieter and lower pitched than his usual hooting (**CD1-35**). This 'location roll' can last for several minutes without interruption. Almost inevitably, it results in the female flying to the nest hole. Imitating it may even cause flushed females to rush back to their nest. By the time location rolling starts, territorial hooting has usually ceased. Engagement song may in fact be a compromise between the two (Glutz von Blotzheim & Bauer 1980): a male may not want to commit himself to an ambivalent female, while he could still lure another one from afar.

It is no wonder that females are fussy about who to mate with and which nest hole to accept. If the breeding attempt is to be successful, they will have to spend the best part of two months indoors. Most nests are in holes excavated by Black Woodpeckers *Dryocopus martius*. In fact, Tengmalm's Owl breeds hardly anywhere in Europe lacking this woodpecker's services. Sadly, mature forests with lots of holes are becoming rare. Nestboxes have become crucial for the maintenance of Tengmalm's populations, and also make breeding possible in areas without Black Woodpeckers.

Tengmalm's Owl *Aegolius funereus*, female, Kuusamo, Pohjois-Pohjanmaa, Finland, 22 May 2014 (*Dick Forsman*)

When the male comes to the nest, protocol must be followed. He, arriving with his hard-won prey, is wary of the larger female. She is wary of anything arriving at the nest hole that is not her mate.

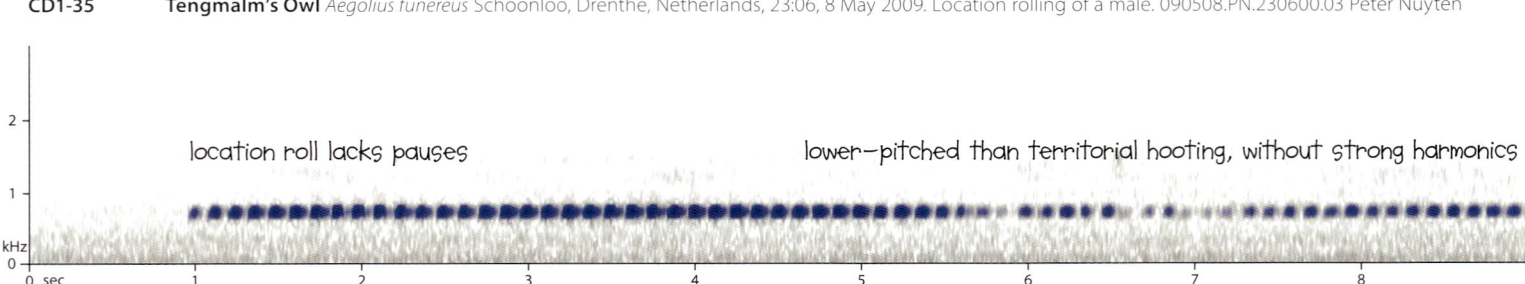

CD1-35 **Tengmalm's Owl** *Aegolius funereus* Schoonloo, Drenthe, Netherlands, 23:06, 8 May 2009. Location rolling of a male. 090508.PN.230600.03 Peter Nuyten

She is particularly vulnerable to Pine Martens *Martes martes* and Beech Martens *M foina*. Scratch the bark at the bottom of her tree, and she will appear at the entrance immediately. Early in the breeding season, the male announces imminent arrival with 'flight rolls', a much shorter version of the location roll. After a while, these are replaced by unobtrusive contact calls, which have a rising, questioning intonation reminiscent of a little owl *Athene*. The female version is somewhat hoarser and higher-pitched than the male version (König 1968). She only uses it after her antagonism towards the male has melted away, towards the end of courtship.

On hearing the male arrive, the female very often responds with her soliciting call, a short, extremely high-pitched sound, in the range of a Hazel Grouse *Tetrastes bonasia* or a Goldcrest *Regulus regulus* (**CD1-36**). Other names for it include 'peeping call' (Bondrup-Nielsen 1984) and 'nest call' (König 1968). Female Tengmalm's Owls do not use their soliciting call as often as most other owl species.

Tengmalm's Owl *Aegolius funereus* Lapua, Ostrobothnia, Finland, 01:16, 16 May 2009. Peeping calls of first-summer female, when male arrives at the nestbox with food. Before each peeping call, she gives a low, rising contact call. Background: chittering calls of several four-week-old young, Black Grouse *Tetrao tetrix* and Northern Lapwing *Vanellus vanellus*. 090516.MC.011600.01   CD1-36

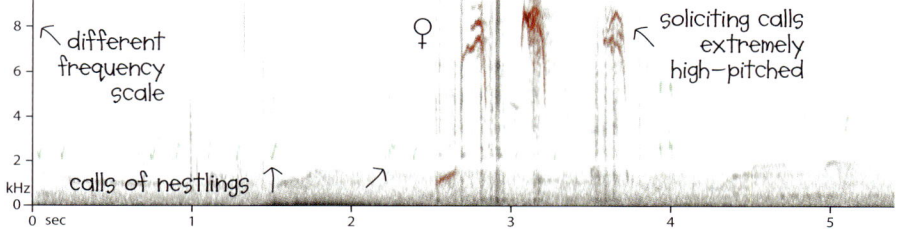

When the young are still very small, the female tears up their food and gives them tiny pieces while uttering a feeding call (**CD1-37**). In rhythm and context this call is similar to the flight roll of the male. Despite being higher-pitched and hoarser, it may have prompted at least some reports of 'female song'.

Tengmalm's Owl *Aegolius funereus* Lapua, Ostrobothnia, Finland, 00:49, 16 May 2009. Feeding calls of female, with chittering of several four-week-old young. Background: Black Grouse *Tetrao tetrix*, Northern Lapwing *Vanellus vanellus* and Eurasian Woodcock *Scolopax rusticola*. 090516.MC.004920.12   CD1-37

A month or slightly more after hatching, the young are ready to leave the nest. They make their first flight from the nest itself, skipping the branch-hopping stage typical of many other forest

Tengmalm's Owl *Aegolius funereus*, nestlings, Hauho, Kanta-Häme, Finland, 24 May 2009 (*Dick Forsman*). Young of c four weeks old, about to fledge within days. It is very rare to find a nest in a natural cavity as the species practically always uses a Black Woodpecker *Dryocopus martius* nest or a nestbox.

enough for him to keep track of them, but without attracting unwelcome attention. Three quarters of juveniles never complete their first year (Schwerdtfeger 1991). Northern Goshawks *Accipiter gentilis* kill many, but Ural Owl *Strix uralensis* is probably their worst enemy. Håkan once had a memorable experience in central Sweden that taught him how dangerous Ural Owl can be.

It was 13 May 1984, a calm evening with clear sky. As the light faded, Håkan was standing on a dirt track in swampy forest. First he whistled a Eurasian Pygmy Owl *Glaucidium passerinum* song, and a male came to perch in the top of a spruce. Then he whistled Tengmalm's Owl. There was no answer, but a Ural Owl came gliding directly towards him and landed in a tree quite close behind. After a couple of minutes it flew back into the forest, the Pygmy mobbing it as it went. Håkan whistled Tengmalm's again. The Ural came silently, stayed a while then disappeared, exactly the same as before. Håkan hooted and the Ural answered; it was a male. For a while they hooted to each other, but the Ural stayed where it was. After a new Tengmalm's imitation, the optimistic Ural came again immediately but left empty-handed. The whole procedure was repeated a fourth time.

Tengmalm's Owl *Aegolius funereus*, fledglings, Evo, Kanta-Häme, Finland, 1 June 2008 (*Dick Forsman*)

owls. The three young begging in **CD1-38** are ready for the big adventure. After they are all out, the male will gradually lead them towards good hunting areas. Their begging calls have to be loud

Tengmalm's Owl *Aegolius funereus* Lapua, Ostrobothnia, Finland, 22:13, 16 May 2009. Begging calls of three nearly fledged young. Background: Redwing *Turdus iliacus*. 090516.MC.221300.12

CD1-38

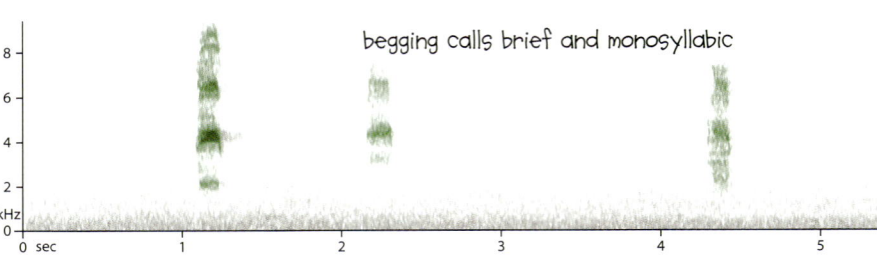

Shortly afterwards there was a sharp *tsyuck* quite close by: a real Tengmalm's Owl had arrived. Håkan whistled some 'song' again, and moments later the Tengmalm's was performing a war dance just a metre and a half in front of him: flying left and right at full speed with the sharpest possible turns. When it perched in a thin alder on the other side of the track, facing him, he saw its silhouette clearly against the sky, showing the oversized, heart-shaped head. With a Ural Owl just 50 m away, the situation was very tense; 10 seconds later he saw the Ural gliding towards the Tengmalm's – approaching it from behind. Suddenly there was a wild chase over the forest track: the Tengmalm's Owl with the Ural Owl just one metre behind.

Håkan whistled again a couple of minutes later to learn the Tengmalm's Owl's fate. The Ural Owl came directly, for a fifth time. So the Tengmalm's had survived after all. The Pygmy Owl, who was still around, dived aggressively towards the Ural's head, and the big owl flew back into the forest. With a *po-po-po-po-po-po... po-po-po-po-po-po...* it answered a final challenge from Håkan. Then silence.

Surviving juveniles disperse from late summer onwards. Their movements peak in September in the far north and October further south, coinciding with those of adult females. When the vole population crashes, Tengmalm's Owls can move on a massive scale. Matti Suopajärvi from the Kemi region at the north end of the Gulf of Bothnia has heard five to eight simultaneously. He sometimes hears them approaching from far off. When one *tsyucks*, any others within 400 m or so are very likely to answer.

In **CD1-39**, a Tengmalm's Owl is on the move in Białowieża forest, Poland. It calls at long intervals, arriving from far to the left and passing to the right by 1:46. No imitation or tape lure was required: this was spontaneous behaviour. At longer distances, the *tsyuck* call appears to change from a 'vertical', short and broad-frequency sound to a 'horizontal' one, long lasting and limited to a narrow frequency range. Only the lowest frequencies travel far, and they leave a 'sound tail' in the resonant forest. For a Tengmalm's, it must be fairly easy to judge the distance.

Tengmalm's Owl *Aegolius funereus* Białowieża forest, Podlaskie, Poland, 03:35, 9 October 2012. *Tsyuck* calls passing slowly, at long intervals. Background: Song Thrush *Turdus philomelos* and Yellow-necked Mouse *Apodemus flavicollis*. 121009.MR.033538.00 CD1-39

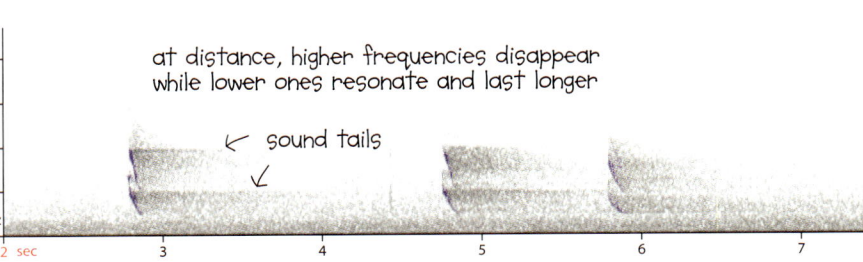

Since they clearly like to stay in vocal contact, the intriguing possibility exists that Tengmalm's Owls wander in loose flocks or 'boids'. There is no proof, but occasional parallel movements seem to suggest this. In Sweden, two females that bred as neighbours 1 km apart in 1981 moved 70 km and bred 2 km apart in 1982 (Löfgren et al 1986). All three male Tengmalm's discovered in the Netherlands in 2010 changed territory during that spring. Two that had been neighbours moved a few kilometres and defended adjoining territories at a second site (Ottens & Jonker 2010).

Białowieża forest includes tracts where no tree has ever been planted and where the ecosystem is closer to natural equilibrium than anywhere else in lowland Europe. A year before my visit, several species of trees had been very generous. A glut of acorns and other seeds had given the forest rodents plenty to eat. Yellow-necked Mice *Apodemus flavicollis* and Bank Voles *Myodes glareolus* bred profusely in response, and so did the owls. They had their best breeding season in living memory. Now another bumper crop of acorns was falling from the trees, making for crunchy night walks along the forest tracks. I could hear rodents quite often, both by their squeaks and squabbles and by the rustle of litter on the forest floor.

When I imitated a Tengmalm's Owl with my voice, the forest's resonance gave me compliments I didn't deserve. The *tsyuck* calls that often followed could be surprisingly loud (**CD1-40**). Occasionally they could be longer, plaintive, descending squeaks (**CD1-41**). Defence, challenge and contact variants of the *tsyuck* call probably differ in ways that we have yet to decipher. In autumn it is almost impossible to know whether we are listening to a male defending his territory or a young bird looking for one. Both seem to use *tsyuck* calls.

Male Tengmalm's Owls sometimes respond to intrusions, whether real or simulated, with a stretched-out *kyuweck*, which can sound surprisingly similar to a Tawny Owl *S aluco*. **CD1-42** illustrates this call at a lower level of intensity. With growing excitement, the ending becomes louder and rougher.

CD1-40 **Tengmalm's Owl** *Aegolius funereus* Białowieża forest, Podlaskie, Poland, 21:08, 4 October 2012. A single *tsyuck* call at close range. 121004.MR.210806.00

CD1-41 **Tengmalm's Owl** *Aegolius funereus* Białowieża forest, Podlaskie, Poland, 22:33, 4 October 2012. A series of rather drawn-out *tsyuck* calls at close range. 121004.MR.223330.00

CD1-42 **Tengmalm's Owl** *Aegolius funereus* Mäntyharju, Savonia, Finland, 23 February 2009. *Kyuweck* calls of an adult. Background: Northern Hawk-Owl *Surnia ulula* and Long-eared Owl *Asio otus*. Hannu Jännes.

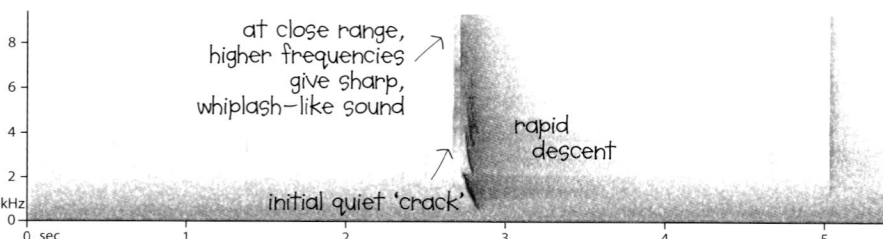

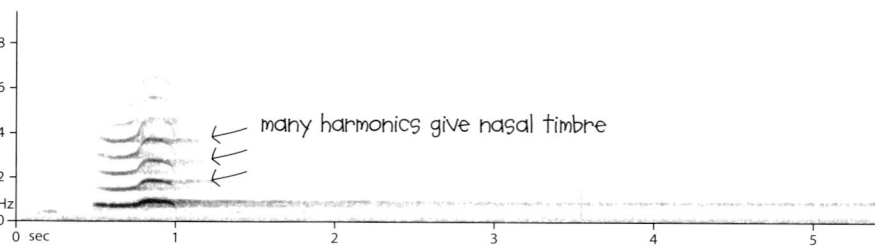

When planning an autumn trip for Tengmalm's Owls, the sound I hoped to capture was 'autumn song', which can occasionally be heard "on windless, clear and usually quite cold evenings and nights, as September turns to October" (Kuhk 1953). When I arrived on 2 October 2012 the weather seemed perfect, so I took a long night walk through mature spruce forest. After nearly six hours without hearing any 'song', I assumed it was safe to go and sleep for a few hours. I left my equipment recording in a clearing where rodents were foraging under a patch of young European Hornbeams *Carpinus betulus*.

Only 20 minutes after I left, a Tengmalm's Owl started singing so far away that, even when amplified, I could only just hear it. Melting into the primeval forest, the five individual hoots of each series were a faint throbbing hum on a single pitch, once every few seconds. The sharp metallic ticks of Song Thrushes *Turdus philomelos* migrating overhead could hardly have contrasted more. I walked many more kilometres over the following nights, but I never heard him again.

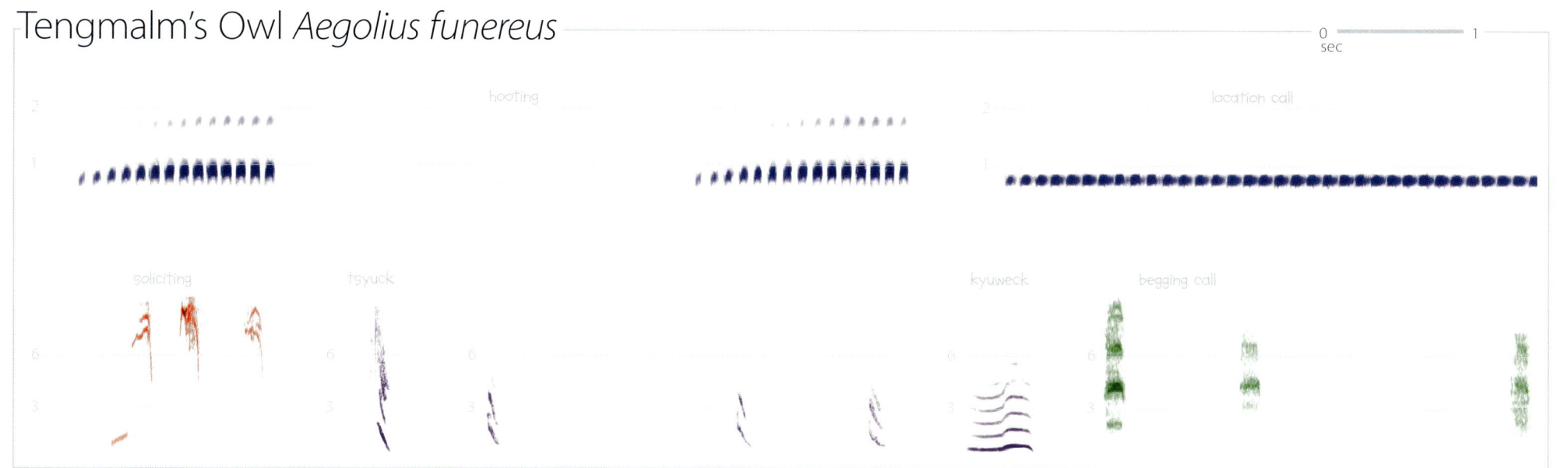

Tengmalm's Owl *Aegolius funereus*

Chapter 3: *Athene*

Little Owl

It was not until I lived in Portugal that I became intimate with little owls *Athene*. I could recognise their voices easily enough, but they always seemed to be inventing new sounds. Gradually I learned to live with their Latin temperament, and with the help of a comprehensive 'dictionary' (Exo & Scherzinger 1989), I eventually learned their language.

Once I was able to sort their calls into types, I was thrilled to find that I could distinguish two different little owl species by ear, both living in the Western Palearctic. The big surprise was that of the many possible taxa it was *vidalii* that was the odd one out. This is not an owl I need to sit five hours on a plane to go and visit, but one I have lived with in Britain (where it was introduced in 1842), Holland and Portugal. A new genetic study (Pellegrino et al 2014) recently confirmed a large genetic difference between this and the other European little owls, and clarified their distribution. Since *A vidalii* is the best known taxon in the English-speaking world, the familiar name Little Owl seems appropriate for it. All the others share a diagnostic battle cry, which several Mediterranean languages use to identify them. We will do the same, and group them together as Cucumiau *A noctua*.

Athene owl calls are highly volatile. Each one seems capable of morphing into others of higher and lower emotional intensity. In the following account, the progression is from relative calm through increasing excitement to decisive action. The notes become shorter with each successive call type as they become more and more explosive. It helps to be familiar with these call-types in Little Owl before learning how they differ to varying degrees in Cucumiau.

Little Owl *Athene vidalii*, Rosmaninhal, Idanha-a-Nova, Portugal, 28 June 2010 (*René Pop*)

Habitat of Little Owl *Athene vidalii*, Rosmaninhal, Idanha-a-Nova, Portugal, 29 June 2010 (*René Pop*). The area where CD1-43 to 44 were recorded.

Hearing a male Little Owl hooting his long, rising notes on a warm, windy night in late February (**CD1-43**), you would never suspect his fiery temper. By the light of a gibbous moon, he calmly surveys his small patch of Holm Oak *Quercus ilex* montado. Nearby there is a small, uninhabited cottage. A couple of donkeys keep the grass cropped under the scattered trees. The nearest inhabited building is 2 km away, so for once there are no dogs barking. Only a croaking Natterjack Toad *Bufo calamita* and some rustling leaves put the owl in his living context.

In early spring, males hoot day and night with a strong peak at dusk and a lesser one at dawn. A bout of hooting may last several minutes or longer. As it progresses, the overall pitch and volume gradually rise. When the male reaches the highest pitch he can hoot loudly, the hoots gradually level out. Females can also hoot, but only in short series of up to about five lower-pitched, shorter hoots (Exo 1984). In **CD1-44** both members of a pair are hooting, the much quieter one being the female. She only starts in earnest at 0:14 and then her series consists of just three short hoots.

CD1-43   **Little Owl** *Athene vidalii* Rosmaninhal, Idanha-a-Nova, Portugal, 20:20, 25 February 2010. Hooting of a male, with others hooting and giving excitement calls in the distance. Background: Natterjack Toad *Bufo calamita*. 100225.MR.202044.21

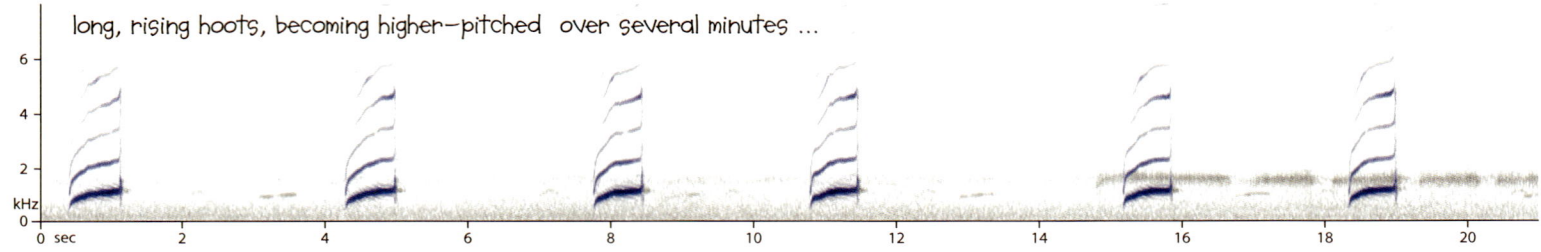

CD1-44   **Little Owl** *Athene vidalii* Rosmaninhal, Idanha-a-Nova, Portugal, 19:26, 25 February 2010. Hooting of a male, with quiet excitement calls of female changing into hooting from 0:14. Background: Natterjack Toad *Bufo calamita*. 100225.MR.192642.30

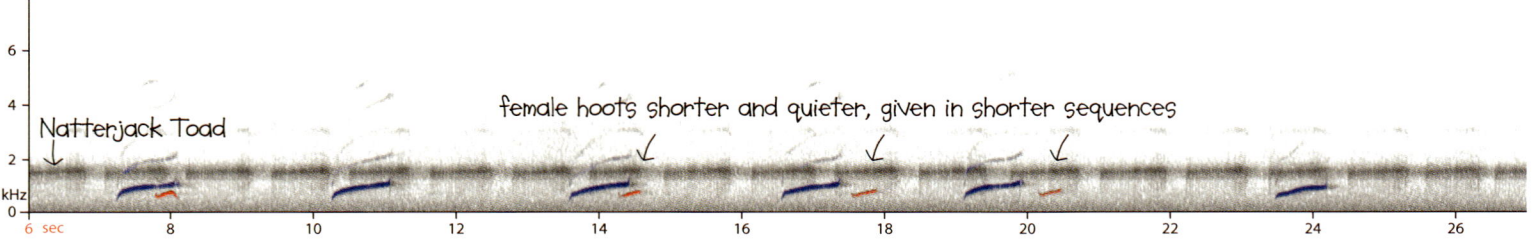

Athene owls are unusual in preferring open habitats and not being dependent on forests. Although they often breed in tree holes, at some point in their evolution they started to recognise cavities in cliffs and piles of rocks as alternatives. This allowed them to colonise arid and barren areas where they were often the only species of owl. The inflections in Little Owl hooting may have evolved as a consequence. Without forest resonance to extend a sustained, even pitch beyond its length, there is little advantage in producing one. Instead, Little Owls can afford to distinguish themselves with a rising hoot.

The Little Owls that I know best breed around Rosmaninhal in eastern Portugal. The village is full of owls, but recording them involves negotiating an acoustic minefield. When one dog gets a fright, it may be 10 minutes before the wave of unrest has made it around the village. Otherwise it is a quiet place, with almost no traffic at night. The human population is mainly elderly, and at a guess I'd say that over half of the houses are unoccupied.

In early March, a 500 m walk along the northern fringe of the village could take you through around six Little Owl territories. In the orange glow of the streetlights, these not-so-sharp-sighted owls are able to stay active all night long. I recorded **CD1-45** underneath a lamppost where one male liked to hoot. It shows how Little Owl calls 'grade' into one another. Here, hooting emerges from two much quieter call types.

At the other extreme, hooting often leads into higher-pitched 'excitement calls' (Exo & Scherzinger 1989). Their contour is highly variable but always rises before it falls. A series may be fairly long, but excitement calls are by nature unstable. Often they escalate into aggressive song, alarm calls or cackling, depending on the course of the interaction. Alternatively, things may calm down until all we hear is subdued hooting. In **CD1-46** it is 02:40 in the morning. Except for one or two insomniacs, the dogs are asleep, but goat bells are still tinkling. The Little Owls are wide awake and socialising. At least six different individuals give excitement calls at high intensity. Over the course of five minutes a Mexican wave of these excitement calls passed slowly from right to left as each pair tested its neighbours.

Aggressive song, the best-known sound in Little Owl's large repertoire, consists of a burst of particularly shrill excitement calls: *MIAU...MIAU...MIAU*...etc. Because so much energy is required to produce such an outburst, it never lasts very long. Very often, both pair members participate as a duet, triggering their neighbours as well. In **CD1-47**, at least four birds are performing aggressive song, with others also calling in the

CD1-45   **Little Owl** *Athene vidalii* Rosmaninhal, Idanha-a-Nova, Portugal, 23:23, 3 March 2010. The first call is half 'contact call' and half 'beckoning call'. After 0:17 there is a contact call, then the bird starts to hoot loudly. Contact calls play a role in close range communication between pair members during the whole year. Beckoning calls are single notes similar to hooting but much quieter and usually shorter. They are used to reassure or appease. Contact and beckoning calls are often heard in association (Exo & Scherzinger 1989). Background: Barbary Dove *Streptopelia risoria*. 100303.MR.232312.11

CD1-46   **Little Owl** *Athene vidalii* Rosmaninhal, Idanha-a-Nova, Portugal, 02:40, 18 March 2012. A chorus of excitement calls involving at least six individuals, part of a 5-minute 'Mexican wave'. Background: Southern Tree Frog *Hyla meridionalis* and Iberian Green Frog *Pelophylax perezi*. 120318.MR.024017.12

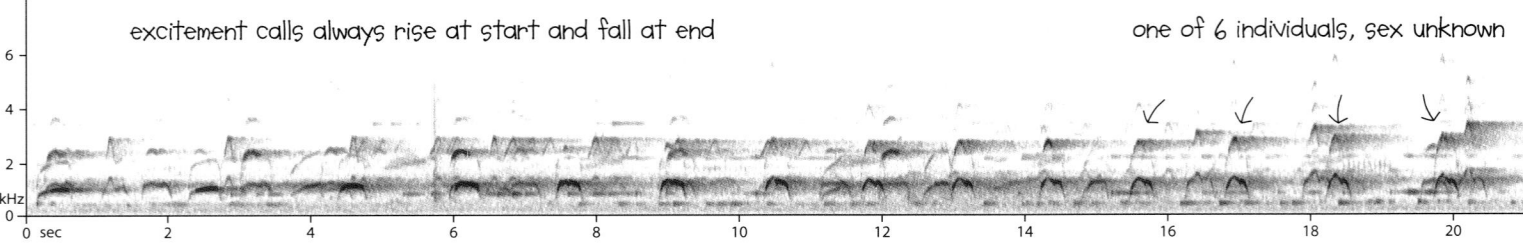

CD1-47 **Little Owl** *Athene vidalii* Rosmaninhal, Idanha-a-Nova, Portugal, 22:45, 6 March 2009. Aggressive song of at least four individuals. Background: Southern Tree Frog *Hyla meridionalis* and Iberian Green Frog *Pelophylax perezi*. 090306.MR.224526.30 background. After a couple of beckoning calls, the pair in **CD1-48** perform shrill aggressive song as a duet. This gives way to a long series of more tempered excitement calls.

Little Owl *Athene vidalii*, adulte (left) and juvenile, Rosmaninhal, Idanha-a-Nova, Portugal, 28 June 2010 (*René Pop*)

CD1-48 **Little Owl** *Athene vidalii* Rosmaninhal, Idanha-a-Nova, Portugal, 22:25, 6 March 2009. Aggressive song of a pair, gradually giving way to excitement calls. Background: Southern Tree Frog *Hyla meridionalis* and Common Barn Owl *Tyto alba*. 090306.MR.222541.01

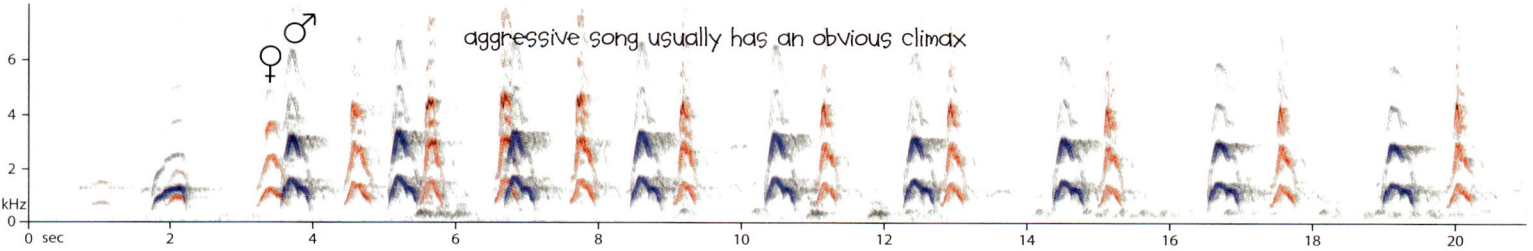

CD1-49 **Little Owl** *Athene vidalii* Cabo Espichel, Sesimbra, Portugal, 06:00, 11 October 2010. Aggressive song at dawn in autumn. Background: the sea. 101011.MR.060052.12

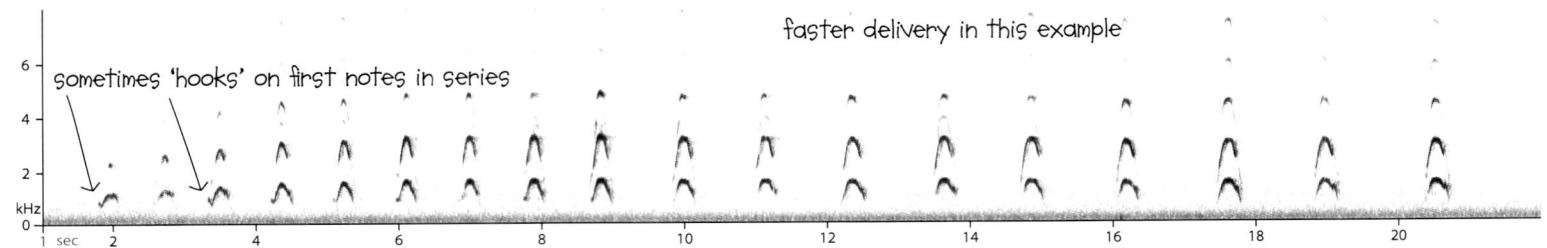

Aggressive song is used throughout the year and plays a prominent role during autumn when young birds are dispersing and competing with adults for territories. When I record night migration in October and November, I often hear it during calm nights. There are peaks at dawn and dusk, especially in areas of high population density. **CD1-49** was recorded in autumn at a disused monastery perched high above the sea, about 75 minutes before sunrise.

Sometimes when discovering and chasing off intruders, aggressive song escalates into the 'alarm call' (Exo & Scherzinger 1989). In Little Owl this usually consists of at least two notes. The complete call may be given in isolation or repeated several times. The 'alarm call' may also be used to warn family members about potential predators. If young are begging nearby, they immediately fall silent.

The two-note alarm calls in **CD1-50** were given by an adult accompanying fledged juveniles, when it became nervous about my presence. **CD1-51** illustrates the less common single-note alarm call, given by a surprised owl as it flew round the corner of the clifftop monastery.

CD1-50 **Little Owl** *Athene vidalii* Rosmaninhal, Idanha-a-Nova, Portugal, 21:57, 15 June 2009. Two-note alarm calls of an adult accompanying fledged juveniles. Background: Iberian Green Frog *Pelophylax perezi* and juvenile humans *Homo sapiens*. 090615.MR.215752.01

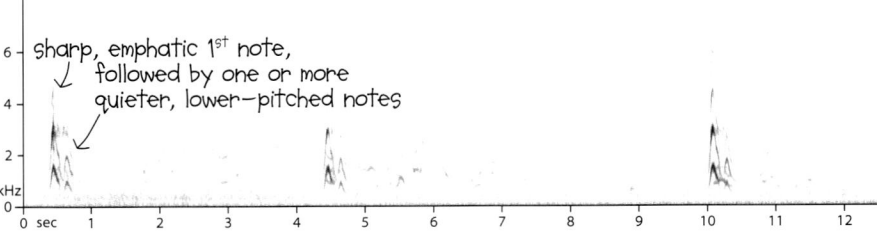

CD1-51 **Little Owl** *Athene vidalii* Cabo Espichel, Sesimbra, Portugal, 06:32, 29 September 2009. Single-note alarm calls in autumn when surprised by recordist. 100929.MR.063226.01

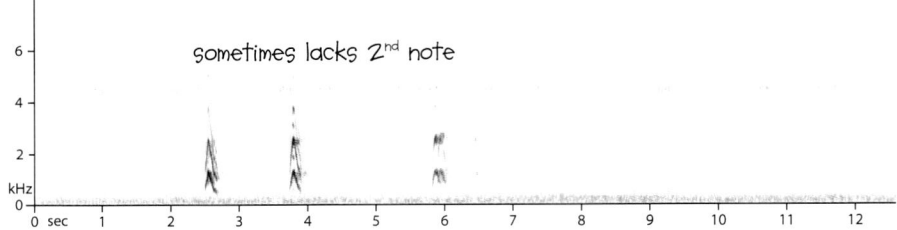

Cackling is Little Owl's most explosive call. It conveys extreme excitement in a variety of situations that include disturbances near the nest, encounters with enemies (I once heard it when a barn owl suddenly appeared), territorial disputes and squabbles with partners. In **CD1-52** the caller arrives from the left and completes the series from a perch. Cackling is in some ways an escalation of the alarm call and structurally related to it. Unlike the alarm call, which contains a warning, cackling usually accompanies decisive action. Of all Little Owl sounds, this is the one most often given in flight. It may ring out quite unexpectedly or mark the end of a longer interaction. We can hear it at any time of year.

you to see whether you can pick them all out, and for me to find out whether I have described them adequately.

After several years of recording Little Owls in Rosmaninhal, I thought I knew their sounds well, but I had never actually recorded at a nest. In an isolated small ruin near my home northwest of Lisbon, I found one hidden in a corner of the loft. To my amazement, almost every sound I recorded there was new to me. I shouldn't have been so surprised. Exo & Scherzinger's (1989) comprehensive account listed at least 22 clearly separate call types that in turn evolved from five basic originals.

CD1-52 **Little Owl** *Athene vidalii* Rosmaninhal, Idanha-a-Nova, Portugal, 06:05, 26 February 2010. Cackling in flight, then perched. Background: Red-legged Partridge *Alectoris rufa* and Woodlark *Lullula arborea*. 100226.MR.060516.01

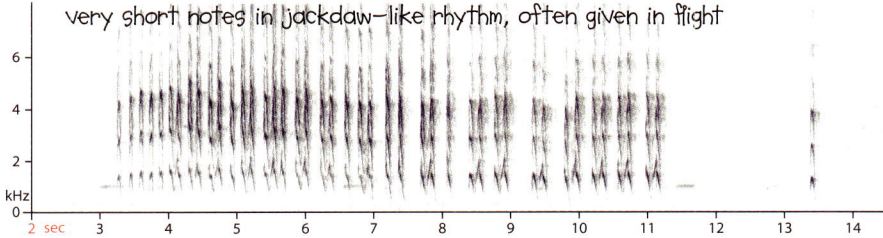

CD1-53 shows Little Owl social dynamics at their most fluid. All of the loud call types that we have covered so far are included, except for cackling. The recording can serve as a little test: for

CD1-53 **Little Owl** *Athene vidalii* Rosmaninhal, Idanha-a-Nova, Portugal, 23:29, 5 March 2009. Calls of a pair perched on a lamppost, interacting with their neighbours. The most prominent sounds include hooting, alarm calls, aggressive song, beckoning calls and excitement calls. Background: Common Barn Owl *Tyto alba*. 090305.MR.232940.11

The first surprise was that during the last couple of weeks before egg-laying, most close-range communication between the partners was with husky, highly variable soliciting calls that I had hardly noticed before. In **CD1-54**, a male and female are both using these, a few days before the start of egg-laying. The context is courtship feeding. This ritual not only cements the pair bond but also establishes how much food is available in the territory. As for the male, he uses this call to placate his partner when he needs to come close.

The female of my local pair laid eggs in mid-April. During the three weeks prior to this, the pair seemed to use almost all the quieter sounds in their vocabulary. In the lead up to copulation they used a great variety of sounds, most of them very quiet. Only the final, high-pitched twitter would have been audible more than a few metres away. **CD1-55** illustrates the whole call sequence before and after copulation.

The month of incubation was very quiet. After hatching, the young were virtually inaudible for the first few days. Even with the microphones just 2 m away, they barely registered. In **CD1-56**, the adult male arrives on the right, then scampers across the floorboards to the nest. I believe he is probably the one giving a single soliciting call as he hands over prey to the female, while she then uses a long series of staccato 'feeding calls' to encourage her nestlings to eat.

CD1-54   **Little Owl** *Athene vidalii* Galamares, Sintra, Portugal, 03:23, 11 April 2012. Soliciting calls of male and female, with the female giving longer calls on the left ('begging-snoring' in Exo & Scherzinger 1989). 120411.MR.032357.02

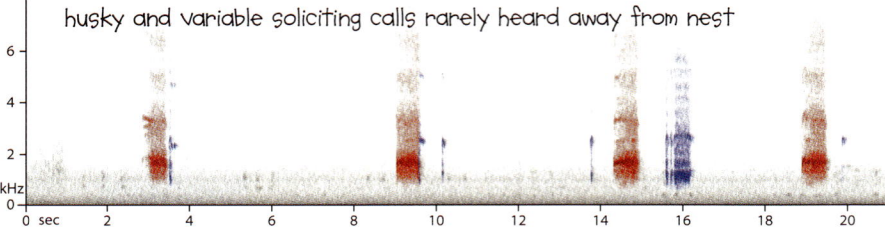

CD1-55   **Little Owl** *Athene vidalii* Galamares, Sintra, Portugal, 03:06, 3 April 2012. Call sequence leading to copulation. The rising, yelping calls belong to the female while the chugging and beckoning calls are the male, as well as the copulation twitter at 0:23. The female gives a few husky soliciting calls at the end. 120403.MR.030646.03

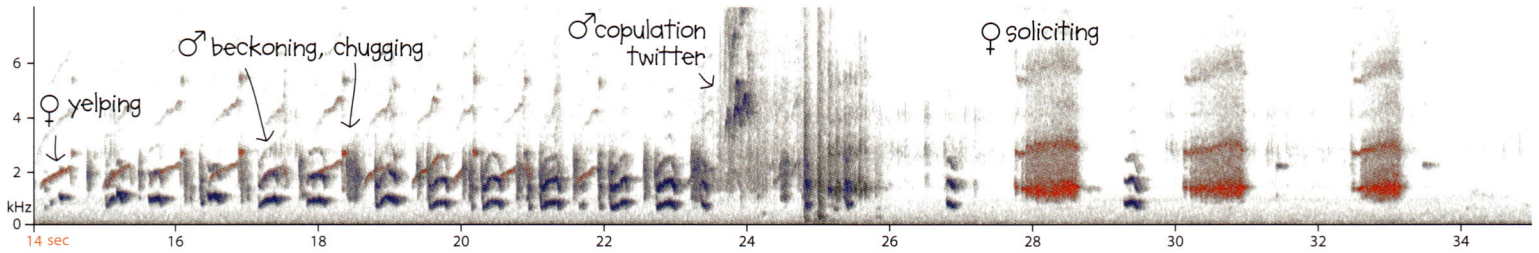

CD1-56 **Little Owl** *Athene vidalii* Galamares, Sintra, Portugal, 03:52, 18 May 2012. Male arrives at nest and scampers across the floorboards. Then there is a single soliciting call (the male?) and a long series of feeding calls (the female?). Two or three tiny nestlings call faintly in the background. 120518.MR.035220.02

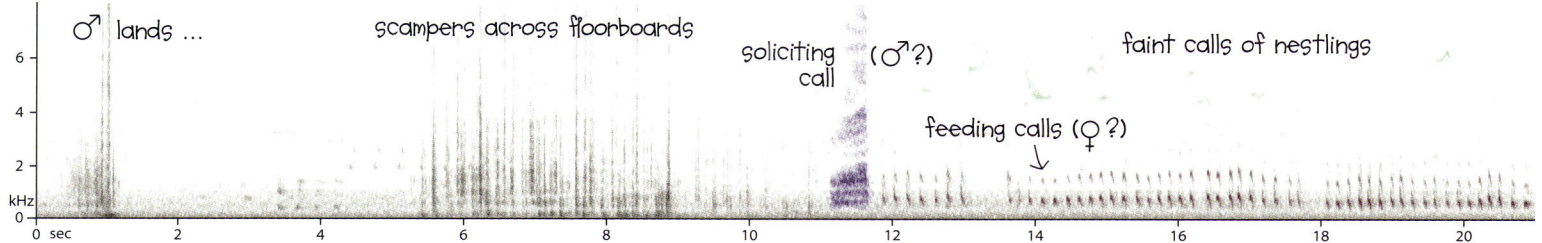

By the time Little Owls fledge, an alert birder passing close by can hardly fail to hear them. In late June, begging calls can be heard all round Rosmaninhal. The challenge is to separate those of Little from the rather similar begging calls of Common Barn Owl. Little Owls beg much more quietly, so confusion is only possible if we misjudge the distance. This quietness also makes them challenging to record. I finally succeeded one early July night when a juvenile landed just 3 m away, apparently oblivious to me (**CD1-57**). When I gently lifted my binoculars it flew off with a single alarm call.

Little Owl *Athene vidalii*, juvenile, Rosmaninhal, Icanha-a-Nova, Portugal, 28 June 2010 (*René Pop*)

Little Owl *Athene vidalii* Rosmaninhal, Idanha-a-Nova, Portugal, 00:57, 4 July 2009. Begging calls of a fledged juvenile, then a single alarm call when it noticed the recordist. Background: a singing dog! 090704.MR.005712.01

CD1-57

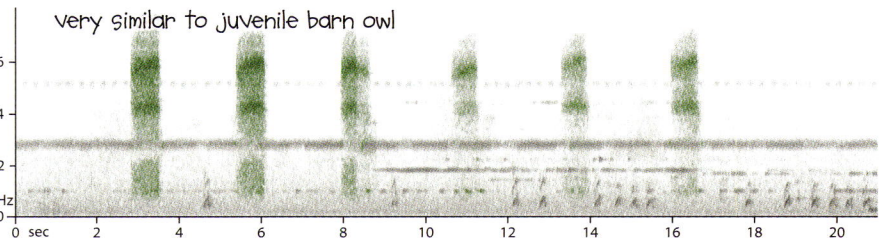

Little Owl *Athene vidalii*, Tahivilla, Andalucia, Spain, 9 September 2012 (*Dick Forsman*)

Juveniles gradually increase their activity radius, but return to their natal territory several times before finally severing ties with their parents in late September or early October. By the beginning of November, most have settled somewhere else. A typical dispersal distance for juveniles is less than 20 km. Fewer than 10% disperse over 100 km (van Nieuwenhuyse et al 2008). Occasionally, Little Owls from the introduced British population have headed out across the Irish Sea, colonising the island of Skomer, plundering British Storm Petrels *Hydrobates pelagicus* on Skokholm (Alexander 1935), and occasionally straggling to the Isle of Man and the east coast of Ireland (Glue 2002).

Such long distance movements are exceptions that highlight a general truth. Owls of the genus *Athene* are, on the whole, rather sedentary. There is none of the continent-wide mixing of genes so typical of Tengmalm's Owl *Aegolius funereus*. Being more sedentary allows them to adapt to regional conditions. In the past, there several species evolved on Mediterranean islands. *A angelis* (Mourer-Chauviré et al 1997) lived on Corsica and Sardinia, *A trinacriae* (Pavia & Mourer-Chauviré 2002) was a contemporary of the giant barn owls and dwarf elephants of Sicily, *A cretensis* lived on Crete (Weesie 1982), and *A vallgornerensis* has recently been described from Mallorca (Guerra et al 2012).

With this in mind, it should not be so surprising that there are still two species surviving. The real surprise is that it has taken so long to learn how to tell them apart.

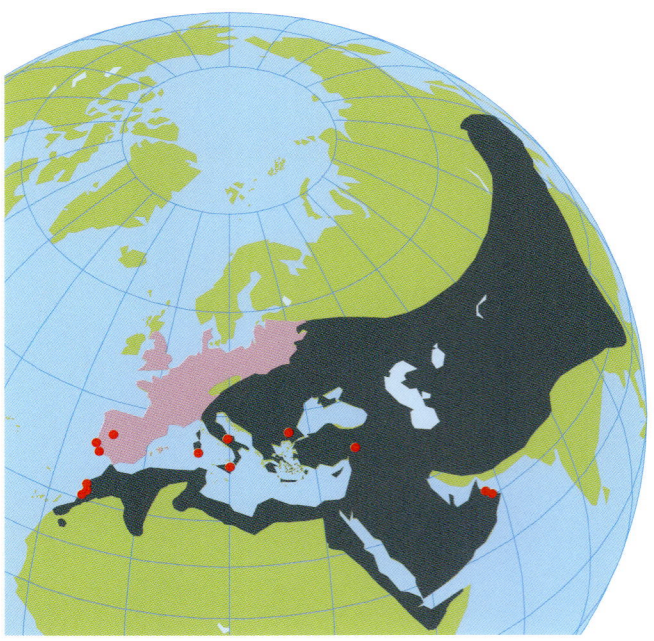

Approximate breeding distribution of Little Owl *Athene vidalii* ■ and Cucumiau *A noctua* ■. Recording locations indicated by ● dots.

Little Owl *Athene vidalii*

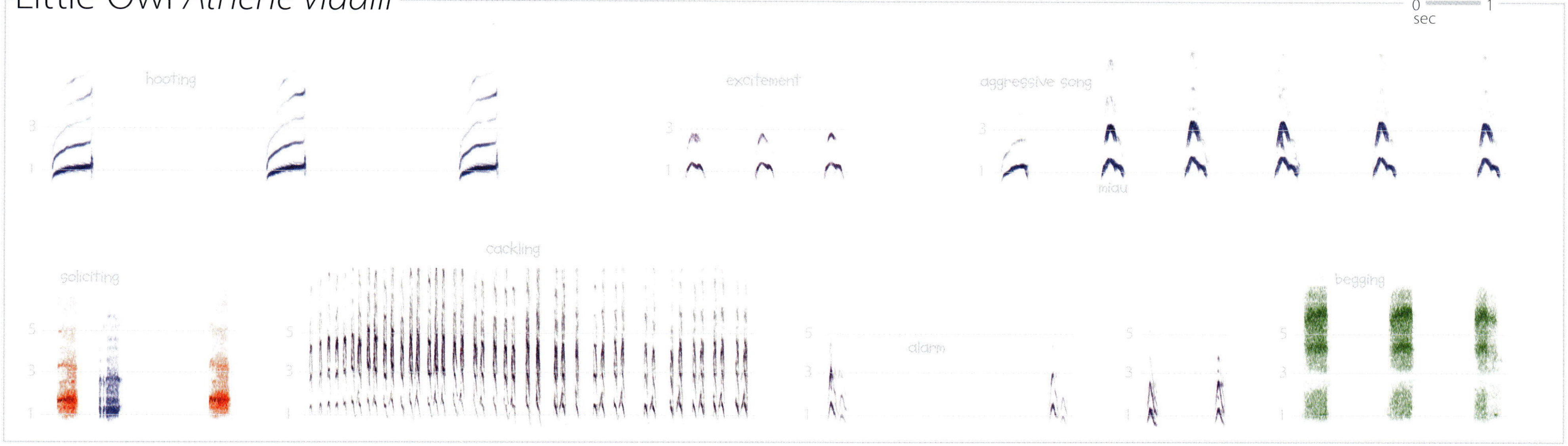

Cucumiau *Athene noctua*

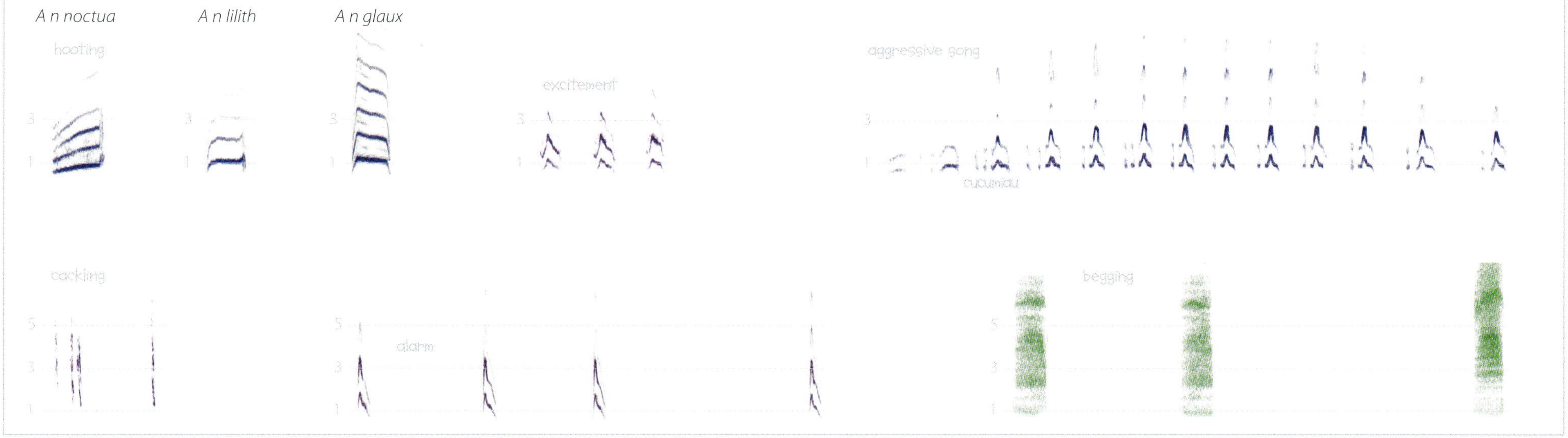

A n noctua *A n lilith* *A n glaux*

Cucumiau

In 1981, fast-flowing streams of lava poured down the north-western flank of Mt Etna on Sicily, narrowly missing the town of Randazzo. The lava solidified into a jagged no man's land, then slowly greened as a variety of plants found pockets of fertile soil. Sicilian Partridges *Alectoris whitakeri* found this habitat very much to their liking, and that was why Arnoud and René spent the night there in April 2007. Some orchards narrowly missed by the lava contained many Eurasian Scops Owls *Otus scops*. Nearby, cavities in the lava offered perfect nesting opportunities for Cucumiaus *Athene noctua*. In **CD1-58**, you can hear several males hooting at once.

CD1-58   **Cucumiau** *Athene noctua* Northern slopes of Mt Etna, Castiglione, Sicily, Italy, 20:20, 21 April 2007. Hooting of several males. Background: hooting and (from 0:22) *twiu* calls of a Eurasian Scops Owl *Otus scops*. 07.017.AB.03036.12

Three years later I visited the same area on a frustrating quest to record the sounds of Lanner Falcons *Falco biarmicus*. Andrea Corso, top birder and all-round obsessive zoologist, had entrusted me to wildlife sculptor Nino Patti. Nino could only stay with me for short periods between working at a museum in Catania and looking after his then 99-year-old grandmother, so I had to drive behind him in my hire car. I could only just keep up. Nino lives in the village of Malvagna, on the northern side of the same broad valley where Arnoud had been three years previously. Elevated on a ridge leading to the Peloritani range, it is a great place to make bird sculptures, offering stunning views over the surrounding countryside and south towards Mt Etna.

Unfortunately the owls were quiet during that visit, probably because they were incubating. By the time I returned with Andrea a year later, Nino's grandmother had completed her century and I had recorded Lanners elsewhere. It was late March and this time the owls were in full voice. The male in **CD1-59** hooted non-stop for hours.

Cucumiau *Athene noctua* Malvagna, Sicily, Italy, 20:49, 23 March 2011. Hooting of a male. 110323.MR.204920.01   CD1-59

While some sounds of Cucumiau are very distinctive, its hooting is very similar to that of Little Owl. In southern Italy I could hear no difference from the Little Owls of northern Europe. However, Cucumiau has several subspecies, and subtle differences started to emerge as I listened to recordings of some of the others. In the following set of recordings, Arnoud takes us clockwise around the Mediterranean, via subspecies *noctua* in Bulgaria and *lilith* in southern Turkey, ending up with *glaux* and *saharae* in Morocco. There is a gradual change from rising to falling pitch in the hoots.

Cucumiau *Athene noctua noctua*, Popovets, Bulgaria, 2 June 2009 (*Arnoud B van den Berg*). Same month and region as in CD1-60 but different bird.

CD1-60 **Cucumiau** *Athene noctua noctua* Madzharovo, Haskovo, Bulgaria, 01:26, 26 June 2009. Hooting of a male. Background: Woodlark *Lullula arborea*. 090626.AB.012608.01

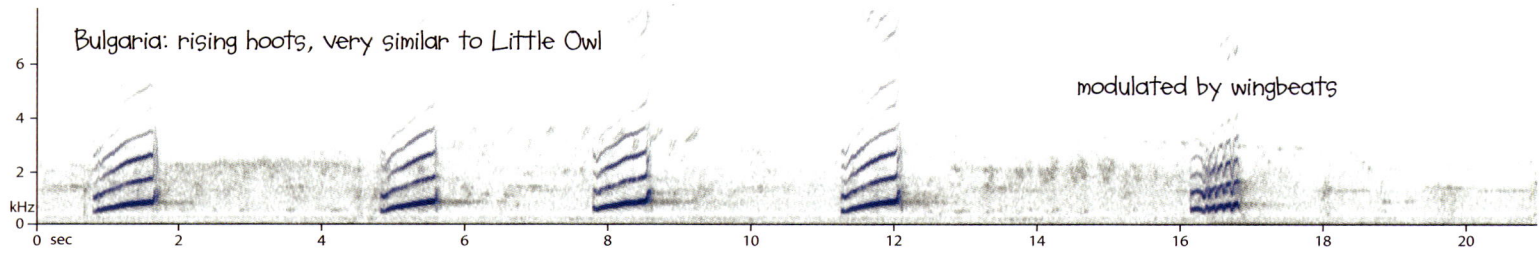

CD1-61 **Cucumiau** *Athene noctua lilith* Payamlı Koyu, Şanlıurfa, Turkey, 04:51, 17 June 2009. Hooting of a male. Background: domestic fowl *Gallus gallus domesticus*, See-see Partridge *Ammoperdix griseogularis*, Collared Dove *Streptopelia decaocto*, European Turtle Dove *S turtur*, Crested Lark *Galerida cristata* and Desert Finch *Rhodospiza obsoleta*. 090617.AB.045128.11

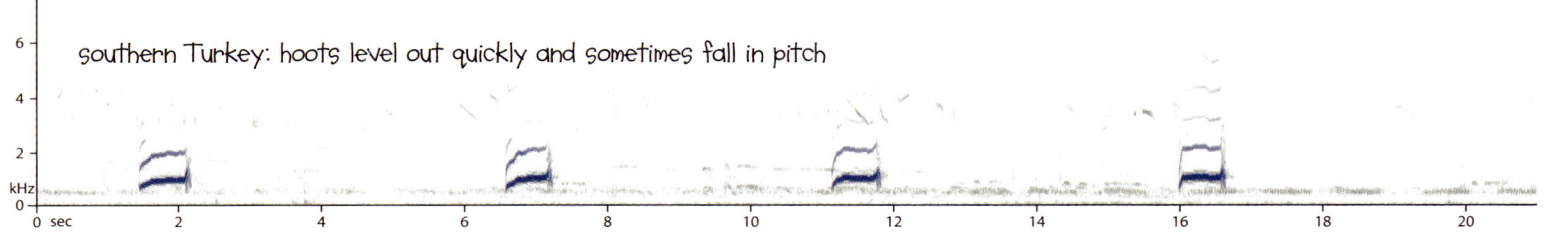

CD1-62 **Cucumiau** *Athene noctua glaux* Taroudant, Souss, Morocco, 23:54, 11 April 2010. Hooting of a male. 100411.AB.235431.21

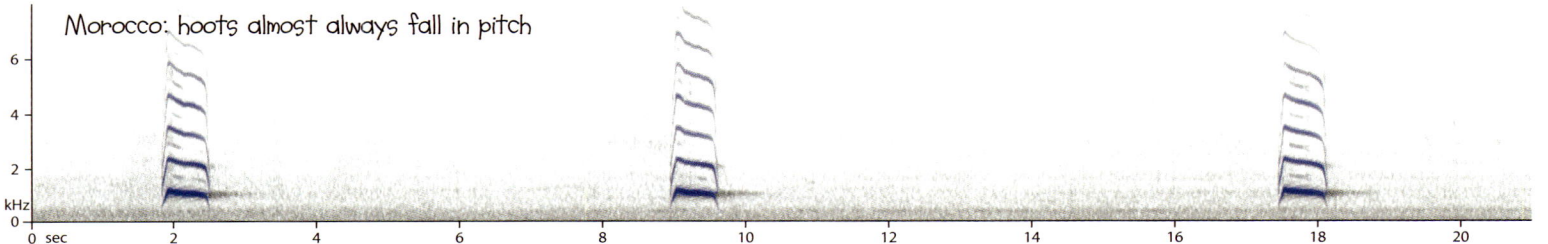

In **CD1-60** we are in a small town in southern Bulgaria. The recording starts with rising hoots. At 0:36 the male changes perch, causing one hoot to be modulated by its wingbeats. From then on, he hoots more intensely and the contour of each hoot levels out.

In **CD1-61**, we are in south-eastern Turkey, listening to subspecies *lilith*. During the stillness just before a desert storm, a male hoots into a great emptiness of rolling, herb-carpeted hills. As the tension builds, each hoot's inflection gradually changes from rising to slightly falling. Although not unheard of in Little Owl, this is certainly more common in Cucumiau, especially east and south of the Mediterranean.

In **CD1-62**, we are in a small fortified market town in southern Morocco, situated in the broad valley between the High Atlas and the Anti-Atlas mountain ranges. A male *glaux* hoots from a pole sticking out of a roof, close to the old city wall. His hoots are strongly descending, except for a lower one about halfway through the series. Arnoud made several recordings of this male and in all of them, descending hoots were the rule.

In **CD1-63**, we have moved about 90 km southwest to Oued Massa on the Atlantic coast. It is mid-morning, and a male *saharae* is hooting from a lone tree in sandy agricultural land between rocky desert and a brackish river. Although the first hoot is rising, most of those that follow are descending, at least in their overall contour.

CD1-63 **Cucumiau** *Athene noctua saharae* Oued Massa, Agadir, Morocco, 09:25, 6 April 2004. Hooting of a male. Background: Collared Dove *Streptopelia decaocto*, Common Bulbul *Pycnonotus barbatus*, yellow wagtail *Motacilla*, Eurasian Reed Warbler *Acrocephalus scirpaceus*, Zitting Cisticola *Cisticola juncidis*, European Goldfinch *Carduelis carduelis*, Common Linnet *Linaria cannabina*, European Greenfinch *Chloris chloris* and Corn Bunting *Emberiza calandra*. 04.008.AB.02947.11

Cucumiau *Athene noctua lilith*, male, Payamlı Koyu, Şanlıurfa, Turkey, 17 June 2009 (*Arnoud B van den Berg*). Same bird as in CD1-61.

Cucumiau *Athene noctua saharae*, Oued Massa, Morocco, 20 March 2014 (*Arnoud B van den Berg*). Same site as in CD1-63 & 67 but in different year.

One of the people who helped me most during my travels in Italy had better remain nameless. It was during secret outdoor trysts that he discovered some of the best places for me to sound record Cucumiaus. A very quiet lane with a ruined farm building and a small copse proved perfect for both activities. Based on our anonymous friend's suggestion, my friends and I went there several times to make recordings.

If nothing happened for too long, Andrea would encourage the owls with some excellent imitations. Their first reaction was usually hooting, but this would often progress towards excitement calls. When these escalated into aggressive song, they began to sound very different from Little Owl.

As Cucumiau's name suggests, every loud *MIAU* of the aggressive song is preceded by one or two low, chugging sounds: *cucuMIAU, cucuMIAU, cucuMIAU*.... By contrast, Little Owl has an aggressive song composed of just a single type of sound: *MIAU, MIAU, MIAU* etc. It was while listening to the 'lover's lane' pair (**CD1-64**) that I first noticed the difference.

Cucumiau *Athene noctua lilith*, adult, Kızılkuyu, Şanlıurfa (near Syrian border), Turkey, 12 June 2009 (*Arnoud B van den Berg*). Same bird as in CD1-65.

At first I thought I had discovered something unique to Italian little owls. Later, when I checked recordings of other taxa, I learned that *vidalii* is the only Western Palearctic *Athene* owl that *lacks* chugging notes in its aggressive song.

CD1-64   **Cucumiau** *Athene noctua* San Giovanni in Galdo, Molise, Italy, 18:58, 18 March 2011. Aggressive song and excitement calls of a pair. Background: Italian Tree Frog *Hyla intermedia*. 110318.MR.185819.01

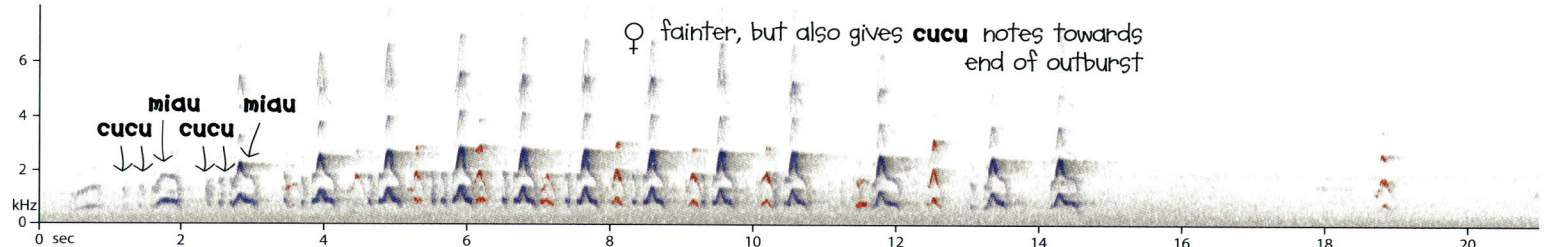

Since aggressive song is arguably the most important long distance signal in their repertoire, this striking difference seems to me to be highly significant.

Aggressive song follows broadly the same pattern in all subspecies of Cucumiau. **CD1-65**, **CD1-66** and **CD1-67** provide examples of subspecies *lilith*, *glaux* and *saharae*. Note that in all three there are also some strongly descending excitement calls. Just as with hooting, this descending contour seems to become steeper as we go clockwise around the Mediterranean.

CD1-65 **Cucumiau** *Athene noctua lilith* Kızılkuyu, Şanlıurfa, Turkey, 05:10, 12 June 2009. Aggressive song and excitement calls of an adult. Background: Rock Dove *Columba livia*, Collared Dove *Streptopelia decaocto* and Barn Swallow *Hirundo rustica*. 090612.AB.051046.11

These taxa – *glaux*, *lilith*, *noctua* and *saharae* – are quite diverse in their appearance, not just in coloration but even to some degree in structure (Cramp 1985). It may seem surprising that *vidalii*, which looks rather similar to *noctua*, is the odd one out. But the genetic evidence for this is compelling. Pellegrino

CD1-67 **Cucumiau** *Athene noctua saharae* Oued Massa, Agadir, Morocco, 09:18, 6 April 2004. Excitement calls and aggressive song of a pair. Background: Eurasian Coot *Fulica atra*, Common Blackbird *Turdus merula*, Zitting Cisticola *Cisticola juncidis*, European Goldfinch *Carduelis carduelis* and Corn Bunting *Emberiza calandra*. 04.008.AB.02440.11

et al (2014) found a very big difference between a north-western group (my 'Little Owl') and a south-eastern group (my 'Cucumiau'). They described this as "towards the upper end of the range" for genetic distances between sibling species.

So there can be little argument about splitting the little owls in two, and the more pertinent question is whether there should be further splits. The vocal evidence for this is subtle, but the various Cucumiau subspecies do seem to show slight differences in both hooting and excitement calls. Although I am convinced that these differences are real, the ones I hear between Little and Cucumiau aggressive song are much clearer. So what does the genetic evidence say about subdivisions within Cucumiau?

Pellegrino et al (2014) used an amazing 326 samples from across Europe. One of their most important findings was that the

CD1-66 **Cucumiau** *Athene noctua glaux* El Kasbah, Aysir, Safi, Morocco, 21:46, 25 June 2010. Aggressive song of one adult, followed by excitement calls of another closer to the microphones. 100625.AB.214600.11

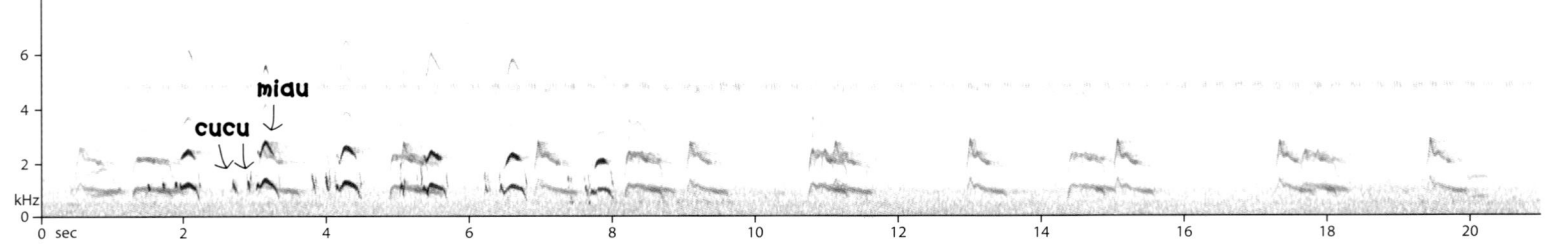

long-neglected subspecies *sarda* from Sardinia (presumably including the few little owls that live on Corsica) forms the oldest known branch within the south-eastern group. It has been evolving separately from other Cucumiaus for around half a million years. We were caught out by this, but Davide De Rosa kindly supplied me with some recordings by a friend. The calls in **CD1-68** seem pretty eccentric, and I am not even sure whether to call them hooting or excitement calls. Other recordings he sent establish that *sarda* has aggressive song like that of its closest relatives in Italy. Davide told me that its Sardinian name is in fact... "Cucumiau"!

Within southern Europe, there are two other well-defined subgroups. One them is confined to southern Italy and Sicily, although its genes do occasionally crop up further north. The other is distributed from the Maritime Alps of France through the northern half of Italy to at least the Balkans and Cyprus. It probably goes much further east, but Pellegrino et al (2014) only studied the situation in Europe. Since the type specimen of *noctua* came from Krain in modern-day Slovenia, we are obliged to use this name for the northern Italian-Balkan

group. This renders another, later established subspecies name obsolete. Owls from Greece, the taxonomic home of '*indigena*', are genetically and vocally indistinguishable from those of northern Italy. On these grounds at least, *indigena* becomes a synonym of *noctua*.

CD1-68   **Cucumiau** *Athene noctua sarda* Sella del Diavolo, Cagliari, Sardinia, 19:37, 16 April 2009. Calls perhaps intermediate between hooting and excitement calls. Fabio Cherchi.

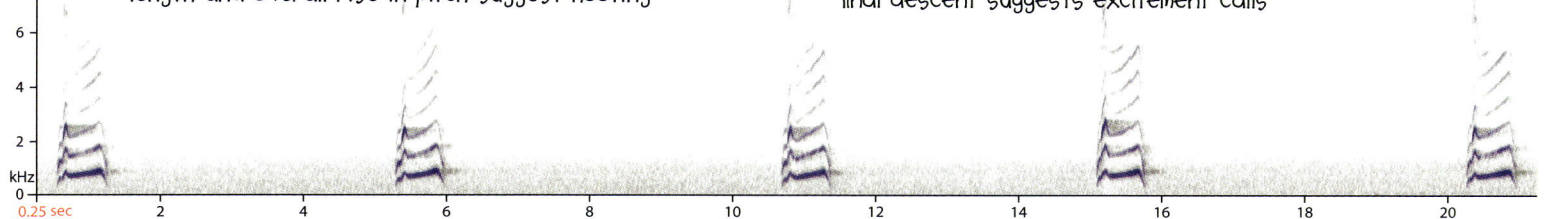

Pellegrino et al (2014) probably did not set out to split species or change names, but their work has two further implications for taxonomy. One is that the population from southern Italy and Sicily, which I always assumed to belong to *noctua*, lacks a scientific name. The other is that birds from Cyprus, traditionally included in subspecies *lilith*, are indistinguishable from the northern Italian-Balkan group that we are now calling *noctua*. It remains to be seen whether *lilith* from other parts of the range are genetically distinct, but an older study suggests they are possibly not.

Beyond Europe, we only have Wink (2008) to go on. He studied just 11 individuals, but included specimens of *'indigena'* from Greece, *lilith* from Cyprus, Israel and Turkey, *glaux* from Israel and *plumipes* from Mongolia. He found almost no genetic difference between *'indigena'* and *lilith*, and that *glaux* was a very close relative of both.

Arnoud once recorded a family of four fledgling *glaux* within earshot of the Atlantic, underneath a clifftop village in Morocco. Only a few sandy fields and a high dune separated the cliff from the sea. The nest was in a large cavity in the lower, sandy part of the cliff, and the young were already venturing outside. Arnoud had placed his microphones about 3 m from the nest and after a while, two of the owlets actually perched on them. One of them even proceeded to pull fibres out of the furry windshield. We'll spare you the sensation of having the hairs plucked out of your scalp, but in **CD1-69** you can hear how a juvenile Cucumiau might sound if it perched on your shoulder. At a certain point, Arnoud decided to rescue his equipment. One of the adults reacted with a form of cackling as he walked towards the nest (**CD1-70**).

Cucumiau *Athene noctua glaux* El Kasbah, Aysir, Safi, Morocco, 07:05, 19 June 2010. Begging calls of two juveniles, one of them perched right beside the microphones. Background: Barn Swallow *Hirundo rustica*, Sardinian Warbler *Sylvia melanocephala*, Zitting Cisticola *Cisticola juncidis*, European Goldfinch *Carduelis carduelis* and House Sparrow *Passer domesticus*. 100619.AB.070507.21

CD1-69

Cucumiau *Athene noctua glaux* El Kasbah, Aysir, Safi, Morocco, 07:09, 19 June 2010. Cackling of adult as recordist moved in to retrieve equipment. Background: Common Quail *Coturnix coturnix*, European Serin *Serinus serinus* and House Sparrow *Passer domesticus*. 100619.AB.070956.22

CD1-70

On other occasions too, when adult Cucumiaus felt their young to be threatened we have recorded sharp, staccato calls similar to cackling in Little Owl. In **CD1-71**, recorded in Oman, these particularly sharp calls silenced the young immediately. They gave no begging calls for several minutes afterwards. The family was living in a disused irrigation pipe, about 1.5 m above the ground.

Cucumiau *Athene noctua*, Sohar, Al Batinah, Oman, 14 April 2010 (*René Pop*). Same month and site as in CD1-71 but different bird.

CD1-71 **Cucumiau** *Athene noctua* Sohar, Al Batinah, Oman, 19:09, 13 April 2010. Begging of a juvenile, which is then silenced by an adult giving cackling calls. Background: Collared Pratincole *Glareola pratincola*. 100413.MR.190907.02

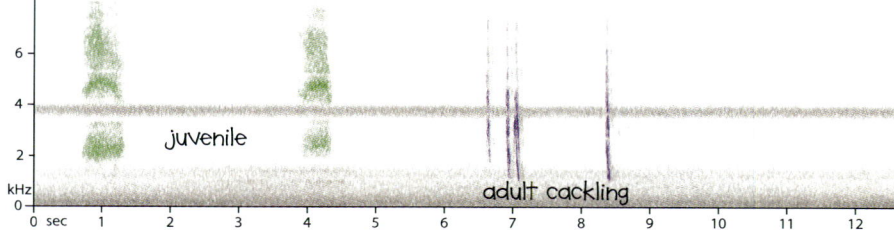

In Cucumiau, alarm calls usually have just a single note (**CD1-72**). The two-note version is rare in Cucumiau but common in Little. If Cucumiau does give a two-note alarm call, the first and second notes are much further apart.

CD1-72 **Cucumiau** *Athene noctua* Khatmat Milahah, Al Batinah, Oman, 18:50, 12 April 2010. Alarm calls of an adult at dusk. 100412.MR.185034.02

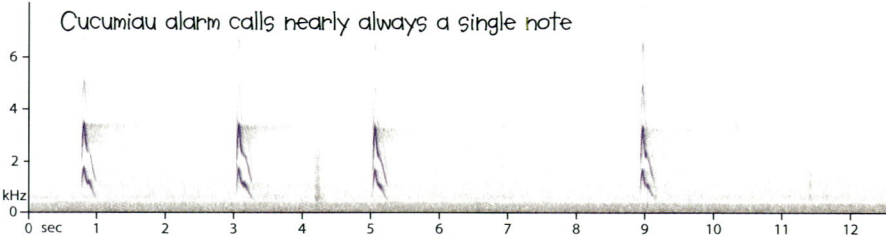

This book only covers the Western Palearctic, but the range of 'little owl' stretches all the way to the Pacific. It remains to be discovered whether several Asian taxa should be included in Little Owl or Cucumiau, or gain recognition as species in their own right.

Cucumiau *Athene noctua*, Kyzylkol, South Kazakhstan, Kazakhstan, 11 September 2009 (*René Pop*)

Our next owl has a range that stretches just as far, but much further north. Its voice is one of the most beautiful sounds of the taiga.

Chapter 4: Surnia

Northern Hawk-Owl

"You're wasting your time", said Dick, "they never call during the day." The road had been long, straight and snowy, and Mark had fallen asleep. When Dick spotted the Northern Hawk-Owl *Surnia ulula* perched in a tree on the other side of the field, everyone sprang into action. Mark pointed his parabolic dish despite Dick's discouragement and an air temperature of -10°C. Perhaps through the sheer power of his will, the owl did call, and an obsession with hawk-owls was born.

The area around Yläne has a lot of forest, more than usual for south-western Finland. Fairly large patches of old growth remain but otherwise it is commercial, dotted with small farms and fields. The previous autumn a surplus of voles had attracted irruptive owls to settle in the area. At the end of winter the snow could have melted too quickly, causing the vole population to crash and the owls to move on. In March 2003, however, the blanket was still flawless and the owls were preparing to breed.

Towards the end of the next day, Dick and Killian dropped Mark off at the same spot. He rested his microphones on the snow, uncoiled 20 m of cables and stood at the far end. On his side of the road there was a ploughed field. On the other the forest blocked his view. For an hour, all remained silent and still. When a very distant hawk-owl finally became active at dusk, its voice emerged as if from nothing. Muted by snow and distance, it sounded like the whistle of an American freight train but diffuse, rising and rippling slightly. Mark was completely enthralled.

Moments later a rickety old tractor with snow chains rumbled into earshot. Punishing Mark slowly, it made its way along an invisible path through the trees directly behind him, then appeared on the road while the owl continued to hoot in the distance. The tractor stopped at the nearby farm. By now the temperature had dropped to -17°C, so when the driver got out he left the engine running and chatted to the farmer on his doorstep. Just when Mark's nerve was beginning to crack, the noise stopped and something happened that thrilled him to the core. A second hawk-owl called in flight nearby. Settling a short distance behind him, much nearer than the first, it started to hoot in answer to the distant bird (**CD1-73**).

Northern Hawk-Owl *Surnia ulula* Yläne, Turku Pori, Finland, 9 March 2003. Hooting of two males, one near and one far. Background: farmers chatting. 03.006.MC.12430.11   **CD1-73**

The generic term 'hooting' describes the territorial and mate attraction signal of Northern Hawk-Owl less well than those of most other owls. Nevertheless, each rippling series is a string of tiny hoots, gradually rising in frequency over anything from

Northern Hawk-Owl *Surnia ulula*, juvenile, Inari, Lapland, Finland, 18 July 2014 (*Dick Forsman*)

1 to c 30 seconds. They are delivered so quickly that I can only count them accurately with the help of sonagrams. Females occasionally hoot a similar song, especially when unpaired. According to Mebs & Scherzinger (2004) theirs is more variable in pitch and can sound a bit careless.

Despite being known as a diurnal species, hawk-owls generally hoot in the dark, especially near the start and end of the night. According to Finnish astronomer Harry Lehto their morning session usually begins at the start of nautical twilight, when the stars are still bright in the sky but you start to see the horizon clearly. Their hooting disappears with the stars, at the start of civil twilight.

In **CD1-74**, a male Northern Hawk-Owl is hooting in the broad daylight of a June morning. Dick recorded it at a typical breeding site in northern Finland, situated in sparse old forest on the edge of a huge clear-fell with some remaining woodlots and a few really old trees. When the weather is cold, northern Finnish forests like this sound dead, but with a rise in temperature everything bursts into song; the change is almost magical. This

CD1-74 **Northern Hawk-Owl** *Surnia ulula* Kuusamo, Finland, 06:54, 8 June 2010. Hooting of a male. Background: Common Cuckoo *Cuculus canorus*, Eurasian Wryneck *Jynx torquilla*, Northern Raven *Corvus corax*, Bohemian Waxwing *Bombycilla garrulus*, Song Thrush *Turdus philomelos*, Common Redstart *Phoenicurus phoenicurus*, Brambling *Fringilla montifringilla* and Glip Crossbill *Loxia curvirostra* type C. 100608.DF.065440.01

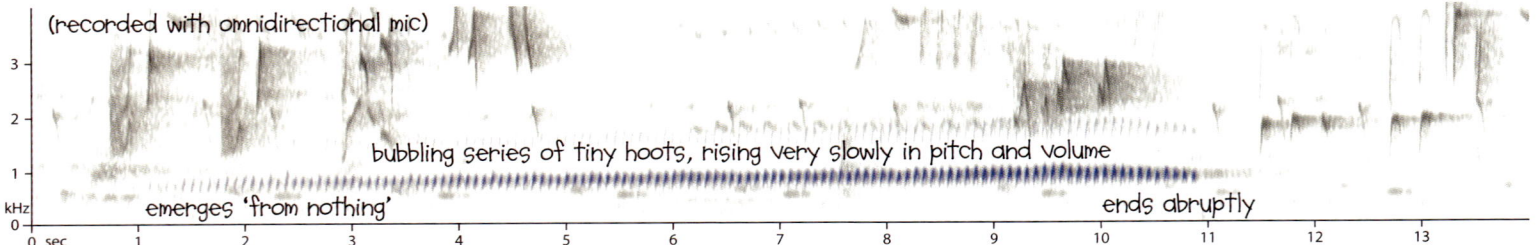

one is especially rich, and the nearby bogs host Spotted Redshank *Tringa erythropus*, Jack Snipe *Lymnocryptes minimus* and Broad-billed Sandpiper *Calidris falcinellus*. Just a few 100 m from the nest, a Brown Bear *Ursus arctos* wintered inside a huge anthill.

Northern Hawk-Owls usually breed in vast stretches of forest interspersed with open areas. Nowadays, most pairs breed on or beside large clear-fells, often with remnant stands of older trees. Open areas provide food while older trees provide nests. Since they can move easily even through rather dense vegetation, they can also breed deep in the forest where we are less likely to find them. They only stop to breed in areas with a very high density of voles. If there is food they will somehow find a suitable nest, which may be in a hollow stump, or in a hole excavated by a Black Woodpecker *Dryocopus martius*. In the far north where there are only stunted birches, they even breed in old nests of Hooded Crows *Corvus cornix*.

Long series of hoots at a medium, slowly rising pitch propagate well in the relatively sparse taiga. Any creature listening can judge distance from the degree of blurring by echoes from trees. Other kinds of hooting might have worked just as well, but 'microhooting' was still available in the vast taiga forests of the far north when the Northern Hawk-Owl appeared on the scene. There is nothing else that sounds quite like one throughout its vast Palearctic breeding range.

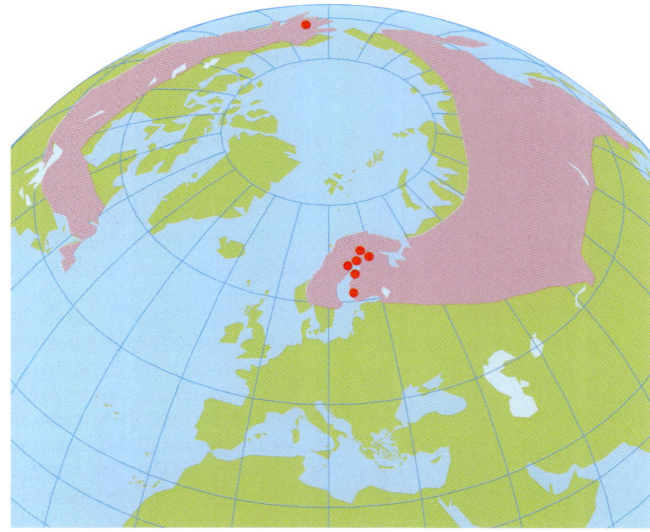

Approximate breeding distribution of Northern Hawk-Owl *Surnia ulula* ■ Recording locations indicated by ● dots.

I learned this by comparing 10 *caparoch* with 11 Eurasian *ulula* (up to three series each). On average, *caparoch* hoots 12.6% more slowly and rises more steeply to a higher maximum pitch. There is also a difference in the shape of the individual hoots. It is conceivable that *caparoch* may have evolved a slower but more strongly rising song to differentiate itself from Eastern Screech Owl *Megascops asio*, which has a faster rippling song on an even pitch. Although their ranges do not overlap today, *caparoch* occurred at least as far south as Tennessee, USA, during the Late Pleistocene (Parmalee & Klippel 1982).

So far, nobody has published a DNA comparison of *ulula* and *caparoch*, so we do not know how long they have been evolving separately. Ecologically, *caparoch* is much less dependent on voles. When the 10-year cycle in the population of the Snowshoe Hare *Lepus americanus* is at its peak, young hares form 40-50% of *caparoch*'s diet (Rohner et al 1995).

In Alaska and Canada, darker-faced and broader-barred subspecies *caparoch* does sound very subtly different (**CD1-75**).

Courtship plays out in a brief whirlwind of threats, chases and tenderness. In fading light or darkness it is often difficult to

CD1-75   **CD1-75 American Hawk-Owl** *Surnia ulula caparoch* Nelson's Clearwater, Fairbanks, Alaska, USA, 15:00, 27 June 1972. Hooting of a male in response to playback. Background: Olive-sided Flycatcher *Contopus cooperi*, Tree Swallow *Tachycineta bicolor*, Swainson's Thrush *Catharus ustulatus*, Dark-eyed Junco *Junco hyemalis*, American Yellow Warbler *Setophaga aestiva* and Myrtle Warbler *S coronata*. Leonard J Peyton and The Macaulay Library at the Cornell Lab of Ornithology.

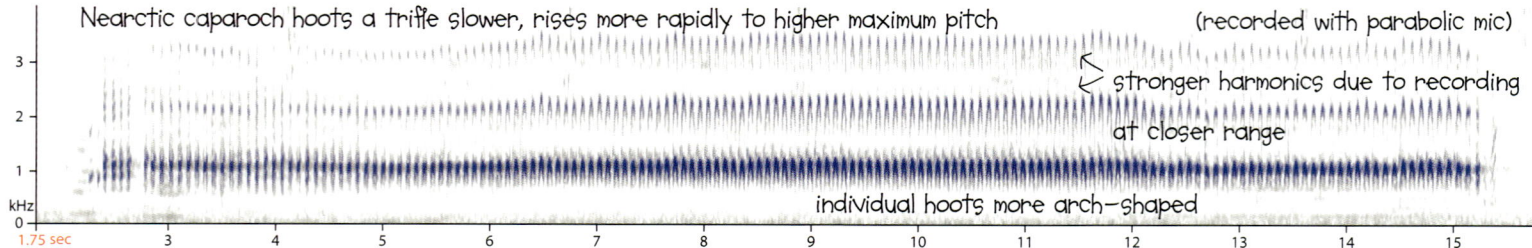

tell the sexes apart, but the tension between them is obvious. In **CD1-76**, a perched male gives a long series of *kirrirritt* calls, which Håkan describes as "like a mean, sharp-voiced, giant Crested Tit". He continues to call *kirrirritt* as he flies across to the female perched nearby. She responds with a smoother version of the same call which melts into an ecstatic, lower-pitched croon. Håkan has also heard the *kirrirritt* call in winter. He had been watching a hawk-owl that seemed to be perched happily on the top of a dead tree when suddenly it flew some 200 m at high speed and with forced wingbeats. It gave a loud *kirrirritt* as it shaved the crown of a Ural Owl *Strix uralensis* perched at the edge of the forest. The Ural seemed almost completely indifferent.

On another occasion, Håkan was owling at midnight. A female Northern Hawk-Owl had been begging persistently, and he could see her bowing forward against the full moon. Copulation seemed imminent. Her mate was hooting, but not the usual long series with 15-20 second gaps between them. Instead he gave short series that followed one another closely, forming an

CD1-76   **Northern Hawk-Owl** *Surnia ulula* Raahe, Ostrobothnia, Finland, 18:15, 11 March 2003. *Kirrirritt* calls of a presumed male flying towards a female, followed by her ecstatic-sounding response. 03.002.KM.00057.11

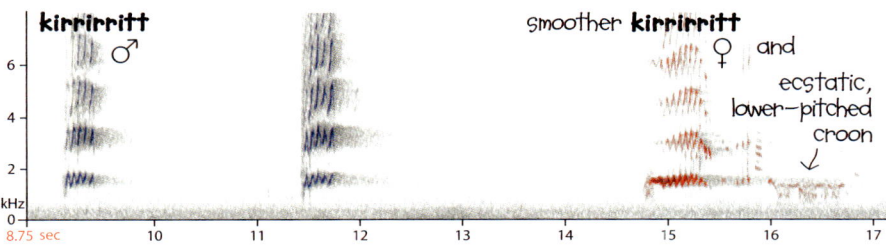

intense duet with the female's *kshyyyy-lip* calls. Suddenly he shifted to a distinctive, quite different sound. The familiar ripple was interrupted about twice a second by lower-pitched notes that sounded like inhalations.

In the struggle to find a name for this call, I have borrowed one from studies of chimpanzees. Let's call it 'pant-hooting'. The Sound Approach has never been lucky enough to record pant-hooting, but **CD1-77** is a recording by Ove Stefansson of a pair that he observed mating. After one of the birds pant-hoots, the other bird gives a series of very high-pitched squeals. This must be Northern Hawk-Owl's copulation call.

The soliciting call is a *kshyyyy-lip* that sounds surprisingly similar to the perennial screech of a barn owl *Tyto*. Most commonly it accompanies soliciting behaviour of females, either for food

Northern Hawk-Owl *Surnia ulula*, fledgling, Keminmaa, Lapland, Finland, 5 June 2010 (*Dick Forsman*). Out of nest only for c two days and c 100 m from nest. Same as in CD1-79 & 82.

or copulation. The male also sometimes calls *kshyyyy-lip* when he brings food to the nest. Later in the breeding cycle it may be used in more stressful situations. We have twice recorded *kshyyyy-lip* from nervous hawk-owls with young as they confronted us in the heart of their territory. **CD1-78** was

CD1-77   **Northern Hawk-Owl** *Surnia ulula* Brännberg, Norrbotten, Sweden, 30 March 2007. A pair copulating: first 'pant-hooting' and then copulation calls. Ove Stefansson.

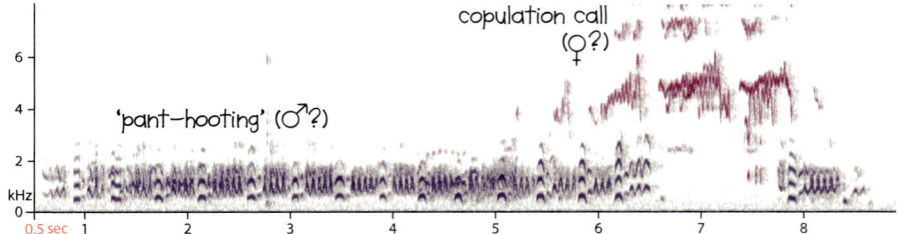

CD1-78   **Northern Hawk-Owl** *Surnia ulula* Haapalahti, Lapland, Finland, 15:30, 5 June 2003. Loud *kshyyy-lip* calls of a presumed female near a nestbox. Background: Wood Sandpiper *Tringa glareola*, Common Snipe *Gallinago gallinago*, Willow Warbler *Phylloscopus trochilus*, Pied Flycatcher *Ficedula hypoleuca*, Redwing *Turdus iliacus* and Common Redstart *Phoenicurus phoenicurus*. 03.007.KM.10154.01

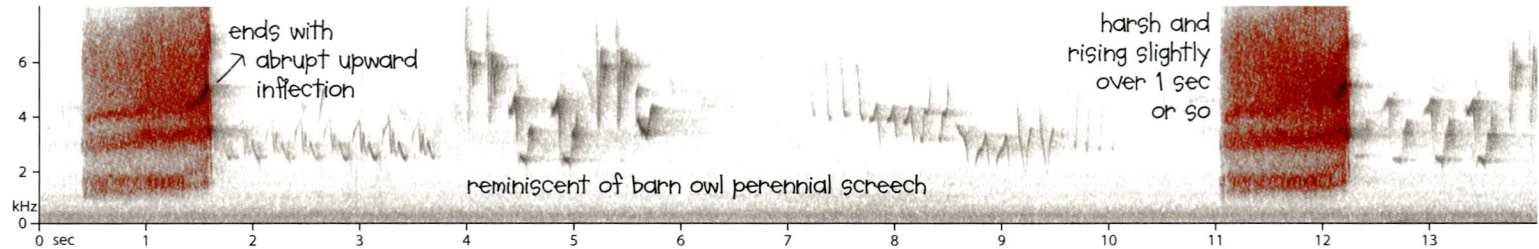

CD1-79   **Northern Hawk-Owl** *Surnia ulula* Tornio, Lapland, Finland, 19:44, 5 June 2010. Begging calls of fledged young. Background: Willow Warbler *Phylloscopus trochilus*. 100605.DF.194406.0

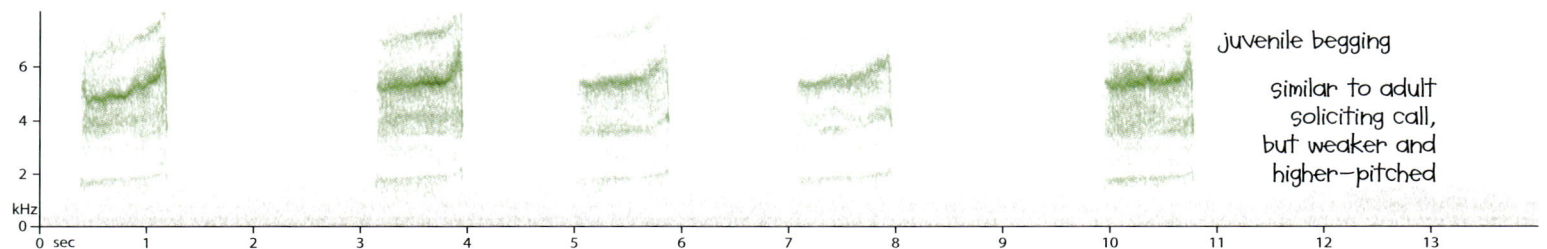

recorded near a nestbox in northern Finland that contained fairly small-sounding young.

Young Northern Hawk-Owls have a begging call very similar to the adult *kshyyyy-lip* but weaker and higher-pitched. In **CD1-79**, there were five young, and they had moved 100 m from the nest since fledging. The young also have a chitter call that they use to express discomfort. It is so quiet that it seems unlikely to attract much attention from a distance. Kilian was very close to the nestbox and using a directional microphone when he recorded **CD1-80**.

CD1-80   **Northern Hawk-Owl** *Surnia ulula* Haapalahti, Lapland, Finland, 16:25, 5 June 2003. Very quiet chitter call of nestling. Background: Redwing *Turdus iliacus* and Brambling *Fringilla montifringilla*. 03.007.KM.12100.01

Northern Hawk-Owls are powerful, aggressive creatures, and they often attack larger owls and raptors. They may also attack people when their young seem threatened, making really nasty attacks. Mark was oblivious to the danger when he recorded **CD1-81**. The excitement call, a persistent *vit-vit-vit*, often precedes attack as indeed it did on this occasion.

Northern Hawk-Owl *Surnia ulula*, fledgling, Keminmaa, Finland, 5 June 2010 (*Dick Forsman*). Same as in CD1-79 & 82.

CD1-81 **Northern Hawk-Owl** *Surnia ulula* Haapalahti, Lapland, Finland, 5 June 2003. *Vit-vit-vit* calls of an adult near a nestbox with young. Background: Common Snipe *Gallinago gallinago*, Willow Warbler *Phylloscopus trochilus* and Pied Flycatcher *Ficedula hypoleuca*. 03.021.MC.03130.01

CD1-82 **Northern Hawk-Owl** *Surnia ulula* Tornio, Lapland, Finland, 19:44, 5 June 2010. *Vit-vit-vit* calls of male (more distant) and female (closer) with begging calls of young. Background: Willow Warbler *Phylloscopus trochilus*. 100605.DF.194406.01

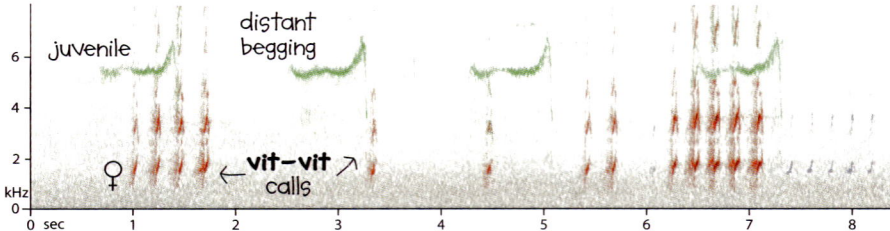

In **CD1-82**, Dick is the one risking life and limb. Several young are begging while the distant, left of centre male calls *vit-vit-vit* and the closer female calls both *vit-vit-vit* and *kshyyyy-lip*, fuller and lower-pitched than the young.

The classic winter view of a hawk-owl is of one perched silently, turning its head quickly now and then, without warning. When it flies, you might hear its fast, purposeful wingbeats. When it perches again, all you hear is its powerful aura. On two days in April 2012, a pair of Parrot Crossbills *Loxia pytyopsittacus* mobbed a hawk-owl that Håkan and I were watching on the edge of a clearing (**CD1-83**). Surveying the scene silently from its favourite dead pine, it seemed interested in everything but them.

CD1-83 **Parrot Crossbills** *Loxia pytyopsittacus* Västerås, Västmanland, Sweden, 15:55, 18 April 2012. Excitement calls of a pair mobbing a Northern Hawk-Owl *Surnia ulula*. Background: Song Thrush *Turdus philomelos* and Common Chaffinch *Fringilla coelebs*. 120418.MR.155526.01

Håkan once saw a hawk-owl terrifying a Hooded Crow with a mere glance of its stern, yellow eyes. The owl was perched on a telephone wire when the crow landed a couple of metres away. It jumped nearer and nearer but the owl took no notice. When it was just 30 cm away, the owl made a sudden turn of its head and the crow just catapulted away.

A hawk-owl's eyes are powerful weapons indeed. By contrast, its sound-gathering facial disk is poorly developed, and its head appears small for an owl. Hawk-owls rely primarily on vision rather than hearing to detect their prey, as suggested by their diurnal habits and noisy flight. When the ground is covered by snow, they give up on their preferred diet of Field Voles *Microtus agrestis* and Root Voles *M oeconomus*, which live in clear-fells. Instead they turn to smaller Bank Voles *Myodes glareolus* living in mature forest (Nybo & Sonerud 1990). Field and Root Voles move underneath the snow, whereas Bank Voles often move on the surface where they are easier to detect.

Unlike Tengmalm's Owls *Aegolius funereus*, hawk-owls of both sexes leave when the vole population crashes, only to return when numbers are approaching peak levels again two years later. This means that they are absent for at least half of each four-year vole cycle (Sonerud 1994). There are no records of either sex staying in an area through the worst of a vole cycle (Sonerud 1997). Most movements take place in autumn and spring. Adult males and juvenile females usually winter within the breeding range, where males claim the best breeding territories as early as possible. Adult females and to a lesser extent juvenile males compete for the best winter territories in lowlands where they have a wider variety of prey and less snow to contend with (Byrjedal & Langhelle 1986).

Northern Hawk-Owls are highly nomadic and may wander great distances in search of voles. Two Finnish juveniles were recovered east of the Urals, 2795 and 2659 km from where they had been ringed. Three turned up 1200-1400 km away in southern Norway (Saurola 2002). American Hawk-Owls have even been known to cross the Atlantic, one being captured alive on board a collier off Cornwall in March 1830, and another flying onto a ship off Las Palmas in the Canary Islands in 1924 (Harrop 2010, Rosmay & Roselaar 2013).

Northern Hawk-Owl *Surnia ulula*, juvenile/first-winter, Hanko, Uusimaa, Finland, 13 September 2013 (*Dick Forsman*)

Vagrants from northern Eurasia have thrilled many birders in recent years, although hawk-owls hardly require the element of surprise to turn them into dream birds. Personally, I prefer to see them in the vast taiga of the far north, exactly where they belong. Their closest Palearctic relative is a tiny twitcher that prefers not to see hawk-owls at all. Although it thinks nothing of adding the odd 'mega' to its larder, it all too often ends up as owl fodder itself.

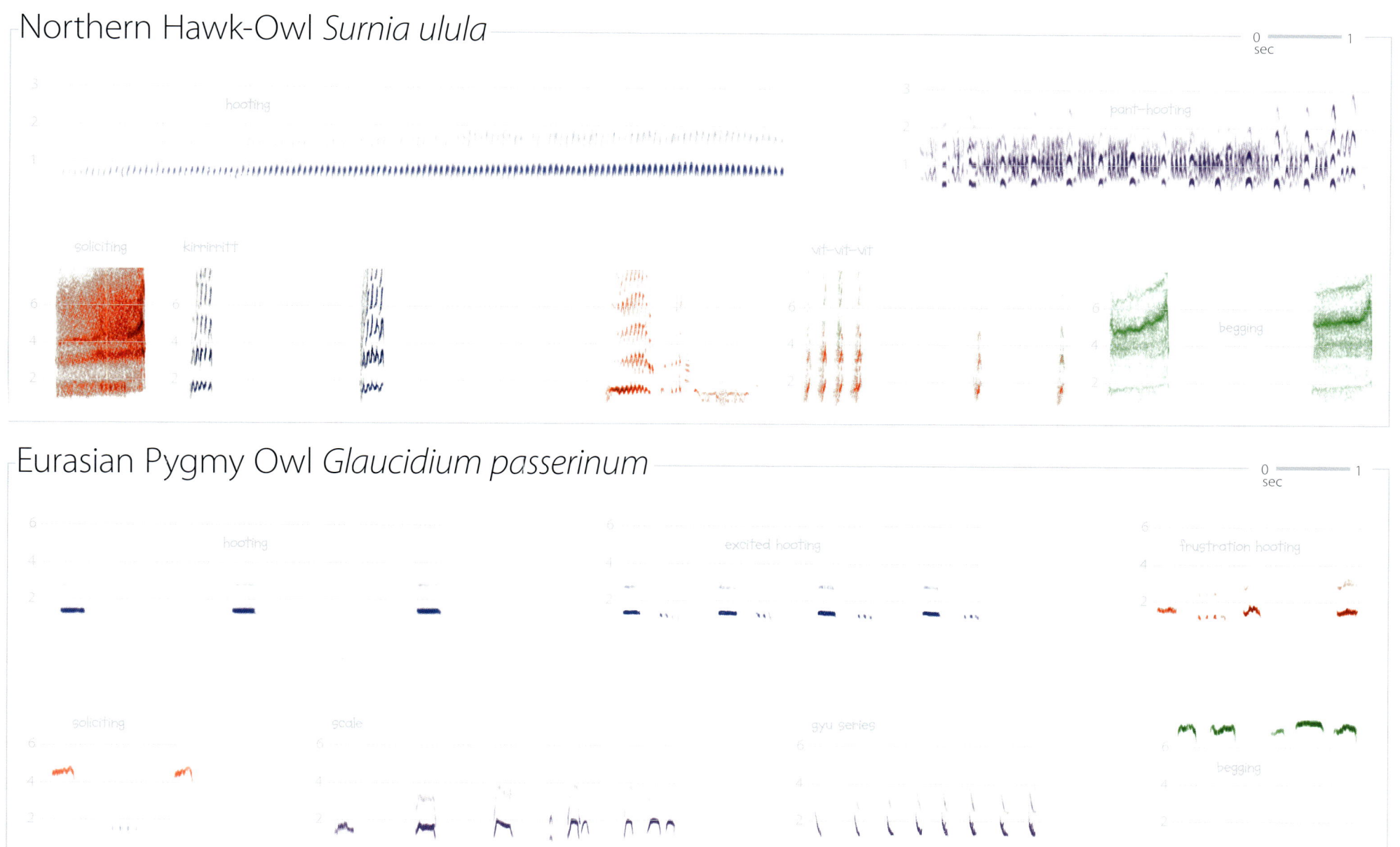

Chapter 5: *Glaucidium*

Eurasian Pygmy Owl

By March, the Common Cranes *Grus grus* have returned to Niedersachsen, Germany, and their distant unison calls radiate bright harmonic spectra through the dim forest. On a small, exposed ridge in a clearing, a tiny owl perches boldly on top of a small European Hornbeam *Carpinus betulus*. His movements are quick and nervous. The hawks have gone to roost but the larger owls are yet to emerge. For a short period after sunset, the Eurasian Pygmy Owl *Glaucidium passerinum* is raptor in chief.

Every two seconds he advertises for a mate. His tail twitches slightly with each soft-edged *beep*, high-pitched for an owl but low considering his size. Recording a mobile pygmy owl in ambient stereo is a challenge. In the course of 15 minutes he changes perch often, broadcasting in all directions and frustrating my attempts to sneak a microphone underneath him. Now a gust has just passed and there is a gap between planes. In a few minutes the first Tawny Owl *Strix aluco* will call. He grants me one last chance, and then falls silent until dawn (**CD2-01**).

In **CD2-02**, a neighbour of the first male, wound up by a whistled imitation from us, replies with 'excited hooting'. In this variant he inserts *du* notes between the usual hoots. At first, several of these combine into a short trill. Then the number of *du* notes gradually decreases until the series ends without them. If you imitate a pygmy owl or use playback, excited hooting is very likely to be the response. Paired males like this one also sometimes reply to their mate with excited hooting. Much less often, a bachelor may produce it on hearing a rival in the distance, or when a female ventures onto his territory (Scherzinger 1970).

CD2-01 **Eurasian Pygmy Owl** *Glaucidium passerinum* Lüneburger Heide, Niedersachsen, Germany, 17:50, 6 March 2008. Hooting of an unpaired male. Background: Common Blackbird *Turdus merula*. 080306.MR.175046.01

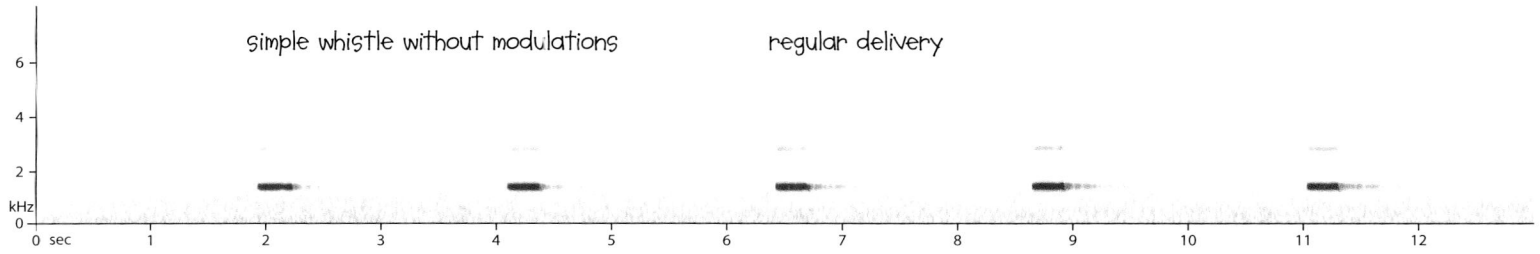

Eurasian Pygmy Owl *Glaucidium passerinum*, female, Hauho, Kanta-Häme, Finland, 10 June 2009 (*Dick Forsman*).

CD2-02   **Eurasian Pygmy Owl** *Glaucidium passerinum* Lüneburger Heide, Niedersachsen, Germany, 20:58, 30 April 2008. Excited hooting of a paired male. Background: Eurasian Woodcock *Scolopax rusticola*, Common Blackbird *Turdus merula* and European Robin *Erithacus rubecula*. 080430.MR.205804.12

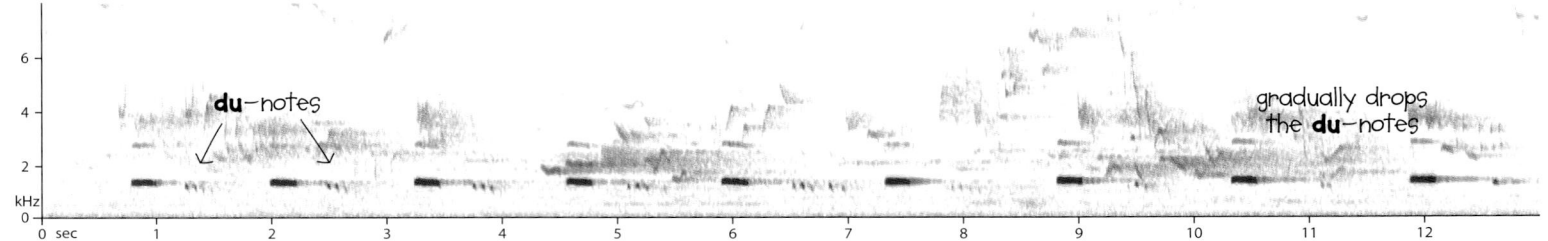

Håkan has been attacked several times after whistling a Eurasian Pygmy Owl, most recently when I was with him in March 2014. Seeing so small a creature hitting him on the head with its talons made me laugh. For a Star Wars fan, it would be like Yoda taking on Count Dooku. Anyway, judging from his exclamation, it really hurt! More than once, an owl has continued to attack him even when he was walking away like a good boy. His nastiest experience started once when he was trying to find out if some perfect-looking habitat was occupied. There was no response to his whistling, but suddenly he received a hard slap on the forehead. Only after this did the owl hoot from close range. Usually it is other owls and carnivorous mammals that bear the brunt of pygmy owl attacks. When one pygmy attacked a Ural Owl *Strix uralensis* in May, it gave a quick, sharp and very shrill chitter call as it dived at the owl's back.

Eurasian Pygmy Owls have good reason to be wary of other owls. Mikkola (1983) found 11 individuals in the prey remains of five other owl species. Even predation by Tengmalm's Owl *Aegolius funereus* has been recorded four times (Korpimäki &

Hakkarainen 2012). When Dave McAdams discovered his first pygmy owl in the forest where this chapter began, it was calling from the top of a conifer at dusk. Dave started to use a 'Hazel Hen' whistle to imitate some female or juvenile calls. It reacted immediately, flying down and straight at him, skimming over his head by a fraction and giving him quite a fright. The pygmy owl remained very close and then, surprisingly, a Tengmalm's Owl appeared and flew at it. Dave could hear excited calls from one or both owls. The Tengmalm's remained perched nearby for a few seconds (it was only then he identified it), before noticing him and flying off.

There is no Palearctic owl smaller than a Eurasian Pygmy Owl, but if there was it would surely feature on Pygmy's menu. As the mobbing in **CD2-03** suggests, small birds form an important part of its diet, especially during periods when birds are more easily available than rodents. Small forest birds in winter travel in easily heard flocks. In the harshest conditions they need all their time to find food, which means cutting down on vigilance. Pygmy owls roam along the fringes of flocks, staying in the tree crowns in order to ambush from above. The birds caught most easily are those small, peripheral species like Goldcrest *Regulus regulus* and Coal Tit *Periparus ater* that are less able to compete with larger species like Crested Tits *Lophophanes cristatus* and Willow Tits *Poecile montanus* for the safer central parts of the trees (Kullberg 1995).

CD2-03   **Eurasian Pygmy Owl** *Glaucidium passerinum* Ysen Lake, Hälsingland, Sweden, 06:06, 26 March 2014. Coal Tits *Periparus ater*, Common Chaffinches *Fringilla coelebs* and a Eurasian Siskin *Spinus spinus* mobbing a hooting male. Background: Northern Raven *Corvus corax*. 140326.MR.060606.00

Among the more surprising birds that Eurasian Pygmy Owls catch are aquatic species like Black-bellied Dipper *Cinclus cinclus* (Voous 1988) and large ones like Mistle Thrush *Turdus viscivorus*, twice the weight of the owl (Cramp 1985). In summer, they even catch Common Swifts *Apus apus* (Kellomäki 1977), presumably by entering their nesting cavities in mature forest. Such a prolific bird hunter is bound to catch the odd rarity from time to time. On 27 October 2005, a first-winter female Siberian Rubythroat

Calliope calliope was found freshly dead in a pygmy owl nestbox at Kokkola (van den Berg & Haas 2005). It was only the third for Finland.

Not every hunt is successful, and Eurasian Pygmy Owls of both sexes may express internal conflict with a special kind of song called frustration hooting ('Konfliktgesang'). In females it is probably their only kind of hooting. Frustrated hooting includes *du* notes, but differs from excited hooting in having a 'wobbly' pitch. Internal conflicts of various kinds can trigger it. In **CD2-04**, a female gives two short series of frustration hooting in response to Dave's imitation of a male (not included). Approaching the source, she expects to meet her mate for the first time that evening. Instead, she finds herself facing us birders. The three very high-pitched soliciting calls in the middle of the recording are presumably attempts to call her mate.

CD2-04 **Eurasian Pygmy Owl** *Glaucidium passerinum* Lüneburger Heide, Niedersachsen, Germany, 17:56, 7 March 2008. Frustration hooting and soliciting calls. Background: Song Thrush *Turdus philomelos*, Common Blackbird *T merula* and Goldcrest *Regulus regulus*. 080307.MR.175649.32

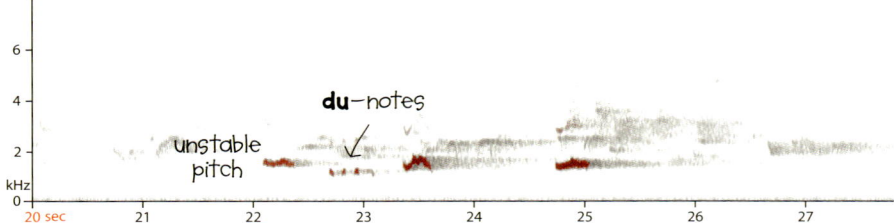

During the breeding season and for much of the year, hooting and soliciting calls are the basic clues for us to identify male and female, respectively. Most interactions start with these two sounds and their variants. Food exchanges, nest selection and copulation all subsequently require close proximity of the pair, and several short-range sounds then help these highly aggressive owls to overcome their mutual intolerance.

CD2-05 illustrates a sequence of calls accompanying copulation. The male announces himself with a single hoot while the female produces a series of soliciting calls. Flying in to join her, the male gives a series of low trills. As he mounts the female, we hear several piercing shrieks. Based on sonagrams, these come from the male (contra Scherzinger 1970). Immediately afterwards he departs to a safe distance with a series of rising whistles. He is smaller than the female, and rarely stays close to her for long.

For most of the year, the soliciting call is in fact the female's most characteristic sound, to such an extent that Scherzinger (1970) called it the 'female-specific call'. She uses it to indicate where she is, and as a begging call towards her mate. She even uses it in various situations when she is alone (Scherzinger 1970). Soliciting calls can be long or short, rising in pitch or level, but all variants have in common that they reach an extremely high pitch for an owl.

During food passes the sequence of calls is very similar, especially for the male. First he announces his presence and his mate answers. Then he uses one type of call to approach

CD2-05 **Eurasian Pygmy Owl** *Glaucidium passerinum* Hauho, Kanta-Häme, Finland, 31 March 2002. Soliciting calls of female, hoot and low trills of male. Copulation call at 0:19. Background: Common Blackbird *Turdus merula*, Great Tit *Parus major* and Northern Bullfinch *Pyrrhula pyrrhula pyrrhula*. 02.003.KM.01045.11

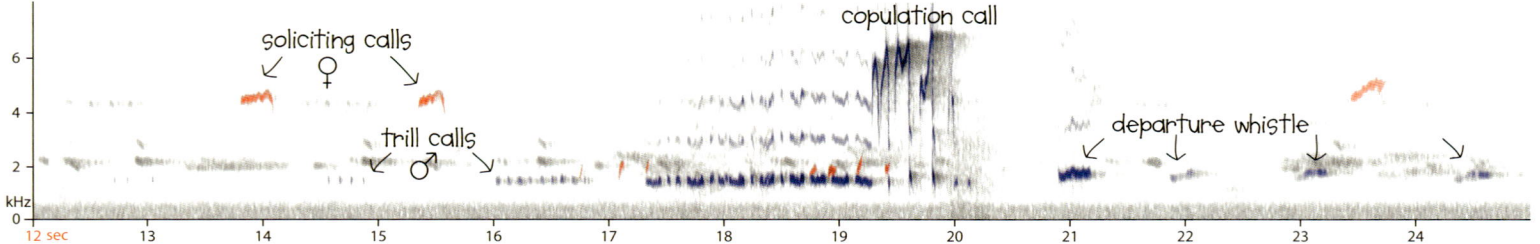

CD2-06   **Eurasian Pygmy Owl** *Glaucidium passerinum* Porras, Kanta-Häme, Finland, 22:00, 10 June 2009. A food pass, with hooting and trills of male, soliciting calls of female and chittering of nestlings. One of the adults also chitters at the moment of transfer. The male departs with rising whistles. Background: Eurasian Bittern *Botaurus stellaris*, Eurasian Woodcock *Scolopax rusticola* and European Robin *Erithacus rubecula*. 090610. DF.220000.01

and another to depart. **CD2-06** starts with the male hooting not far from a nestbox and the female replying with soliciting calls. The nestlings also hear the male and one of them chirps quietly. The female moves to the nestbox entrance and begs impatiently with her soliciting call. Using a series of trills, the male indicates that he is ready to hand over the prey. The female flies out to join him. When she arrives, the male interrupts a trill to give a shrill chitter call. He flies away as soon as he can, giving a series of departure whistles, very similar to the whistles when departing after copulation. These are higher-pitched than hooting, and usually begin with a rising intonation. The female continues to solicit and soon flies off after the male. A nestling chitters discontentedly in the nest. Perhaps the female scared the male away before he was able to hand over the prey.

Eurasian Pygmy Owl *Glaucidium passerinum*, with chicks, Hauho, Kanta-Häme, Finland, 24 May 2009 (*Dick Forsman*). Same as in CD2-06 but two weeks earlier.

CD2-07 is a more successful food pass at the same nest, recorded 18 days earlier. As usual it starts with a male-female

CD2-07   **Eurasian Pygmy Owl** *Glaucidium passerinum* Porras, Kanta-Häme, Finland, 21:47, 23 May 2009. Food pass at same nest as in CD2-06, 18 days earlier. Hooting of male, soliciting call of female and faint calls of young. Beckoning calls at 0:32-36, then trills of male followed by two departure calls. Feeding calls of female from 1:09. Background: Eurasian Woodcock *Scolopax rusticola*, Great Spotted Woodpecker *Dendrocopos major* and European Robin *Erithacus rubecula*. 090523. DF.214700.11

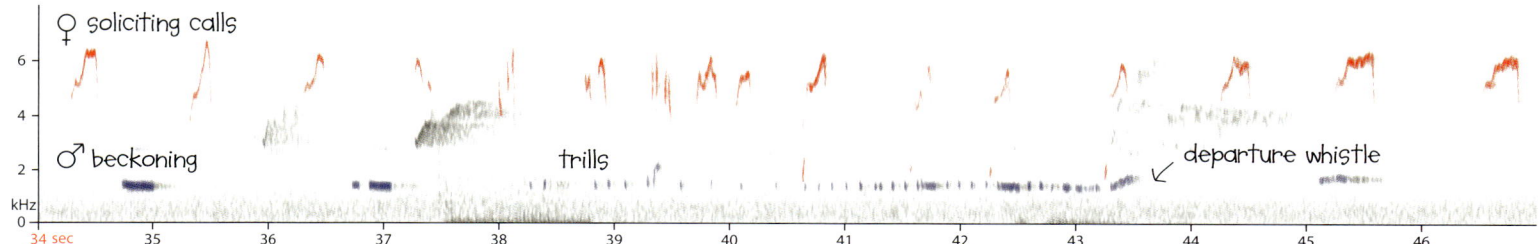

duet. The male's last hoots turn into two-part 'beckoning calls', and then he trills while handing over the prey. His departure is marked by two single, rising whistles. This time the female returns to the nestbox where she divides the food while giving short bursts of feeding calls.

Begging calls of juvenile Eurasian Pygmy Owls start as weak and very short squeaks but evolve into a sound similar to the soliciting call of the female. After the young leave the nest, these calls help them to stay together and allow the adults to

Eurasian Pygmy Owl *Glaucidium passerinum* Hattula, Hauho, Kanta-Häme, Finland, 16:36, 10 June 2009. Begging calls and chitters of nestlings with *gyu* calls of adult female. Background: Common Chaffinch *Fringilla coelebs* and European Robin *Erithacus rubecula*. 090610.DF.163600.01

CD2-08

Eurasian Pygmy Owl *Glaucidium passerinum* Porras, Hauho, Kanta-Häme, Finland, 21:47, 23 May 2009. *Gyu* calls in a series. Background: Song Thrush *Turdus philomelos*. 090523.DF.214700.31

CD2-09

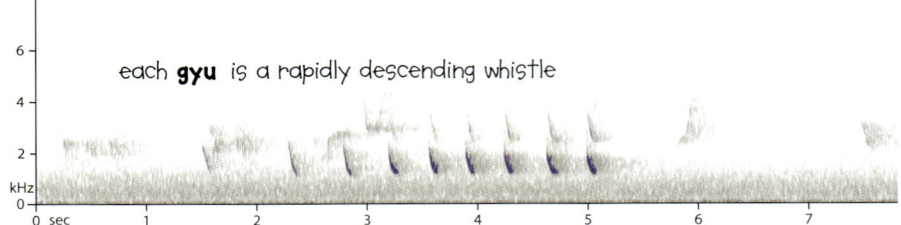

Eurasian Pygmy Owl *Glaucidium passerinum*, juvenile, Luopioinen, Pirkanmaa, Finland, 10 June 2009 (*Dick Forsman*)

find them. The brood in **CD2-08** was still about a week from fledging. Besides their begging calls, there are several very quiet *gyu* calls of the adult female, an excitement call often heard when the young are in danger. Sometimes *gyu* calls can be heard as the first sign of activity in the morning or as the last call given when flying to the roost at night. At higher levels of excitement they may be strung into a series as in **CD2-09**, recorded at a nest in Finland.

Adult Eurasian Pygmy Owls are among the more sedentary of Western Palearctic owls. If necessary, a pair will move from a summer territory with better nest holes, sometimes in deciduous forest, to a winter territory nearby with better cover, usually offered by Norway Spruce *Picea abies*. A few adult females do change location from one breeding season to the next (Wiesner 1992), but most pairs are able to stay within a very limited area all year round. Occasionally, mass movements occur in Scandinavia and the Baltic countries in years when the vole population crashes, but these mostly involve juvenile females (Polakowski et al 2008).

Eurasian Pygmy Owl has never been recorded in Britain, not even as Pleistocene remains. Finding the first will of course be largely a matter of luck, but knowing its autumn sounds may help. Antero Lindholm (in litt) reports that pygmies are the most vocal of several owl species that pass through the south-western corner of Finland in autumn. Their commonest autumn call is the 'scale' (König 1968, Scherzinger 1970), which they also sometimes use in spring. In early March, the German pair from the start of the chapter 'scaled' quite often but usually just once, which made recording the sound very difficult. So I went to Poland in autumn.

Eurasian Pygmy Owl *Glaucidium passerinum*, Białowieża forest, Podłaskie, Poland, 16 June 2005 (*Magnus Robb*)

Białowieża forest has a healthy population of Eurasian Pygmy Owls, and 2012 had been a particularly good breeding season. On my first day, I arrived long after sunset. For the rest of that evening, the pygmy owls were silent, but Tengmalm's Owls and Tawny Owls called from time to time. Finally, at quarter to one in the morning, a single very loud scale shattered the silence like a fanfare, possibly in reaction to some distant *tsyuck* calls of Tengmalm's. In **CD2-10**, after two introductory whistles that descend in pitch, the notes of the 'scale' gradually rise and accelerate to a climax that resonates for several seconds through the forest.

Eurasian Pygmy Owl *Glaucidium passerinum* Białowieża forest, Podłaskie, Poland, 00:46, 3 October 2012. Scale at close range in autumn. Background: Tengmalm's Owl *Aegolius funereus* and European Robin *Erithacus rubecula*. 121003.MR.004626.01

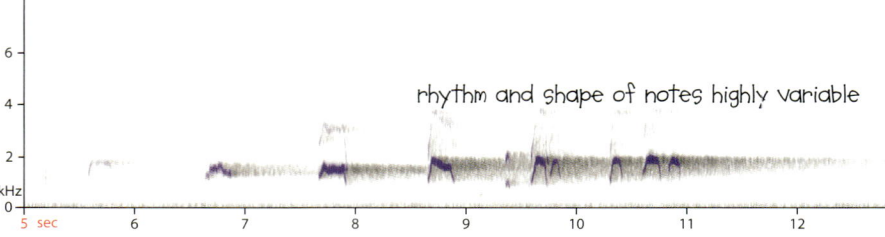

It was only towards the end of the night that scales began to ring out more regularly. There was an obvious peak around one hour before sunrise, when they came from all directions, two or three individuals per minute. Sometimes a wave of them would approach then recede as neighbour responded to neighbour across several kilometres of suitable habitat. In **CD2-11** there are three. The first and last calls are much more similar to each other than either is to the second, so probably both came from the same individual. Some chitter calls precede the first scale, perhaps betraying fear of the Northern Goshawk *Accipiter gentilis* already awake in the distance. After the last call in the recording, the pygmy owls fall silent till dusk.

CD2-11 **Eurasian Pygmy Owl** *Glaucidium passerinum* Białowieża forest, Podłaskie, Poland, 06:14, 8 October 2012. Scale calls, the closest pass of a 'Mexican wave' crossing the forest. Background: Northern Goshawk *Accipiter gentilis*, Eurasian Skylark *Alauda arvensis*, Dunnock *Prunella modularis*, Common Blackbird *Turdus merula*, Eurasian Jay *Garrulus glandarius*, Common Chaffinch *Fringilla coelebs* and Common Reed Bunting *Emberiza schoeniclus*. 121008.MR.061419.02

The only other owl in the Western Palearctic with hooting similar to Eurasian Pygmy Owl is the slightly larger Eurasian Scops Owl *Otus scops*. The genuses they belong to could hardly be more different. Pygmy owls are smaller, yet they tend to go for larger prey. Scops Owls are far more intrepid travelers. With our recognition of Cyprus Scops Owl *O cyprius* and the recent addition of Rinjani Scops Owl *O jolandae* (Sangster et al 2013), *Otus* has 50 species, most of which are tropical and 34 of which are endemic to islands. Some of these islands are far out in the ocean. *Glaucidium* has 25 species, again mostly tropical, only one of which - Cuban Pygmy Owl *G siju* – is endemic to an island (Mikkola 2012). Cuba is less than 200 km from the nearest mainland.

The English Channel is only 34 km wide but Eurasian Pygmy Owl, now breeding as close as Belgium (Sorbi 2013), has never crossed it. As for the warmth-loving Eurasian Scops Owl, the top UK destination for vagrants is the windswept, treeless Shetland Islands, an overshoot of 1500 km or more.

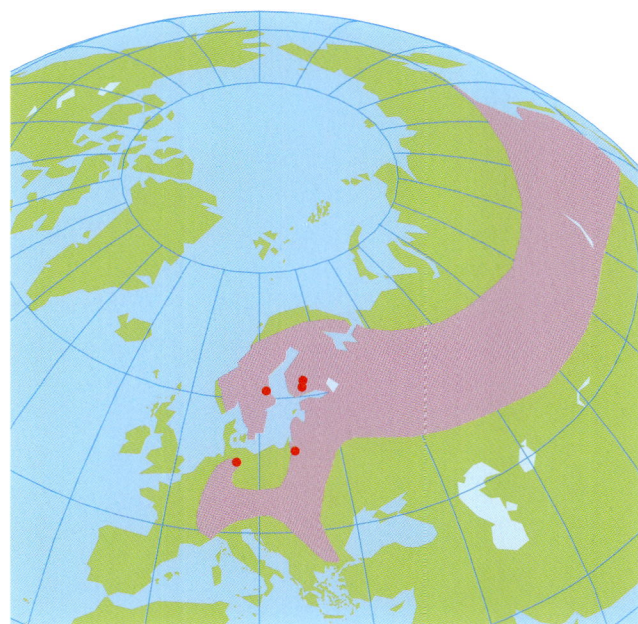

Approximate breeding distribution of Eurasian Pygmy Owl *Glaucidium passerinum* ■. Recording locations indicated by ● dots.

Chapter 6: *Otus*

Eurasian Scops Owl

Over the last five summers I have spent far too many hours under the spell of Eurasian Scops Owls *Otus scops*. By night they tantalise me with their obvious presence; by day they vanish into thin air. When roosting, their 'ears' break up an otherwise rounded profile and their cryptic plumage makes them look like a bark-covered stump. They are also tiny, no larger than a Common Starling *Sturnus vulgaris*. Mediterranean summer nights would not be the same without their musical toot, roughly every three seconds. There they reach higher breeding densities than any other Western Palearctic owl. A diet of large insects precludes them from breeding in northern Europe. In summer they can count on a steady food supply, not fluctuating from year to year. Winter survival is more difficult. In all but the warmest pockets of their breeding range they are obliged to migrate south to winter in the tropics.

One of my Eurasian Scops Owl sites is a small, secluded valley only 18 km from the busy Algarve coast of Portugal. It is a pleasant place to be, especially during the coolness of the night. Arriving in the heat of the afternoon, I spend an hour or two searching the scattered Holm Oaks *Quercus ilex* for roosting owls and nests. After climbing to inspect a few holes, which I can discount due to the presence of spider webs, I usually end up playing 'spot the cicada'. *Cicada orni*'s camouflage against the tree bark is every bit as good as a scops owl's, but 'singing' loudly in the afternoon makes it much easier to find.

After dark, up to five male Eurasian Scops Owls call at once, accompanied by crickets and the occasional Southern Tree Frog *Hyla meridionalis*. Now and then a distant dog barks or a feral pig squeals. Three other owl species are quiet, including two – Eurasian Eagle-Owl *Bubo bubo* and Tawny Owl *Strix aluco* – that are sworn enemies of Scops (Mikkola 1983). There is little to inhibit the four singers in **CD2-12**, or to distract me from listening to them. Three of the four males converge around the same pitch, a slightly sharp E for a musician or 1333 Hz for a scientist.

Hooting Eurasian Scops Owls can sound quite similar to Eurasian Pygmy Owls *Glaucidium passerinum*. However, the individual notes are lower-pitched and more modulated than those of Pygmy, and the gaps between them are longer (Lindén 2013). If in doubt, one of the most reliable things to listen for is an initial *t-* sound in Scops, as opposed to a softer *p-* in Pygmy. In sonagrams, this corresponds to a rapid initial descent in Scops; the notes appear L-shaped. In Pygmy an L-shape is rarely visible in sonagrams and never strong enough to be clearly audible. Vagrants of either species need to be identified with care.

Eurasian Scops Owl *Otus scops*, at nesting site, Rosmaninhal, Idanha-a-Nova, Portugal, 20 July 2013 (*Magnus Robb*). Same as in CD2-22.

CD2-12   **Eurasian Scops Owl** *Otus scops* Vale da Ribeira das Mercês, São Bras de Alportel, Portugal, 19:31, 19 March 2009. Hooting of four males. Background: crickets and Southern Tree Frog *Hyla meridionalis*. 090319.MR.193136.11

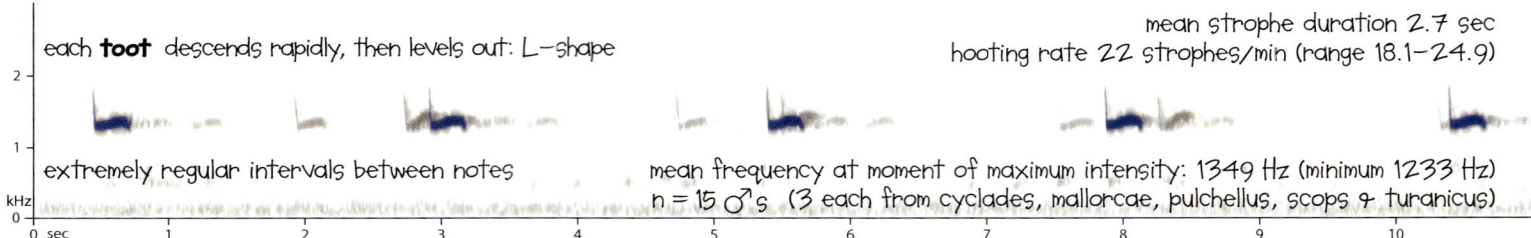

each **toot** descends rapidly, then levels out: L-shape

mean strophe duration 2.7 sec
hooting rate 22 strophes/min (range 18.1–24.9)

extremely regular intervals between notes

mean frequency at moment of maximum intensity: 1349 Hz (minimum 1233 Hz)
n = 15 ♂'s (3 each from cyclades, mallorcae, pulchellus, scops & turanicus)

Eurasian Scops Owls breed in a band of suitable habitats from Morocco and Iberia across southern Europe, skirting the Black Sea and the Central Asian steppes all the way to Lake Baikal in eastern Russia. Remarkably, their hooting sounds very much the same across the whole of this vast range. Of the taxa usually included in Eurasian Scops, only *cyprius*, a resident of Cyprus, sounds markedly different, which is why we regard it as a separate species.

In **CD2-13**, several Eurasian Scops Owls are hooting in a wooded gorge in southern Kazakhstan. Two of them sing a musical E just like in the Algarve, and the third is only slightly lower-pitched. The two groups of males are over 6500 km apart, but the only difference I can hear is that the hoots in Kazakhstan sound slightly shorter. This is partly because the acoustics are drier; the more resonant Algarve valley makes the hoots seem longer than they really are, and the omnidirectional microphone I used in Portugal captures more reflections than the parabolic one I used in Kazakhstan.

Eurasian Scops Owl *Otus scops* Berkhara Gorge, Karatau mountains, Kazakhstan, 19:00, 13 May 2000. Hooting of three males. The nearest one has an intermittent and very faint second note or *bip*. Background: Eastern Nightingale *Luscinia megarhynchos golzii*. 00.028.MR.04010.02   **CD2-13**

Over much of Eurasian Scops Owl's range, the Common Midwife Toad *Alytes obstetricans* produces a confusingly similar sound (**CD2-14**). The toad's call is not only shorter but lacks any audible inflection in pitch, which in scops owls is usually easy to hear. In Spain and Portugal, Iberian Midwife Toad *A cisternasii* can sound even more similar to Eurasian Scops because its song-notes are slightly longer. Add a bit of resonance, and it can be really hard to tell a distant one from a Scops. With **CD2-15**, I was convinced that I was recording my first autumn scops owl, until I noticed that the rhythm was too irregular and the notes were a bit too flat.

One important variant of Eurasian Scops Owl hooting seems to have gone almost unnoticed in the literature. Roughly two thirds of the way between each toot and the next, there is often a very quiet, short *bip*. To my ear, it precedes the main toot as a kind of 'up-beat'. To illustrate

CD2-14   **Common Midwife Toad** *Alytes obstetricans* Manteigas, Serra da Estrela, Portugal, 22:56, 18 July 2013. Song of two males in a cabbage patch. Background: other males, and a Tawny Owl *Strix aluco*. 13071E.MR.225614.01

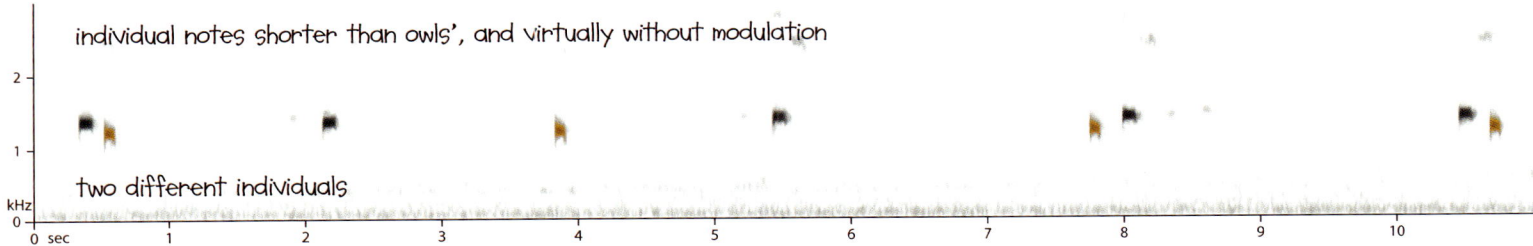

CD2-15   **Iberian Midwife Toad** *Alytes cisternasii* Rosmaninhal, Idanha-a-Nova, Portugal, 21:25, 24 September 2009. Song of a distant male. Background: rutting Red Deer *Cervus elaphus* and fish in the Tagus river. 090924.MR.212512.02

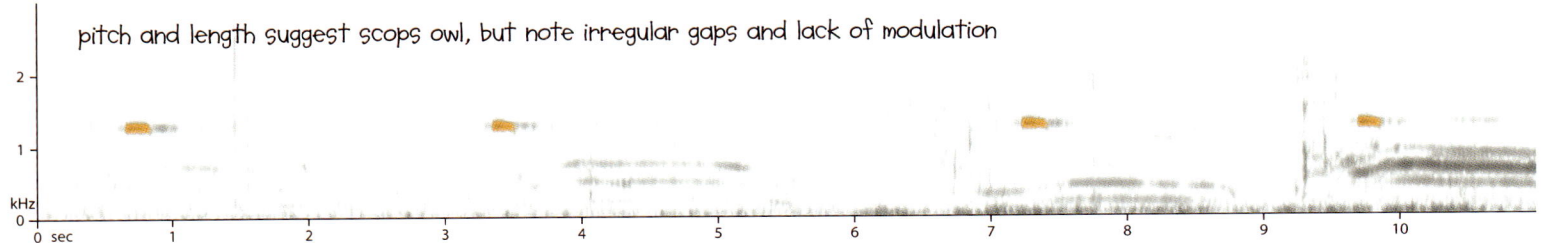

Nesting site of Eurasian Scops Owl *Otus scops*, Rosmaninhal, Idanha-a-Nova, Portugal, 20 July 2013 (*Magnus Robb*). The area where many recordings of this species come from (CD2-16 & CD2-20 to 22).

it well, I have chosen an exceptionally clear example, this time a male from Portugal. His *bips* could be heard from a distance of 400 m, although I went much closer to make the recording. Normally the *bip* is only audible at very close range. It is also present in the recording from Kazakhstan (cf, **CD2-16**), where it is much harder to hear. Can you pick it out?

Hooting with an additional *bip* occurs at a low incidence in all regions where Eurasian Scops Owl occurs, including Pakistan where Roberts & King (1986) showed it in a sonagram. In Cyprus Scops Owl *O cyprius*, *bips* are the rule and very audible. Oriental Scops Owl *O sunia* and its close relative the Socotra Scops Owl *O socotranus* also have one or more quiet, lower-pitched notes

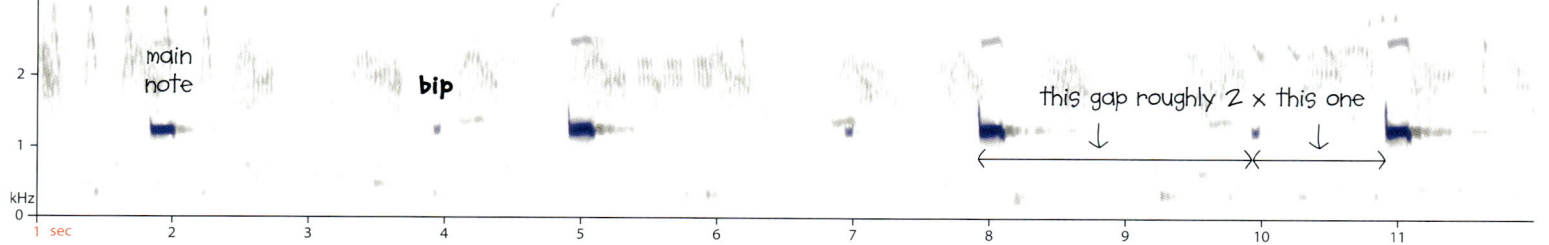

CD2-16 **Eurasian Scops Owl** *Otus scops* Rosmarinhal, Idanha-a-Nova, Portugal, 00:53, 13 May 2012. Hooting with prominent *bip* preceding main note. Background: Iberian Green Frog *Pelophylax perezi*, Common Nightingale *Luscinia megarhynchos*. 120513.MR.005304.01

preceding the main hoot (Pons et al 2013), so these may be a throwback to a common ancestor. Their presence or absence in Eurasian Scops seems to be a matter of individual variation. Sometimes an individual gives just an occasional *bip*. Most individuals do not *bip* at all and amazingly, a 26-page study of individual variation in hooting (Dragonetti 2007) fails to mention it at all.

Individual male scops owls can often be identified by their hooting. König (1973) found that she could play back recordings in perfect synchrony with their performer, even when the recordings were several years old. Rate of delivery is the most reliable feature. The shape of the hoots and the average pitch of their sustained part are nearly as consistent (Dragonetti 2007, Galeotti & Sacchi 2001). A minority of males have two clearly different types of hoots in their repertoire (Dragonetti 2007). The way they alternate is by 'eventual variation', ie, AAABBB rather than 'immediate variation' or ABABAB. This can lead to overestimates of the number of males present in a given area.

Pitch matters to male Eurasian Scops Owls. The lower the hoot, the fatter the male (Hardouin et al 2007). Dimensions such as wing length are irrelevant; it is weight that counts. Fat reserves are a better indication of a male's condition than his length or wingspan. Playback experiments have shown that males are able to vary the pitch of their hoots and 'lie' about their fitness. When played a recording of an unusually low-pitched male, 20 out of 26 males responded by lowering the pitch of their own hoots (Hardouin et al 2007). Curiously, males tend to respond more vigorously to higher-pitched than to lower-pitched playback, suggesting that they exercise greater caution when reacting to heavy strangers. Males with lower-pitched hoots are the most successful breeders, even when their hoots are lower than expected from their body condition. This may be due to the advantage their low-pitched hoots give them when competing for the best territories (Hardouin et al 2009).

Eurasian Scops Owls are famous for their monotony. It can be difficult to avoid being hypnotised and keep track of what is going on. Sexing them is often far from straightforward, and may not always be possible. After the courtship period, however, females hoot very little. Often two Scops apparently hooting together are simply two males on different pitches. I made a breakthrough when I worked out that many hoot-like sounds,

especially in females, are actually something else. These *twiu* calls as I call them are equivalent to the soliciting calls of other owls: I hear them especially when the owls are exchanging food and copulating. In the three other Western Palearctic scops owls they are more obviously different from hooting and easier to recognise. But before I give examples of *twiu* calls, how do females sound when they really do hoot?

Paired females hoot with a more variable pitch than males, as well as sounding weaker or quieter, and sometimes slightly hoarse. When these characteristics are combined with a much higher overall pitch and they are perched close to a typical-sounding male, we can identify them with confidence (**CD2-17**). Paired females hooting at a more male-like pitch must be sexed more carefully by listening for as many clues as possible: they may eventually switch to a higher-pitched version. Unpaired females may not always be possible to sex with confidence (König 1973).

In late April 2007, Arnoud happened to be on Sicily when pair formation was at a peak. Many of the Eurasian Scops Owl recordings he made there were of a pair breeding in an abandoned orchard beside a lava field on the northern slopes of Mt Etna. In **CD2-18**, the male and female are both hooting. The female is the closer bird hooting at a high pitch, while the male gives a few lower-pitched hoots before falling silent. Then from 0:28 the female drops to a slightly lower pitch and utters a series of *twiu* notes that have an audibly different shape.

CD2-19 was recorded earlier in the night. It starts with the male giving his own lower-pitched version of the same *twiu* note, which he delivers more quickly than his hooting. At 0:34 the female arrives hooting, before giving her own *twiu* from 0:41-

CD2-17 **Eurasian Scops Owl** *Otus scops* Northern slopes of Mt Etna, Castiglione, Catania, Sicily, 20:54, 21 April 2007. Hooting of a female, with a lower-pitched hoot from her mate at 0:20. There are also *twiu* calls towards the end of the recording. Background: Sicilian Partridge *Alectoris whitakeri*, Cucumiau *Athene noctua* and other Eurasian Scops Owls. 07.017.AB.04717.32

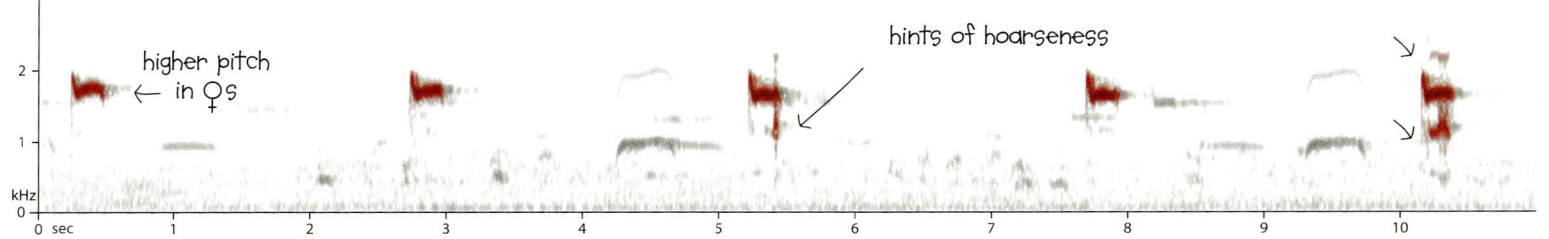

CD2-18 **Eurasian Scops Owl** *Otus scops* Northern slopes of Mt Etna, Castiglione, Catania, Sicily, 05:13, 22 April 2007. Hooting of female and male, followed by *twiu* soliciting calls of female. Background: Cucumiau *Athene noctua* and Common Nightingale *Luscinia megarhynchos*. 07.019.AB.02958.11

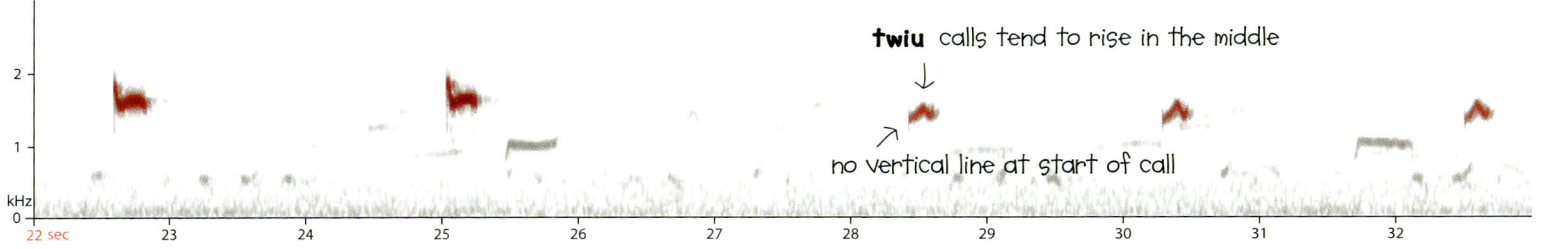

CD2-19 **Eurasian Scops Owl** *Otus scops* Northern slopes of Mt Etna, Castiglione, Catania, Sicily, 21:17, 21 April 2007. *Twiu* soliciting calls of male and female, then hooting of both, leading to copulation at 0:58. Background: other Eurasian Scops Owls. 07.017.AB.05212.31

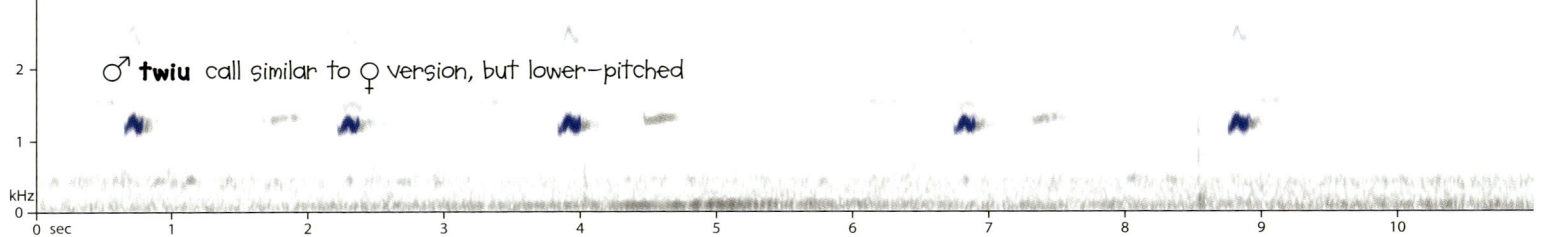

0:46. When the male starts to hoot (with additional *bip* notes), she briefly reverts to her own high-pitched hooting. The sequence ends with copulation, accompanied by a shrill twitter from the male and a croaking, lower-pitched *dr-r-r-r* from the female.

Eurasian Scops Owl *Otus scops* Rosmaninhal, Idanha-a-Nova, Portugal, 03:29, 14 May 2012. Hooting of male, *twiu* calls of female, then copulation twitter of male. Background: Iberian Green Frog *Pelophenax perezi*. 120514.MR.032950.00 **CD2-20**

Once I recognised the copulation twitter, which is only ever given by the male, I started hearing it often, sometimes far into the breeding season. In **CD2-20**, the microphones were placed within two metres of a cavity in a Holm Oak that a pair appeared to be adopting as a nest (they ended up nesting elsewhere). The male of the nearby pair had two types of loud hoot, one of which was disyllabic. Surprisingly, the female often sounded lower-pitched than he, something that was not supposed to happen. The recording starts with the male hooting and the female giving a series of what I now know to be *twiu* calls. Another male is hooting some distance away (if you are listening on headphones, he should be on the right). At 0:29 the female flies right and lands heavily on a twig beside the microphone where she carries on giving her low-pitched *twiu*. At 0:51 the male's wingbeats can be heard as he flies a short distance. The female flies to join him from 1:02. At 1:09 the copulation twitter is overlaid on one of the female's *twiu* calls, and my sexing is confirmed.

On another occasion, I ruined a recording of the lead-up to copulation by returning in my car at just the wrong moment. I had left the equipment running for two hours so I was very unlucky that the only action happened right then. Fortunately the climax occurred only after I had stopped the motor (**CD2-21**). I include it here to draw attention to the croaking call (König 1973), which sounds like an amphibian, perhaps a Common Frog *Rana temporaria* or a Natterjack Toad *Bufo calamita*. I am referring to the soft, low-pitched, croaking *drrrr... drr..* that the female does at the end of the male's copulation twitter (it was also present in **CD2-19**). This croaking call is similar in structure

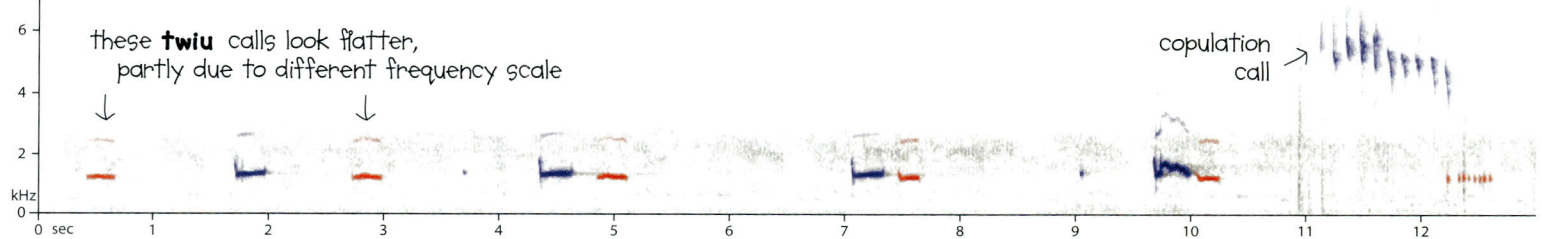

CD2-21   **Eurasian Scops Owl** *Otus scops* Rosmaninhal, Idanha-a-Nova, Portugal, 00:01, 13 May 2012. Copulation, starting with hooting of male and *twiu* calls of female. Immediately after male's copulation twitter, female gives croaking call. Background: Iberian Green Frog *Pelophenax perezi*. 120513.MR.000157.00

to the feeding calls of other owls, but the adults use it for more than just feeding. König (1973) heard them croaking both when offering and demanding favours, as well as when distributing food to the young.

It was only by the skin of my teeth that I managed to record juvenile Eurasian Scops Owls for this book. Every time adult behaviour at night suggested the location of a nest, daytime searching revealed nothing. This went on for years. At Rosmaninhal in Portugal, I searched for nests in early June on an evening when the males were frustratingly quiet. Without hearing them I had no idea where they were. At one point my impatience got the better of me and I tried a little playback. Within seconds a scops owl hit me hard on the side of my head. I could feel the sharp claws, although they failed to draw blood. I never did find this male's nest, and when I eventually found his neighbours' nest it was through more patient fieldcraft.

I now realise that most of my efforts were simply too early. Scops owls time their breeding to coincide with the maximum abundance of large insects, and adults may be feeding fledglings long after most other owls have finished. Egg-laying is from mid-May to mid-June. With an incubation period of about 24 days and the owlets being fed for up to 60 days (Mebs & Scherzinger 2004), late juveniles may only attain independence in the first half of September.

For two years, I made a big effort to find the nest of a particular pair near Rosmaninhal (cf, **CD2-20** & **CD2-21**). In the second year, in 2013, I made a special trip in early June to try to find the nest, or at least to study the adults' behaviour. The owls were copulating at least six times a night, so it seemed that egg-laying was imminent. I tried climbing a few Holm Oaks where they had been, and peering into holes. All kinds of things were inside, Wood Mice *Apodemus sylvaticus*, Spotless Starlings *Sturnus unicolor*, even a latrine belonging to Common Genets *Genetta genetta*, but no scops owls. When I returned in the evening of 19 July, I finally heard juvenile begging calls coming at incredibly low volume from one of their four favourite trees. The calls were barely audible, even at about 10 m distance.

I placed the microphones close to the nest and left, recovering them in the morning. During the night, the parents fed the young frequently, often several times per hour. With the help of photographs in König (1973), I aged the young at about 15 and 17 days old. In **CD2-22**, one of the adults announces its arrival with two *twiu*-like calls. After a few seconds it goes to the nest, and the young start begging intensely with an almost puppy-like panting. The striking thing about these begging calls is the very fast rate of their delivery, up to around 70/minute. König (1973) found 30/minute to be typical of relaxed situations, rising to twice that rate when the young were being fed. From 0:21, the adult gives some croaks, used here as food-offering calls. One of the young gives a few very high chitters of discontent, eg, at 0:33 and 0:43.

Begging calls increase gradually in volume until the young leave the nest on around their 21st day. From then on, they rock their body when begging. This looks like an exaggeration of the way perched raptors use parallax, rocking their head from side to side when fixing the location of prey. From about the 30th day, the begging call takes on an increasingly voiced or tonal quality. Then from the 60th day, the gestures decrease. König's (1973) sonagram of 124-day-old female shows a mostly tonal begging call that has almost evolved into a *twiu* call.

Eurasian Scops Owl *Otus scops*, nest with chicks, Rosmaninhal, Idanha-a-Nova, Portugal, 20 July 2013 (*Paulo Monteiro*). Same as in CD2-22.

CD2-22   **Eurasian Scops Owl** *Otus scops* Rosmaninhal, Idanha-a-Nova, Portugal, 22:20, 19 July 2013. Adult announces arrival with *twiu*-like calls, then croaks as a feeding call. Two nestlings beg and give occasional high-pitched chitters. Background: crickets and Iberian Green Frog *Pelophenax perezi*. 130719.MR.222054.21

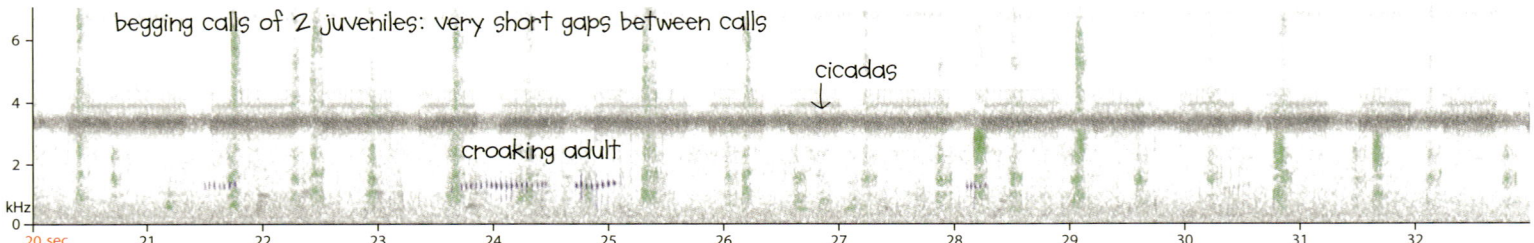

them, so I suspect the predator was a bird. Two is a very small brood size for Eurasian Scops Owl, so perhaps the predator had taken one or two young before I found them. In my recordings, two suspects emerge. An Azure-winged Magpie *Cyanopica cooki* called several times uncomfortably close to the nest during the night, and one of the adults got very excited when a Little Owl *Athene vidalii* appeared nearby.

One call of Eurasian Scops Owl actually sounds very similar to a Little Owl, so much so that it forms an identification pitfall. When we went through our database searching for any recordings of Little Owl and Cucumiaus *A noctua* from strange places, we found a couple that were really Scops giving excitement calls. Although we may hear these at any point from spring to at least autumn, I have heard them most often after the young leave the nest. **CD2-23** and **CD2-24** date from this period. While recording them, I nearly made what would have been an embarrassing mistake. I knew that the excitement

Eurasian Scops Owl *Otus scops*, Rosmaninhal, Idanha-a-Nova, Portugal, 20 July 2013 *(Paulo Monteiro)*. Within 2 m of the nest in CD2-22.

Sadly, I never had the chance to follow the development of these young. A few days after my visit the nest was predated, and the juveniles' delicate body feathers were scattered on leaf litter under the tree. Some had beak-shaped nips taken out of

Eurasian Scops Owl *Otus scops* Vale da Ribeira das Mercês, São Bras de Alportel, Portugal, 22:47, 13 August 2011. Varied excitement calls of an adult. Background: juvenile Eurasian Eagle-Owl *Bubo bubo* at 0:35 and 0:44. 110813.MR.224710.11   CD2-23

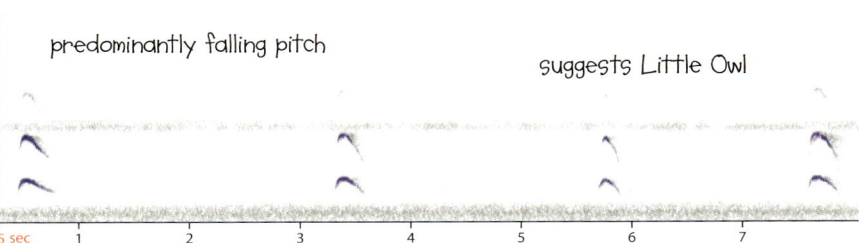

Eurasian Scops Owl *Otus scops* Vale da Ribeira das Mercês, São Bras de Alportel, Portugal, 22:51, 13 August 2011. Excitement calls, including a whinnying variant. Background: feral pigs. 110813.MR.225126.11   CD2-24

calls were coming from an adult Scops, but I could also hear a juvenile owl in the same valley. Its calls seemed too loud and were repeated with gaps too long to be juvenile Scops. With the adult alarming nearby, however, I started to wonder if my assumptions about Scops begging calls were correct. The juvenile was in fact a Eurasian Eagle-Owl. No wonder the adult Scops was getting so excited!

In areas such as southern Spain (König 1970) and Crete (Streseman 1943) where Eurasian Scops Owls are resident, they sometimes hoot in autumn and winter. I myself once heard several in the Ebro Delta, Catalonia, in late September. Males are said to hoot occasionally during autumn migration (Mebs & Scherzinger 2004), although this seems to be rare. At Sagres in the extreme south-western corner of Europe, where migration has been monitored extensively by teams of observers since 1990, Scops are present each autumn but Ricardo Tomé, one of the project coordinators, tells me that none have ever been heard calling. Only one of my friends in Portugal has heard a scops owl in autumn at a site where they do not breed (Georg Schreier pers comm).

Eurasian Scops Owls wintering in Africa call very little during their stay (Moreau 1972, Cramp 1985), and this combined with their visual similarity to African Scops Owl *O senegalensis* makes them very difficult to study. We still know very little about the half of their life spent outside Europe, and I wonder what some well-designed tracking experiments might reveal. When Mori et al (2014) did a winter survey in Italy, they found that the few Eurasian Scops wintering there respond more strongly to playback of Cucumiau than they do to Eurasian Scops.

Eurasian Scops Owl *Otus scops*, Lesvos, Greece, 26 April 2001 (*René Pop*)

During northward migration, Eurasian Scops Owls can be surprisingly vocal. Andrea Corso told me about orchards along the Sicilian coast where, if you imitate one on the right day in spring, you receive many replies but a few weeks later there are none. In mid-April, I once heard hooting at dawn, coming from thick tamarisk scrub on Fuerteventura in the Canary Islands, where no Scops Owls breed. In Portugal, I have sometimes heard hooting during a single spring night in places where I never heard one before or after.

Spring is also the time when the great majority of vagrant Scops Owls overshoot into northern Europe. In Britain and Ireland, there were 96 records up to the end of 2012 (rarebirdalert.co.uk). April, May and June have an almost equal share of the total. Many were shot during the 19th century, when there were even three records involving more than one individual. Older distribution maps (eg, in Mikkola 1983) show the species breeding further north than it does today, especially in France and Russia, so overshooting was probably commoner back then. In recent decades agriculture has intensified so much that large insects have become scarce. Insecticides have certainly contributed, but so has the disappearance of suitable habitats. In Portugal, for example, most olive oil is now produced in intensively managed plantations with much reduced insect life and trees too young to have holes.

All the more reason to cherish the traditional olive groves, orchards and open Mediterranean woodlands where they still enchant in good numbers. Could an ecological revolution in farming, coupled with global warming, result in a return to former breeding sites in the north? Or are we in for a genetically modified, critter-free countryside, where even Tawny Owls become a thing of the past? I hope the owls know who needs their hypnotherapy the most.

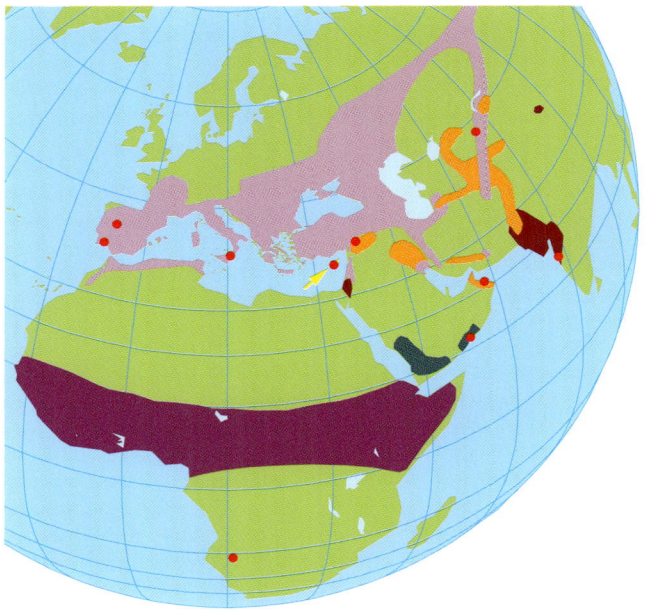

Approximate breeding and winter distribution of Eurasian Scops Owl *Otus scops* (■ and ■) and Pallid Scops Owl *O brucei* (■ and ■) and breeding distribution of Cyprus Scops Owl *O cyprius* ■ (Cyprus only) and Arabian Scops Owl *O pamelae* ■. Recording locations of Eurasian, Cyprus, Pallid, Arabian, Oriental Scops Owl *O sunia* and African Scops Owl *O senegalensis* indicated by ● dots.

Cyprus Scops Owl

Cyprus is a magnet for anyone interested in endemic island birds and their sounds. Its central Troodos Mountains rise to 1952 m, hiding traditional villages, Byzantine monasteries and a variety of endemic taxa in their folds. On the lower slopes, it is not difficult to find Cyprus Wheatears *Oenanthe cypriaca* and Cyprus Warblers *Sylvia melanothorax*. Up on top, forests of Black Pine *Pinus nigra* are home to Cyprus Coal Tits *Periparus ater cypriotes*, Cyprus Short-toed Treecreepers *Certhia brachydactyla dorotheae* and Cyprus Crossbills *Loxia curvirostris guillemardi*, all of which sound in some way different from their mainland counterparts.

Having spent the early daylight hours of 26 March 2000 walking through snow on north-facing, 1700 m high slopes in bright sunlight, a Cyprus Scops Owl *Otus cyprius* was the last thing I expected to hear. The first was a male, some distance away in a sun-warmed patch of pine forest. It gave a series of two-note songs, repeated every 3.5 seconds. A prominent *bip* preceded each louder *toot* by about a second (**CD2-25**).

More than half a century ago, Bannerman & Bannerman (1958) described two-note hooting in Cyprus Scops Owl, which they interpreted as a male-female duet. Over the next few decades, the number of birders on the island grew exponentially, but it was not until the early 1990s that somebody challenged this interpretation. Observing a local male by daylight, David Whaley (1991) discovered that a single individual could produce both notes. Several years later, Peter Flint and Jeff Gordon became interested and confirmed Whaley's observations, also by visual means. While taking a holiday on the island, Mark heard about this discovery from Jeff, but remained unconvinced. When I decided to visit Cyprus in spring 2000, he suggested I check it out.

When I whistled an imitation, the high-altitude, daytime male came a little closer while still remaining out of sight. Soon a female added her own two-note song, somewhere close to the male. Hers was slightly higher-pitched than his, and

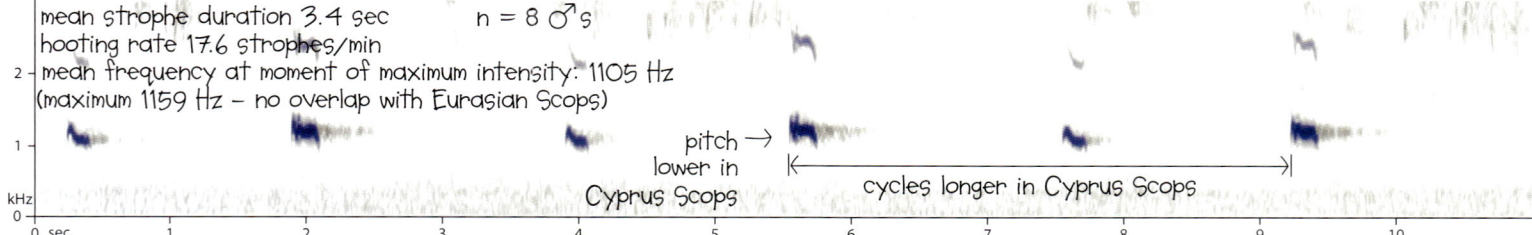

CD2-25   **Cyprus Scops Owl** *Otus cyprius* Troodos, Limassol district, Cyprus, 12:40, 26 March 2000. Hooting of a male. Background: Cyprus Coal Tit *Periparus ater cypriotes* and Cyprus Short-toed Treecreeper *Certhia brachydactyla dorotheae*. 00.002.MR.04040.11

Habitat of Cyprus Scops Owl *Otus cyprius*, Lefkara, Larnaca, Cyprus, 27 June 2013 (*René Pop*). Site where CD2-35 & 36 were recorded.

they were almost but not quite in synchrony. With slightly differing phrase lengths, they very gradually moved out of phase. The exact sequence of the four notes in the duet – his two and her two – changed subtly with every repetition,

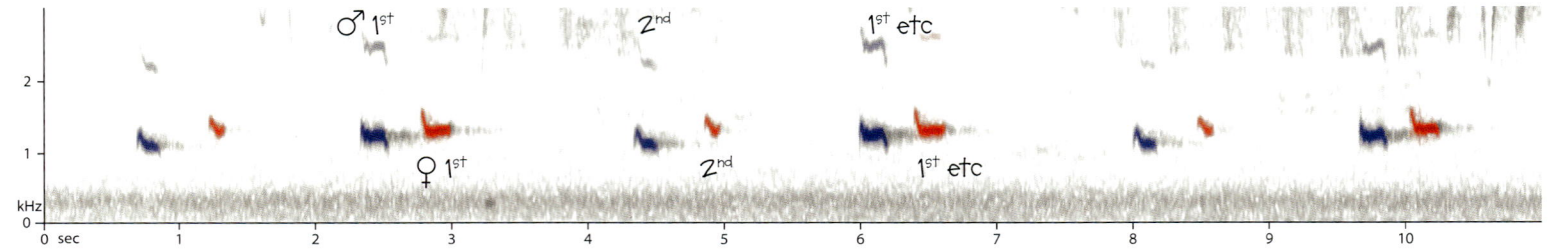

CD2-26 **Cyprus Scops Owl** *Otus cyprius* Troodos, Limassol district, Cyprus, 12:40, 26 March 2000. Hooting duet of male and female. Background: Cyprus Coal Tit *Periparus ater cypriotes* and Cyprus Short-toed Treecreeper *Certhia brachydactyla dorotheae*. 00.002.MR.03858.00

resulting in a musical composition that a minimalist like Steve Reich would have been proud of (**CD2-26**).

As I explored the island over the next couple of weeks, I often heard Cyprus Scops Owls. Sustained bouts of hooting always consisted of two notes in a rigid sequence: quiet note, short silence, loud note, long silence. One time I managed to confirm visually for myself, by daylight, that one individual could produce both notes. I am convinced that this is always the case, not least because I know that Eurasian Scops Owl sometimes has a two-note song too. On my return, I told Mark that I believed David, Jeff and Peter were right.

In Cyprus Scops Owl the *bip* is always strong while in Eurasian Scops Owl it tends either to be absent or exceedingly quiet, to the extent that very few publications have ever clearly acknowledged its presence (Roberts & King 1986, Rasmussen & Anderton 2005). There are two other ways in which Cyprus Scops hooting differs from that of Eurasian Scops Owl: delivery rate and pitch. On average, Cyprus Scops gives 17.6 phrases per minute, whereas Eurasian Scops gives 22. The mean frequency of the loudest point in the call is 1105 Hz for Cyprus Scops and 1349 Hz for Eurasian, with little or no overlap.

In the Far East, Oriental Scops Owl *O sunia* also has *bips* between its louder hoots. Northern populations *O s stictonotus* and *O s japonicus* hoot more rapidly than Cyprus Scops Owl, and usually have two *bips* before each *toot*. Southern populations of Oriental Scops show more variation, including modulation of the main toot, which becomes *trrt* (**CD2-27**). Oriental Scops used to be included in Eurasian Scops Owl, but recent DNA studies have shown that it is a member of a group of about a dozen other species from southern Asia and the Indian Ocean, to which Eurasian Scops does not belong (Fuchs et al 2008, Pons et al 2013). Only one of those species, Socotra Scops Owl *O socotranus*, sounds very similar to Oriental Scops. At one time, I wondered if Cyprus Scops might be related to Oriental Scops and Socotra Scops. However, genetic studies place it extremely close to Eurasian Scops. With an mtDNA difference of just 0.1%,

CD2-27 **Oriental Scops Owl** *Otus sunia rufipenr is* Bhagwan Mahaveer Wildlife Sanctuary, Goa, India, 03:42, 9 January 2013. Hooting of a male, joined by a female from 0:40. 130109.AB.034200.01

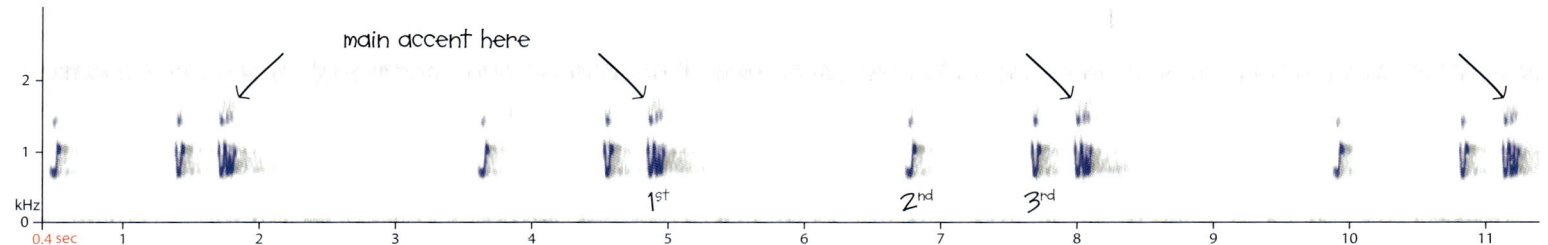

it must have diverged very recently, during the last major glacial cycle (Flint et al submitted manuscript).

Towards the end of my stay in Cyprus, I recorded a pair of Cyprus Scops Owls near a stream passing an old Byzantine chapel. The male had two versions of the louder hoot in his song, one higher-pitched than the other. In **CD2-28**, he switches between them at 0:26 and again later. At 1:00 he hesitates briefly, inserting an extra *bip* before continuing as before. The extra *bip* has the effect of creating a longer, 'three-note strophe'. Cyprus Scops often does this, and I have even heard the odd 'four-note strophe'. Such strophes are usually scattered among normal ones, although **CD2-29** gives an exceptional example of consecutive 'three-note strophes'. So far, I have never come

Cyprus Scops Owl *Otus cyprius* Ayias Minas, Paphos district, Cyprus, 13:02, 2 April 2000. Hooting of a male, with an unusual example of two consecutive 'three-note strophes'. Background: Eurasian Blackcap *Sylvia atricapilla* and Great Tit *Parus major*. 00.010.MR.00314.00

CD2-29

CD2-28 **Cyprus Scops Owl** *Otus cyprius* Ayias Minas, Paphos district, Cyprus, 20:13, 2 April 2000. Hooting of a male, with others in the distance. At 0:26 he changes to an alternative version of the louder note. At 1:00 there is a 'three-note strophe'. Background: Middle East Tree Frog *Hyla savignyi*. 00.010.MR.01218.00

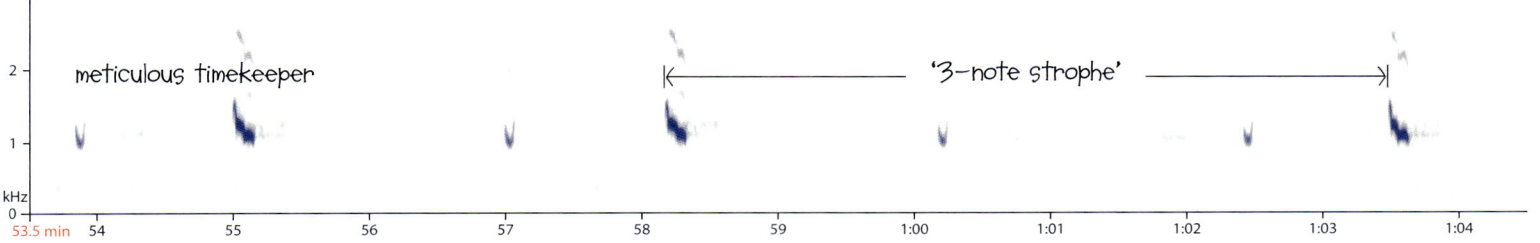

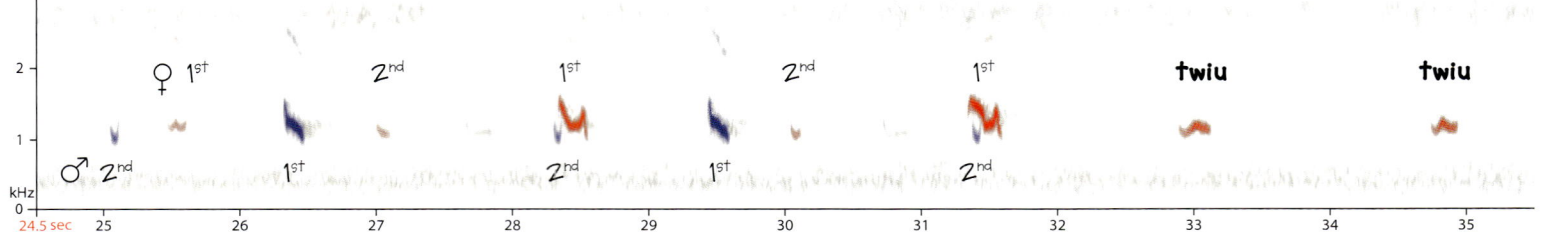

CD2-30   **Cyprus Scops Owl** *Otus cyprius* Ayias Minas, Paphos district, Cyprus, 20:06, 2 April 2000. Hooting of a male, including a 'four-note phrase' at 0:06. The female joins in with a series of quiet *twiu* calls, then gives two phrases of hooting from 0:27, starting with a *bip*, before returning to *twiu* calls again. Background: Middle East Tree Frog *Hyla savignyi* 00.010.MR.00154.00

across them in Eurasian Scops Owl. To me, such strophes sound like tidy discontinuities. Scops owls are exceedingly meticulous timekeepers. Any distraction or hesitation, whatever the cause, is immediately assimilated within their strict sense of rhythm.

Female Cyprus Scops Owls usually have two-note hooting very similar to males but slightly higher-pitched, weaker and more modulated. They also have a *twiu* call very similar to that of Eurasian Scops Owl, which only exists in a single-note version (**CD2-30**). The observation that female Cyprus Scops hoot with two notes but *twiu* with just one strongly supports recognition of the *twiu* as a different call type.

My understanding of Cyprus Scops Owl sounds was enriched thanks to the help of Johannes Honold, who spent several months in Cyprus in 2013. Johannes and I came into contact when he sound recorded two Asian Buff-bellied Pipits *Anthus rubescens japonicus* on the island in March. When I realised there was a savvy sound-recordist staying on the island, I challenged him to find a Cyprus Scops nest and record some sounds that we still needed. He found several, and had a lot of fun while doing so.

At one of those nests, Johannes recorded a very amphibian-like version of the croaking call, apparently coming from a brooding female (**CD2-31**). Other recordings from the same evening included begging calls of tiny nestlings. I believe that the female was croaking while offering food to her young.

Cyprus Scops Owl *Otus cyprius* Klavdia Pyrga, Larnaca district, Cyprus, 23:41, 7 June 2013. Croaking of a female in a nest with tiny nestlings. 130607.JH.234100.01 Johannes Honold   **CD2-31**

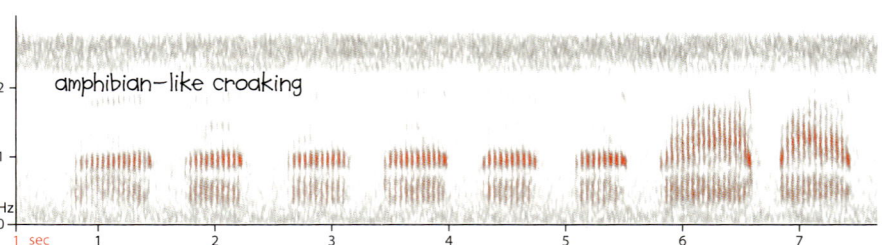

Johannes's most important contribution was to confirm a vocal difference between Cyprus Scops Owl and Eurasian Scops Owl excitement calls that I had previously only suspected, based on a single call. The one in **CD2-32** was surprisingly low-pitched, reaching a maximum frequency of 1084 Hz. Johannes recorded alarm calls of at least a further eight individuals. When I calculated the 'means of means' for all nine individuals, the maximum frequency in Cyprus Scops turned out to be 1227 Hz, while the mean duration was 0.36 seconds. In 10 Eurasian Scops from a variety of subspecies, the 'means of means' were 1572 Hz for maximum frequency and 0.3 seconds for duration. So, excitement calls of Cyprus Scops average lower-pitched and longer than those of Eurasian Scops.

Cyprus Scops Owl *Otus cyprius*, adult, Panagia, Paphos, Cyprus, 29 June 2013 (*René Pop*). Possibly one of the birds in CD2-33.

CD2-32 **Cyprus Scops Owl** *Otus cyprius* Ayias Minas, Paphos district, Cyprus, 2 April 2000. Excitement call, possibly of a female. A male hoots very slowly with phrases 3.7 seconds long, or just 16.2 phrases per minute. 00.010.MR.02301.31

In **CD2-33**, two owls are excitement-calling from a nest in an abandoned monastery: a distant, higher-pitched individual followed by a much nearer and lower-pitched one that calls several times while moving away from us. It was mainly in July that Johannes recorded higher-pitched excitement calls like the more distant bird, suggesting to me that they may have been females. A month before, many would still have been in the nest, either incubating or brooding small young. Some pairs breed earlier than others, however, and one of Johannes's earlier recordings also has excitement calls of two individuals (**CD2-34**).

CD2-33 **Cyprus Scops Owl** *Otus cyprius* Panagia tou Sinti, Paphos district, Cyprus, 22:30, 4 July 2013. Excitement calls of a pair near their nest, one near and one far. Background: Common Barn Owl *Tyto alba*. 130704.JH.223000.01 Johannes Honold

CD2-34 **Cyprus Scops Owl** *Otus cyprius* Klavdia-Pyrga, Larnaca district, Cyprus, 21:22, 14 June 2013. Excitement calls of a pair near their nest in an ancient olive tree. 130614.JH.212200.11 Johannes Honold

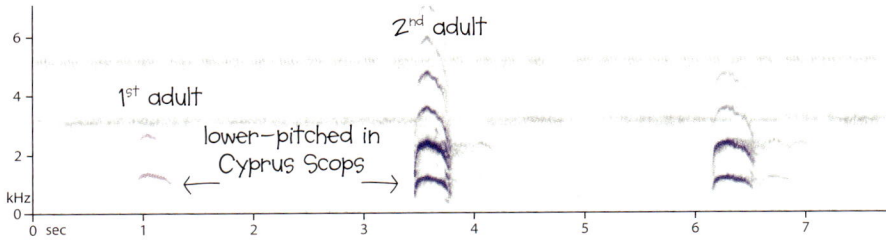

Cyprus Scops Owl *Otus cyprius*, juveniles, Lefkara, Larnaca, Cyprus, 27 June 2013 (*René Pop*). Same as in CD2-35 & 36.

The one giving the very first call is slightly higher-pitched than the other that calls from then onwards. My comparison between Cyprus Scops Owl and Eurasian Scops Owl excitement calls ought to be repeated with birds of known sex. Nevertheless, I have no strong reason to suspect a sexual bias in the recordings I used.

Another of Johannes's sites was an ancient olive grove, a paradise for scops owls. By the time he recorded **CD2-35**, at least two young had fledged. One of them is begging and when an adult arrives, its begging intensifies. The adult gives a few excitement calls as it feeds the youngster, which gradually returns to a more relaxed calling rate. It is clear from this recording that begging calls of Cyprus Scops Owl are very similar to those of Eurasian Scops Owl. One family of each is not much to compare, but if anything the Cyprus juveniles sound slightly less disyllabic than their cousins from Portugal. After fledging, this family stayed in the olive grove, where René managed to photograph them. By this time their calls carried about 100 m, although Johannes recorded **CD2-36** from much close range.

CD2-36 **Cyprus Scops Owl** *Otus cyprius* Lefkara, Larnaca district, Cyprus, 22:25, 27 June 2013. Begging calls of several fledged juveniles, six days later than CD2-35. 130627.JH.222500.01 Johannes Honold

CD2-35 **Cyprus Scops Owl** *Otus cyprius* Lefkara, Larnaca district, Cyprus, 21:25, 21 June 2013. Begging of a juvenile, which is then fed by an adult. The adult gives several excitement calls including one that is particularly loud. 130621.JH.212500.01 Johannes Honold

Cyprus Scops Owl *Otus cyprius*, juveniles, Lefkara, Larnaca, Cyprus, 26 June 2013 (*René Pop*). Same as in CD2-35 & 36.

Breeding takes place several weeks earlier than in most populations of Eurasian Scops Owl. Small young of Cyprus Scops Owl have been found from late April onwards (Peter Flint in litt), suggesting incubation from early April and fledging from the second half of May. Eurasian Scops typically breeds very late. When I finally found a nest in Portugal, the young were set to fledge in late July. Even in North Africa, egg-laying time is May to early June (Heim de Balsac & Mayaud 1962), so fledging may be just as late as in Portugal. The earlier breeding of Cyprus Scops raises some interesting questions. Is their diet somehow different from that of their Eurasian relatives? Do they winter on the island, or do they migrate?

A study of birdliming (Horner & Hubbard 1982) shed virtually the only light on Cyprus Scops Owl movements. Sadly, despite being illegal, catching migrants by such cruel means is still common in Cyprus. The number of owls involved is shocking. During the spring of 1968, 136 migrating Eurasian Scops Owls and 14 Cyprus Scops were limed at Paralimni, near the south-eastern coast. They could be identified by their plumages. Cyprus Scops is dark, like all the other bird taxa endemic to the island, existing only in a dark grey morph (Flint & Stewart 1992). The black streaks on both the upperparts and the underparts are heavier, white spots on hindneck and mantle are larger and more contrasting than in Eurasian Scops, and the spotting often extends to the crown and scapulars (C S Roselaar in Cramp 1985). Although wintering seems difficult to exclude, the Cyprus Scops at Paralimni were probably returning from overseas. Two specimens collected in Israel in or before March, closely resembling Cyprus Scops, support this hypothesis (Flint et al submitted manuscript). In the liming study, Cyprus Scops were present only between 12 March and 3 April, whereas Eurasian Scops arrived between 16 March and 8 May, with most in mid-April. So, the Cyprus Scops were back before the bulk of Eurasian Scops passed through.

In Turkey just to the north, Eurasian Scops Owls are migratory in all but a few warm coastal pockets (Eken 1997). A slight cooling of the climate might eliminate those wintering sites, and also render Cyprus itself unsuitable for wintering scops owls. Cyprus Scops Owl has wings as long as most Eurasian Scops, suggesting that migration has always at least been retained as an option. A scarcity of winter records on the island suggests that wintering abroad may be commoner than previously thought (Flint et al

Cyprus Scops Owl *Otus cyprius*, juvenile, Lefkara, Larnaca, Cyprus, 27 June 2013 (*René Pop*). Same as in CD2-35 & 36.

submitted manuscript). Alternatively, the owls may simply be less territorial when not breeding.

On Madeira in the North Atlantic, subfossil remains have shown what happened to an insular scops owl that stopped migrating altogether. The recently described Madeira Scops Owl *O mauli* evolved much longer legs than Eurasian Scops Owl and a largely terrestrial lifestyle. It may have become extinct as recently as 600 years ago. When humans arrived on Madeira, they altered habitats and introduced mammalian predators that the owls would have been ill equipped to deal with (Rando et al 2012). In the Azores, the slightly smaller São Miguel Scops Owl *O frutuosoi* survived until at least 49 BC (based on radiocarbon dating) and more likely until Europeans arrived. It was also a weak flier, spending most of its time on the predator-free floor of the once extensive Azorean laurisilva forests (Rando et al 2013).

Cyprus Scops Owl challenges many of our ideas about what constitutes a species. Two important vocalisations differ from Eurasian Scops Owl, and yet its mtDNA hardly differs at all. Its plumage is subtly distinct but its structure is not. Large numbers of Eurasian Scops migrate through Cyprus, and yet it remains distinct. Clearly, this taxon represents something more interesting than the various subspecies of Eurasian Scops. It certainly deserves much closer attention than it has received up to now.

Cyprus Scops Owl breeds at remarkably high densities; its population has been estimated at 4000-8000 pairs (Snow & Perrins 1998). Evening birders in parks, around villages and in lightly wooded areas in Cyprus, can hardly fail to notice it. The same cannot be said of Pallid Scops Owl *O brucei* of the Middle East and Central Asia. In city parks, its inconspicuous sounds are easily lost in the traffic. Even in dry wadis when the wind lies still, a birder's footsteps can drown out its sounds. If ever there was an owl that requires careful listening then Pallid Scops is surely it.

Pallid Scops Owl

An ancient Elb Tree *Ziziphus spina-cristi* stands proudly in the middle of a deep, flat-bottomed wadi in northern Oman. Several thick trunks radiate at angles from its thick, gnarled base, their coarse bark easy to climb. Halfway up one of them, a rounded stone nestles in a fork, a reminder of the occasional flash floods that leave little else behind. Higher still, Egyptian Fruit-eating Bats *Rousettus aegyptiacus* flap to and fro, plucking small yellow fruits from the broad, undulating crown.

A Pallid Scops Owl *Otus brucei* in a neighbouring tree hoots with metronomic regularity. **CD2-37** is as loud as he gets, barely

Pallid Scops Owl *Otus brucei* Al Jabal Al Akhdar, Al Batinah, Oman, 23:47, 23 March 2013. Hooting of a male, with Egyptian Fruit-eating Bats *Rousettus aegyptiacus*. 130323.MR.234759.32

CD2-37

Habitat of Pallid Scops Owl *Otus brucei*, Al Jabal Al Akhdar, Al Batinah, Oman, 20 March 2013 (*René Pop*). From this tree we recorded not only Pallid Scops Owls but also the first Omani Owls *Strix omanensis*.

enough for a faint aura of collective echoes. For eight nights this male led me on a little tour of his section of the wadi. Each time I managed to work out which tree he was in, I chose it as the site for the next night's recordings. He had about 40 in his territory and unluckily for me, during those eight nights he never hooted in the same tree twice. This was as close as I got.

A month later I was back, this time with Arnoud. I decided to try my luck in a narrower section of the wadi with only a handful of trees about 800 m to the north. Glowing through a saffron veil of desert dust, the full moon betrayed leaf-toed geckos *Asaccus* even before they darted away across huge round boulders.

After several hours of reverie but no point blank recording, I noticed a vague dent in the side of the moon: an eclipse had started. I walked back to ask how Arnoud was faring and have a bite to eat. As I arrived at the old territory the usual pair called from an old Elb that I had tried at least once previously. After they moved on, I approached with the thought of once again placing my equipment high in that tree. It was then that I noticed the LED lights of Arnoud's recorder. He had chosen this tree for his very first attempt, and must have just made a fantastic recording! René later taught me a funny Dutch word to give vent to my frustration, which would have come in handy on this occasion. Krijgdeovermaassehazewindhondenkorenmolenpestpokke! So here is how a hooting Pallid Scops sounds at a distance of just a few metres, gradually building up steam while silhouetted against a partially eclipsed full moon (**CD2-38**).

The hooting begins almost inaudibly, a peculiarity of Pallid Scops Owl. Gradually over a couple of minutes it becomes louder and slightly higher-pitched. This male's 65.6 hoots/minute is almost identical to the 65.5 of one month previously. His nearest neighbour was equally consistent at around 90 hoots/minute. In **CD2-39**, Arnoud recorded both hooting together.

Hearing two Pallid Scops Owls duetting like this, apparently close together with one faster and slightly higher-pitched

CD2-38   **Pallid Scops Owl** *Otus brucei* Al Jabal Al Akhdar, Al Batinah, Oman, 01:53, 26 April 2013. Hooting of a male at very close range. Background: domestic goat. 130426.AB.015348.02

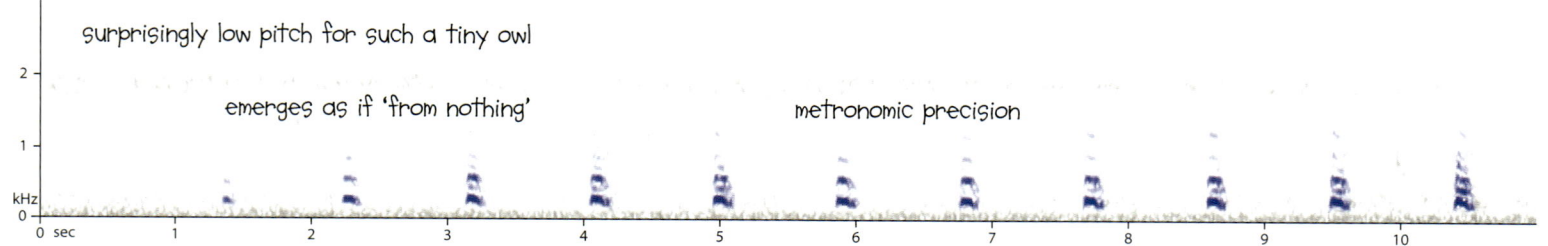

than the other, it is easy to imagine a pair. I had been determined to find out whether this was true. In fact all but a few of these apparent 'duets' concern neighbouring males, just as in **CD2-39**. Females do occasionally hoot, but only briefly. Before giving any examples, however, I would like to illustrate the female's commonest call, which is quite different.

Female Pallid Scops Owls have a soliciting call directly equivalent to the *twiu* of Eurasian Scops Owl. In Pallid, however, hooting and soliciting are easy to tell apart, creating the illusion that the female Pallid solicit more frequently. Sometimes their soliciting calls sound harsh (**CD2-40**), and at other times the timbre is

Pallid Scops Owl *Otus brucei*, singing, Al Jabal Al Akhdar, Al Batinah, Oman, 30 May 2013 (*Arnoud B van den Berg*). One of the males of CD2-39.

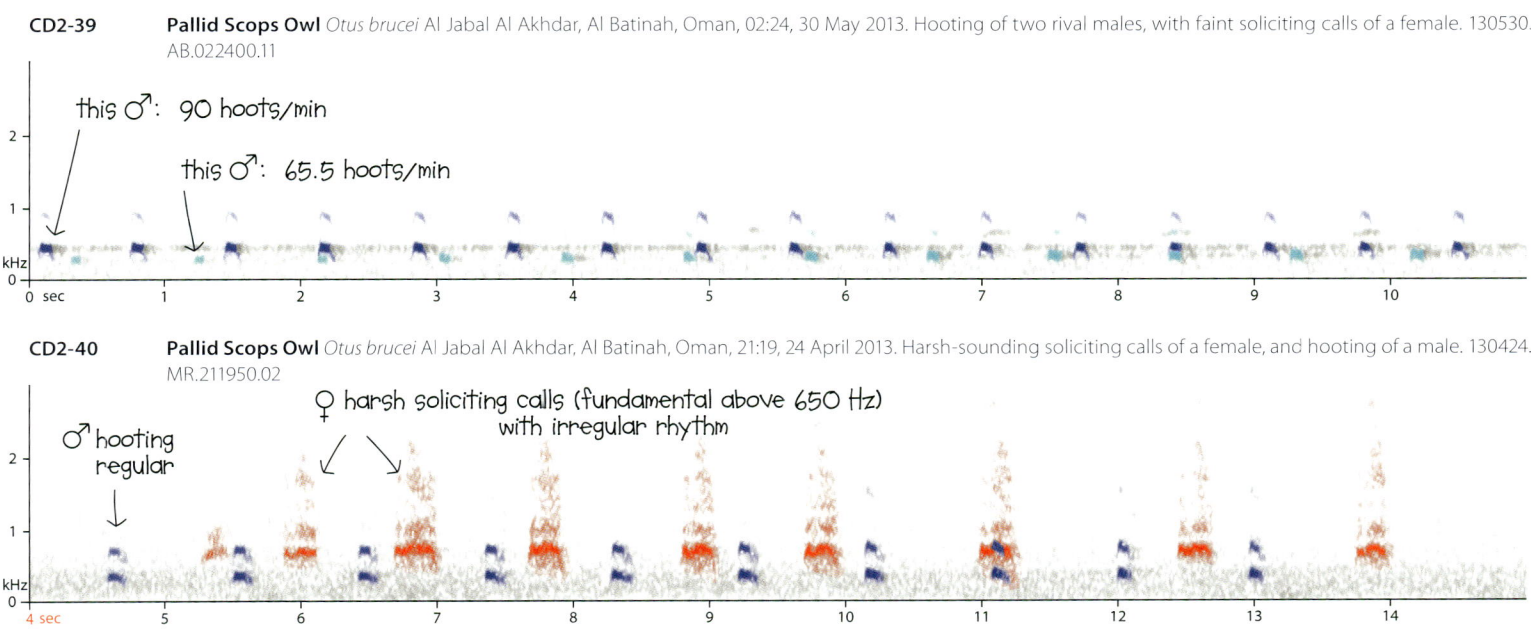

CD2-39   **Pallid Scops Owl** *Otus brucei* Al Jabal Al Akhdar, Al Batinah, Oman, 02:24, 30 May 2013. Hooting of two rival males, with faint soliciting calls of a female. 130530. AB.022400.11

CD2-40   **Pallid Scops Owl** *Otus brucei* Al Jabal Al Akhdar, Al Batinah, Oman, 21:19, 24 April 2013. Harsh-sounding soliciting calls of a female, and hooting of a male. 130424. MR.211950.02

smooth (**CD2-41**). At first I thought these were different call types, until I noticed that smooth turns to harsh as soon as the dominant frequency goes above about 650 Hz. Now I hear them as gradations of the same call. By May harsher variants are uncommon, so perhaps they are more aggressive and no longer required after the partners have become more familiar with one another. Over 50 of our 213 recordings of Pallid Scops Owl contain female soliciting calls, but we have only one example from a male (**CD2-42**).

During the night of 12 April 1982, a party of Swiss birders heard Stock Dove *Columba oenas*-like calls while camping on the shores of the Euphrates in south-eastern Turkey. The next morning they discovered a pair of Pallid Scops Owls (Hüni 1982). A year later, other Pallid Scops were found in a tea park just south of the centre of the nearby town of Birecık. They were easy to see in the artificial lighting, and seemed hardly to be bothered by the loud music and crowds of people. Within a couple of years the owls became a strong additional incentive, besides the

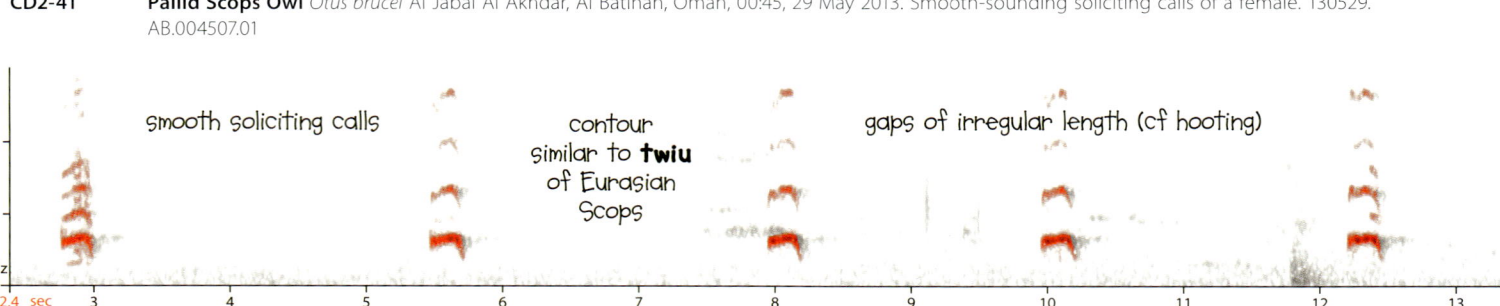

CD2-41　　**Pallid Scops Owl** *Otus brucei* Al Jabal Al Akhdar, Al Batinah, Oman, 00:45, 29 May 2013. Smooth-sounding soliciting calls of a female. 130529.AB.004507.01

CD2-42　　**Pallid Scops Owl** *Otus brucei* Al Jabal Al Akhdar, Al Batinah, Oman, 02:40, 20 May 2013. Soliciting calls of a male. Background: domestic goat. 130520.AB.024002.12

Pallid Scops Owl *Otus brucei*, Al Jabal Al Akhdar, Al Batinah, Oman, 30 May 2013 (*Arnoud B van den Berg*). Probably same as in CD2-42.

famous colony of Northern Bald Ibis *Geronticus eremita*, for birders to visit the area. The trick was to order a cup of tea and only then inquire about the whereabouts of the owls. At this, a waiter would happily lead the way to a roosting owl or a nest.

On 3-5 May 1987, Arnoud and about 100 other visitors to the tea park could see the owls well as they preyed on beetles and other insects. They even hunted underneath people's chairs. Their hooting was almost inaudible even at distances below 10 m (van den Berg et al 1988). In May 2001, I visited Birecık too.

Pallid Scops Owl *Otus brucei*, entering nest, Birecık, Sanliurfa, Turkey, 8 June 2009 (*Arnoud B van den Berg*). Same garden as in CD2-43 but eight years on.

Pallid Scops Owl *Otus brucei*, foraging, Birecık, Sanliurfa, Turkey, 11 June 2009 (*Arnoud B van den Berg*). Same garden as in CD2-43 but eight years on.

In **CD2-43**, a tea park female gives three smooth soliciting calls, then two hoots that morph into a series of faster and slightly harsher soliciting calls. At the same time a male, probably her mate, hoots at a lower pitch in the background. A few minutes later the female hooted a longer sequence, but the recording was spoiled by traffic.

CD2-43   **Pallid Scops Owl** *Otus brucei* Birecık, Sanliurfa, Turkey, 18 May 2001. Soliciting calls and brief hooting of a female, with hooting of a male. 01.021.MR.00123.12

case, the female hooted for brief periods before reverting to her usual soliciting calls, while the male hooted for much longer periods. **CD2-44** starts with the male hooting. The female joins in with a single soliciting call, gives four hoots, and then reverts to soliciting. Hooting of this particular female was only slightly higher-pitched than her mate's, with maximum frequency between 400 and 520 Hz. Another female reached a maximum of just under 650 Hz.

Most Pallid Scops Owl sounds are remarkably low-pitched, but males have a very high-pitched copulation call similar to that of Eurasian Scops Owls. **CD2-45** starts with a soliciting call of

Pallid Scops Owl *Otus brucei*, 'Wadi Mac', Al Hajar mountains, Al Batinah, Oman, 22 October 2014 (*Mike Watson/Birdquest*)

In Oman, we gradually amassed further evidence for female hooting. In May 2013, Arnoud made three recordings where both members of our favourite pair hooted together. In each

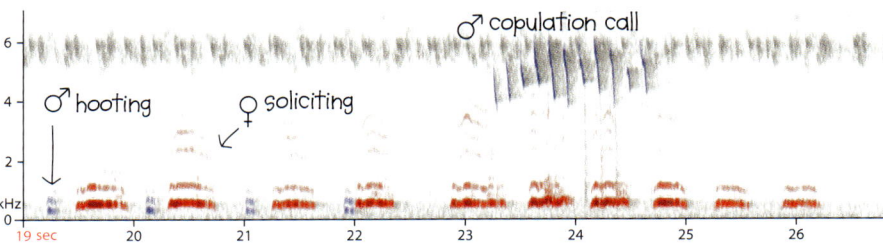

Pallid Scops Owl *Otus brucei* Al Jabal Al Akhdar, Al Batinah, Oman, 03:40, 21 May 2013. Male hooting and female soliciting calls, ending with male's copulation twitter. 130521.AB.034000.02   CD2-45

CD2-44   **Pallid Scops Owl** *Otus brucei* Al Jabal Al Akhdar, Al Batinah, Oman, 04:27, 21 May 2013. Hooting of a male, then hooting and soliciting calls of a female. Background: Desert Lark *Ammomanes deserti*. 130521.AB.042700.00

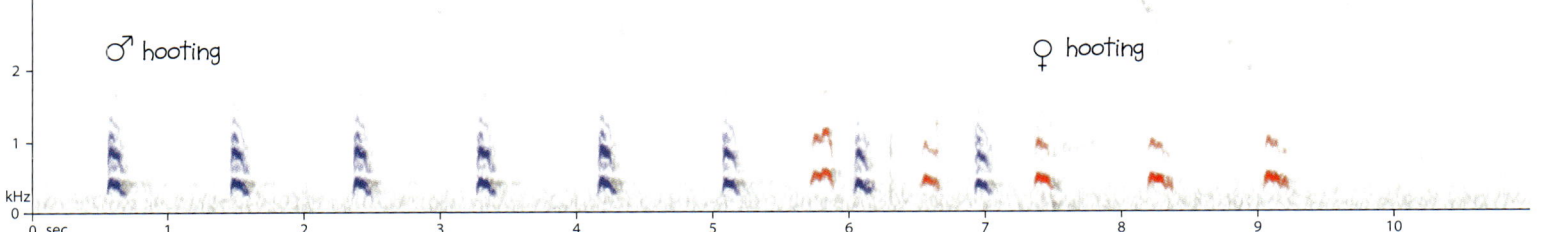

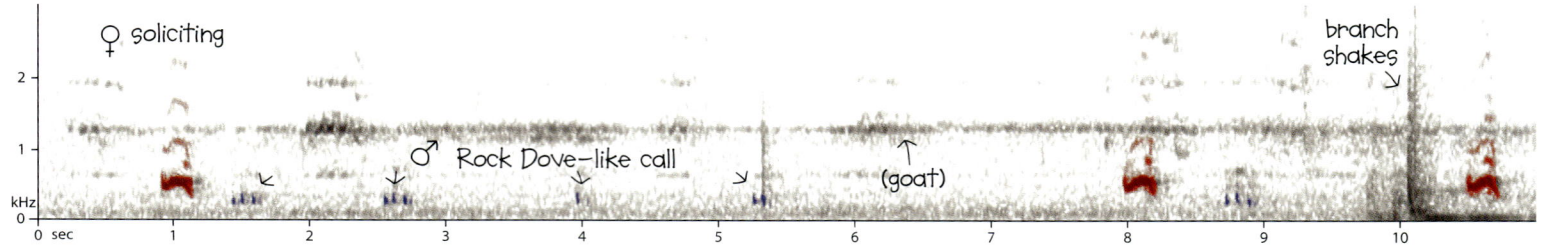

CD2-46   **Pallid Scops Owl** *Otus brucei* Al Jabal Al Akhdar, Al Batinah, Oman, 02:38, 23 May 2013. Soliciting calls of a female and dove-like *rukutu* of a male. Also sounds of preening. 130523.AB.023800.01

a female. Her mate starts hooting, and gradually she becomes more excited. The male's copulation call comes towards the end.

A quiet, dove-like *rukutu* may be Pallid Scops Owl's equivalent to the croaking call of Eurasian Scops Owl. **CD2-46** starts with three soliciting calls of a female, and then we heard the male's *rukutu*. Every now and then one of the owls preens vigorously enough to shake the small branch supporting the microphones. On another occasion, Arnoud recorded calls that seemed to morph from normal male hoots into this *rukutu* sound.

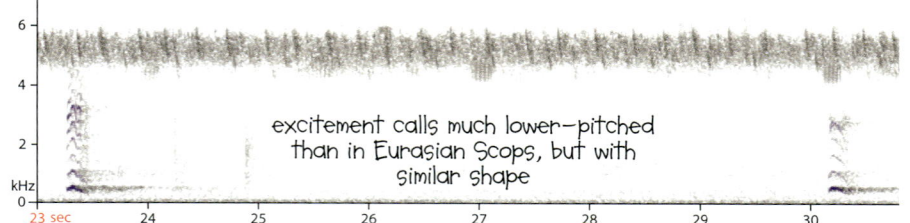

CD2-47   **Pallid Scops Owl** *Otus brucei* Al Jabal Al Akhdar, Al Batinah, Oman, 00:04, 27 March 2013. Excitement calls. The rising, nasal background sound near the start baffled us for a long time. Eventually, Arnoud traced it to a leaf-toed gecko *Asaccus*. 130327.MR.000429.12

Pallid Scops Owl's excitement calls have an arched shape like those of the other three Western Palearctic *Otus* owls. Pallid is the lowest (**CD2-47**), and Eurasian is the highest-pitched in both call-types.

Breeding takes place about a month earlier than in Eurasian Scops Owl, with a peak from mid to late April in Arabia (Jennings 2010), and probably no later than the first week of May in Turkey (van den Berg et al 1988). Pallid Scops Owl is highly nocturnal although in April 2010, René and I heard one hooting in broad daylight. In Oman, where Pallid Scops is resident, the main period of hooting starts in January (Sargeant et al 2008), and we have found May to be a peak month. In mid-July, Arnoud heard no calls at all.

Juvenile Pallid Scops Owls have begging calls very similar to those of Eurasian Scops Owls, just slightly lower-pitched. In late May 2014, I found three broods in Oman by listening for their very short, frequently repeated hissing calls. In **CD2-48**, up to four fledglings are begging in a small tree right above the microphones. I first detected these calls from a distance of at least 75 m.

CD2-48   **Pallid Scops Owl** *Otus brucei* Al Jabal Al Akhdar, Al Batinah, Oman, 01:28, 28 May 2014. Begging calls of four fledged juveniles while being fed by an adult. An adult male hoots in the distance. Background: clangs of metal crash barrier cooling down. 140528.MR.012844.01

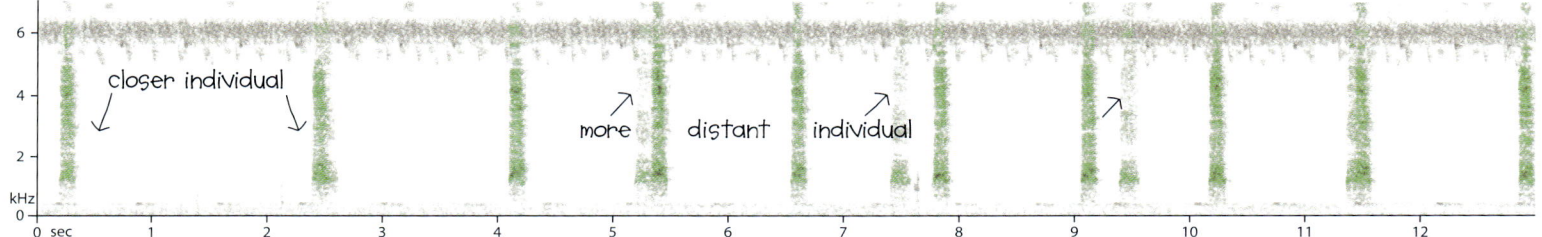

In southern Israel, Pallid Scops Owl is a migrant and winter visitor. During a study of their ecology and distribution over two winters, Lerman et al (2006) located 24 individual owls, all of which were roosting in acacias located in desert washes in the Arava valley. James Smith, one of the authors of the study, told me: "I never once heard a wintering Pallid Scops Owl call in southern Israel. I did try to hear vocals on several occasions, making sure that I was close to known roosting birds at dusk and even tried playback couple of times. The birds appear to be silent whilst wintering, at least during my experiences with them (annual from 1997 through to current date). I've never heard mention of other observers hearing them either…" The only winter sound that has ever been described is bill-clicking in the hand (Mundkur 1986).

I never found a Pallid Scops Owl during the day, and have rarely seen them even at night. Once I was lying on a flat rock under a full moon, listening and drifting close to the threshold of sleep. My equipment was doing the hard work under an Umbrella Thorn up on the opposite slope, where I hoped that an owl would hoot. About 2 m away from me was a small bush, and suddenly something fell from it, maybe a large leaf or a twig. I looked round, but in the moonlight I could see nothing untoward. A couple of minutes later some flapping quickened

my senses. I felt something touching my forehead and looked up to see a Pallid Scops Owl fluttering right over my face for a moment, before flying off to the nearest tree. I sometimes wonder if I dreamed this.

When Sclater coined the word 'Palæarctic' in 1858, he included Africa north of the Atlas, Europe, Asia Minor, Persia and Asia north of the Himalayas, northern China, Japan and the Aleutian Islands. *Palaios* is a Greek word meaning 'old', referring to the Old World, and *arktikós* means 'northern' or literally, 'of the bear'. The Ural River is a convenient and universally accepted border between the Eastern and Western Paleartic in the north. A southern border is more difficult to define.

Popular opinion, based mainly on 'BWP' (Cramp 1985), includes most of the Sahara in but only the northernmost part of Arabia. As we worked on *Undiscovered owls*, we began to question why southern Arabia had been excluded. Roselaar's (2006) well-reasoned definition of the Palearctic includes most of the peninsula. To keep things simple we went a step further and included the whole of Arabia. This added three more species to the book, including one final scops owl that was brought to light by a spy.

Arabian Scops Owl

In the summer months, the Dhofar region of southern Oman benefits from the Southwest Monsoon. The skies become overcast, and the hillsides turn lush and green. Several species that are best known from Africa, such as Bruce's Green Pigeon *Treron waalia*, Diederik Cuckoo *Chrysococcyx caprius* and Grey-headed Kingfisher *Halcyon leucocephala* arrive for the wet season to breed. To the north and east, 700 km of barren desert form a barrier preventing these species spreading any further. Other African specialities stay there all year round, such as Black-crowned Tchagra *Tchagra senegala* and African Paradise Flycatcher *Terpsiphone viridis*. So it is hardly surprising that, until very recently, two of the owls of this region were treated as subspecies of widespread African species.

When George Latimer Bates (1937b) described Arabian Scops Owl *Otus pamelae*, he classified it as a subspecies of African Scops Owl *O senegalensis*, although his formal description only mentioned differences, not similarities to that species. The type series of specimens on which he based his description came from Wadi Bisha in south-western Saudi Arabia (Bates 1937a).

Some locals had given an adult and three fledglings to Harry St John Philby, an Arabist, explorer and writer known to them as 'Sheikh Abdullah'. Philby was also a British spy and incidentally the father of Kim Philby, later a notorious double agent and member of 'the Cambridge Five'. It was at Philby senior's suggestion that Bates named the new subspecies *pamelae*. His club in London, the Athenaeum club, had an owl as its emblem and one Pamela Lovibond was its librarian.

Arabian Scops Owl is a widespread resident in 'Arabia Felix', the part of Arabia blessed with the highest rainfall and the most fertile land. In southern Oman and much of Yemen, it occurs in Common Myrrh *Commiphora myrrha* and 'acacia' scrub. In the mountainous Asir region of Saudi Arabia it lives on dry wooded slopes, in lush vegetation and *Ficus* thickets, as well as montane juniper forest. Most sites are close to a freshwater source (Jennings 2010). African Scops Owl breeds as close as Eritrea, just across the Red Sea, and in Somalia, which is just across the Gulf of Aden.

CD2-49 is a typical male Arabian Scops Owl, recorded in Dhofar in April. He hoots at intervals of nine seconds, about three times

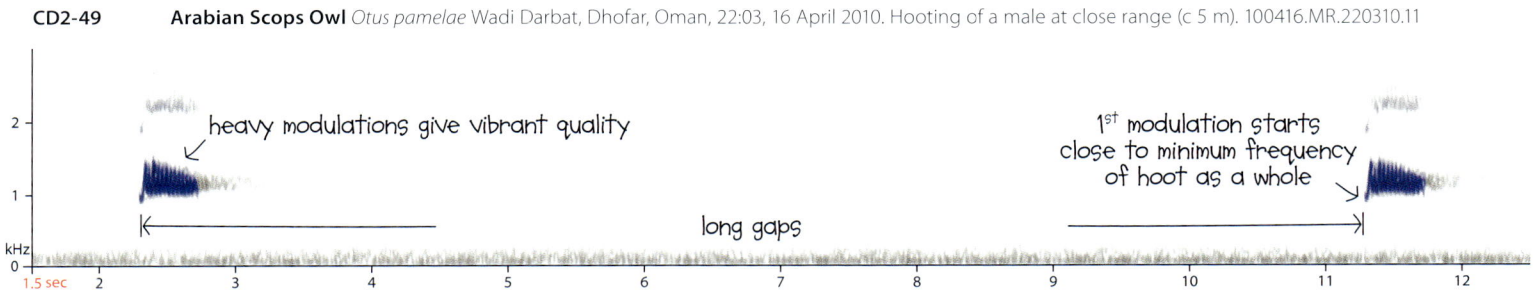

CD2-49   **Arabian Scops Owl** *Otus pamelae* Wadi Darbat, Dhofar, Oman, 22:03, 16 April 2010. Hooting of a male at close range (c 5 m). 100416.MR.220310.11

slower than Eurasian Scops Owl. The pitch is slightly lower than in Eurasian Scops but much higher than in Pallid Scops Owl *O brucei*.

Arabian Scops Owls in Dhofar start breeding in autumn, when Eurasian Scops Owl and some Pallid Scops Owl are migrating south. The majority of callers have been reported from September to November, with some from December to February and April, suggesting that most breeding takes place there after the Southwest Monsoon and may continue until April (Jennings 2010). Elsewhere, in Yemen and Saudi Arabia, breeding is more in line with other northern hemisphere birds (Bates 1937a, Jennings 2010).

A wide expanse of desert separates the sedentary Arabian Scops Owl from the breeding range of Pallid Scops Owl in northern Oman. Some Pallid Scops do arrive in Dhofar and Yemen during the 'winter', although they probably come from Central Asia (Jennings 2010). Eurasian Scops Owls are regular migrants in Oman, with most individuals probably continuing on into Africa.

Arnoud spent several nights in Dhofar at the start of the monsoon in July. The owls were not very vocal, but at least there was nobody to disturb his efforts. It was the month of Ramadan, so nearly everybody was spending the evenings with family. The rain and high humidity bring millions of biting insects to

Arabian Scops Owl *Otus pamelae*, Wadi Darbat, Dhofar, Oman, 17 July 2013 (*Arnoud B van den Berg*). Same male as in CD2-50 & 56.

Wadi Darbat, but with stoical perseverance Arnoud managed to make both photographs and sound recordings of one particular male. Its hoots were slightly higher-pitched than the one in **CD2-50**, and delivered at slightly shorter intervals of 7.9 seconds.

CD2-50   **Arabian Scops Owl** *Otus pamelae* Wadi Darbat, Dhofar, Oman, 01:02, 17 July 2013. Hooting of a male at close range. Background: Dhofar Toad *Bufo dhufarensis*. 130717. AB.010201.01

It is unrecorded whether St John Philby told George Bates about any sounds he may have heard from Arabian Scops Owl. Its hooting does actually sound very similar to that of African Scops Owl. Both species have single-note hoots with a buzzing timbre caused by rapid modulations. There is only one African Scops in our own sound collection, but as of 11 June 2014 you can listen to 17 at the online archive www.xeno-canto.org. Previous authors have noted that African Scops has lower-pitched, shorter hoots than Arabian Scops (König et al 2008, Pons et al 2013), and you can hear this in **CD2-51**. Most other African Scops conform to this pattern, although of the 17 on Xeno-canto, two from Zambia are as high-pitched as Arabian

Arabian Scops Owl *Otus pamelae*, Ayn Hamran, Dhofar, Oman, 4 November 2014 (*Mike Watson/Birdquest*)

CD2-51   **African Scops Owl** *Otus senegalensis* Etosha, Namutoni, Namibia, 23:10, 22 March 1999. Hooting of a male. Background: Monotonous Lark *Mirafra passerina*. 99.004.AB.01202.21

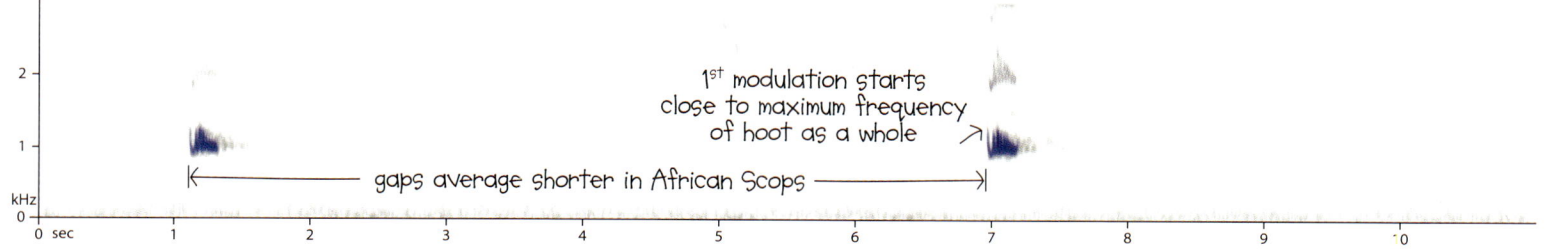

Scops and one from Ghana has hoots that are just as long. I have indicated some other differences in the sonagrams.

Hooting of female Arabian Scops Owls is similar to that of males but quieter. In **CD2-52**, the male hoots first, then the female joins in and they form a duet. Surprisingly for a female owl, she is lower-pitched than the male. In **CD2-53**, recorded a couple of minutes later, the same female uses *twiu* soliciting calls that are very similar to those of Eurasian Scops Owl. **CD2-54** starts with the male hooting and the female giving *twiu* calls, but ends with copulation. The male gives a high-pitched twitter while the female gives a few very short notes that may be related to the croaking call of Eurasian Scops (**CD2-54**).

Arabian Scops Owl *Otus pamelae*, female, Wadi Darbat, Dhofar, Oman, 12 November 2013 (*Dick Forsman*). Paired with the male photographed on the same day.

Arabian Scops Owl *Otus pamelae*, male, Wadi Darbat, Dhofar, Oman, 12 November 2013 (*Dick Forsman*). Hooting.

CD2-52   **Arabian Scops Owl** *Otus pamelae* Waci Darbat, Dhofar, Oman, 19:20, 26 February 2014. Hooting duet of female and male perched in the same tree. 140226.MR.192015.01

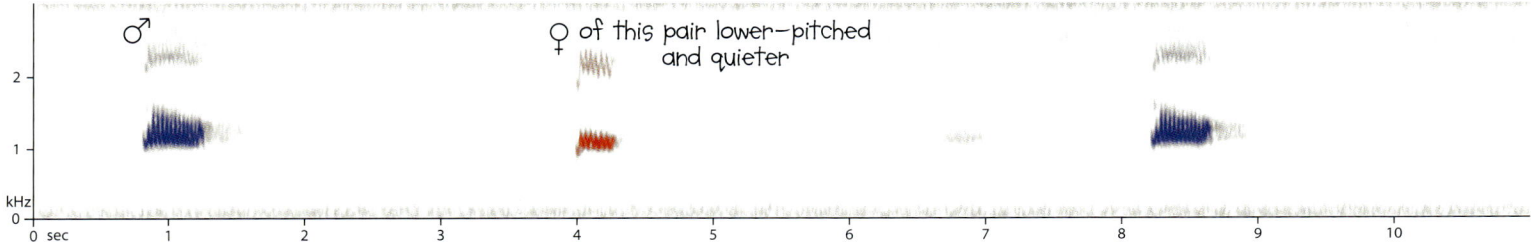

CD2-53   **Arabian Scops Owl** *Otus pamelae* Wadi Darbat, Dhofar, Oman, 19:20, 26 February 2014. *Twiu* soliciting calls of a female, and hooting of a male. 140226.MR.192015.01

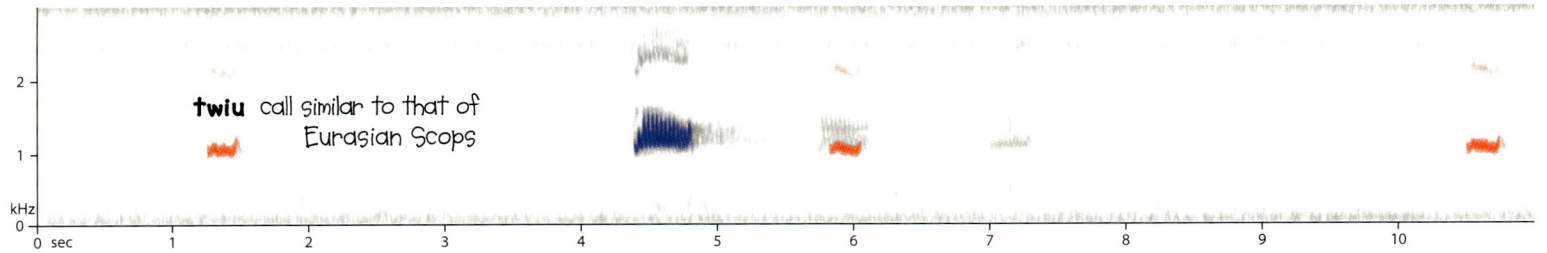

CD2-54   **Arabian Scops Owl** *Otus pamelae* Wadi Darbat, Dhofar, Oman, 19:20, 26 February 2014. Copulation, starting with *twiu* calls of female and hooting of male. Copulation calls of male at 0:31. Background: excitement calls and hooting of other individuals. 140226.MR.192015.01

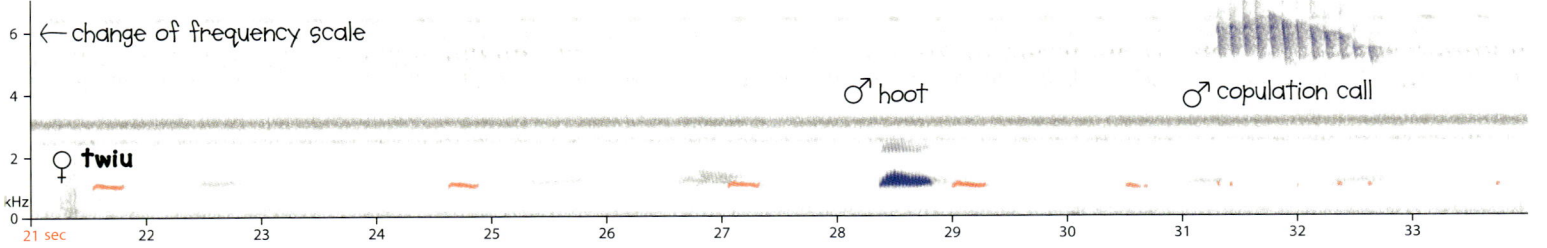

Excitement calls of Arabian Scops Owl follow the classic *Otus* blueprint, although they seem to be unusually variable in pitch and timbre. The calls in **CD2-55** for example are lower-pitched and harsher than those in **CD2-56**. During our visits in February, April and July, these calls were common.

Much remains to be discovered about Arabian Scops Owl. We did not manage to record any juvenile sounds, for instance. We would love to have recorded a larger repertoire but events elsewhere in Arabia, described in the final chapter, stole our attention during the final year of fieldwork for this book. Perhaps somebody else would like to take up the challenge.

CD2-55 **Arabian Scops Owl** *Otus pamelae* Wadi Darbat, Dhofar, Oman, 19:45, 26 February 2014. Excitement calls. Background: Arabian Eagle-Owl *Bubo milesi*. 140226.MR.194522.01

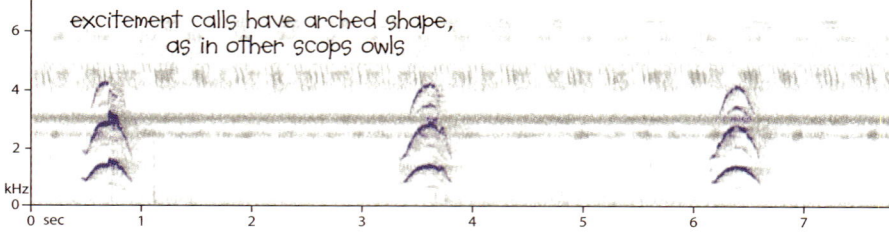

CD2-56 **Arabian Scops Owl** *Otus pamelae* Wadi Darbat, Dhofar, Oman, 19:35, 15 July 2013. Excitement calls. 130715.AB.193500.22

Arabian Scops Owl has a much longer wing than African Scops Owl, and this was what convinced Bates that *pamelae* was a new taxon. Its plumage is also much paler with less prominent streaks on the breast and a less distinct scapular stripe. The two species are genetically distinct, with a 4% difference in mtDNA. They are not even each other's closest relatives (Pons et al 2013). Arabian Scops Owl branched off earliest, followed by Eurasian Scops Owl and two island species from either side of Africa, leaving African Scops as the most recently evolved species.

Arabian Scops Owl *Otus pamelae*, Wadi Darbat, Dhofar, Oman, 17 July 2013 (*Arnoud B van den Berg*). Same male as in CD2-50 & 56.

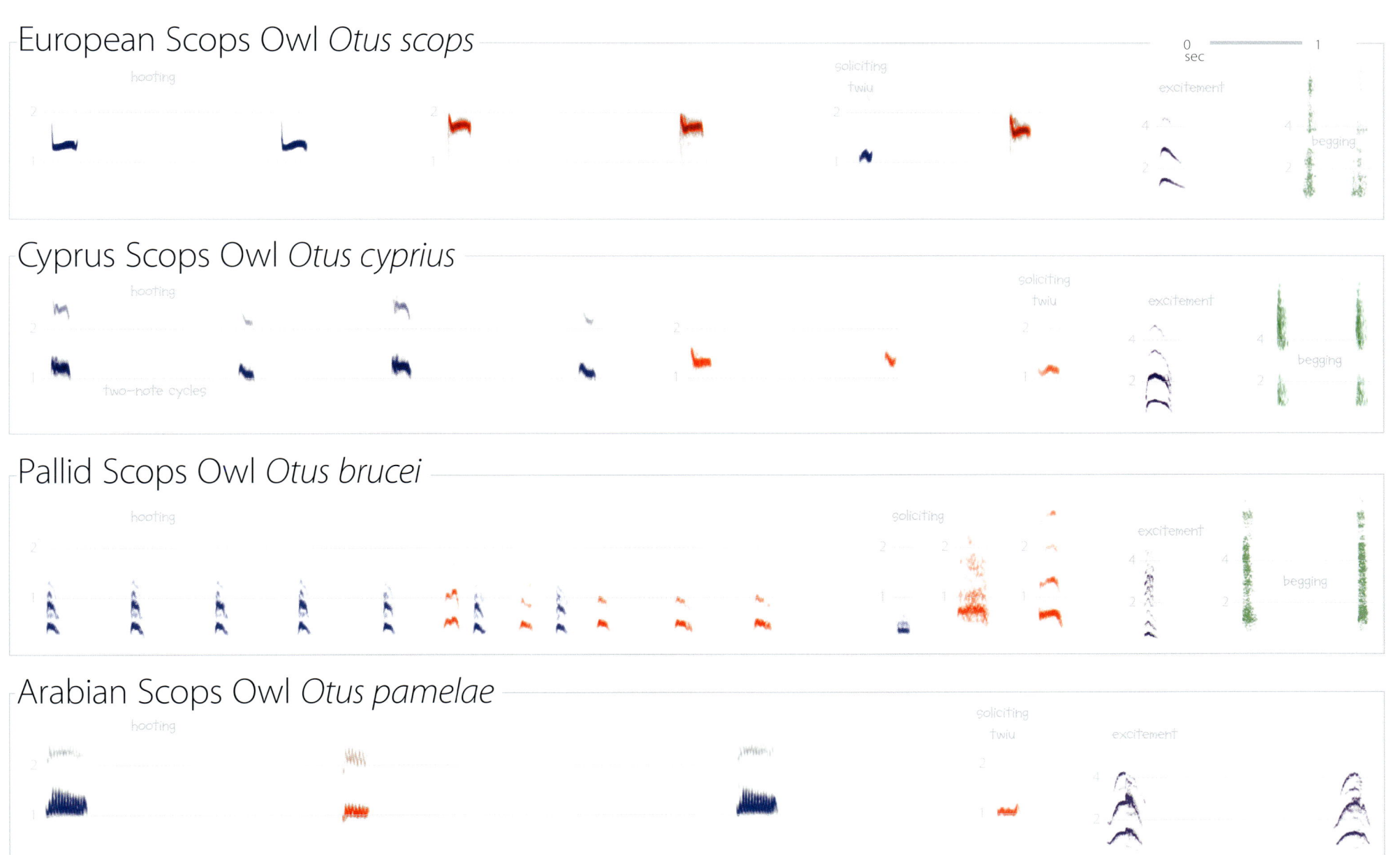

Chapter 7: *Asio*

Long-eared Owl

Imagine yourself in a Harry Potter story, visiting Eeylops Owl Emporium. Which owl would you choose? A screeching Common Barn Owl *Tyto alba*, perhaps a rare Turkish Fish Owl *Bubo semenowi* or the one Hagrid chose for Harry, a huge Snowy Owl *Bubo scandiacus*? For Mark it would have to be a Long-eared Owl *Asio otus*.

It's easy to become obsessed with Long-eared Owls. For a start they are stealthy. They live longer that way. Often they hide right under our muggle noses. Camouflaged against bark and twigs, dozens hide themselves in urban parks, then glide out incognito into the darkness. When winter ends they find new ways to escape our attention. The simple, repeated hoot of a male Long-eared Owl could hardly be subtler (**CD2-57**). Once noticed, its deep smoothness is to be savoured. Without traffic,

Long-eared Owl *Asio otus*, Hanko, Uusimaa, Finland, 14 March 2012 (*Dick Forsman*)

CD2-57   **Long-eared Owl** *Asio otus otus* Pancas, Benavente, Portugal, 23:25, 28 February 2013. Hooting of a male in open Holm Oak *Quercus ilex* woodland, with large pools here and there following heavy rain. Background: Mallard *Anas platyrhynchos* and Tawny Owl *Strix aluco*. 130228.MR.232502.01

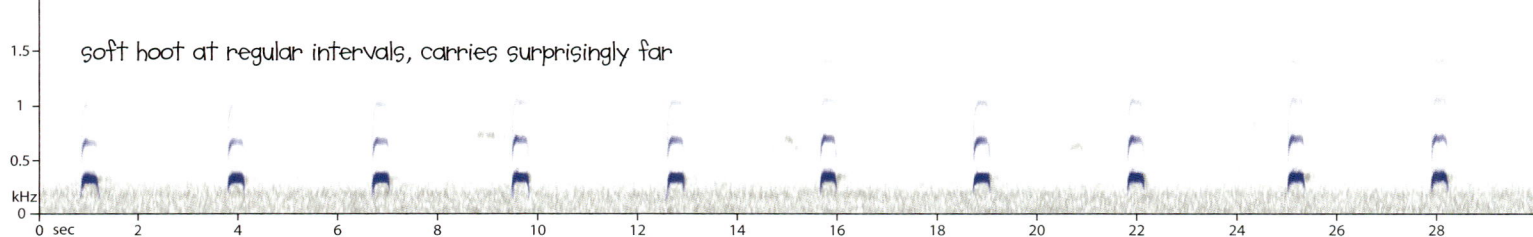

Long-eared Owl *Asio otus*, Hanko, Uusimaa, Finland, 3 March 2005 (*Dick Forsman*)

Among all the recordings in this book it is this next one from Portugal that makes Mark jealous. Despite huge efforts, he has never managed to make a good recording of a Long-eared Owl. The male in **CD2-58** is the same as in **CD2-57**, but now he is at the centre of a much livelier scene. Amazingly, his neighbour sounds almost as loud despite being 30 times more distant.

Achieving such projection is all about choosing the right songpost. The trick is to take advantage of interference between direct and reflected sound waves (Catchpole & Slater 2008). Sit at the wrong elevation and the wave bouncing off the ground will be half a wavelength out of phase with the one travelling directly to the listener: they will cancel each other out, causing attenuation of the sound. Choose the right elevation and the two different waves will differ by one wavelength: they will sum with each other. The sound will be intensified and carry further. As **CD2-58** unfolds, we hear several Tawny Owls *Strix aluco*, the gradual approach of a migrating Water Rail *Rallus aquaticus* (from 0:10), a loud Southern Tree Frog *Hyla meridionalis* (from 0:11) and the grazing of a herd of young bulls. Then at 0:28 a female Long-eared Owl joins in with her *Vvvw* call, the loudest sound in the recording.

Occasionally, individual males depart from their usual smooth timbre and produce slightly strained-sounding hoots. One that I recorded in 2012 consistently hooted with a harsher timbre. Otherwise, his behaviour was very typical. In **CD2-59**, he takes off after 29 hoots, giving a series of single wingclaps while flying a circuit around the nesting area. At 1:25 his mate gives several loud *Vvvw* calls, then flies right with almost identical wingclaps. Long-eared Owls clap underneath the body, never above it

planes or wind to drown it out, it can travel half a kilometre or more. Usually, however, nobody will notice.

CD2-58 **Long-eared Owl** *Asio otus otus* Pancas, Benavente, Portugal, 00:46, 20 February 2013. Hooting of two males. At 0:28 a female joins in with her *Vvvw* call, the loudest sound in the recording. Background: besides the munching of a herd of young bulls there are several Tawny Owls *Strix aluco*, flight calls of a gradually approaching Water Rail *Rallus aquaticus* (from 0:10), and a loud Southern Tree Frog *Hyla meridionalis* (from 0:11). 130220.MR.004658.31

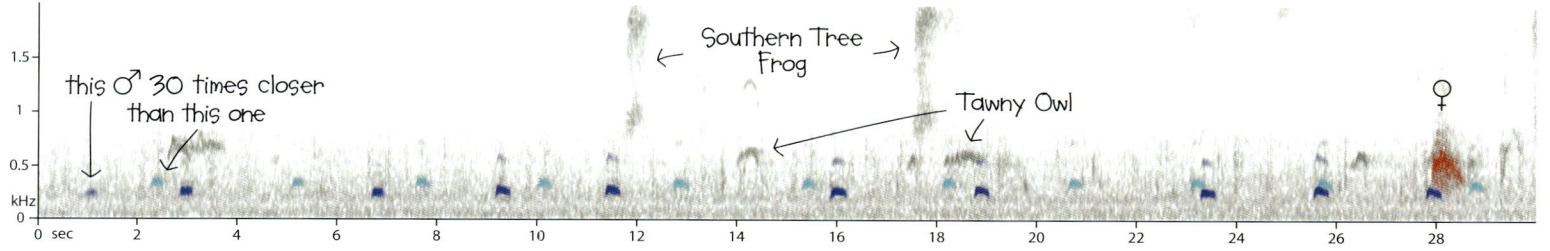

CD2-59 **Long-eared Owl** *Asio otus otus* Pancas, Benavente, Portugal, 04:52, 16 April 2012. Unusually harsh hooting of a male, then wingclaps. From 1:25 *Vvvw* calls of female, then her wingclaps. Background: European Tree Frog *Hyla arborea*, Little Owl *Athene vidalii*, Tawny Owl *Strix aluco* and Common Nightingale *Luscinia megarhynchos*. 120416.MR.045255.11

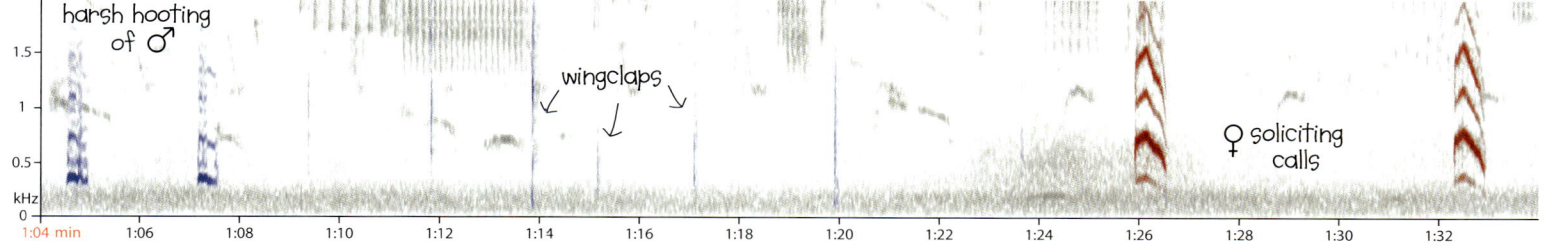

(Scott 1997). Males clap much more often than females, often while flying from a songpost to join their mate. Unpaired males hoot, but they do not clap (Hawley 1966).

The female's *Vvvw* is a soliciting call and her most characteristic sound during the breeding season. It is much more nasal and higher-pitched than male hooting, and usually repeated at intervals of 5 seconds or more. The interval between male hoots is rarely more than 3.3 seconds. Shaped like a heavy sigh, the *Vvvw* descends and fades out towards the end. If you have ever tried the old game of humming through a comb covered in cigarette paper (or Izal, that crispy and perhaps obsolete toilet paper that scratches your backside), well, the timbre is a lot like that. **CD2-60** has smooth-sounding, humming *Vvvw* calls that could be confused with male hooting were it not for the very long gaps. **CD2-61** is a slightly richer-sounding individual, one that already featured in **CD2-59**. Finally, **CD2-62** is a rather harsh-sounding female at very close range.

CD2-60 Long-eared Owl *Asio otus otus* Kennemerduinen, Bloemendaal, Netherlands, 23:25, 2 June 2012. *Vvvw* calls of a female, smooth variant. Background: Common Nightingale *Luscinia megarhynchos*. 120602.AB.232530.01

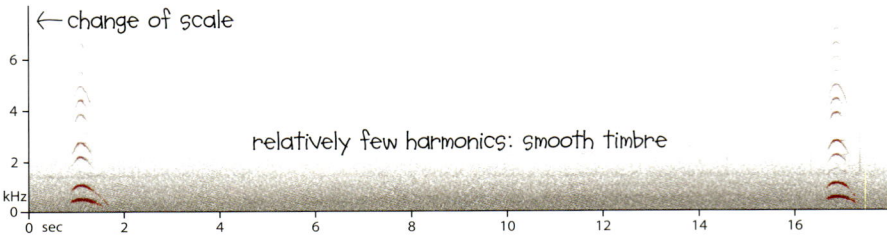

CD2-61 Long-eared Owl *Asio otus otus* Pancas, Benavente, Portugal, 00:06, 7 April 2012. *Vvvw* calls of a female, typical variant. Background: Tawny Owl *Strix aluco* and Common Nightingale *Luscinia megarhynchos*. 120407.MR.000616.01

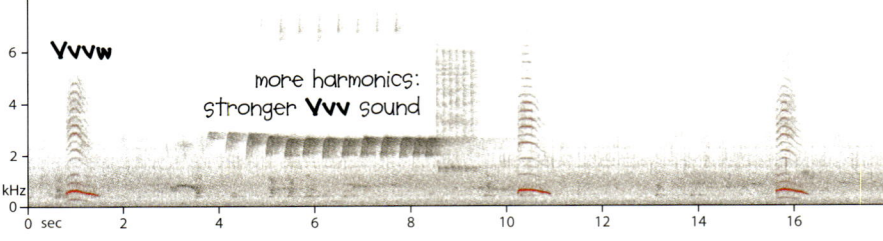

CD2-62 Long-eared Owl *Asio otus otus* Pancas, Benavente, Portugal, 00:17, 1 March 2013. *Vvvw* calls of a female, harsh variant. Background: Tawny Owl *Strix aluco*. 130301.MR.001748.02

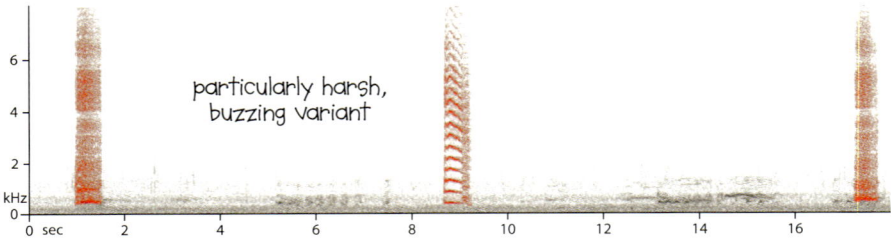

A rich texture of harmonics makes *Vvvw* calls seem louder than male hoots at close range, but from a couple of 100 m they are barely audible. This is because the harmonics decay so rapidly with increasing distance. From the courtship period until sometime after the young hatch, the female calls frequently from the nest, usually one built by corvids or raptors, or from elsewhere in the same tree. For this reason the *Vvvw* is sometimes called the 'nest call'. Before selecting one, she may *Vvvw* from anywhere in the wood (Hawley 1966).

Across the whole of Eurasia, only one population is distinct enough to merit separation as a subspecies, being smaller and

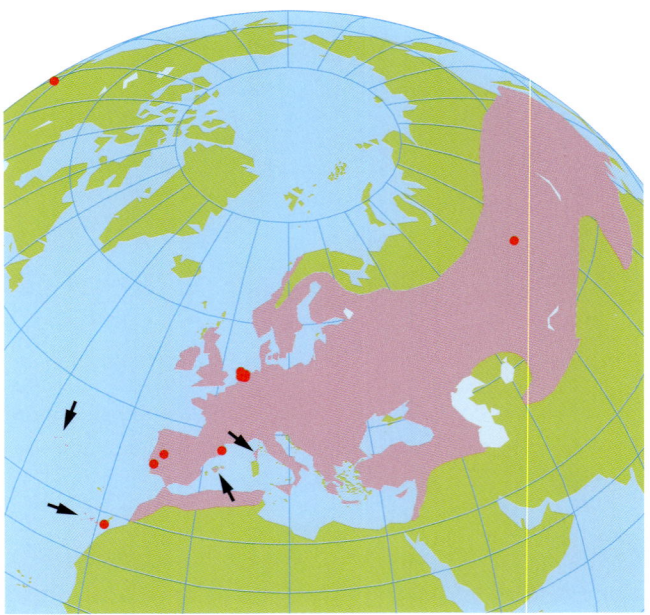

Approximate breeding distribution of Long-eared Owl *Asio otus* ■. Recording locations of Long-eared and Wilson's Owl *A wilsonianus* (in North America) indicated by ● dots.

more heavily marked, with reddish eyes. Canarian Long-eared Owl *A o canariensis* is fairly common on well-wooded islands such as Gran Canaria and Tenerife, but has only recently been found breeding on Fuerteventura (López-Darias et al 2006).

Canarian Long-eared Owl *Asio otus canariensis*, Betancuria, Fuerteventura, Canary slands, 22 January 2010 (*René Pop*). Bird from the same tiny roost as the male in CD6-63.

By searching one of the few pine forests on that island, René Pop and I found a winter roost holding at least four. About 40 African Northern Ravens *Corvus corax tingitanus* arrived to spend the night there just when the owls were leaving. As the sky darkened, the cacophony gradually died down. From within the owl roost, we heard some familiar-sounding wingclaps. Then not far away, a male started to hoot. A week later we returned, better prepared. I left my equipment recording in a clump of pines, more or less where I thought the male had been. Fortunately, he chose the same songpost and hooted bravely among the ravens (**CD2-63**).

Canarian Long-eared Owl *Asio otus canariensis* Betancuria, Fuerteventura, Canary Islands, 18:54, 29 January 2010. Male hooting in the middle of an African Northern Raven *Corvus corax tingitanus* roost. 100129.MR.185427.01

CD2-63

Given that they are around 10% smaller (Cramp 1985), it seems surprising that neither this male nor another recorded by Moreno (2000) sounded different from their relatives on the mainland. Perhaps *canariensis* only evolved very recently. Genetic studies show no clear distinction from continental *otus* (Wink et al 2008). Long-eared have also colonised the Azores, but without evolving a distinctive appearance at all (Bannerman & Bannerman 1966).

The long-eared owl that occurs in North America – let's call it Wilson's Owl *Asio wilsonianus* – has been evolving separately for much longer. Its mtDNA differs from that of its Palearctic relatives by 1.13% (Johnsen et al 2010), suggesting around half a million years of isolation. Wilson's has two subspecies: *wilsonianus* in the east and *tuftsi* in the west. Both share yellow irides, a more golden-rufous facial disk outlined by a blacker ruff, and much heavier cross-barring on the underparts than Long-eared Owl. Hooting of Wilson's averages higher-pitched

CD2-64   **Wilson's Owl** *Asio wilsonianus tuftsi* Walla Walla county, Washington, USA, 20:30, 20 April 1990. Hooting of a male. David S Herr and The Macaulay Library at the Cornell Lab of Ornithology.

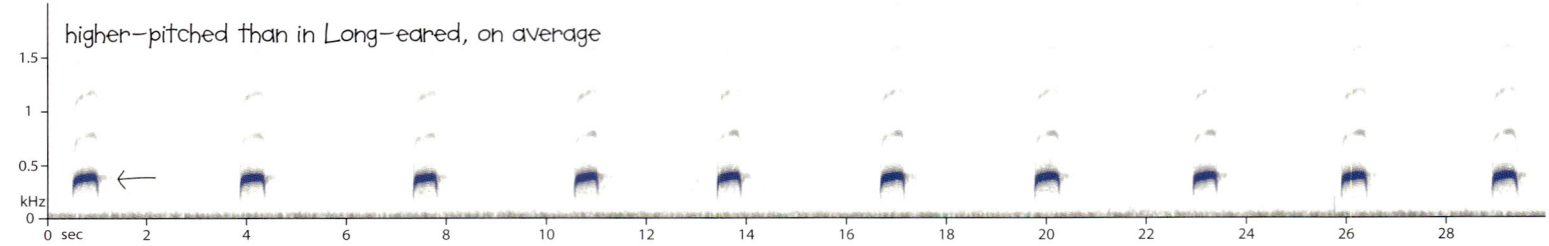

(**CD2-64**), as I discovered by comparing 10 individuals from widely spread locations on each continent.

Female Long-eared Owls occasionally hoot, and when they do, their pitch is higher than that of males. So beware of claiming a Wilson's Owl in Europe! In **CD2-65**, the context was rather unusual, involving two females and a male. An intruding female had the audacity to give *Vvvw* calls in flight close to a nesting tree while another female was in it. The latter had then reacted by flying a little circuit, wing-clapping and giving a very rapid series of hoots, before landing back in her nest and rustling it noisily. Over the course of 25 minutes she switched several times between *Vvvw* calls and a high-pitched form of hooting with long notes. I interpreted her hoots as aggression towards the second female while the *Vvvw* calls were directed at the male. He, meanwhile, spent much of the time hooting normally some distance away.

The 'nest-showing call' (Mebs & Scherzinger 2004) is a speeded-up version of hooting. Again females are higher-pitched than males. In **CD2-66**, a male and female are flying around a

Long-eared Owl *Asio otus*, juvenile, Helsinki, Uusimaa, Finland, 10 July 2014 (*Dick Forsman*)

CD2-65 **Long-eared Owl** *Asio otus otus* Pancas, Benavente, Portugal, 00:16, 1 March 2013. Hooting of a female and a more distant male. From 2:04, female *Vvvw* calls. Background: Red Fox *Vulpes vulpes*, Mallard *Anas platyrhynchos*, Common Barn Owl *Tyto alba* and Tawny Owl *Strix aluco*. 130301.MR.001644.02

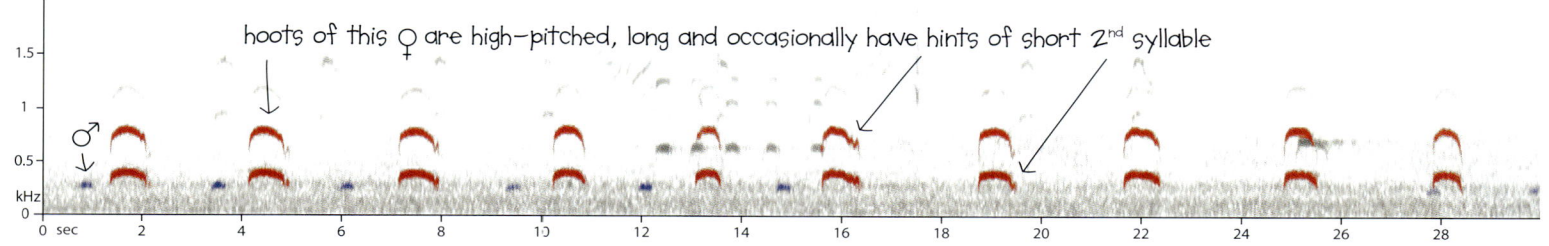

CD2-66 **Long-eared Owl** *Asio otus otus* Pancas, Benavente, Portugal, 01:01, 7 April 2012. Nest-showing calls and wing-clapping of a male and a female. Background: Mallard *Anas platyrhynchos* and Common Nightingale *Luscinia megarhynchos*. 120407.MR.010155.01

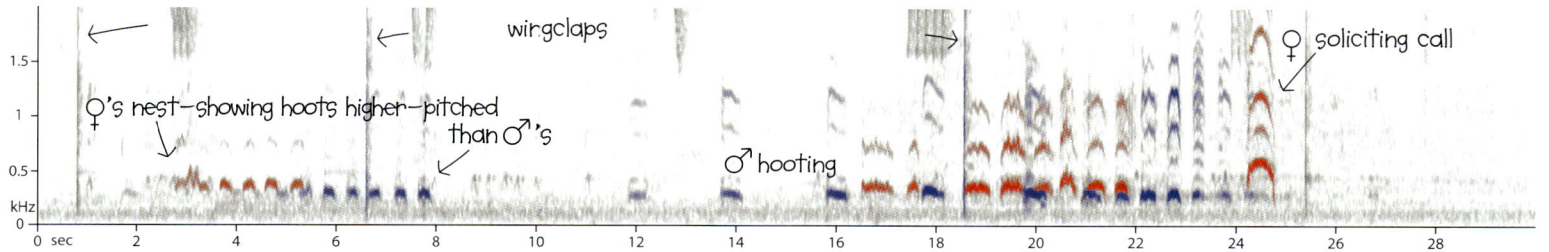

small clump of pines during an early stage of courtship. Both are using the nest-showing call and both are wing-clapping, especially the male. At 0:08 they appear to land briefly, then at 0:24 the female gives a loud *Vvvw* call as the male flies off.

Wingclaps of Long-eared Owls come in two variants: single and double. The latter are doubled so quickly that this seems to have escaped anyone's attention so far. A single bird produces both claps: these are not duets. Exactly how the double clap is produced is still a mystery. In **CD2-67** the first few claps are

Long-eared Owl *Asio otus otus* Kennemerduinen, Bloemendaal, Netherlands, 19:22, 6 April 2008. Wingclaps of male – single then double – followed by high-pitched calls and bill-snaps, indicating close contact or possibly copulation. 080406.MR.192202.02 **CD2-67**

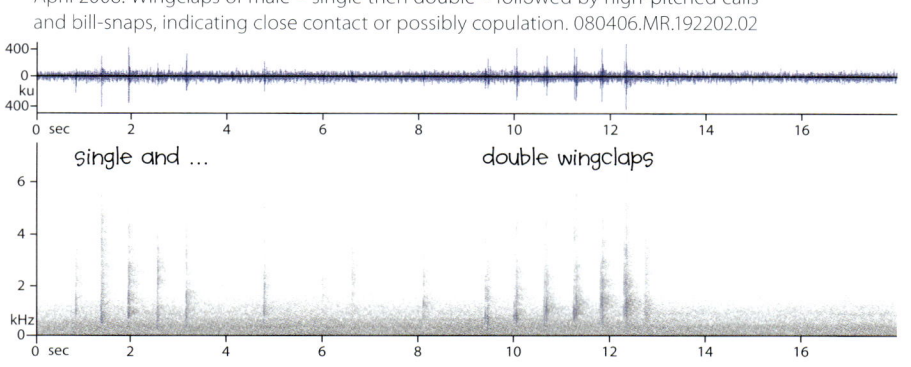

single, then from 0:09 there follows a series of double claps. Towards the end of the recording there are some faint, high-pitched calls accompanied by bill-snaps. These fit sketchy descriptions of copulation calls in the literature (eg, Scott 1997), but I could not confirm what happened. I only know that the male and female were in close physical proximity when I heard those calls.

In southeast Dorset where Mark lives, Long-eared Owls are rare. Reading an article in the Norfolk Bird Report (Kemp 1981), he became inspired to search for calling young. Over two summers and twenty-plus nights he found... none! More often, juveniles are the only clue that finally gives a breeding attempt away. Their piercing, eerie begging calls carry far. Usually, they only become conspicuous during the last of three weeks that the young are in the nest. The youngest owlet calls more often and at a higher pitch than its larger siblings. In **CD2-68**, the pitch difference between the two fledglings is obvious. Between them, the young may keep a stream of these loud calls going

Long-eared Owl *Asio otus*, fledgling, Kirkkonummi, Uusimaa, Finland, 10 June 2014 (*Dick Forsman*). Bird perhaps fledged the day before.

CD2-68   **Long-eared Owl** *Asio otus otus* Rosmaninhal, Idanha-a-Nova, Portugal, 01:22, 15 May 2012. Begging calls of two fledglings. In this case the younger, higher-pitched fledgling calls only slightly more often than its older sibling. Background: Woodlark *Lullula arborea* and Common Nightingale *Luscinia megarhynchos*. 120514. MR.012236.01

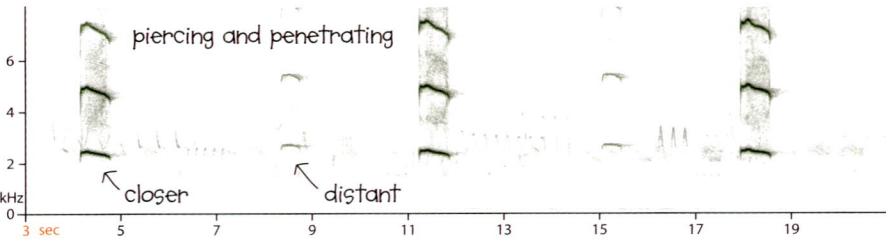

virtually all night long until they are 7 or 8 weeks old. Some may even beg until 14 or 15 weeks of age, long after they are able to catch prey for themselves (Scott 1997). I often wonder how they can afford to make themselves so conspicuous.

If you approach a brood of Long-eared Owls, sooner or later you will probably hear some gruff, rising barks, most likely in threes or fours. Since the juveniles ignore them and carry on begging, Wendland (1957) concluded that barking calls do not warn about danger but express irritation. Females also bark, for example, if a male takes too long to bring food to the nest (Cramp 1985). Males occasionally bark too (eg, Saurola 1995).

The four young in **CD2-69** are all within 15 m of one another. The female barks frequently, probably because of me, while two of the juveniles beg nearby. When the male arrives with prey she gives some very harsh *Vvvw* calls. The male leaves almost immediately, giving a series of quickly repeated coarse hoots known as 'departure calls'. The female then takes off after him, perhaps because he failed to deliver prey.

Juveniles also have barking calls, although these lack any hint of gruffness and are as high-pitched as their begging calls (**CD2-70**). The rhythmic pattern is very similar in juveniles and adults.

CD2-69   **Long-eared Owl** *Asio otus otus* De Weerribben, Overijssel, Netherlands, 22:00, 3 June 2005. Juvenile begging calls and adult female barking. From 0:38, female *Vvvw* calls and from 0:46, departure calls of male. Background: Common Cuckoo *Cuculus canorus*, Common Blackbirds *Turdus merula* and Bluethroat *Luscinia svecica*. 05.014.MR.10048.11

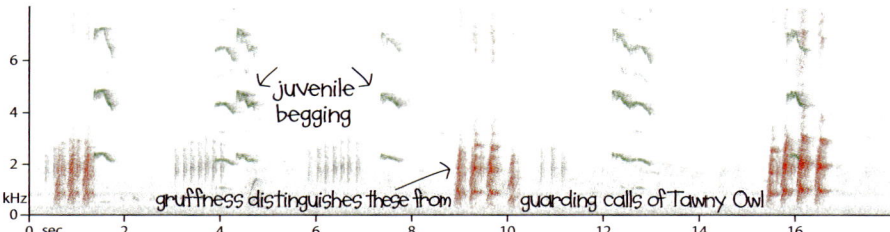

Long-eared Owl *Asio otus otus* Kolarovo biological station, Tomsk, Russia, 03:10, 6 July 2011. Juvenile barking and begging calls. Background: Siberian Rubythroat *Calliope calliope*. 110706.AB.031002.31   CD2-70

By this late stage in the breeding cycle, the female no longer repeats her *Vvvw* call in long, song-like sequences. Instead, she uses a harsh version briefly when the male arrives with prey, and sometimes also when feeding the young (Mebs & Scherzinger 2004). The male has his own version, which he uses most often at this time. If anything, his is coarser, deeper and harder sounding, and certainly never a hum. He often announces himself with a *Vvvw* just before delivering prey, often forming a duet with the female. In **CD2-71**, a male and female are both using harsh *Vvvw* calls, with the female more prominent than the male.

Long-eared Owl *Asio otus otus* De Weerribben, Overijssel, Netherlands, 22:00, 3 June 2005. *Vvvw* of female and begging calls of fledglings. Male visits briefly at the start, giving 'departure calls' as he moves off to the right, followed by a series of distant *Vvvw* calls. At around 0:45 he returns to deliver prey, giving a brief *Vvvw* at close range followed by 'departure calls' and one last *Vvvw* after returning to the right. Background: Northern Lapwing *Vanellus vanellus*, Eurasian Curlew *Numenius arquata*, Common Snipe *Gallinago gallinago* and Bluethroat *Luscinia svecica*. 05.014.MR.10400.01   CD2-71

Once Killian and I found a brood of Long-eared Owls in eastern Portugal. As we approached them the two fledglings, which were barely able to fly, stopped calling and hid inside a bush. At this point I was distracted by chaotic flapping sounds and screams about 20 m away. It sounded as some unfortunate creature was fighting for its life. Then I understood. An adult was trying to distract me away from the young. When it happened again I made a brief recording (**CD2-72**). The fledglings remained

Long-eared Owl *Asio otus otus* Rosmaninhal, Idanha-a-Nova, Portugal, 21:40, 30 May 2011. Distraction display of an adult. 110530.MR.214032.13   CD2-72

Long-eared Owl *Asio otus otus* Rosmaninhal, Idanha-a-Nova, Portugal, 21:47, 30 May 2011. *Vvvw* calls of adult male and female. Background: Iberian Green Frog *Pelophylax perezi*. 110530.MR.214700.02

CD2-73

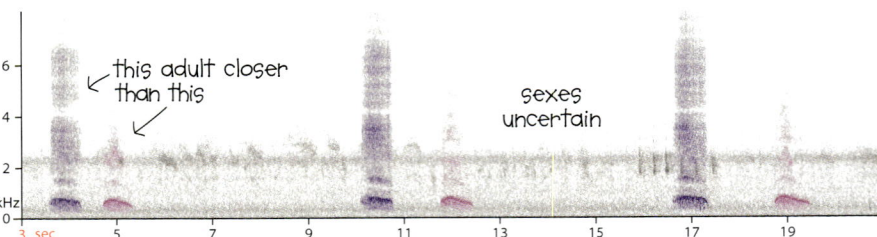

silent. When I moved away from the bush, both adults started giving harsh *Vvvw* calls from some tall pines nearby (**CD2-73**).

It is always a treat to actually see a Long-eared Owl. Sometimes, we flush one by accident. Other times, we might sense a pair of eyes watching us after following a Yellow-browed Warbler *Phylloscopus inornatus* deep into a thicket. Arnoud sometimes catches them while ringing migrants, especially in August-November. He caught the adult female in **CD2-74** at his regular site. Its bill-snaps and hisses are universal owl language, used to issue threats at close quarters when escape is not possible.

Long-eared Owl *Asio otus otus* Van Lennep ringing station, Bloemendaal, Noord-Holland, Netherlands, 10:32, 13 October 2011. Hissing and bill-snapping of an adult female in the hand. 111013.AB.103211.11

CD2-74

Autumn hooting is rare, but I recorded it once in the Ebro Delta, Spain. Two individuals were hooting in the same small area, close to where Ricard Gutiérrez told me there had been a nest in the spring. One of them sounded like a typical male, but the other sounded very strange. It gave hoots with the same rhythm as a male, but with a higher-pitched, hoarse voice reminiscent of

CD2-75 **Long-eared Owl** *Asio otus otus* L'Eucalyptus, Catalonia, Spain, 00:59, 28 September 2014. Hoarse hooting of a presumed female in autumn. Background: migrating European Robin *Erithacus rubecula*. 140928.MR.005940.11

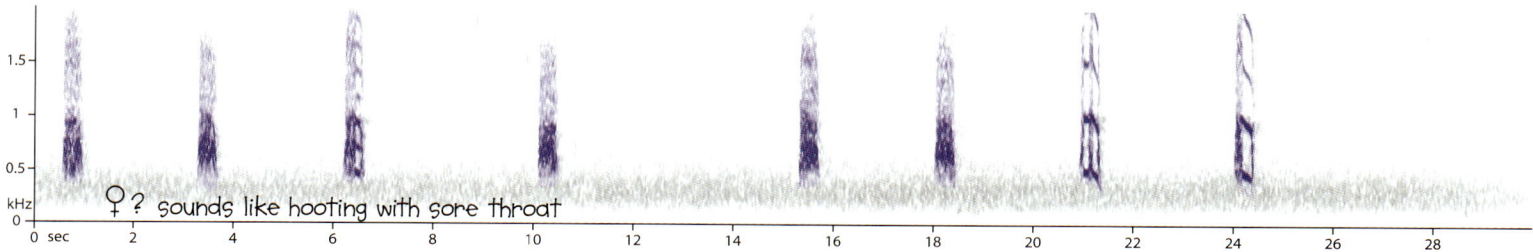

soliciting calls (**CD2-75**). I presume that it was a female, although it sounded nothing like the one in **CD1-65**.

Long-eared Owls are famous for roosting communally during the winter, sometimes on a spectacular scale. In Kikinda, Serbia, the town square hosts up to 750 in a single roost. In the Netherlands, many roost in urban areas but in more moderate numbers. Arnoud always shows them on his five-day Limosa Holidays winter birding tours. During a scouting trip in February 2008, he visited a roost just 2 km from Schiphol airport. At dusk, the owls gave faint calls as they prepared to go hunting (**CD2-76**). These were unfamiliar to both of us at the time, but now I realise they have a rhythm similar to barking calls. Recorded from just 5 m, they were very quiet indeed.

CD2-76 **Long-eared Owl** *Asio otus otus* Vijfhuizen, Noord-Holland, Netherlands, 18:14, 19 February 2008. Very quiet barking calls before leaving roost. Background: Common Blackbird *Turdus merula*. 080219.AB.181427.32

Long-eared Owls' excellent hearing allows them to hunt voles and other small mammals in near total darkness (Payne & Drury 1958). One might imagine that their extra long 'ear tufts'

Long-eared Owl *Asio otus*, two at winter roost of c 10, Swifterbant, Flevoland, Netherlands, 7 February 2014 (*Arnoud B van den Berg*). Similar situation as in CD2-76.

enhance their hearing. In fact these pinna are not receivers of any kind, but transmitters. Like other head ornaments, which include bright orange irides, white 'eyebrows' and 'chinstrap', and blackish 'harlequin's tears' above and below the eyes – they can be activated by raising or flattening different feather tracts. Such ornaments communicate mood, but only if they can be seen. Galeotti & Rubolini (2007) showed that species with more ornaments tend to hunt more by daylight and live in more open habitats. Only the latter applies to Long-eared Owls.

Unlike Common Barn Owls or Short-eared Owls *A flammeus*, Long-eared Owls rarely call in flight, except in the Netherlands where they give a trumpeting nasal *honk-honk* or a staccato *kip-kip-kip* as they fly past at night…. Curiously, this *kip-kip-kip* is the same flight call that Common Barn used to give, but only in Britain. Different birding cultures have their own traditions, and sometimes they perpetuate errors. The nasal *honk-honk* is in fact a Eurasian Coot *Fulica atra* flight call and the *kip-kip-kip* belongs to Common Moorhen *Gallinula chloropus* (Constantine et al 2012). The British barn owl tradition was politely deconstructed by Bunn et al (1982), while de Wijs (2009) whacked the Dutch Long-eared Owl fallacy hard on the head.

Nocturnal flight calls of other marshland birds somehow never became part of these traditions. How many observers would recognise a Little Grebe *Tachybaptus ruficollis* if it flew overhead in spring? Or a Short-eared Owl, chasing a rival away from vole-rich mire on a late autumn night?

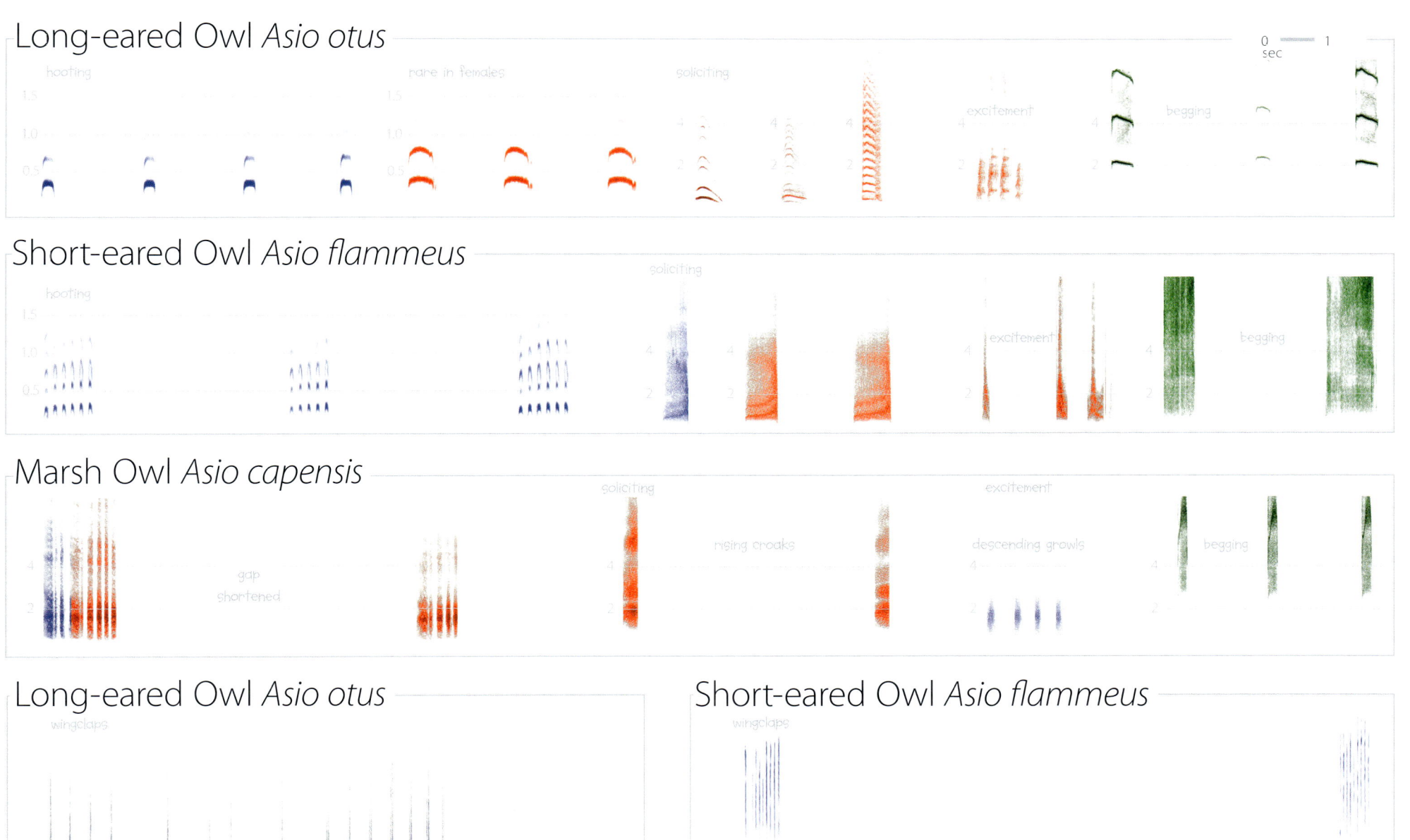

Short-eared Owl

Short-eared Owls *Asio flammeus* are complete bastards to record. They hoot mainly in flight and often at a great height. Getting close is almost impossible; you can't just leave a recorder near a songpost. If one hoots right overhead, its next series of hoots will seem far away. We all had a go at one time or another, for the best part of a decade. On the island of Texel, where Arnoud and I tried for several years to record them, they hoot in the late afternoon. Parachute jumpers, the Royal Dutch Air Force, car and bicycle traffic all conspired against us. I finally succeeded while revisiting another island, after realising that they also hoot at dawn and in the middle of the night.

When I was a child I spent all my summer holidays in Orkney. As we travelled round the islands, I learned to pay attention

Habitat of Short-eared Owl *Asio flammeus*, from Stenness, looking towards Orphir, Orkney, Scotland, June 2012 (*Eric Meek*). Most recordings of this species are from Orkney (CD2-77 to 79, CD2-82 to 84 & CD2-86 to 87).

whenever pasture gave way to rough grassland or bog. Often a Short-eared Owl would be perched on a fencepost or a Hen Harrier *Circus cyaneus* would be skimming the tussocks on raised wings. Orkney supports the UK's only Common Voles *Microtus arvalis*, brought from the continent in Neolithic times (Haynes et al 2003). Not only are they abundant, but since arriving in the archipelago they have increased in size. Orkney has no natural ground predators, which benefits not only the voles but also ground-nesting birds like Short-eared Owls. Given such advantages, it is no surprise that Orkney has one of their healthiest populations in north-western Europe.

In 2010 I took my own family on holiday to Orkney for the first time. By day we shared the pleasures of beachcombing and singing to Grey Seals *Halichoerus grypus*. By night I went off to record Short-eared Owls. In order to minimise disturbance, I left the recording equipment in a well-chosen spot and went back to get some sleep. There were two pairs that I could follow. One already had tiny nestlings so the male was not hooting very much. The male of the other pair was still displaying. In **CD2-77**, he gives several volleys of quiet, low-pitched hoots. As he

CD2-77   **Short-eared Owl** *Asio flammeus* Naverdale, Orkney, Scotland, 01:11, 11 June 2010. A male hooting in flight. Background: Hen Harrier *Circus cyaneus*, Eurasian Curlew *Numenius arquatus* and Sedge Warbler *Acrocephalus schoenobaenus*. 100611.MR.011153.21

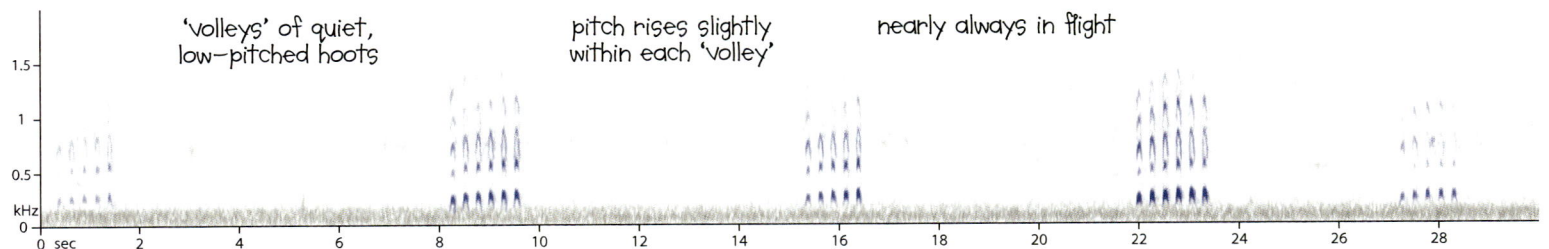

passes out of earshot, a Eurasian Curlew *Numenius arquata* sings. Then he is back, with only a distant Sedge Warbler *Acrocephalus schoenobaenus* for company as he hoots right overhead.

Nearly two hours later, the male flies over again while performing a different display flight (**CD2-78**). Although it is only 02:53, the dawn chorus is well underway, and curlews ripple gently in all directions. Over this murmur, the owl gives four series of hoots interspersed with rapid volleys of wingclaps. During the long gaps, a Common Snipe *Gallinago gallinago* drums close by, and a Red Grouse *Lagopus scotica* displays in the distance.

Like many other ground-nesting birds, male Short-eared Owls use altitude to project their sound and to be seen. Think of a skydancing Hen Harrier, or a Eurasian Skylark *Alauda arvensis* singing as a speck up in the sky. Curiously, their wing-clapping often seems to project further than their hooting. On the steppes of northern Kazakhstan, I once followed a male displaying until he was so high up that I could barely hear either sound. Wing-clapping at such a high altitude is a courtship display, whereas low-altitude clapping is primarily aggressive.

CD2-78　**Short-eared Owl** *Asio flammeus* Naverdale, Orkney, Scotland, 02:53, 11 June 2010. Wingclaps and hooting of a male. Background: Red Grouse *Lagopus scotica*, Common Pheasant *Phasianus colchicus*, Eurasian Oystercatcher *Haematopus ostralegus*, Eurasian Curlew *Numenius arquata*, Common Snipe *Gallinago gallinago*, Eurasian Skylark *Alauda arvensis* and Common Reed Bunting *Emberiza schoeniclus*. 100611.MR.025328.02

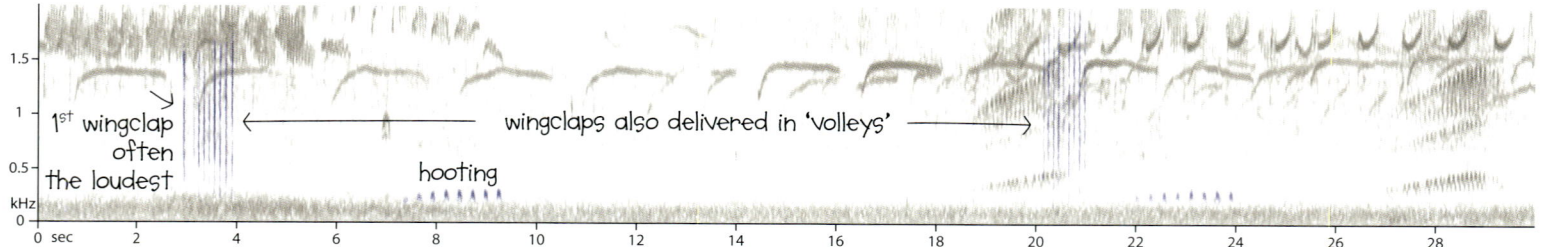

Aggressive wing-clapping typically consists of one volley or just a few volleys, each of which contains about 10 claps. It occurs during direct, rapid flight where the bird's obvious intent is to chase another owl, or less often when returning to its territory from a chase (Clark 1975). In **CD2-79**, a male was recovering his composure after chasing off a Peregrine Falcon *Falco peregrinus*. Wing-clapping is performed both by paired and unpaired male Short-eared Owls, unlike Long-eared Owl in which only paired males wing-clap (Hawley 1966). It is limited to the breeding season, and autumn wing-clapping is only possible if a freak rodent plague encourages breeding at the 'wrong' time of year. In the 1950s, for example, three Dutch pairs bred in December (Bakker 1957).

CD2-79   **Short-eared Owl** *Asio flammeus* Finstown, Orkney, Scotland, 11:58, 13 June 2010. A single volley of wingclaps, followed by hoarse *rrrrAH* calls Background: Eurasian Curlew *Numenius arquata*, Eurasian Skylark *Alauda arvensis*, Hooded Crow *Corvus cornix* and Common Reed Bunting *Emberiza schoeniclus*. 1006˙3.MR.115818.01

Treeless habitats and partly diurnal habits make Short-eared Owls conspicuous, so the visual aspect of their displays is highly developed. In courtship flights, the male ascends with characteristic 'rowing' wingbeats, which are rhythmic but only moderately deep. He interrupts these now and then to perform wingclaps. "With increasing altitude the male Wingclaps less frequently and does some occasional soaring... The bird intersperses hovers with relatively shallow descending glides that end with a Wingclap. Then he climbs again. The routine generally ends in a spectacular descent with a flight somewhat peculiar to this situation." This display is called the Sashay flight, "as the bird appears to rock back and forth with its wings held in a deep dihedral" (Clark 1975).

Display flights are visible continuously, making it possible for Short-eared Owls to economise on sounds, and this perhaps helps to explain why they hoot and wingclap in short volleys. The visual display continues during the long silence between volleys. Physiological limits also play a role. It would be impossible for an owl to maintain flight and give volleys of wingclaps or hoots at very short intervals. No owl that I know of ever hoots in flight for more than a few seconds at a time.

A few weeks after our Orkney holiday, Peter Nuyten was on Ameland, a Dutch island that also offers special conditions for Short-eared Owls. It is the only Waddeneiland supporting

Common Voles and since 1984 it has also had Field Voles *M agrestis* (Broekhuizen et al 1992). Unlike nearby Terschelling and Texel, which have Stoats *Mustela erminea*, Ameland has no natural ground predators. The pair that Peter recorded seemed intent on nesting on a high dune in an area subject to flooding by the nearby Waddenzee. In **CD2-80**, the male is hooting at night, with a variety of wetland birds for company.

CD2-80 **Short-eared Owl** *Asio flammeus* Ameland, Friesland, Netherlands, 00:32, 24 April 2010. A male hooting in flight at night. Background: Mallard *Anas platyrhynchos*, Eurasian Oystercatcher *Haematopus ostralegus*, Lesser Black-backed Gull *Larus fuscus* and Common Nightingale *Luscinia megarhynchos*. 100424.PN.003210.01 Peter Nuyten

Territorial displays can have a male calling and wing-clapping as it circles high 600 or 700 m away from a female who responds from the ground. Attempts to record this joint display have frustrated us the most. While we don't have an example that captures the three dimensional scale and distance, we do have a closer version of it. In **CD2-81**, the Ameland male hoots several times as he arrives with prey. The female replies with *rrrrAH* soliciting calls that quickly sound frenzied, as she demands that he hand over the prey. This is the female's commonest call during the breeding season, equivalent to the *Vvvw* of Long-eared Owl.

Male hooting and female soliciting calls are subject to individual variation. The male in **CD2-82** belongs to the second pair I recorded in Orkney. Every time this male hooted, his voice had a markedly gruff timbre. In this recording he hoots three times. The female goes out to meet him, giving a very short, slightly descending variant of her soliciting call.

Short-eared Owl *Asio flammeus* Finstown, Orkney, Scotland, 00:41, 7 June 2010. Gruff hooting of a male with short soliciting call of a female. Background: Eurasian Oystercatcher *Haematopus ostralegus*, Eurasian Curlew *Numenius arquata* and Common Snipe *Gallinago gallinago*. 100607.MR.004112.01 **CD2-82**

At other times, the same female gave more typical soliciting calls, often in long series. In **CD2-83**, she is the bird closer to the microphones. The male arrives at the start, giving a couple of

CD2-81 **Short-eared Owl** *Asio flammeus* Ameland, Friesland, Netherlands, 00:32, 24 April 2010. Hooting of a male and *rrrrAh* calls of a female, becoming frenzied as the male delivers prey. Background: Eurasian Oystercatcher *Haematopus ostralegus*, Lesser Black-backed Gull *Larus fuscus* and Common Nightingale *Luscinia megarhynchos*. 100424.PN.003210.01 Peter Nuyten

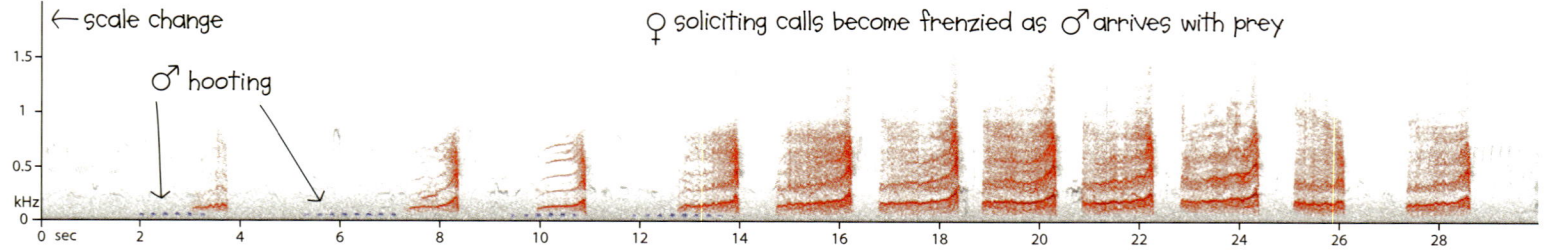

quiet, low grumbles. Then he perches at a distance and at 0:25 and 0:34 he replies to the much closer female with his own slightly lower-pitched soliciting calls. After a short series of hoots at 1:02, he eventually brings food to the nest. We hear his wingbeats and the female's increased excitement as he approaches.

Clark (1975) could distinguish male and female soliciting calls at four different nests, the male sounding lower-pitched and more disyllabic than the female, with a more rasping first syllable. In **CD2-84**, the male is the closer individual that calls once at the start, and the female replies several times. For me the only striking difference is in their pitch.

Male Short-eared Owls sometimes use their soliciting call in territorial defence displays, the two most important of which are the 'Underwing' and the 'Skirmish' (Clark 1975). In the Underwing, the male flies around with exaggerated wingbeats, raising his wings high above his back to show their whitish undersides to his rival. Males often use this low-intensity display to reinforce their mutual territorial borders. In the Skirmish, the rivals fly up at one another, presenting their talons if the encounter becomes more intense. In extreme cases, talon-locking with spiralling falls may result.

Traditionally, up to 10 subspecies of Short-eared Owl have been recognised (del Hoyo et al 1999). Based on starkly contrasting soliciting calls, they can be placed in two groups. *A f flammeus* is the Short-eared Owl of northern Eurasia and North America.

CD2-83 **Short-eared Owl** *Asio flammeus* Finstown, Orkney, Scotland, 03:33, 7 June 2010. Female soliciting calls, with two low grumbling calls of a male. Then soliciting call exchange between male and female. Male hoots at 1:03 then brings food to the nest. Background: Eurasian Curlew *Numenius arquata*, Common Redshank *Tringa totanus* and Common Snipe *Gallinago gallinago*. 100607.MR.033306.01

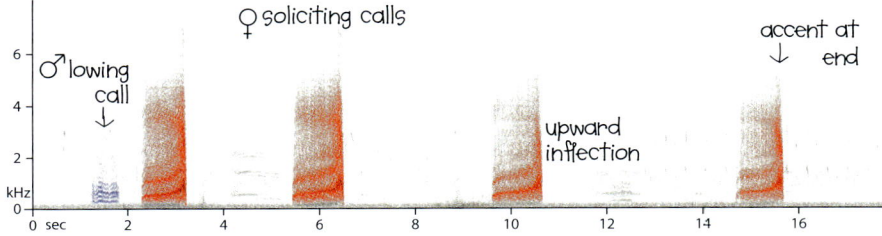

CD2-84 **Short-eared Owl** *Asio flammeus* Finstown, Orkney, Scotland, 13:36, 13 June 2010. Male soliciting call once close by at start, followed by several female replies. Background: Eurasian Curlew *Numenius arquata*, Eurasian Skylark *Alauda arvensis* and Meadow Pipit *Anthus pratensis*. 100613.MR.133618.01

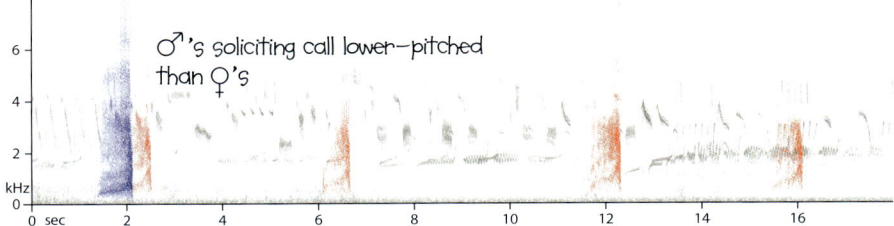

Field Owl *Asio domingensis sanfordi* Kidney Island, Falkland Islands, 23 December 1970. Adult moaning calls emanating from tussock grass. Kidney Island is free of introduced rats and mice (Woods & Woods 1997), and well known for its breeding penguins Spheniscidae, Sooty Shearwaters *Puffinus griseus* and other seabirds. Background: Magellanic Penguin *Spheniscus magellanicus* and Austral Thrush *Turdus falcklandii*. Ian J Strange. **CD2-85**

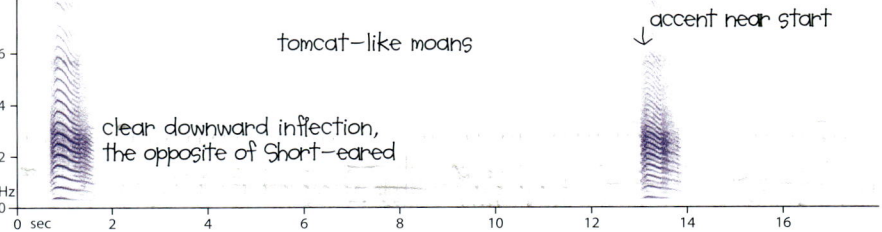

Most of the others live in or near the Caribbean and South America, except for *sandwichensis* of Hawaii and *ponapensis* of the Caroline Islands, Micronesia, the only one for which I could find no recordings. On vocal grounds, there is evidence for a northern group with rising *rrrrAh* soliciting calls and a Caribbean/South American group with very different-sounding, tomcat-like, moaning soliciting calls. **CD2-85** is an example from the latter group: subspecies *sanfordi*, endemic to the Falkland Islands. By contrast the even more isolated *sandwichensis*, known in Hawaii as the Pueo, has a *flammeus*-like soliciting call and presumably evolved from northern stock.

None of the southern group have ever occurred in the Western Palearctic. Besides *sanfordi*, they include *domingensis* and *portoricensis* of the Greater Antilles, *bogotensis*, *pallidicaudatus* and *suinda* of continental South America, and the isolated *galapagoensis* of the Galapagos Islands. Through most of Latin America, they are called 'lechuza campestre' or 'búho campestre', both of which translate as 'field owl'. The oldest named southern taxon is *domingensis* so in the event of a split, we can call the southern species Field Owl *A domingensis*.

In Orkney, Short-eared Owls are called 'Cattie-face'. The female of the second pair I recorded there gave soliciting calls to demand voles whenever the male appeared. After taking one, she would encourage her tiny nestlings to accept little morsels with her 'feeding calls' (**CD2-86**). These are quiet calls, probably impossible to hear under normal field conditions. The rhythmic pattern of feeding calls is similar in all owl species.

Short-eared Owl *Asio flammeus* Finstown, Orkney, Scotland, 15:54, 13 June 2010. **CD2-86** Feeding calls of a female. Background: Eurasian Curlew *Numenius arquata*, Meadow Pipit *Anthus pratensis*, Eurasian Skylark *Alauda arvensis* and Common Reed Bunting *Emberiza schoeniclus*. 100613.MR.155438.01

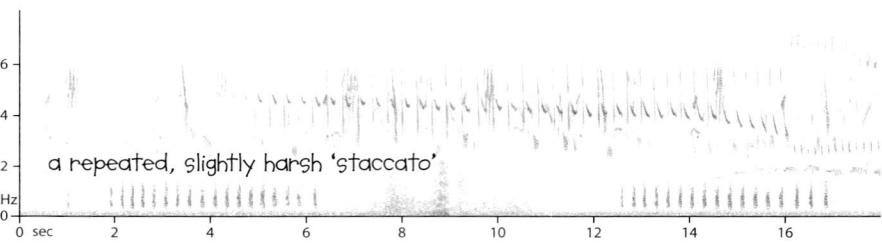

During the two nights I spent recording this family, one week apart, they were constantly fighting with a Peregrine Falcon. I am not sure whether the Peregrine, a known predator of Short-eared Owls (Mikkola 1983), was actually targeting the owls or simply passing by. In **CD2-87**, the female attacks the Peregrine ferociously. As she takes off from the nest, two tiny young peep quietly for a few seconds. There is a harsh, descending bark from the female followed by the whoosh of the Peregrine's wings. The female barks several more times and snaps her bill loudly at the enemy. From 0:15 the Peregrine calls and the owl gives two last barks. Gradually calm returns.

The reaction to ground predators is very different. Like waders and other birds that nest on the ground, as well as a few owls that don't, Short-eared Owls have a well-developed distraction display. Dick witnessed this while approaching a nest in Lapland where the young were in the process of hatching. The male came flying in through the trees and threw himself on the ground, dragging his wings. The next day Dick was better prepared, but

CD2-87 **Short-eared Owl** *Asio flammeus* Finstown, Orkney, Scotland, 13:05, 13 June 2010. Female attacks a Peregrine Falcon *Falco peregrinus*. Her tiny nestlings peep faintly in the background (beware of confusion with alarm calls of closer Meadow Pipit *Anthus pratensis*). Background: Eurasian Curlew *Numenius arquata* and Eurasian Skylark *Alauda arvensis*. 100613.MR.130503.11

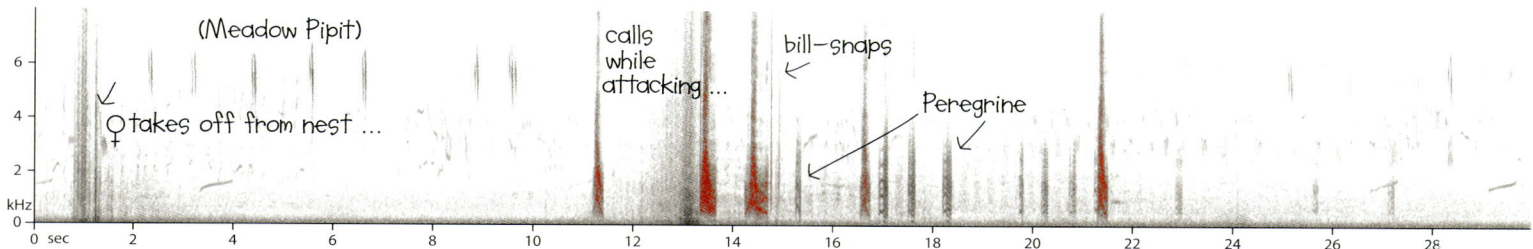

Short-eared Owl *Asio flammeus*, attacking Arctic Fox *Vulpes lagopus*, Nome, Seward Peninsula, Alaska, USA, 1 June 2004 (*René Pop*)

Short-eared Owl *Asio flammeus*, Tornio, Lapland, Finland, 7 June 2010 (*Dick Forsman*). Same territory as in CD2-88.

age of just two weeks. They can move surprisingly far in just a short time, eg, 175 m in just four days (Clark 1975). Begging persistently and loudly like a Long-eared Owl is not an option, so their calls are weaker and saved largely for when an adult arrives with food. To help adults locate them quickly, the owlets ruffle the body feathers and vibrate their wings close to the body. "As the intensity of begging increases, the owlet extends and flutters the wings. Finally, at full intensity, the fully extended wings are rotated so that the ventral surface is directed forward (showing the lighter coloration of the underwing to the approaching parent), and are fluttered in this position almost to the point of flapping" (Clark 1975). As soon as they stop this display, their grass-like camouflage makes them virtually invisible once again.

Begging calls of juvenile Short-eared Owls have a rising intonation, like the soliciting call of adults (**CD2-89**). By contrast, those of Field Owl have the same descending contour as the adult's moans. Each taxon's begging call probably develops into its adult soliciting call. In **CD2-90**, a juvenile *sanfordi* gives a continuous stream of begging calls, while an adult barks in excitement.

the display was less intense. In **CD2-88**, the calls are all given in flight, not on the ground, but I still find them impressive.

CD2-88 **Short-eared Owl** *Asio flammeus* Tornio, Lapland, Finland, 03:29, 7 June 2010. Calls associated with distraction display, although here given in flight. Background: Eurasian Curlew *Numenius arquata* and Willow Warbler *Phylloscopus trochilus*. 100607. DF.032900.02

The dangers of nesting on the ground are so great that Short-eared Owls flee into the vegetation like young waders at the precocious

Short-eared Owl *Asio flammeus* Manitoba, Canada, 11 June 1969. Begging calls of a captive juvenile. Richard J Clark and The Macaulay Library at the Cornell Lab of Ornithology.   CD2-89

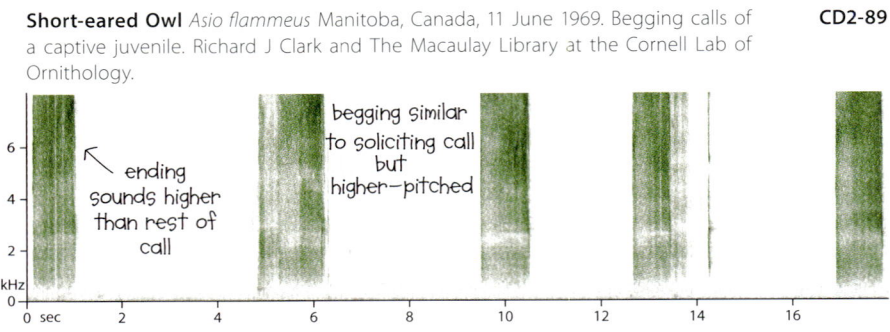

CD2-90 **Field Owl** *Asio domingensis sanfordi* Kidney Island, Falklard Islands, 23 December 1970. A brood of juveniles beg and an adult flies over giving excitement calls. Background: Austral Thrush *Turdus falcklandii*. Ian J Strange.

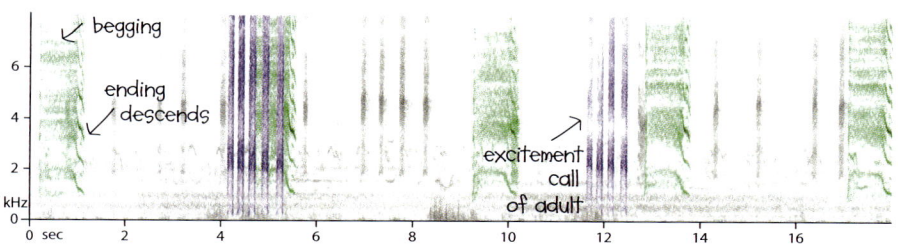

After learning to fly, Short-eared Owls lose none of their wanderlust. They are among the most nomadic of owls, flying long distances in search of abundant food supplies. A few even cross the Sahara, the only WP owl other than Eurasian Scops Owl *Otus scops* known to do so. With movements like this, it is not surprising that Short-eared Owls have reached far-flung oceanic islands like Hawaii. More surprising perhaps is that apart from Iceland, they have not colonised any of the more distant North Atlantic islands. They do turn up from time to time in the Azores, and it is not impossible that they bred in the Selvagens before the introduced House Mouse *Mus domesticus* population was eradicated (Rafael Matias pers comm). A century ago, breeding was also suspected on Porto Santo or associated islets in the Madeira archipelago (Bannerman 1965).

Over the last few autumns I have been visiting the tiny island of Berlenga, just off continental Portugal. By day I count migrants and search for vagrants; by night I listen to nocturnal migration and the odd Grant's Storm Petrel *Oceanodroma*. During my first autumn visit, I was thrilled to hear Short-eared Owls in the dark. There were at least two on the island, and a month later there were six. Berlenga has many Black Rats *Rattus rattus*, presumably the main attraction for the owls. It is thrilling to hear the occasional storm petrel and owl duet on Berlenga, a combination I never managed to capture in a recording. The calls I hear there in autumn are mainly variants of the soliciting call and a coarse barking sound similar to the one Short-eared uses when mobbing a raptor. Elsewhere, it is not uncommon to hear calls like these whenever several of the owls winter together in a restricted area.

My most magical Portuguese encounter with Short-eared Owls took place one autumn night when I went to record migration in the hours before dawn. At the end of a peninsula called Cabo Espichel, there is a picturesque former convent. I sat under its walls hoping to hear migrating passerines and maybe see a few lit up in the floodlights. Surprisingly, it was five Short-eared that I saw, flying in slow, untidy circuits, high above the convent. Now and then when they met in mid-air, they gave a very faint, high-pitched tinkling sound unlike anything I have heard at any other time.

I began to suspect that like me, they were there for the migrating passerines. When a Song Thrush *Turdus philomelos* came in off

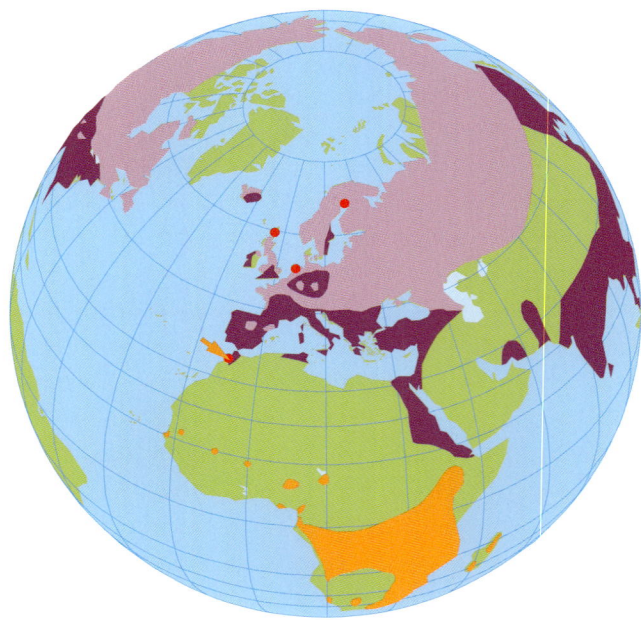

Approximate breeding distribution of Short-eared Owl *Asio flammeus* ■ and Marsh Owl *A capensis* ■ (note arrow) and winter-only distribution of Short-eared ■. Recording locations indicated by ● dots.

the sea, two of them went for it. Later, I read Canário et al's (2012) account of exactly the same behaviour at Sagres, the south-western corner of Portugal. Arnoud also saw Short-eared Owls catching passerines near a lighthouse in the Netherlands (van den Berg 1974).

Short-eared Owls do not breed in Portugal, so they were migrants too. In a week or two the songbird passage would be over and they would have to hunt elsewhere. Would they stay in Portugal, or might they head south for a meeting with their darker, more raucous African cousin?

Marsh Owl

Just over 100 km south of the Strait of Gibraltar, in Morocco, a narrow channel divides sand dunes formed by Atlantic gales. Seawater meets freshwater from several small rivers, creating a lagoon 7 km long and 3.5 km wide. Its name – Merja Zerga – means 'blue lagoon'. Arnoud and Cecilia have been visiting the area for decades. Slender-billed Curlew *Numenius tenuirostris* used to be the main attraction until it became extinct. Since 1995, the lagoon's most endangered bird has been *Asio capensis tingitanus*, the isolated northern subspecies of Marsh Owl. Morocco's human population is growing fast, and some 8000 people live in small villages scattered around the lagoon. Most earn a living from fishing, livestock, and by making mats from rushes. A handful try to earn a few extra dirhams by flushing Marsh Owls out of their roosts, and even breeding sites, for any visiting birder unscrupulous enough to pay.

In **CD3-01**, it is dusk. A breeding pair croaks in flight, their voices overlapping at the start. Marsh Owls do not hoot, and these short strophes of irregular length croaks are their most important

Marsh Owl *Asio capensis*, Merja Zerga, Moulay Bousselham, Rharb, Morocco, 20 March 2005 (*James Lidster*)

vocalisation. Let's call them 'song croaks'. The owls croak at roughly 20-second intervals, nearly always in flight. Individual variation is strong but each owl's song croaks are consistent and recognisable, especially regarding the rhythm at the start.

CD3-01   **Marsh Owl** *Asio capensis* Merja Zerga, Douar Rouissia, Rharb, Morocco, 21:08, 10 June 2010. 'Song croaks' of a pair, overlapping at the start. 100610.AB.210800.1

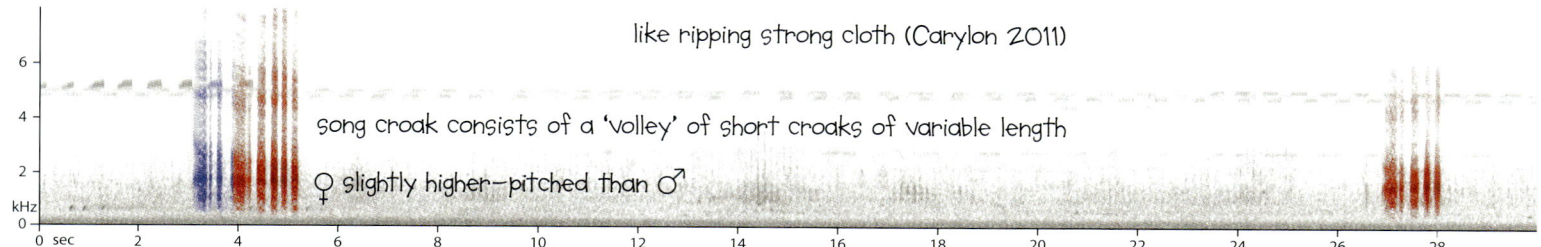

Curiously, none of Arnoud's 84 recordings of Moroccan Marsh Owls contain any wing-clapping. Matt Pretorius from South Africa who knows Marsh Owl *A c capensis* well, having worked with African Grass Owls *Tyto capensis* in the same habitat, tells me that wing-clapping is commonest just before and during the breeding season. He adds that if a predator or a researcher flushes a Marsh, it may wing-clap aggressively at any time of year. In Matt's experience, Marsh only gives single claps like Long-eared Owl, not volleys as in Short-eared Owl.

Marsh Owl is the African ecological equivalent of Short-eared Owl, and a very close relative (Wink et al 2009). Both live in open habitats and nest on the ground. There have been no detailed studies of Marsh Owl sounds, but I hear many parallels with Short-eared. Despite their very different timbre, Marsh song croaks and Short-eared hooting share some obvious similarities, such as their temporal pattern, including the long silences in between. Both are normally given in flight.

Marsh Owls are social, sometimes breeding in dense clusters of territories. Suitable habitat is often limited, sometimes leading to the formation of loose colonies (Carlyon 2011). They are also well known for roosting communally. In **CD3-02**, recorded in October, at least two owls fly out of their roost. There is one croak at close range, then by the time other croaks follow the owls are already distant.

Marsh Owl *Asio capensis* Merja Zerga, Moulay-Bousselham, Rharb, Morocco, 18:21, 5 October 2007. Several song croaks as at least two different individuals leave their communal roost. Background: Common Blackbird *Turdus merula*. 071005.AB.182111.31   CD3-02

During the breeding season, Marsh Owls croak as they make long display flights in wide circles with deliberate wingbeats and periodic wing-clapping (Smith & Killick-Kendrick 1964).

Both sexes produce song croaks. According to Fry et al (1988), the female's voice is higher-pitched and softer than the male's.

CD3-03 **Marsh Owl** *Asio capensis* Merja Zerga, Douar Rouissia, Kénitra, Morocco, 19:00, 26 March 2006. Song croaks of male and female, emerging from their breeding territory at dusk. Background: Moroccan Toad *Amietophrynus mauritanicus* and Crested Lark *Galerida cristata*. 06.002.AB.01038.01

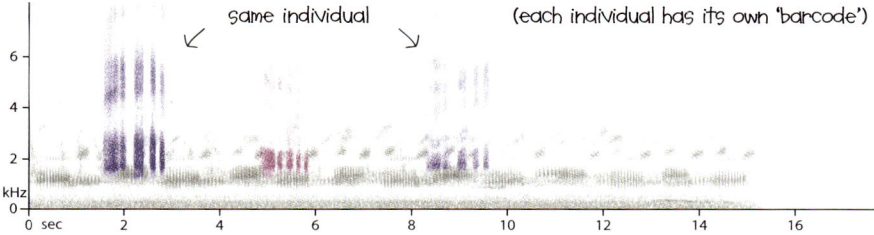

CD3-04 **Marsh Owl** *Asio capensis* Merja Zerga, Douar Rouissia, Kénitra, Morocco, 18:37, 25 March 2006. A series of rising croaks from the ground. Background: Moroccan Toad *Amietophrynus mauritanicus*. 06.001.AB.02825.01

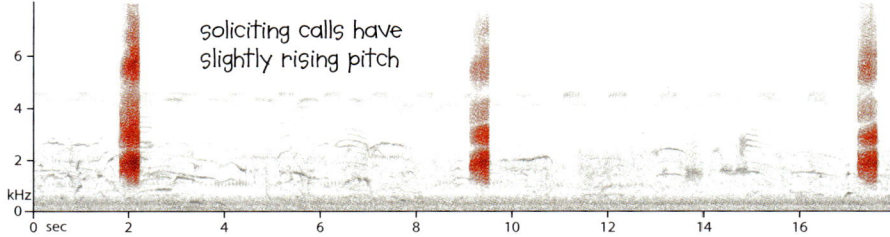

In **CD3-03**, from the main courtship period in March, a male and female are emerging from their breeding territory at dusk. In this recording, any pitch difference between the two individuals is negligible and I hear no difference in timbre or 'softness', so I have left them unsexed.

Marsh Owl's soliciting call is a short rising croak, equivalent to the *rrrrAh* of Short-eared Owl. In Arnoud's recordings of this sound, the caller was always perched. In **CD3-04**, it is egg-laying time and a presumed female Marsh gives a series of rising croaks at dusk.

Hamida Hammouradia, a warden at Merja Zerga, made a special effort to find a Marsh Owl nest for Arnoud. When he succeeded, Arnoud and Cecilia immediately drove down from the Netherlands to Morocco. When Hamida showed them the nest, it contained three young around 12 days old. Arnoud left his equipment recording there for a couple of hours and moved to a respectful distance. Two days later they had dispersed into the grass, just like two-week-old Short-eared Owls.

During the last half hour of Arnoud's recording session, adults landed at the nest six times. In **CD3-05** one, probably the female, gives a song croak before landing, and then walks into the tunnel in the grass where the nest is situated. Once at the nest she starts giving rising croaks while the nestlings beg with high, rising whistles. These begging calls almost certainly develop into the rising croaks of adults. In the background the other adult gives a series of descending growls from a perch nearby. Arnoud recorded these growls most frequently when he was close to the nest, both from perched and flying Marsh Owls. They were usually single (**CD3-06**), but with increasing excitement they could be grouped into short, fairly rapid series (**CD3-07**).

Marsh Owl *Asio capensis* Merga Zerja, Douar Rouissia, Rharb, Morocco, 20:55, 24 June 2010. Two descending croaks at close range. 100624.AB.205500.21   CD3-06

Marsh Owl *Asio capensis* Merga Zerja, Douar Rouissia, Rharb, Morocco, 22:27, 20 June 2010. A fairly rapid series of descending croaks in flight. 100620.AB.222748.21   CD3-07

In **CD3-08**, an adult that has just brought prey to the nest gives a series of very quiet, low-pitched croaks. These are Marsh Owl's feeding calls. The youngsters in the recording respond with begging calls, but they also produce some chitter calls, signalling discomfort.

Marsh Owl *Asio capensis* Merga Zerja, Douar Rouissia, Rharb, Morocco, 22:17, 20 June 2010. Feeding calls of an adult with begging calls and a few faint chitter calls of nestlings. 100620.AB.221729.01   CD3-08

During the same trip to Morocco, Arnoud recorded a family of Marsh Owls at Oued Loukkos, a freshwater marsh 35 km to the north. Oued Loukkos has long been known for Marsh Owls, although this was their first breeding record for many years. The juveniles in **CD3-09** were among three that had already learned to fly and were perched on fence posts along the edge of the marsh.

CD3-05   **Marsh Owl** *Asio capensis* Merga Zerja, Douar Rouissia, Rharb, Morocco, 22:29, 20 June 2010. Song croak of adult, presumed female, which then visits nest. Begging calls and occasional chitters of young, descending barks of presumed male outside, and rising croaks of presumed female in nest. When the male takes off at 2:27, he gives a few bill-snaps. 100620.AB.222952.01

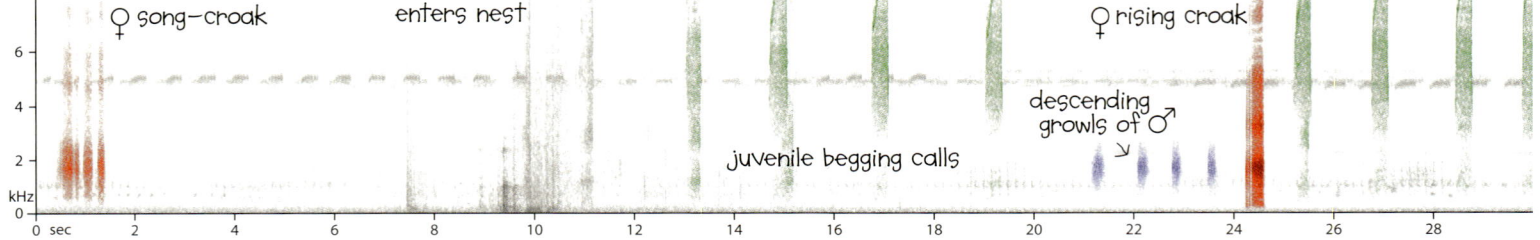

Marsh Owl *Asio capensis*, Merja Zerga, Douar Mghayetan, Rharb, Morocco, 3 October 2010 (*Arnoud B van den Berg*). At roost in south-east of lagoon.

Nowadays, Marsh Owl barely clings to survival in north-western Africa, and it may become extinct there without stricter protection. The population was certainly healthier in recent history, but would have been common thousands of years ago, when the Sahara received more rainfall than at present. A major study of Saharan conditions 6000 years ago, based on pollen and plant macrofossil data, identified only two sites in southern Egypt that were desert at that time. "All other Saharan sites were either steppe, at low elevation, or temperate xerophytic woods/scrub, or even warm mixed forest in the Saharan mountains" (Jolly et al 1998). Marsh Owl's North African heyday probably ended around the time of the ancient Egyptians when the desert gradually expanded to its current size, and most forms of life were pushed towards its fringes.

As recently as the late 19th century, Marsh Owl showed up regularly in Europe. M F Favier, a French collector who died in Morocco in the mid-19th century, described Marsh Owl as "a common resident near Tangier, usually frequenting wet swampy ground, feeding chiefly on insects. Some pass over to Europe in March and April, returning in November and December" (Irby 1895). In Cádiz, Spain, Howard Irby found eight Marsh Owls, up to three at a time, "within a space of about a square mile". He flushed them all while hunting snipe in October and November, but others also found them there during the winter months. March, May and August visits failed to produce any owls (Irby 1895). This hotspot probably concerned a roost, but elsewhere in Iberia there are suggestions that the owls may even have bred.

One of my favourite owl recording locations in Portugal is Pancas on the Tagus Estuary. I have sound-recorded seven species there, including Short-eared Owl. In the 19th century there was an eighth. Dom Carlos de Bragança, a keen collector who happened to be the king, shot two Marsh Owls at Pancas

CD3-09   **Marsh Owl** *Asio capensis* Oued Loukkos, Larache, Morocco, 04:45, 8 June 2010. Begging calls of two perched fledglings. Background: Cucumiau *Athene noctua glaux*. 100608.AB.044500.02

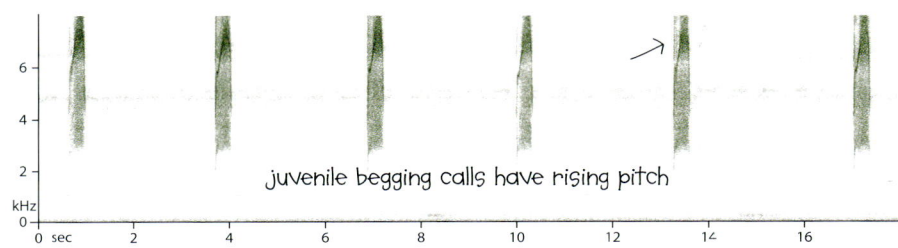

in his youth, one in December 1887 and the other in January of an unrecorded year. In February 1908 he suffered the same fate. According to Dom Carlos, Marsh Owl was a sedentary species, and "one or two could always be found in the marsh at Pancas, in summer or winter" (Carlos de Bragança in Catry et al 2010).

It was almost dark when Arnoud returned to pick up his equipment from the nest that Hamida had found. As he reappeared some distance away, an adult went out with a growl and flew some distance away. **CD3-10** documents what happened next. First we hear Arnoud moving through the sedge. Then there are some high-pitched squealing sounds, moving fairly rapidly from left to centre. Arnoud assumed that this sound was coming from the young, since the adult had flown some distance away. However, the rapid movement does not fit easily with a nestling and we never recorded those sounds at any other time. With the benefit of hindsight, I suggest that an adult approached unseen by Arnoud and performed a distraction display to try to lure him away from the nest. The sounds are remarkably similar to distraction sounds of other *Asio* owls (cf, **CD2-72** & **CD2-87**).

CD3-10   **Marsh Owl** *Asio capensis* Merga Zerja, Douar Rouissia, Rharb, Morocco, 22:17, 20 June 2010. Squealing sounds recorded during a possible distraction display. Most of the movements are Arnoud's, although there are some possible flapping sounds at 0:12 & 0:15. 100620.AB.221729.01

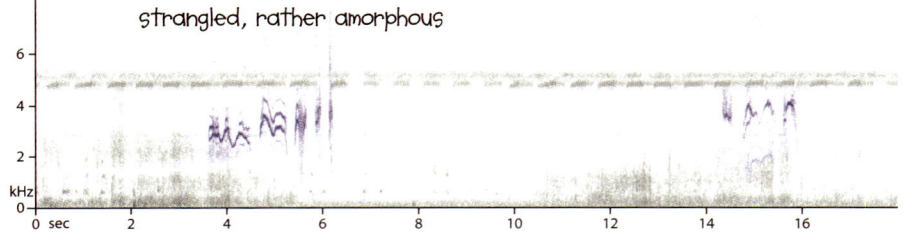

Marsh Owl *Asio capensis*, Merja Zerga, Moulay Bousselham, Rharb, Morocco, 13 September 2012 (*Dick Forsman*)

Like Dick on his return visit to the Short-eared Owls, Arnoud may not have been treated to the full distraction display. According to Smith & Killick-Kendrick (1964), adults disturbed at a nest with well-incubated eggs or tiny young will fly around in tight circles "and then crash to the ground, flapping in the grass and uttering a noise that is best described as a squeal." According to Joubert (1943), adults disturbed at their nest fly round with croaks and a feeble whistle, and much bill-snapping. Matt Pretorius tells me that distraction displays are often preceded by wing-clapping.

After they leave their parents, Moroccan Marsh Owls do not have to disperse very far. The coastal wetlands usually offer sufficient food all year round, even during the dry season. In Sub-Saharan Africa life can be much more difficult. There, the owls often make nomadic movements in search of food and sometimes even follow bushfires, preying on termites and other insects fleeing the flames (Kemp 1987). Breeding takes place when productivity is highest at the end of the rains, and before the worst of the drought. This also applies for Morocco, where the rainy season is from November to March.

Marsh Owls eat a great many insects and arachnids. At some sites in Morocco they also focus on rodents, but at Merja Zerga they hunt birds. During late summer and early autumn, the driest season, migrants pass through in great numbers. Many also stay for the winter. Keijl & Sandee (1996) listed Common Quail *Coturnix coturnix*, Dunlin *Calidris alpina*, small chats and warblers, and possibly even Richard's Pipit *Anthus richardi* in their early November diet, while Bergier & Thévenot (1991) mentioned birds as large as Water Rail *Rallus aquaticus*, European Golden Plover *Pluvialis apricaria* and Common Redshank *Tringa totanus*. The owls hunt mainly at night, suggesting that they snatch some of the passerines from their roosts, before returning to their own roost around an hour before dawn.

On 6 October 2007, Arnoud was ready for them. The cockerels were wide-awake, but the villagers were still sleeping off the previous evening's Ramadan feast. In **CD3-11**, the first owl to return is the same as the first one out the evening before

Marsh Owl *Asio capensis*, Merja Zerga, Moulay Bousselham, Rharb, Morocco, 6 October 2008 (*Arnoud B van den Berg*). At same tree roost as in CD3-02 & 11 but a year later.

(cf **CD3-02**). As the Marsh Owls settle into their roost, some Cucumiaus *Athene noctua glaux* have the last word, scolding the bird hunters in their midst.

Marsh Owl *Asio capensis* Merja Zerga, Moulay Bousselham, Rharb, Morocco, 05:48, 6 October 2007. Song croaks on returning to the roost before dawn. Background: Cucumiau *Athene noctua glaux* and Common Blackbirds *Turdus merula*. 071006. AB.054834.01

CD3-11

Chapter 8: *Bubo*

Arabian Eagle-Owl

Shortly after midnight, a male Arabian Eagle-Owl *Bubo milesi* lands on a sturdy branch overlooking a monsoon pool in southern Oman. Every few seconds he croons two notes, the first longer than the second (**CD3-12**). His voice is languid, not fierce or imposing. Arabian Eagle-Owl is one of the smallest members of the genus *Bubo* and has a diet to match. Soon some Dhofar Toads *Bufo dhufarensis* strike up a chorus. The owl is not here by chance. *Bubo* is here to hunt *Bufo*.

CD3-12   **Arabian Eagle-Owl** *Bubo milesi* Wadi Darbat, Dhofar, Oman, 00:28, 18 July 2013. Hooting of a presumed male. Background: Singing Bush Lark *Mirafra cantillans* and Dhofar Toad *Bufo dhufarensis*. 130718.AB.002826.12

To the best of our knowledge, this is the first sound recording of Arabian Eagle-Owl ever to be published. Up to now, taxonomists have only had museum skins to work with. That is why they lumped Arabian with Spotted Eagle-Owl *B africanus*, a common species in Africa south of the tropical forest and, until recently, Greyish Eagle-Owl *B cinerascens* living to the north of Spotted. To date, there have been no genetic studies involving all three of these former subspecies. They do seem likely to be each other's closest relatives, as they show broad similarities in plumage and size, in vocalisations, and share a similarly varied diet of insects and small vertebrates. However, there are important differences in the tone and patterning of their plumage, their eye colour and their sounds.

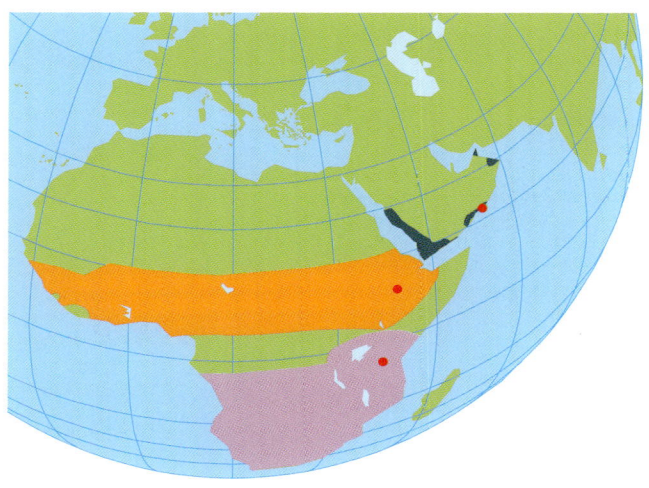

Approximate breeding distribution of Arabian Eagle-Owl *Bubo milesi* ■, Spotted Eagle-Owl *B africanus* ■ and Greyish Eagle-Owl *B cinerascens* ■. Recording locations indicated by ● dots.

The male Arabian Eagle-Owl in **CD3-13** is a different individual that was also hunting toads during the July monsoon. His hooting is slower than most, with phrases 4.3 seconds long. Male Spotted Eagle-Owls also hoot with a high and slightly longer first note followed by a low second one (**CD3-14**). However, their two notes are much shorter than those of Arabian, and the whole phrase is delivered in less than half the time. Hooting of male Greyish Eagle-Owl resembles that of Spotted but is delivered more slowly (**CD3-15**). Despite this, the phrases are much shorter than in Arabian.

Arabian Eagle-Owl *Bubo milesi* and Dhofar Toad *Bufo dhufarensis*, Wadi Darbat, Dhofar, Oman, 16/17 July 2013 (*Arnoud B van den Berg*). Possibly same as in CD3-12. In July, during the monsoon, these toads became vocal and conspicuous, easy prey for Arabian Eagle-Owls.

CD3-13 **Arabian Eagle-Owl** *Bubo milesi* Wadi Darbat, Dhofar, Oman, 20:51, 15 July 2013. Hooting of a presumed male. Background: Arabian Scops Owl *Otus pamelae*. 130715.AB.205100.12

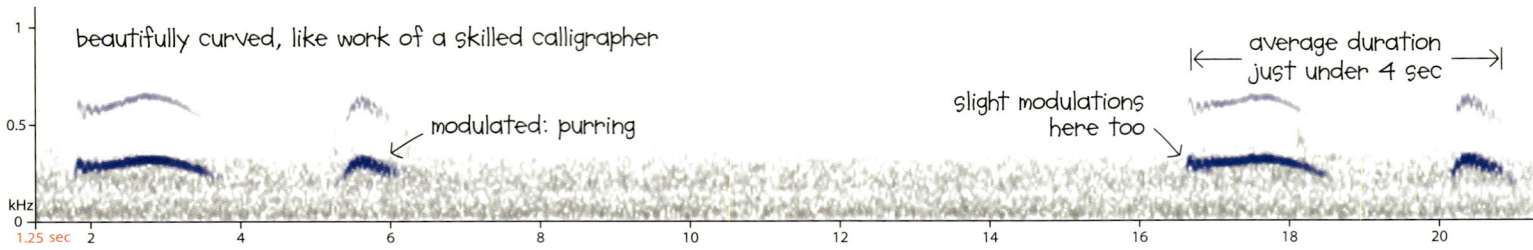

CD3-14 **Spotted Eagle-Owl** *Bubo africanus* Ngorongoro Crater, Tanzania, July 1986. Hooting duet of male and female, starting with the male. David Moyer & The Macaulay Library at the Cornell Lab of Ornithology.

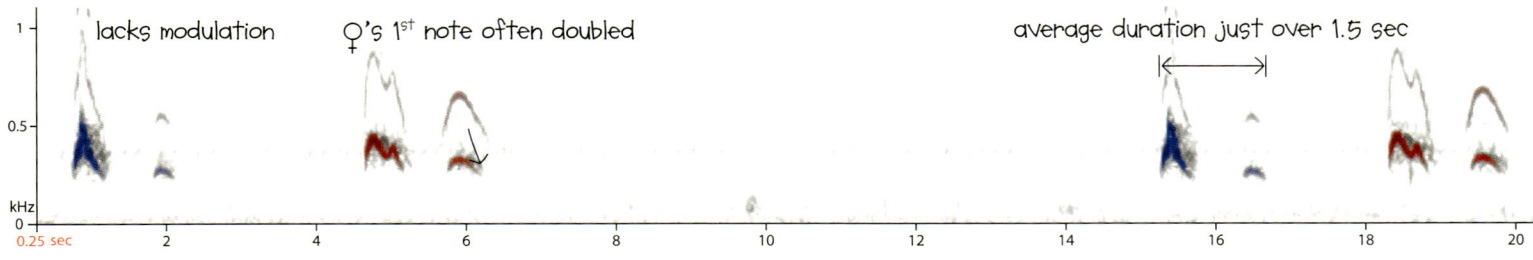

CD3-15 **Greyish Eagle-Owl** *Bubo cinerascens* Langano, Oromia, Ethiopia, 12:30, 17 February 2011. Hooting of a male. The gaps between hoots have been shortened by about 30%. Background: African Mourning Dove *Streptopelia decipiens*, Laughing Dove *S senegalensis* and Rüppell's Starling *Lamprotornis purpuroptera*. Jelmer Poelstra.

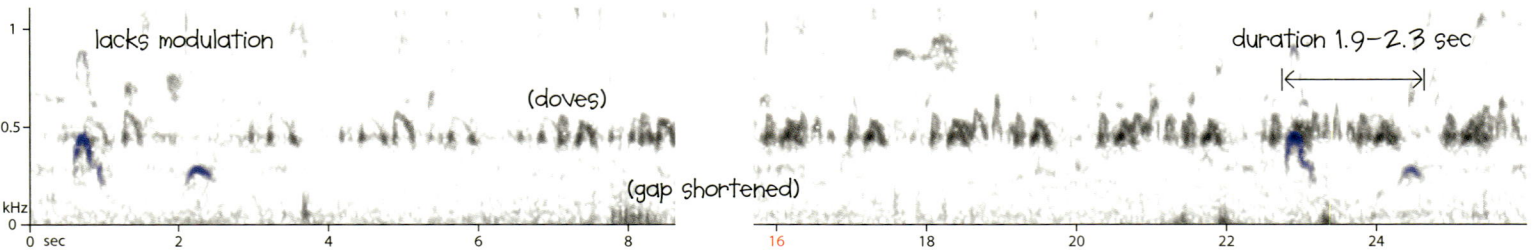

Left: Arabian Eagle-Owl *Bubo milesi*, Wadi Darbat, Dhofar, Oman, 18 July 2013 (*Arnoud B van den Berg*). Centre: Spotted Eagle-Owl *B africanus*, female, Kalahari Gemsbok NP, South Africa/Botswana, 12 March 1995 (*Arnoud B van den Berg*). Compare CD3-14. Right: Greyish Eagle-Owl *B cinerascens*, Langano lake, Oromia, Ethiopia, 23 September 2004 (*Dick Forsman*). At same site as in CD3-15. Arabian Eagle-Owl has bright yellow eyes, surrounded by a black orbital ring (and black spot on eye-lid). The iris of Spotted Eagle-Owl is similar, although it can be more orange. Greyish Eagle-Owl is the odd one out, having dark brown iris with pinkish orbital ring. Owls with dark eyes usually lead the darkest lives (Galeotti & Rubolini 2007). We are not aware of any daytime observations of Arabian but its habitat is fairly open and therefore not very dark. In the Natural History Museum at Tring, England, Arnoud photographed skins of Arabian from Oman and Spotted from South Africa and came to the same conclusion as his old professor (Voous 1988): Arabian is paler, tawnier and slightly smaller than Spotted. The markings are much finer and more speckled or vermiculated, particularly on the head and mantle, where the Spotted has larger white spots. Greyish also has a finely marked head and neck, but differs from both Arabian and Spotted in being darker and having a colder tone to its plumage.

When Richard Bowdler Sharpe described Arabian Eagle-Owl in 1886, he compared it to eagle-owls from Asia, Europe and South America, and to Cape Eagle-Owl *B capensis* from Africa. He was apparently unaware of earlier descriptions of Spotted Eagle-Owl (Temminck 1821) or Greyish Eagle-Owl (Guérin-Méneville 1843). Sharpe had received his holotype from Colonel S B Miles, a British political agent and Consul in Muscat who travelled extensively in southern Arabia from 1872 to 1886. It is surprising that the specimen came from northern Oman, because nobody found the species there again for a century. There are probably no more than 25 pairs in northern Oman today (Jennings 2010). Elsewhere, the breeding range stretches from Dhofar in southern Oman through parts of Yemen to the western highlands of Saudi Arabia, much the same as that of Arabian Scops Owl *Otus pamelae*. This area has a relatively good supply of water, and consequently more woodland than the rest of Arabia.

Arabian Eagle-Owl *Bubo milesi*, Wadi Darbat, Dhofar, Oman, 16 July 2013 (*Arnoud B van den Berg*). Perhaps same bird as in CD3-13.

In July 2013, Arnoud and Cecilia spent a week at Wadi Darbat in Dhofar, southern Oman. That year, the holy month of Ramadan coincided with the start of the monsoon. People remained at home in the evenings to break their fast, and nobody cared about the flooding on the Wadi Darbat road. Perhaps they also preferred to avoid the thick mist of stinging insects that emerge on monsoon nights. The pools on the road filled up with toads and at night, only the owls disturbed them. At every pool along the roadside they saw an owl perched in a tree, jumping down now and then to grab a toad. Arnoud and Cecilia were very lucky. It will be 12 years before Ramadan coincides with the monsoon again.

During an earlier visit in April 2010, René and I heard many Arabian Eagle-Owls but saw none. In **CD3-16**, five Arabian are hooting, although two of them are almost inaudible. From about 0:50 onwards, there seems to be a loose duet between the nearest two birds, a lower-pitched one to the right and a higher-pitched one to the left of the microphones. Given the pitch difference, this may concern a male and a female. There is no real synchronisation, however, and a simple pitch difference between two males is difficult to rule out.

Arabian Eagle-Owl *Bubo milesi* Wadi Darbat, Dhofar, Oman, 19:52, 18 April 2010. CD3-16
Hooting of five individuals at dusk. Background: Arabian Scops Owl *Otus pamelae*.
100418.MR.195242.12

CD3-17 illustrates a different sound of Arabian Eagle-Owl recorded during that same April visit. The first time I heard these single-note, slightly nasal calls, they seemed to be given in reply to another individual that was hooting. In Eurasian Eagle-Owl *B bubo*, a similar but deeper and harsher call is the female's soliciting call, heard especially around the time of egg-laying.

Arabian Eagle-Owl *Bubo milesi* Wadi Darbat, Dhofar, Oman, 19:41, 18 April 2010. CD3-17
Nasal-sounding calls, possibly soliciting calls of female. 100418.MR.194152.01

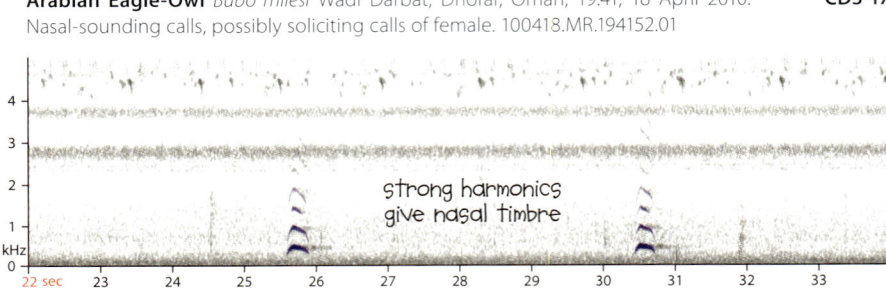

Arabian Eagle-Owl *Bubo milesi*, Wadi Darbat, Dhofar, Oman, 12 November 2013 (*Dick Forsman*)

During our most recent visit in February 2014, the eagle-owls were very quiet. One windy evening, I put a microphone under a cliff from which a male had been calling four years earlier. As it became dark, I recorded a series of deep hoots given in flight (**CD3-18**). It could only have been an Arabian Eagle-Owl, although I have no idea what the sound 'meant'.

With this brief account, we have taken Arabian Eagle-Owl out of obscurity and shown that it sounds very different from its African relatives, but there is still a great deal to learn. For instance, we have not yet heard any juveniles. In Spotted Eagle-Owl, older young have a wheezing begging call (Laidler 2010), higher-pitched than that of Eurasian Eagle-Owl or indeed Pharaoh Eagle-Owl *B ascalaphus*, which also breeds in Arabia.

Arabian Eagle-Owl and Pharaoh Eagle-Owl probably know one another, but not very well. Where they meet, at least one of them is usually rare, and Arabian's preference for wooded areas probably reduces contact to a minimum. When it happens, Pharaoh seems to dominate. Between 1986 and 1991 for example, Pharaoh replaced Arabian at all known breeding wadis near Taïf in Saudi Arabia (Martins & Hirschfeld 1998).

Studies of eagle-owls are not for the faint-hearted. Pharaoh Eagle-Owl is only slightly larger than Arabian Eagle-Owl but a lot more ferocious. In Morocco it is a known predator of Common Barn Owl *Tyto alba* (Thévenot 2006). So the Arabians of Taïf may not have been merely 'replaced'. Should the opportunity arise, *Bubo* may well hunt *Bubo*.

CD3-18   **Arabian Eagle-Owl** *Bubo milesi* Wadi Darbat, Dhofar, Oman, 18:45, 21 February 2014. Series of hoots in flight at dusk. Background: Arabian Scops Owl *Otus pamelae* and Blackstart *Oenanthe melanura*. 140221.MR.184524.12

Pharaoh Eagle-Owl

When Arnoud's airline cancelled a flight home from Morocco in early 2013, this joined a long list of frustrations. The main goal of his trip had been to improve and diversify our recordings of Pharaoh Eagle-Owl *Bubo ascalaphus*, but they had been resolutely silent. By text message, we debated whether strong wind, timing of incubation, or food supply was the cause. The flight cancellation would give him two more nights.

On the second, just as Arnoud was leaving his recording gear under some cliffs, a 4 x 4 vehicle appeared in the distance. Slowly, it made its way towards the gully. Arnoud guessed who would be inside. Some years ago when he and Dick had been drinking coffee at Oued Massa, a photographer had recognised them and shown them some stunning shots of Pharaoh Eagle-Owls. When Arnoud emailed him a few years later to ask where they had been taken, he mentioned Goulimine. It was only after promising secrecy that Arnoud had learned the exact location. He was not even supposed to tell Cecilia, who was travelling with him as usual. That was why the two of them had to sneak out of the gully, creeping from bush to bush so that whoever was in the vehicle would not see them.

In the morning, Arnoud returned alone to pick up his equipment before the local herdsmen appeared. Sure enough it was Torsten the photographer and his wife Kathrin who had arrived for a short holiday the evening before. They had camped and were now preparing a picnic breakfast. Arnoud was invited to join them by their fire for a cup of tea. Torsten told him that the Pharaoh Eagle-Owls had at least two nests to choose from, and changed every other year or so. He thought that the low level of activity this year was down to unusually dry conditions. The gully looked sandier than in previous years, and the usual Long-legged Buzzards *Buteo rufinus* and Lanner Falcons *Falco biarmicus* were not nesting, suggesting that food was scarce. Torsten and Kathrin reported that the wind had died down and they had heard the male Pharaoh from their sleeping bags before dawn. Fortunately, Arnoud's equipment had not let him down (**CD3-19**).

Pharaoh Eagle-Owl *Bubo ascalaphus* Goulimine, Guelmim, Lower Draa, Morocco, 05:06, 13 February 2013. Hooting of a male. 130213.AB.050625.13

CD3-19

Pharaoh Eagle-Owl *Bubo ascalaphus*, Goulimine, Guelmim, Lower Draa, Morocco, 26 March 2010 (*Torsten Pröhl*). Same territory as in CD3-19 but almost three years earlier.

CD3-20 **Pharaoh Eagle-Owl** *Bubo ascalaphus* Jebel Lamdouar, Rissani, Tafilalt, Morocco, 19:54, 11 March 2012. Hooting of a male, with echo. Background: dogs. 120311. AB.195445.02

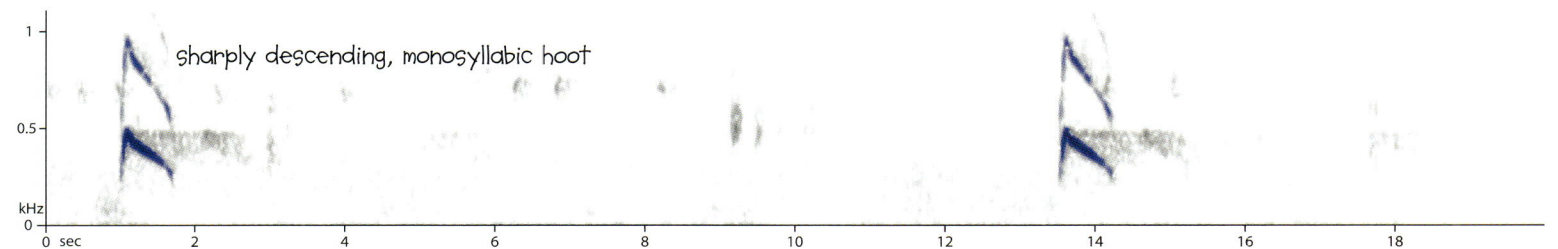

sharply descending, monosyllabic hoot

Pharaoh Eagle-Owl has a very distinctive hoot consisting of a single, rapidly descending and diminishing note. The pitch levels out towards the end, sometimes creating a suggestion of a low final 'syllable', although it is never cleanly separated from the first. **CD3-20** and **CD3-21** were recorded near Rissani, also in Morocco, in different years and territories. Both are typically monosyllabic, although they differ slightly in how quickly the pitch levels out.

CD3-21 **Pharaoh Eagle-Owl** *Bubo ascalaphus* Jebel Ihrs, Rissani, Tafilalt, Morocco, 18:44, 22 March 2004. Hooting of a male. At 0:26 it also gives a series of low grunts. 04.006. AB.04020.11

Pharaoh Eagle-Owl breeds all the way from the Atlantic coast of Africa to the eastern limits of Arabia, although densities are low over much of this vast range. The name '*desertorum*' is sometimes used for Pharaoh in the eastern part of its range (eg, Mikkola 1983). This subspecies is said to be smaller and paler than western birds, but has no basis in sounds. I once recorded a male at Wadi Dana in Jordan and the British Library Sound Archive has recordings from the United Arab Emirates but all sound indistinguishable from Arnoud's Moroccan examples.

Pharaoh Eagle-Owl *Bubo ascalaphus*, Jebel Lamdouar, Rissani, Tafilalt, Morocco, 15 March 2014 (*Arnoud B van den Berg*). Same nesting site as in CD3-20 and CD3-24 but two years later.

CD3-22 **Pharaoh Eagle-Owl** *Bubo ascalaphus* 157 km south of Boujdour, Laayoune-Boujdour, Western Sahara, 21:22, 8 February 2013. Hooting of a presumed female. 130208.AB.212250.12

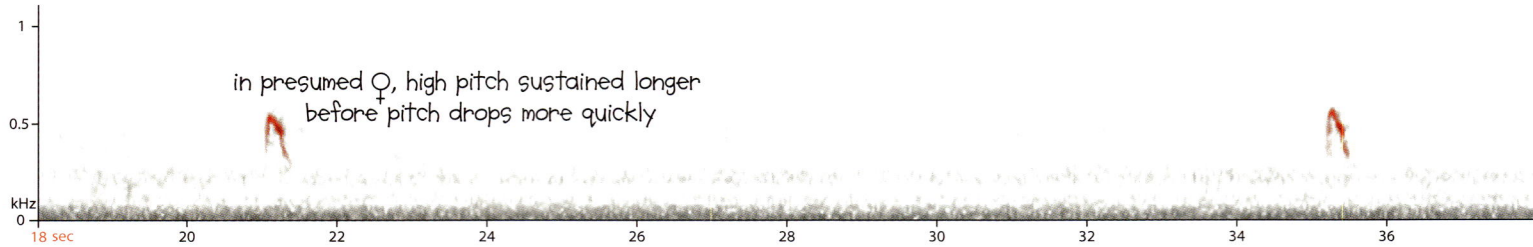

At the other extreme of the breeding range, in Western Sahara, Arnoud did record one slightly different sounding Pharaoh Eagle-Owl. The hooting in **CD3-22** sounds higher-pitched and slightly longer, as if wanting to draw attention to the high pitch, before descending as rapidly as in the other examples. In a weaker recording from the same location (**CD3-23**), this individual is joined briefly by a second one, whose hooting is closer to the other examples you have heard. Although faint, you can hear the second owl several times, eg, at 0:02. Both birds hoot from the same direction, and they seem likely to be a pair in the same territory, with the closer, higher-pitched one being the female. To the best of our knowledge, however, nobody has ever sound recorded hooting of a female Pharaoh Eagle-Owl with certainty, so there is nothing for comparison. According to König et al (2008), females do have a higher-pitched hoot, which would support the provisional sexing of the two individuals in **CD3-23**.

Scouring the internet, I found one call type that was certainly given by a female Pharaoh Eagle-Owl. In a video of a public demonstration at the Centre for Birds of Prey, Charleston, South Carolina (sccontaindergarden 2012), a female demands morsels of food with a very coarse, rising *rrrèh*. This is similar to the soliciting call of female Eurasian Eagle-Owl *B bubo* but noticeably higher-pitched.

We know what sort of prey male Pharaoh Eagle-Owls bring to females, because there have been many studies of the pellets of this species. They clearly prefer small desert mammals, especially jerboas *Jaculus*, gerbils *Gerbillus* and jirds *Meriones*, while invertebrates, especially scorpions and 'camel spiders' Solifugae, are probably their second choice (Boukhamza et al 1994, Rifai et al 2000, Sándor & Orbán 2008, Saint-Girons et al 1974, Shehab & Ciach 2008, Thévenot 2006, Vein & Thévenot 1978). The exact choice depends very much on rare episodes of rainfall. When it comes, the rain can be torrential. Annual plants react by growing new foliage almost immediately, and this in turn provides rodents with the minerals and water

CD3-23 **Pharaoh Eagle-Owl** *Bubo ascalaphus* 157 km south of Boujdour, Laayoune-Boujdour, Western Sahara, 23:38, 8 February 2013. Hooting of a presumed pair, distant. 130208.AB.233850.12

necessary to reproduce and lactate (Shenbrot et al 2010). Owls that live in the desert vary the exact timing of their breeding attempts according to rodent numbers. Perhaps this is why our visits never quite seem to coincide with the main courtship period. In Portugal a few 100 km to the north, Eurasian Eagle-Owls are at their most vocal in January and February. At the same time of year, the Pharaohs of Morocco seem to be much, much quieter.

Once Arnoud, Håkan and Killian were guided to a breeding cliff close to a village. Arnoud positioned his microphones before the male emerged, and as expected it hooted briefly before flying off. Not wanting to leave his equipment overnight for curious villagers to find, Arnoud climbed back up the slope. He was very surprised when the male started hooting again very close by, just as he was rolling up the cables. While Arnoud pressed record and held his breath, Killian accidentally knocked over a tripod some distance away. At this, the owl flew out, giving 'devil's cackles' as it went (**CD3-24**). In the original recording there were three calls in sequence, then Arnoud lost his balance, spoiling the more distant calls.

CD3-24   **Pharaoh Eagle-Owl** *Bubo ascalaphus* Jebel Lamdouar, Rissani, Tafilalt, Morocco, 19:02, 10 March 2012. 'Devil's cackles' of a male. Arnoud's subsequent tumble has been deleted. 120310.AB.190244.21

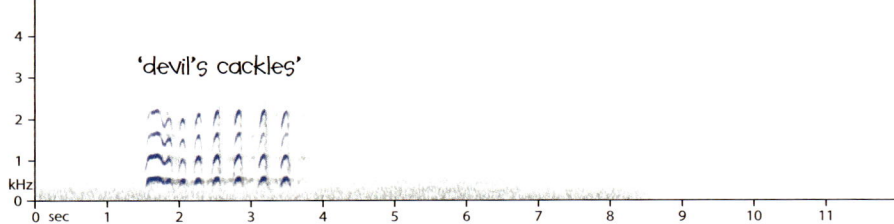

Rissani, where **CD3-24** was recorded, is perhaps the best-known area in Morocco for Pharaoh Eagle-Owls. It is right on the edge of the Sahara. Although there are cultivations around the town, the area is essentially flat desert with high, table-like rocky outcrops. Because of its outstanding beauty, several famous international films have been shot there. Rissani's other claim to fame is that the ground is rich in fossils from the Devonian era, many of which are dug up from dangerous 10 m deep pits.

Pharaoh Eagle-Owl *Bubo ascalaphus*, adult at nest, Momia, Rissani, Tafilalt, Morocco, 30 March 2010 (*Arnoud B van den Berg*). More than 10 weeks later, begging fledglings in CD3-25 & 26 were recorded here.

other territories in the area. In return for up to date information, Arnoud brought customers to Lahcen's cave and made him known to as many birders as possible.

One year, Lahcen told Arnoud about a breeding pair in a natural amphitheatre with beautiful acoustics, surrounded by a vast stretch of open rocky desert. Many centuries ago the Portuguese turned it into a fortress by putting a wall across the opening. The site became famous as a movie set for several films, including *The Mummy* in 1999. When Arnoud and Cecilia arrived to spend the night at this desolate site in mid-June 2010, two young Pharaoh Eagle-Owls haunted the fortress virtually all night long. In **CD3-25**, you can hear one of these fledged juveniles begging persistently at fairly close range. In **CD3-26**, both young are calling at shorter intervals, due to the arrival of a parent. The single hoot towards the end was the only adult call recorded during the entire night.

Pharaoh Eagle-Owl *Bubo ascalaphus* Momia, Rissani, Tafilalt, Morocco, 05:51, 15 June 2010. Begging calls of one of two fledged juveniles. 100615.AB.055100.01   CD3-25

Pharaoh Eagle-Owl *Bubo ascalaphus* Momia, Rissani, Tafilalt, Morocco, 03:55, 15 June 2010. Begging calls of two fledged juveniles, with a single hoot from an adult male. 100615.AB.035500.31   CD3-26

Years ago, Arnoud made friends with a fossil seller named Lahcen Ouacha, who has a stall at a cave entrance on the road out of Rissani towards Alnif. When Lahcen saw tourists striking out into the desert to visit beauty spots they had seen in films, he would cycle after them with his fossils. Arnoud was one of the first birders to visit the area, which has since become popular. When Lahcen and one or two of his colleagues saw birders with binoculars, they offered to show them a Pharaoh Eagle-Owl. In the end, Lahcen got to know the owls rather well. Later, when Arnoud brought birding tour groups to Rissani, Lahcen kept an even closer eye on the owls, and went to look for

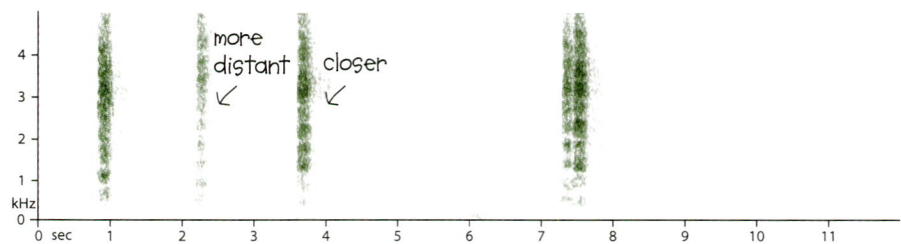

Pharaoh Eagle-Owl *Bubo ascalaphus*, Rissani, Tafilalt, Morocco, 8 April 2010 (*Arnoud B van den Berg*). Roost on cliff 4 km from Monia (CD3-25 & 26) and 3.5 km from Jebel Ihrs (CD3-21).

Pharaoh Eagle-Owl's modern links with Egypt go back to 1809, when Savigny described '*Bubo ascalaphus*' based on a specimen from Upper Egypt, in a 23-volume work on Egypt commissioned by Napoleon. Savigny was well versed in ancient literature,

Pharaoh Eagle-Owl *Bubo ascalaphus*, male, Hurghada, Eastern Desert, Egypt, 15 March 2009 (*Dick Forsman*)

and the scientific name of his owl was based on Askalaphos, a figure from Greek mythology. Askalaphos was the custodian of the orchard of Hades, god of the underworld. After he told the other gods that Persephone had eaten a pomegranate in the underworld, they punished him by turning him into an owl (Ovid, *Metamorphoses* V, 534).

Although Savigny originally described Pharaoh Eagle-Owl as a species, for most of the following two centuries it was considered a subspecies of Eurasian Eagle-Owl. With a body length of 45-50 cm, it is around 75% of the size of Eurasian. The plumage of Pharaoh is much paler, and its ground colour is sandy-pinkish. The eyes are larger in proportion to the head. Diagnostic features include dark streaking on the upper breast but not the rest of the underparts, and a much more strongly marked black outline to the facial disc. Pharaoh is an extremely beautiful owl.

According to Wink et al (2009), Pharaoh Eagle-Owl and Eurasian Eagle-Owl differ by 3.5% in mtDNA, a level typical of species, not subspecies. In fact, Pharaoh is apparently not even the closest relative of Eurasian. That position belongs to Cape Eagle-Owl *B capensis*, an intermediate-sized predator of the Rift Valley, occurring from Eritrea and Ethiopia to South Africa.

What happens when Pharaoh Eagle-Owl meets one of its larger northern relatives? Vaurie (1960) studied museum specimens from the contact zone between *ascalaphus* and the *interpositus* subspecies of Eurasian Eagle-Owl in Israel, and concluded that hybridisation was taking place. There has not been any molecular research to back up this view. Vaurie (1960) also suggested that Pharaoh and Eurasian occurred together on the southern slopes of the Atlas mountains in Algeria, based mainly upon the labels of two museum specimens. There have been no subsequent records and there is no proof that Eurasian ever bred there (Isenmann & Moali 2000), so it seems that only Pharaoh occurs in northern Africa, and that there is no opportunity to study interactions with Eurasian.

When we asked Håkan what he thought would happen when a Eurasian Eagle-Owl met a Pharaoh Eagle-Owl, he told us he had found remains of Ospreys *Pandion haliaetus* in three Eurasian nests. Håkan smiled and said that if they met, the Eurasian would eat the Pharaoh.

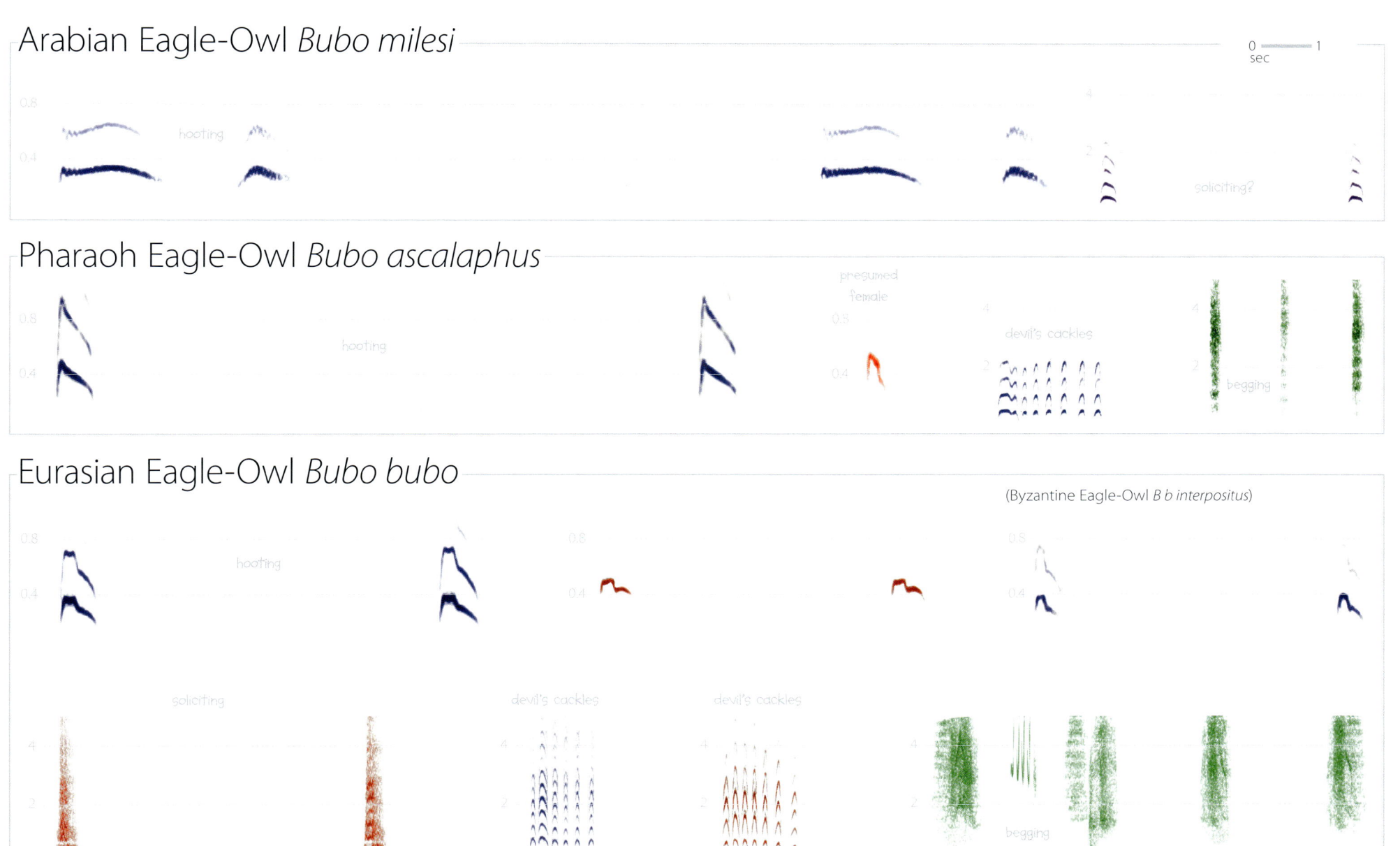

Eurasian Eagle-Owl

A male Eurasian Eagle-Owl *Bubo bubo* plays the landscape like a musical instrument. Crags of a certain shape and orientation to wind, water and forest allow him to project his hoots as far as possible. Each one has a sweet spot, ideal for targeting those listeners that matter the most. 'Floating' males must be repelled at all costs, neighbours should be kept exactly where they were yesterday, and a female's demands must be met.

A disused quarry with a tiny lake inside makes a fine bass drum. This one is in Extremadura, Spain. Normally the resident male plays it from the highest point on its rim. The quarry is tilted slightly towards the east, where neighbours on the cliffs of a gorge will hear him better than most. For listeners inside the quarry, he resonates long and powerfully. I'm sure his mate enjoys the sensation every bit as much as I do.

Tonight there is no wind and the temperature is well below freezing. The roosting Griffon Vultures *Gyps fulvus* might as well be rocks. It is easy to forget a huge dormitory of White Wagtails *Motacilla alba* until the female flies too close and wafts them like dust off a shelf. A great roar of tiny wings tails slowly away as the wagtails return nervously to their perches.

Some time later the male hoots again while taking off and flying across the quarry (**CD3-27**). When he passes just a few metres away, the movement of his echoes reveals the shape of the quarry walls. Each hoot consists of two notes slurred together, the first higher and louder than the second. The female responds with gruff *rrrèh* calls from somewhere down on the right.

CD3-27 **Eurasian Eagle-Owl** *Bubo bubo* Alcántara, Extremadura, Spain, 04:35, 30 January 2012. Hooting of a male in flight, with *rrrrèh* calls of a female. 120130.MR.043528.11

160 km to the south, another pair breeds on a rocky headland overlooking the controversial Alqueva reservoir. Submerged below them, Aldeia da Luz ('village of the light') was sacrificed to the gods of progress when the Guadiana River was dammed in 2002. The owls also lost one of their old homes, a nest that disappeared below the surface. At least the water is good for one thing. It carries the male's hooting over very long distances. In Sweden, Håkan once heard one hooting from an island that turned out to be 5 km away when he measured this on a map.

A huge, well-worn boulder forms the highest point of the headland. With such an obvious songpost, all I need to do is shelter my microphones from the wind, retreat some 500 m and wait. The male calls twice from this boulder during the night. **CD3-28** must be more or less how a male Eurasian Eagle-Owl hears himself. He is much closer to the microphones than his echoes, so the recording lacks the aura of the ones I made in the quarry. In the background, his mate gives *rrrèh* calls from a

CD3-28 **Eurasian Eagle-Owl** *Bubo bubo* Alqueva reservoir, Alentejo, Portugal, 05:11, 9 January 2012. Hooting of a male at a distance of just 2 m, with distant soliciting calls of a female. 120109.MR.051100.00

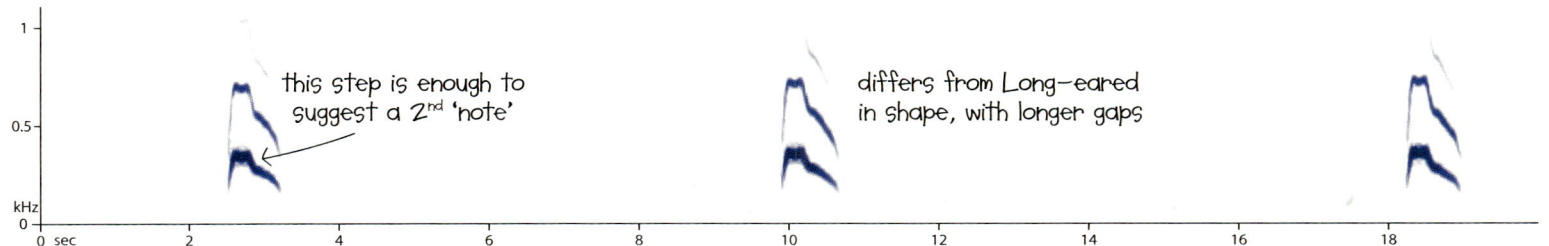

CD3-29   **Eurasian Eagle-Owl** *Bubo bubo* Alqueva reservoir, Alentejo, Portugal, 20:22, 8 January 2012. *Rrrèh* calls or soliciting calls of a female at a distance of just 2 m. Background: Northern Lapwing *Vanellus vanellus*. 120108.MR.202258.01

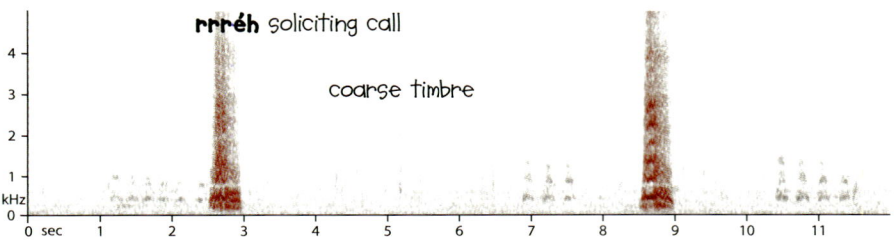

During the autumn and early winter, females are more likely to hoot than to *rrrèh*. In October 2002, Arnoud and I recorded a pair in South Korea, belonging to the far eastern subspecies *kiautschensis*. The hooting started as we were returning from a small wetland, under a bright moon. The first owl in **CD3-30** is a female, and her hooting is much higher-pitched than that of her partner. Now listen to a male and a female hooting in Bulgaria, on the shores of the Black Sea (**CD3-31**). Females not only tend to sound higher-pitched than males; they also have a smaller pitch interval between the first and second notes. In other words, hooting of females descends less than that of males.

lower cliff some 250 m away. Earlier in the night, she gave the same calls from the big boulder (**CD3-29**). Håkan has noticed that during the courtship period, these soliciting calls of the female become smoother and more inviting while still retaining a dangerous tone of voice. They remind him of a female spider, as if she were saying, "come to me… and I will eat you."

In December 2009 I visited the Sierra Norte near Seville, Spain, where Vincenzo Penteriani and colleagues have been studying Eurasian Eagle-Owls for many years. Much of their research has focussed on visible aspects of hooting. Watch an eagle-owl hooting by day, at dusk or under a full moon, and you may notice that with every hoot, a white and more or less rectangular patch or 'badge' appears on its throat. This becomes brighter during the territorial-mating period, and females have brighter badges than males (Penteriani et al 2006). Badges are honest signals of condition: research has shown that

CD3-30   **Eurasian Eagle-Owl** *Bubo bubo* Upo wetland, Gyeongsangnam-do, South Korea, 18:36, 17 October 2002. Hooting duet of female and male, four days before a full moon. Background: Middendorff's Bean Goose *Anser middendorffii* and Mallard *Anas platyrhynchos*. 02.030.AB.10230.31

CD3-31   **Eurasian Eagle-Owl** *Bubo bubo* Cape Kaliakra, Dobrich, Bulgaria, 18:56, 14 February 2012. Female and male hooting on a very cold night when the temperature was -12°C. Background: distant dogs and Mallard *Anas platyrhynchos*. 120214.MR.185642.12

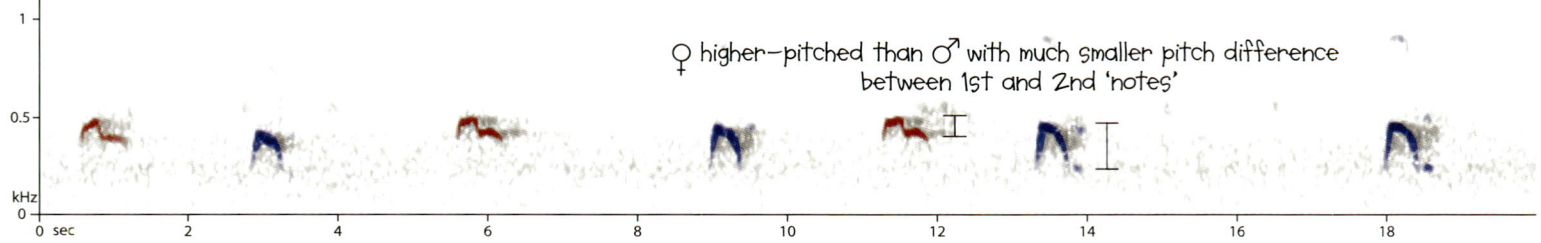

males with brighter ones breed more successfully (Penteriani et al 2007). By hooting most often at twilight, eagle-owls can flash their badges when they contrast most strongly with the background (Penteriani & Delgado 2009). For the same reason, they call more often and move to higher, more conspicuous songposts when there is strong moonlight (Penteriani et al 2010).

At dusk when I recorded **CD3-32**, I was amazed to hear up to four males and one very distant female calling in the space of just two minutes. The nearest two males were only about 500 m apart. At one particular spot, Vincenzo has heard up to eight eagle-owls at dusk, four males and four females. Amazingly, the closest pairs nest only 250 m apart. The area has high densities of European Rabbits *Oryctolagus cuniculus*, no doubt explaining why it is able to support around 40 pairs of eagle-owls in only 100 km2 (Delgado et al 2013). Vincenzo and colleagues have recently discovered hierarchies within this rich social fabric. It seems that in clusters of neighbouring territories, the males hoot in a particular order. The male that hoots first occupies the best territory and raises the most young, and also has the brightest badge and the highest percentage of red blood cells. The other males apparently hold him in such esteem that if he fails to hoot during the evening chorus, they remain silent too (Penteriani et al 2014).

Eurasian Eagle-Owl *Bubo bubo* Sierra Norte, Andalusia, Spain, 18:06, 10 December 2009. Hooting of four males and one female. Background: Azure-winged Magpie *Cyanopica cooki*, Dartford Warbler *Sylvia undata*, Common Blackbird *Turdus merula*, Song Thrush *T philomelos*, European Robin *Erithacus rubecula* and Dunnock *Prunella modularis*. 091210.MR.180602.31

CD3-32

Male hooting peaks during the territorial and courtship phases of the annual cycle, before gradually becoming less frequent through the rest of the breeding season (Delgado & Penteriani 2006). From late August, juveniles start to disperse: they become 'floaters'. From roughly September to December, territorial males direct their hooting mainly at male floaters, which helps to prevent potentially deadly confrontations. They also hoot to maintain stable relations with their neighbours. Then in January and February, they hoot for the female too. During the

CD3-33   **Eurasian Eagle-Owl** *Bubo bubo* Alcántara, Extremadura, Spain, 00:33, 30 January 2012. *Rrrèh* calls of female, hooting of both and from 0:30, nest-showing call of male. Females make the same sound when stimulating nestlings to accept food (Mebs & Scherzinger 2004). 120130.MR.003301.11

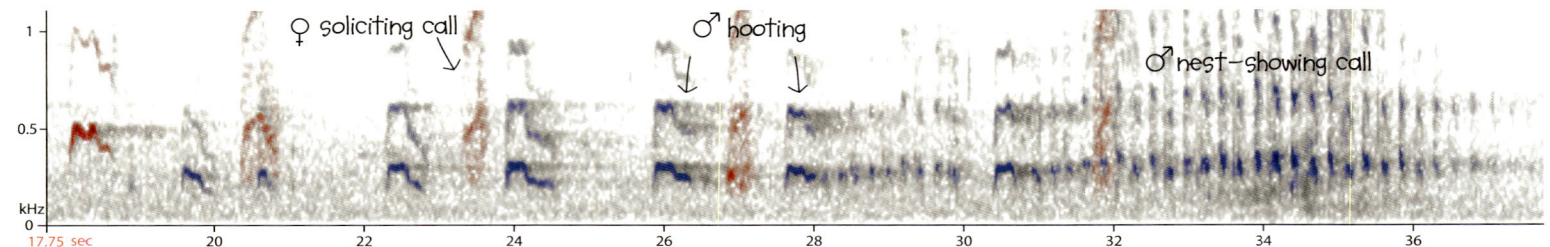

courtship period, male songposts are often lower than during the territorial phase, because the female tends to stay close to the nest (Penteriani 2002).

As with most owls, male Eurasian Eagle-Owls propose nest sites to females who then make the final decision. In **CD3-33**, a male is proposing a nest in the resonant quarry with the Griffon Vulture roost. At the beginning, we can hear his wingbeats as he flies rapidly to a high perch on the left where the female calls *rrrèh*. Both owls hoot, then the male starts adding a few short, extra notes. As he flies down to a proposed nest on the right (from 0:30), he gives a continuous, rather breathless hooting with higher-pitched chitters interspersed. The female does not follow him this time, but comes a little closer without visiting the nest.

Sounds associated with copulation are loud and carry far. **CD3-34** starts with the male hooting on the right and the female giving *rrrèh* calls on the left. The male then flies across to the female, still hooting. Then he erupts into an excited, rapid-fire hooting that has a chimpanzee-like quality. A moment later the female gives a high-pitched whine: her copulation call (0:32). She follows this with one hoot of her own, perhaps a hint of

CD3-34   **Eurasian Eagle-Owl** *Bubo bubo* Alcántara, Extremadura, Spain, 02:16, 30 January 2012. Hooting of male and *rrrèh* calls of female. Then excited, rapid-fire hooting of male and copulation whine of female. 120130.MR.021609.02

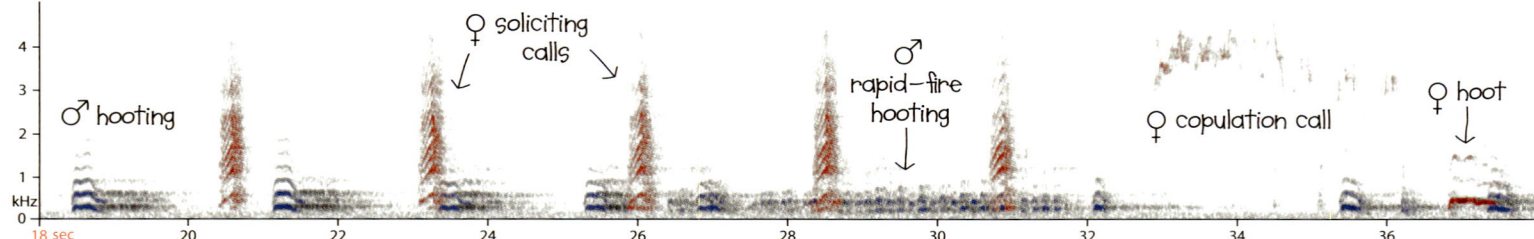

aggression. Then with a series of harsh, impatient *rrrèh* calls, she sends the male off hunting again.

If you go close to an eagle-owl nest without knowing it, you may get the fright of your life. 'Devil's cackles' are excitement calls the owls use not only in this context but throughout the year, and especially during the pre-laying period. Most often, devil's cackles precede or follow pair contact (Delgado & Penteriani 2006). **CD3-35** from the Sierra Norte illustrates them at their most diabolic. **CD3-36** from southern Finland shows how loud and resonant they can be, alongside the hooting of a male.

CD3-35   **Eurasian Eagle-Owl** *Bubo bubo* Sierra Norte, Andalusia, Spain, 20:38, 9 December 2009. 'Devil's cackles' of a female. Background: dogs. 091209.MR.203835.31

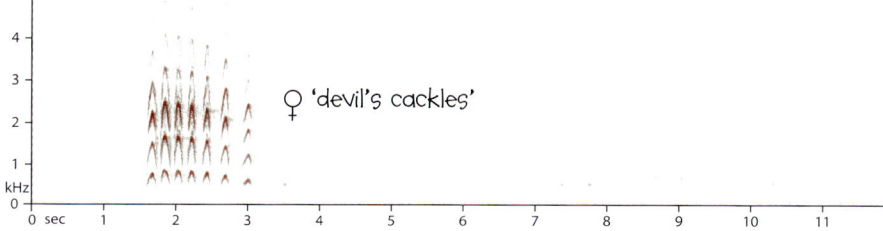

CD3-36   **Eurasian Eagle-Owl** *Bubo bubo* Porkala, Kirkkonummi, Uusimaa, Finland, 21:15, 17 May 2009. 'Devil's cackles' of a female, with hooting of a male. The female was reacting to Dick's reappearance after a fairly long absence. Background: Eurasian Wigeon *Anas penelope*, Mallard *A platyrhynchos*, Common Teal *A crecca*, Eurasian Woodcock *Scolopax rusticola*, Common Cuckoo *Cuculus canorus*, Common Blackbird *Turdus merula*, Song Thrush *T philomelos* and European Robin *Erithacus rubecula*. 090517.DF.215000.02

CD3-37   **Eurasian Eagle-Owl** *Bubo bubo* Sierra Norte, Andalusia, Spain, 06:42, 11 December 2009. Slurred 'devil's cackles' of a female. 091211.MR.064234.12

CD3-38   **Eurasian Eagle-Owl** *Bubo bubo* Parque Natural do Tejo Internacional, Beira-Baixa, Portugal, 21:04, 23 September 2009. Distant 'devil's cackles' of a male, with rutting Red Deer *Cervus elaphus*. Background: Iberian Midwife Toad *Alytes cisternasii*. 090923.MR.210458.31

At times the individual cackles can become slurred together as shown by a female in **CD3-37**, reminding me of the way a dog sometimes slurs its barks. When recording autumn migration I sometimes pick up very distant devil's cackles of eagle-owls from my back yard, where lots of houses have the effect of dispersing the sound and making it sound muffled. There are many dogs in the neighbourhood, so it is easy to miss a distant cackle. **CD3-38** is an autumn example with some more impressive wild mammals: rutting Red Deer *Cervus elaphus*. The owl is clearly a male, because of the low pitch of his devil's cackles. The closer

CD3-39 **Eurasian Eagle-Owl** *Bubo bubo* Sierra Norte, Andalusia, Spain, 23:23, 9 December 2009. 'Devil's cackles' of a male. Background: dogs. 091209.MR.232312.01

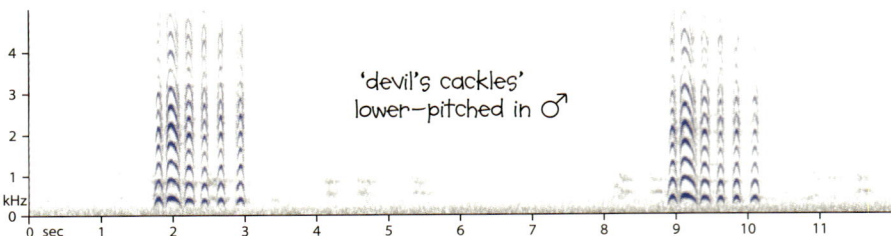

male in **CD3-39** was a Spanish second-winter that had already completed his first breeding season as a territory holding 'adult' (mated to the female in **CD3-35**).

Dick has often visited nests to ring the young. Besides devil's cackles, he tells me that some angry females may give a loud, monosyllabic 'crack', a sign that they are 'losing it completely'. Nevertheless, this is a fairly shy species that rarely attacks humans. Many other creatures are less fortunate. As opportunistic hunters, Eurasian Eagle-Owls will take mammals up to the size of a Brown Hare *Lepus europaeus* or even a young Red Fox *Vulpes vulpes* (eg, Olsson 1979). They often take other owls and raptors, with Common Buzzard *Buteo buteo* and Long-eared Owl *Asio otus* among their favourites (Mikkola 1983). It all depends on what is plentiful and easy to catch in their territory. During peak vole years in northern Europe, their diet may be almost identical to that of the Eurasian Pygmy Owl *Glaucidium passerinum*, which is 30 times smaller by weight.

Being close to the top of the food chain, it is perhaps surprising that eagle-owls have a well-developed distraction display. They only use it as a last resort when all other attempts to warn enemies away from large young have failed. Exposed and fluffed up, a desperate adult looks the intruder in the eye before throwing itself to the ground, dragging its wings and looking quite bedraggled, like a wader feigning injury near its nest. The irregular stream of high-pitched humming and piping that accompanies this display reminds Håkan of a Brown Rat *Rattus norvegicus* being tortured, or perhaps trodden on.

Patrick Franke witnessed a distraction display in June 2013 while taking part in a ringing session in Germany. As the ringer got close to the juvenile, the presumed adult female flew off the nest, landed on the floor of the quarry and feigned injury. Despite a strong wind, Patrick managed to record the owl's weird calls (**CD3-40**).

Eurasian Eagle-Owl *Bubo bubo* Kroppenstedt, Sachsen-Anhalt, Germany, 15 June 2013. Distraction display of adult, presumed female, while juvenile was being ringed. Patrick Franke.

Eurasian Eagle-Owl *Bubo bubo*, female, Sipoo, Uusimaa, Finland, 4 July 2014 (*Dick Forsman*). Showing distraction behaviour, trying to lead intruder away from hidden fledglings (compare CD3-40).

Eurasian Eagle-Owl *Bubo bubo*, female, Kirkkonummi, Uusimaa, Finland, 4 June 2006 (*Dick Forsman*). At same nest as in CD3-36 & CD3-41 to 44 but in a different year.

Nestlings also have some special defensive tactics that they use when they feel threatened. From about 15 days of age, they will hiss and bill-snap in response to any disturbance (**CD3-41**). Some nestlings may also raise their wings in a 'forward-threat posture' common to many owls (Desfayes & Géroudet 1949), which has the effect of greatly increasing their apparent size. Half-grown young may also lie on their backs and raise their claws in threat (Schnurre 1936).

Eurasian Eagle-Owl *Bubo bubo* Getberg, Kirkkonummi, Uusimaa, Finland, 05:30, 8 June 2003. Hissing and bill-snaps of a nestling about five weeks old. Background: Great Spotted Woodpecker *Dendrocopos major* and Willow Warbler *Phylloscopus trochilus*. 03.003.DF.10708.11

CD3-41

Eurasian Eagle-Owl *Bubo bubo*, fledgling, Kirkkonummi, Uusimaa, Finland, 24 June 2009 (*Dick Forsman*). Same as in CD3-42.

Juvenile Eurasian Eagle-Owls beg with a loud, slightly harsh, short hiss. It may carry as far as 1 km (Frey 1973), while seeming to be much closer. This can sometimes lead to confusion with young owls of other species that have much weaker voices and may indeed be much closer to the observer. The two juveniles in **CD3-42**, recorded in Finland in late June, were already very large, and they called virtually all night long.

CD3-42   **Eurasian Eagle-Owl** *Bubo bubo* Porkala, Kirkkonummi, Uusimaa, Finland, 00:16, 23 June 2009. Begging calls of two fledged juveniles. Background: European Nightjar *Caprimulgus europaeus* and Song Thrush *Turdus philomelos*. 090623.DF.001620.01

CD3-43   **Eurasian Eagle-Owl** *Bubo bubo* Inkoo, Uusimaa, Finland, 01:00, 7 June 2009. Chitter calls of a seven-week-old nestling in a quarry, with begging calls of another. Background: Common Redstart *Phoenicurus phoenicurus*. 090607.DF.010000.01

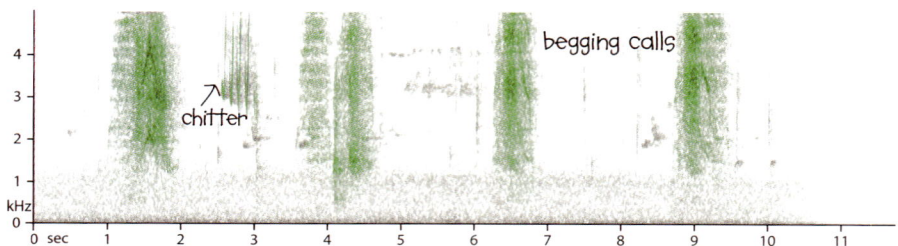

As in other owl species, there is a chitter call used mainly as a signal of discomfort. According to Scherzinger (1974a), chicks start using this a day before hatching when the eggs are turned, then after they hatch it becomes gradually louder. The nestlings in **CD3-43** were seven weeks old.

In **CD3-44**, a whole family reacts to the arrival of an adult male with prey. Female soliciting calls on the right are immediately followed by juvenile begging calls on the left. The male hoots and

CD3-44   **Eurasian Eagle-Owl** *Bubo bubo* Inkoo, Uusimaa, Finland, 01:00, 7 June 2009. Hooting of male, *rrrèh* calls and bill-snapping of female and begging of two nestlings. Background: Mallard *Anas platyrhynchos* and Common Redstart *Phoenicurus phoenicurus*. 090607.DF.010000.01

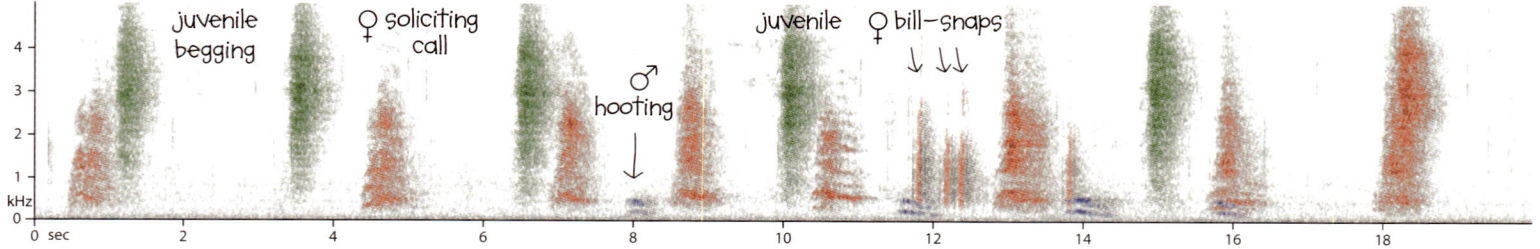

the female bill-snaps, and then a second, fainter juvenile joins the first. Towards the end, the young also engage in bill-snapping, and some deep sounds suggest exercising of wings.

Karla Bloem of the International Owl Center has been studying the vocal development of another eagle-owl, the Great Horned Owl *B virginianus* of the Americas. She is breeding wild injured adults and observing them and their offspring with remote cameras and microphones. On 8 October 2013, she wrote to me: "Very interestingly, the owlets were able to produce 'hoots' of the proper rhythm at just over two weeks of age, albeit in very squeaky little voices. These little hoots only continued for three weeks. The owlets, when separated from their parents at 5 months of age, began hooting again, but their voice quality was like a teenage boy whose voice was changing. All three owlets finally attained their adult voice quality and produced territorial-style hoots indistinguishable from adults when they were between 6.5 and 7 months of age. In all instances, there was no practicing. They simply produced hoots of the proper rhythm in the proper context from the beginning. Even at 2 to 5 weeks of age their heads lowered forward when hooting and their featherless tail stubs tilted upward, although not as much as adults."

Sounds of owls are thought to be 'hard-wired', not learned. Owls are unable to add attractive new sounds to their repertoire or imitate other individuals. The fixed nature of their vocal repertoire is of crucial importance in taxonomy. Owl sounds evolve through natural selection or drift, and this is a slower kind of change than can be achieved through learning. When two populations sound different, it strongly suggests that they are separately evolving lineages, which have not been in contact for a long time.

One population still included in Eurasian Eagle-Owl does seem to sound slightly different. Rothschild & Hartert (1910) described *B b interpositus* or 'Byzantine Eagle-Owl' based on a specimen obtained at Ereğli in southern Turkey, and that happens to be where I first recorded it (**CD3-45**). In the far east of Turkey, Roy Slaterus and I came across another pair a year later (**CD3-46**). Additional recordings from Georgia, Israel and Turkey made by other people gave seven adult *interpositus*, of which four males and two females were hooting. Compared to other Eurasian Eagle-Owls, the lower second note follows the higher first one slightly more quickly in Byzantine. Eurasian can vary quite extensively, so there is almost certainly some overlap in this character.

Such a subtle difference based on a tiny sample would hardly be worthy of comment, were it not for a surprise genetic result. According to Wink et al (2009), a single individual of *interpositus* from Israel was more closely related to Pharaoh Eagle-Owl *B ascalaphus* than to Eurasian Eagle-Owl. Its mtDNA differed from Pharaoh by 2%, suggesting that *interpositus* may even be a separate species.

Other subspecies of Eurasian Eagle-Owl are much easier to identify than *interpositus*, such as the very pale *sibiricus*, breeding in northern Russia from the Urals to the river Ob. Up on the Arctic tundra there is an eagle-owl that can be completely white, but that is a very different creature altogether.

CD3-45   '**Byzantine Eagle-Owl**' *Bubo bubo interpositus* Ereğli, Konya, Turkey, 5 May 2001. Hooting of a male at dusk. Background: Eastern Black-eared Wheatear *Oenanthe melanoleuca*. 01.016.MR.14710.12

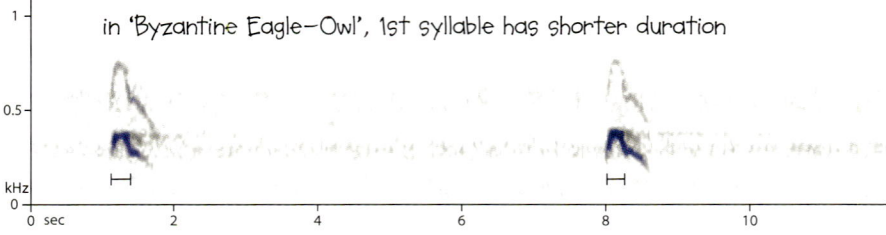

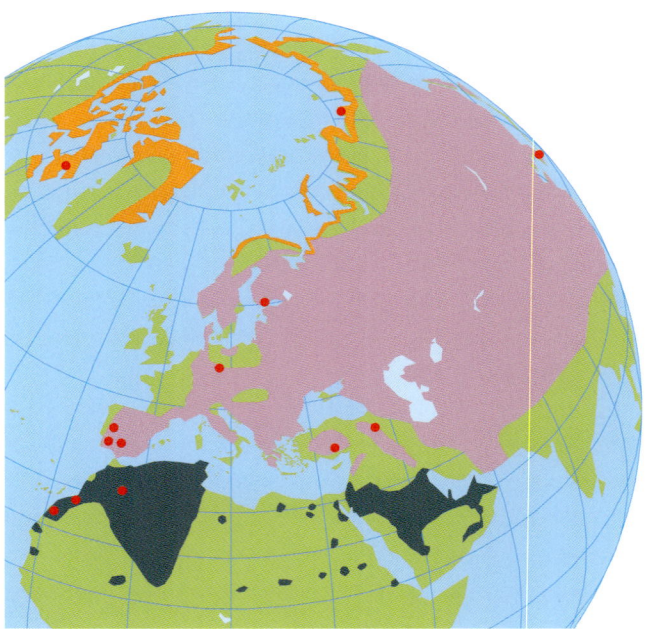

Approximate breeding distribution of Pharaoh Eagle-Owl *Bubo ascalaphus* ■, Eurasian Eagle-Owl *B bubo* ■ and Snowy Owl *B scandiacus* ■. Recording locations indicated by ● dots.

CD3-46   '**Byzantine Eagle-Owl**' *Bubo bubo interpositus* Van, Van, Turkey, 3 June 2002. Hooting of a male at dusk. Background: Variable Toad *Pseudepidalea variabilis*, European Nightjar *Caprimulgus europaeus* and Eastern Black-eared Wheatear *Oenanthe melanoleuca*. 02.032.MR.05403.11

Snowy Owl

Allow me to take you north and east, out of the Western Palearctic to the Lena delta in arctic Siberia. It is June and the sun will not dip below the horizon until early August. Spring is late this year, and temperatures have been below zero for much of the month. Nevertheless, there is plenty for me to record while waiting for the ice to break. Flock after flock of Curlew Sandpipers *Calidris ferruginea* and other waders have been arriving, often in full song, only to huddle together on the gravel banks of a small stream of melt water that has cleared away a little snow.

The wind has been strong most days, and very cold. On a day of mild southerlies, the snow melts. When the wind stops altogether, every creature makes the most of a few precious hours of calm. Pacific Golden Plovers *Pluvialis fulva* whistle, Pectoral Sandpipers *C melanotos* boom and Red-throated Pipits *Anthus cervinus* sing over new claimed territories. Soon a fresh gale starts from some other direction. Blizzards blanket the tundra and all the waders flock to the gravel again.

We are staying at the Lena-Nordenskjöld International Biological Station, situated on the banks of the main channel of the Lena, about 65 km from the nearest town of Tiksi. Its scientific director is Dr Vladimir Pozdnyakov. I have maybe 200 words of Russian while Vladimir and colleague Yuri Sofronov speak about the same amount of English. We are able to talk about a few things, but there is so much more that I would like to ask.

There is no spring here, only a monumental battle as summer wrests power from winter. In front of the station lies an 8 km wide stretch of the river Lena. When I arrived it was covered in a thick layer of ice. At the river's source some 4400 km to the south, winter ended weeks earlier. Here in the delta the ice rose slightly higher each day on the accumulating melt water, cracking here and there until it almost reached the top of the riverbank. Eventually we saw some clear water somewhere far out in the middle of the ice. The break-up was rapid, and on 16 June we awoke to find that the last ice sheet near the station had finally gone.

After several weeks in a tundra landscape of rolling hills, we are navigating a labyrinth of channels between tiny, flat, waterlogged islands. Woolly Mammoth *Mammuthus primigenius* bones still emerge from the banks each year. It is strange to see Willow Grouse *Lagopus lagopus* flying low over the water like

Lena delta, near Lena-Nordenskjöld biological station, Yakutia, Russia, 13 June 2004 (*Magnus Robb*). During the long battle between winter and summer, only one Snowy Owl *Bubo scandiacus* appeared here.

ducks. On making a short stop, we hear the ecstatic long calls of a pair of Ross's Gulls *Rhodostethia rosea*. They are heading for the outer delta, and so are we.

As we make our way towards the island of Nizhny Bobrowski, the big question is whether this will prove to be a 'lemming year'. The four-year lemming cycle suggests it should be, but proof is lacking. Most years, lemming numbers are low and there are no Snowy Owls *Bubo scandiacus* at all in the delta. We did not see many lemmings at the station, but a single male Snowy hunting on its slopes gave me some hope. Vladimir tells me that conditions in the delta itself can be very different. Navigating one channel, I think I see a distant Snowy on the ground. Vladimir is not convinced. Then after flushing a female from the top of a bank, right beside the channel, we jump ashore to investigate.

Snowy Owls do not nest on snow. They prefer windswept places where the snow clears first. The nest of this pair is on a flat area near the highest point of a steep bank. It contains six eggs as well as several dead Siberian Brown Lemmings *Lemmus sibiricus*. I am impressed to find the severed head of a Stoat *Mustela erminea* nearby, among moulted feathers and pellets. While Vladimir and Yuri take measurements for a paper they are working on (Pozdnyakov & Sofronov 2005), I make my first Snowy Owl recordings. At first the male mobs me with furious cackles. Soon he settles on the opposite bank where he fixes me with bright yellow eyes, lowering his wings and holding his body in a horizontal position. He inflates his throat, then hoots while thrusting his head down and cocking his tail at right angles to the ground (**CD3-47**).

Less then 3 km further along the same channel we find a second pair, this time with five nestlings and three eggs. One of them is still hatching, a task that may take up to three days to complete

Snowy Owl *Bubo scandiacus* Lena delta, Yakutia, Russia, 23:00, 24 June 2004. Hooting of a male. Background: Curlew Sandpiper *Calidris ferruginea*, Dunlin *C alpina* and Lapland Longspur *Calcarius lapponicus*. 04.032.MR.05945.31

CD3-47

(Potapov & Sale 2012). The second male does not mob us but starts hooting from the opposite bank almost as soon as we arrive near the nest. The female stays further away. Like all that I recorded, the male in **CD3-48** hoots in two-note 'strophes', the first hoot marginally higher than the second. At other times, they may give single-note hoots. There is no running water in the recording, because I am using a parabolic microphone and have positioned it low, where it has a 'view' of the owl but not the channel. Instead, we can hear at least nine other species of tundra birds.

Besides hooting in threat to enemies like us, male Snowy Owls hoot to other males as a territorial display, and to females to gain their attention. In the Lena delta in 2004, nests were no closer than 1.5 km from one another (Pozdnyakov & Sofronov 2005) so presumably males can hear each other from at least that distance. Human observers have reported hearing hoots at distances from about 1 km (Potapov & Sale 2012), to an incredible 11.3 km (Sutton 1932).

When do Snowy Owls hoot? The extreme difficulties involved in Arctic fieldwork in late winter mean that the beginning is difficult to establish. Schaanning (1907) heard 'courtship notes' in Novaya Zemlya as early as 5 April, and Sutton (1932) heard hooting on Southampton Island from 25 April onwards. Hooting is frequent during incubation and the early nestling phase, based on my own experience. Watson (1957) heard it frequently on Baffin Island until the end of July, with the last male hooting on 23 August, after its young could fly.

While the male Snowy Owl's hooting dominates the spring soundscape, the female hoots rarely and then only close to the nest (Potapov & Sale 2012). I have never been lucky enough to hear female hooting myself, but Scherzinger (1974b), who worked with captive birds, wrote a detailed description. A recording by Claude Chappuis of a captive individual seemed to fit the description (Deroussen & Millancourt 2003). I sent it to Scherzinger and he agreed it was a female. The rhythm and posture are essentially the same as in the male, but the timbre

CD3-48   **Snowy Owl** *Bubo scandiacus* Lena delta, Yakutia, Russia, 00:15, 25 June 2004. Hooting of a male. At 0:14 the female gives a cackle off to the side, and at 1:42 the male gives his own lower-pitched cacking. Background: Bewick's Swan *Cygnus bewickii*, Willow Grouse *Lagopus lagopus*, Black-throated Diver *Gavia arctica*, Temminck's Stint *Calidris temminckii*, Pectoral Sandpiper *C melanotos*, Dunlin *C alpina*, Ruddy Turnstone *Arenaria interpres*, Red Phalarope *Phalaropus fulicarius* and Lapland Longspur *Calcarius lapponicus* 04.032.MR.11132.01

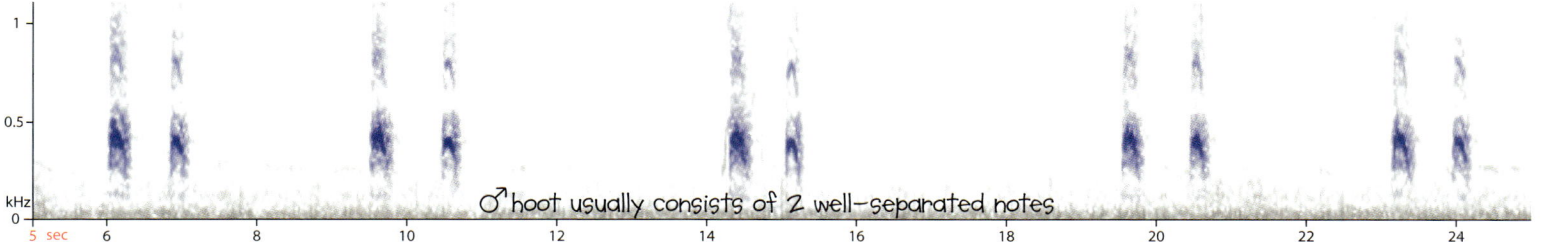

is quite different. Each high-pitched hoot of the female combines a hoarse descending squeak and a sound like a cough or a bark. Being higher-pitched and hoarse, her hoot does not travel very far.

One of the female's commonest calls during the breeding season is her soliciting call, a powerful, shrill and slightly hoarse whinny. As the male approaches, the female crouches and sways her head and the front part of her body, before meeting him with spread wings. In **CD3-49**, the female's whinny appears at 0:03 and 0:12. The guttural clucking from the male at 0:02 after his first double hoot is a sound associated with food-offering, whether by male to female or young, or by female to young (Tulloch 1968). In this case I was standing near their nest, so the food exchange was probably false: a displacement activity. In such situations males often pass food or even clumps of turf to their mate, or else the pair may copulate (Watson 1957).

Snowy Owl is one of those species whose formal description dates back to the founder of modern taxonomy, Carl Linnaeus.

CD3-49 **Snowy Owl** *Bubo scandiacus* Lena delta, Yakutia, Russia, 00:15, 25 June 2004. Hooting of male (also in flight at the end) with soliciting call of female. Also faster food-offering calls of male. Background: Willow Grouse *Lagopus lagopus*, Pectoral Sandpiper *Calidris melanotos*, Ruddy Turnstone *Arenaria interpres* and Red Phalarope *Phalaropus fulicarius*. 04.032.MR.11015.01

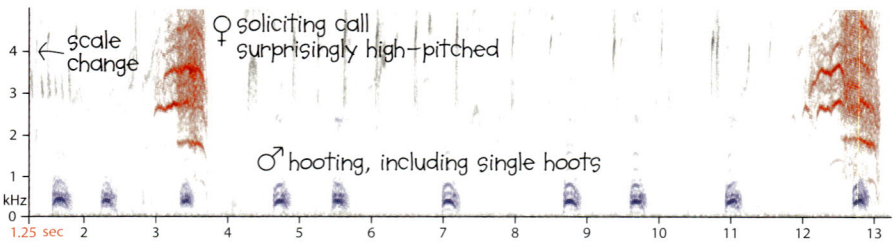

In fact "L.", as he is often called, described two species, *Strix scandiaca* and *S nyctea* (1758), based on drawings by his teacher Olof Rudbeck of a male and female, respectively. Perhaps he also had some experience of them as winter visitors to the farmland around the city of Uppsala, Sweden. *Strix* was the genus in which Linnaeus placed all owls but as it happens, the *Strix* owls in the modern sense are among the Snowy Owl's closer relatives (Wink et al 2009). In the course of a long and complicated taxonomic history, L's two '*Strix*' species were combined into *Nyctea scandiaca*, a name that remained stable for many years, until genetic studies rocked the boat.

Comparison of both mitochondrial and nuclear DNA has shown conclusively that Snowy Owl is in fact an Arctic species of eagle-owl *Bubo*. According to Wink et al (2008, 2009) and Omote et al (2013) its closest known relative is the Great Horned Owl *B virginianus* of the Americas. Most criteria for defining a genus are quite woolly, but two are very clear. A genus should be a 'monophyletic clade', consisting of an ancestral species and *all* of its descendent species, and if new insights mean that two genera have to be merged, the older name has priority. That is why *Bubo* (1806) consumed *Nyctea* (1826) and went on to swallow up *Ketupa* (1830) and *Scotopelia* (1850).

The expanded and now monophyletic genus *Bubo* can be divided into three further clades, each of which branched off at a different point in time. The oldest clade includes the fish owls, formerly *Ketupa*, the fishing owls of Africa, formerly *Scotopelia*, and at least four eagle-owls from Africa and Asia. The next to evolve was the Snowy Owl and Great Horned Owl clade. The most recent clade includes all the other eagle-owls mentioned so far in this book - Spotted *B africanus*, Indian *B bengalensis*, Pharaoh *B ascalaphus*, Cape *B capensis*, Eurasian *B bubo* and presumably also Greyish *B cinerascens* and Arabian Eagle-Owl *B milesi*. The mewing whinny of the female Snowy fits well with this phylogenetic tree. Soliciting calls in both of the older clades are relatively high-pitched mewing or whinnying sounds. Soliciting calls in the most recent clade are very different: Eurasian and its closest relatives beg with harsh sounds that use a wide range of frequencies.

Adult Snowy Owls also use a mewing whinny or whistle in distraction displays, and in the latter part of the breeding season this is the whistle a human intruder is most likely to

hear. Watson (1957) saw many distraction displays, which involved trailing and threshing the wings, spreading the tail and swaying the head from side to side. It was usually the female that whistled during distraction displays, but Watson once heard a male giving a similar call in the same situation.

I never saw any distraction displays in arctic Siberia, although the owls did subject me to other defensive measures. Being dive-bombed by a huge white owl is something I shall not easily forget. It happened that very first time when we jumped

out of the boat, as soon as the male found me alone. During the bombardment he used his 'devil's cackling' call (**CD3-50**).

| CD3-50 | **Snowy Owl** *Bubo scandiacus* Lena delta, Yakutia, Russia, 23:00, 24 June 2004. Devil's cackling of a male. Background: Little Stint *Calidris minuta*, Temminck's Stint *C temminckii*, Lapland Longspur *Calcarius lapponicus*. 04.032.MR.04720.01 |

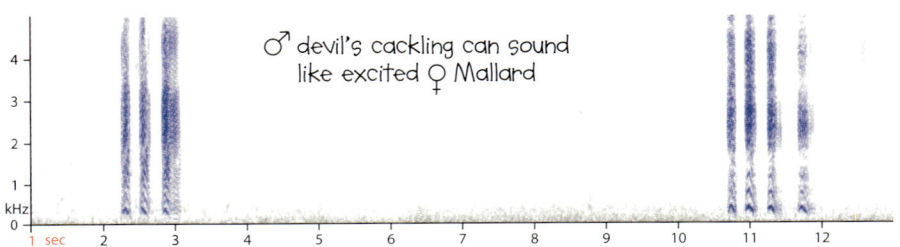

As in Eurasian Eagle-Owl, devil's cackling is an expression of general excitement and not just an alarm call. Snowy Owls cackle in sexual excitement, when attracting a partner to the nest and in response to rivals. In many situations they hold their body horizontally, with the head low, then jerk the tail upwards with each cackle (Scherzinger 1974b). When alarmed, however, they cackle in an upright posture as shown by Håkan's illustration.

Female devil's cackling is easy to tell from that of the male, being distinctly higher-pitched with a squeaky quality. In **CD3-51**, a female cackles at close range. In the long gap between the first and second cackles, the nestlings chitter faintly, eg, at 0:34. At 1:27 the male interrupts his hooting to cackle too.

Snowy Owl *Bubo scandiacus* Lena delta, Yakutia, Russia, 00:15, 25 June 2004. Hooting of male, with cackling of a female prominent at 0:04 and 0:41. Also chittering of nestling. Background: Greater White-fronted Goose *Anser albifrons*, Willow Grouse *Lagopus lagopus*, Red-throated Diver *Gavia stellata*, Temminck's Stint *Calidris temminckii*, Ruddy Turnstone *Arenaria interpres* and Snow Bunting *Plectrophenax nivalis*. 04.032.MR.10530.11

CD3-51

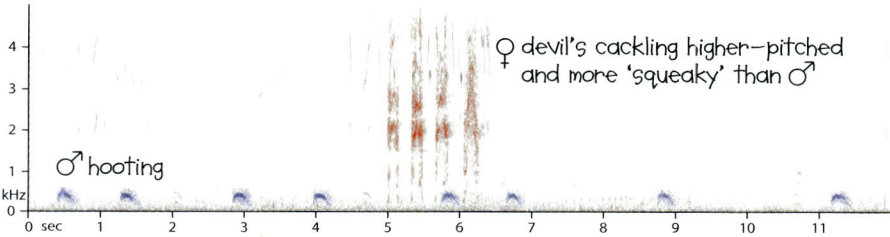

CD3-52 **Snowy Owl** *Bubo scandiacus* Lena delta, Yakutia, Russia, 00:15, 25 June 2004. Chittering of nestlings. Background: Pectoral Sandpiper *Calidris melanotos*. 04.032.MR.11950.00

Nest of Snowy Owl *Bubo scandiacus*, Lena delta, near Lena-Nordenskjöld biological station, Yakutia, Russia, 25 June 2004 (*Magnus Robb*). Chittering nestlings in CD3-52.

When Vladimir and Yuri had finished taking measurements at the nest, I moved in to make a quick recording of the young, the oldest of which was c 10 days old. In **CD3-52**, you can hear two loud series of chitter calls, a sign that the young were cold or stressed. I would have liked to record more of their calls but clearly it was time for me to leave.

When the young leave the nest their bodies and heads are covered with their second downy plumage known as mesoptile. Their wings soon grow white, dark-barred ordinary feathers, which are concealed in the grey mesoptile at rest. A juvenile lying down on the tundra looks like a grey boulder, but when a parent flies in with a lemming, suddenly the boulder stands up and waves white wings. The earliest form of begging call - a short *psu* or *psju* – gradually becomes longer, more whistling

and louder as the nestlings grow. By the time they are fully-grown, their begging calls sound quite like soliciting calls of adult females. **CD3-53** has the falling pitch typical of owls one month or older (Scherzinger 1974b). Juveniles beg until they are

Snowy Owl *Bubo scandiacus* Nunavut, Canada, 24 July 1969. Begging calls of a juvenile over a month old. Philip Taylor & The Macaulay Library at the Cornell Lab of Ornithology.

CD3-53

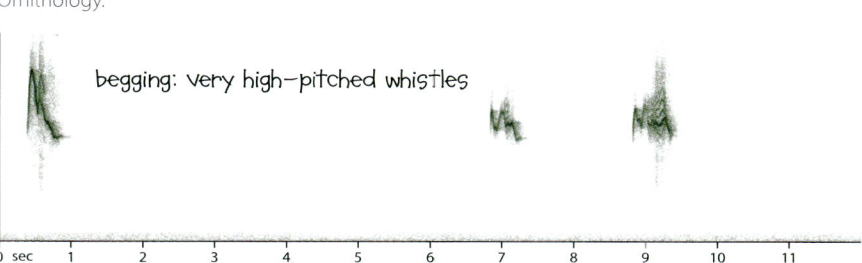

three to four months old. By the time they can fly, their begging calls may be heard from over 1.6 km away (Tulloch 1968).

Snowy Owls are among only a handful of bird species that are capable of wintering in the Arctic. Two of the others, Rock Ptarmigan *Lagopus mutus* and Willow Grouse *L lagopus*, are their most important winter prey when lemmings are not available. Alternatively, some Snowy prey on sea ducks wintering in polynyas in the polar ice (Robertson & Gilchrist 2003). When the midwinter skies are clear, the owls hunt by the stars and the northern lights: there is no daylight at all.

Snowy Owls that winter on grasslands south of the taiga zone thrive on a more varied and plentiful diet of small mammals and birds. Still, it is not exactly the Serengeti. When Mark and Mo crossed southern Canada three decades ago, the temperature was so low and the railway was so straight that the train would freeze into a straight line. When it finally had to turn a corner, men would get out and knock ice off the vestibules with hammers. It was not easy to spot the Snowy Owls they dreamed of seeing, sitting in such a white landscape. The one they did eventually see was flying alongside the train.

When food is plentiful and disturbance is limited, it is sometimes possible to find concentrations of Snowy Owls. Logan Airport near Boston, Massachusetts, USA, has had up to 23 individuals present at one time (Smith et al 2012). Grain terminals in the Duluth-Superior harbour area (Minnesota/Wisconsin) are another 'hotspot', thanks to plentiful Brown Rats *Rattus norvegicus*. Evans (1980) studied territorial interactions between Snowy Owls wintering there, and found that they could be surprisingly vocal. The owls, mostly females, defended their winter territories with "high pitched, drawn out screams".

In the Western Palearctic, Snowy Owls are relatively rare. Håkan has probably seen more wintering in Sweden than anybody else alive, but never more than five together at the same place, and those were always silent. In North America, five is 'peanuts'. In early December 2013, an unprecedented influx of Snowy took place in Atlantic Canada, the north-eastern USA and the Great Lakes region. Nowhere was this more apparent than in Newfoundland. In one weekend, Bruce Mactavish saw 301 Snowy in the south-eastern corner of the island. While this was thrilling for a birder, the owls were close to starvation. Bruce found a dead one, and it was very thin. Owls were flying high and out to sea while others were coming in off the sea. They were pretty tolerant of one another, although they did tend to spread out over a large barren area. With nothing to fight over, none of them were calling.

Migrating Snowy Owls may occur in large concentrations more often than we think, although usually we only see one at a time. Potapov & Sale (2012) developed a fascinating theory after they noticed that as soon as the first Snowy appeared on their study site in the Lower Kolyma in spring, there would always be more at some distance. They believe that almost the entire population of Snowy can be divided into about five to 10 'loose boids', huge but widely dispersed aggregations that move through vast areas of the tundra in spring in the hope of hitting good lemming areas, if any exist that year. The individual owls keep their distance but influence each other's movements, so that a boid may occupy hundreds of km of tundra. Each one is capable of producing 300 to 2000 breeding pairs. Potapov &

Snowy Owls *Bubo scandiacus*, Cape Race, Newfoundland, Canada, 8 December 2013 (*Bruce Mactavish*). Some of the hundreds that month.

Sale (2012) believe that one such boid roams across northern Europe, from Scandinavia and Novaya Zemlya to the Taimyr peninsula, an idea that is at least loosely supported by satellite telemetry (Solheim et al 2008, 2009).

Europe's Snowy Owls have not always been confined to the Arctic. For much of the last million years they occurred widely in southern and western Europe, with records as far south as Gibraltar (Eastham 1968). Their oldest known remains come from Early Pleistocene France, and we know that they bred there in the Middle Pleistocene thanks to immature bones found in Bouches-du-Rhône (Mourer-Chauviré 1975). Much more recently, the Magdalenians of south-western France were obsessed with Snowy. At several sites associated with these sophisticated hunter-gatherers, archaeologists have found unusual numbers of their remains. (In recent times, Inuit have also hunted Snowy Owls, and the Inuit name for Barrow means 'the place where we hunt Snowy Owls'.) Cave art in Trois Frères shows a pair at a ground nest, although Short-eared Owl *Asio flammeus* is difficult to rule out (Eastham 2012, Potapov & Sale 2012). Another more safely identifiable image comes from La Portel cave, and has been dated to 11600 BP (Clottes 2002).

Ice Age remains from North America are much scarcer and mostly Late Pleistocene, leading Potapov & Sale (2012) to suggest that Snowy Owls arrived there after expanding their range from Europe. A different line of thinking leads me to the opposite conclusion. Snowy only breed when there are sufficiently high concentrations of lemmings, and they prefer collared lemmings of the genus *Dicrostonyx* (Dorogov

1987). The form ancestral to this genus, *Praedicrostonyx hopkinsi*, appears in the earliest Pleistocene glacial period in North America, but only later in Asia (Yalden 1999). According to the molecular clock, the ancestral eagle-owl that gave rise to both Snowy and Great Horned Owl lived around 4 million years ago (Wink et al 2009). There is a gap of around 3 million years until the earliest appearance of Snowy in the fossil record. During the intervening period, I envisage a ground-dwelling eagle-owl on the North American prairies that coevolved with its favourite prey and only became white during the course of the Pleistocene, when collared lemmings adapted to live in Arctic conditions.

In the southeast of our region, another very large owl can only survive when some of its habitat remains ice-free. Its range once stretched from the eastern Mediterranean to southern Asia. All that remains is a relict population that was only hypothetical until 2009. We were thrilled to take part in its rediscovery.

Snowy Owl *Bubo scandiacus*

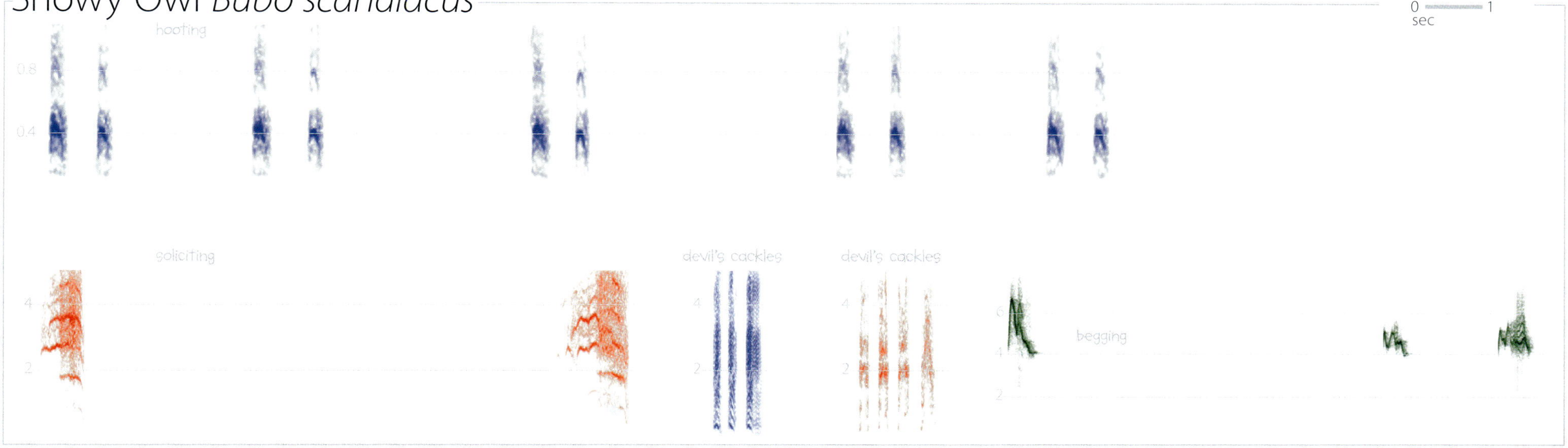

Turkish Fish Owl *Bubo semenowi*

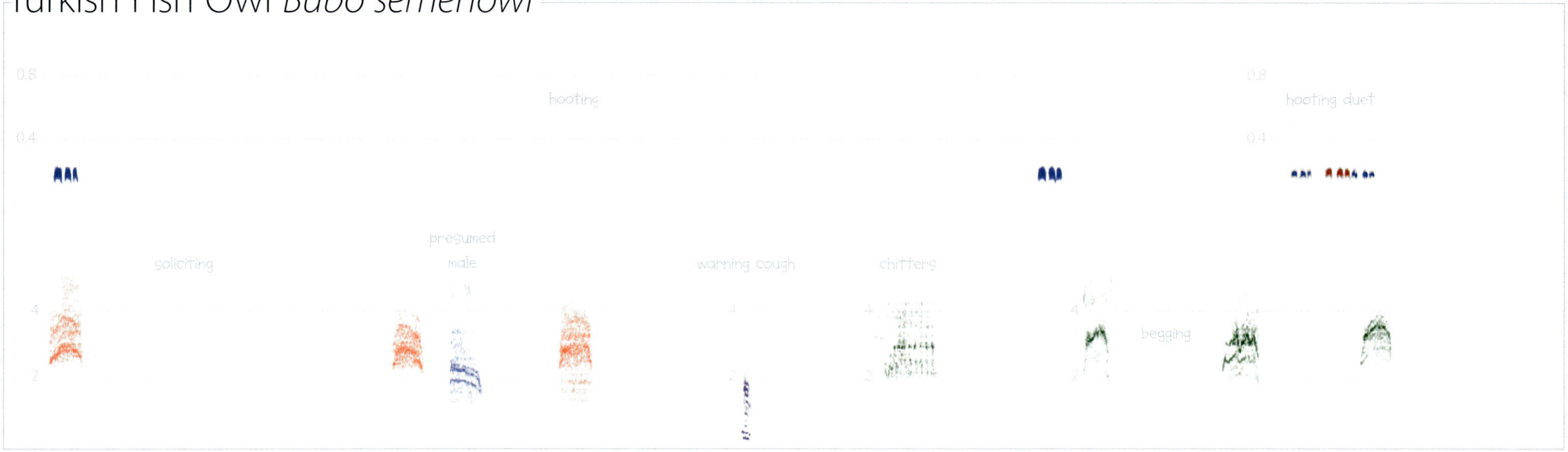

Turkish Fish Owl

When we started work on this book, the Turkish Fish Owl *Bubo semenowi*, known to us at the time as 'Brown Fish Owl *B zeylonensis*', posed an enormous challenge. There had been just a handful of Western Palearctic records in the last 100 years, including two from its last known stronghold: southern Turkey. In late April 1990, a fisherman caught one alive on a hook near Adana (Magnin 1991). This became the only record for Turkey in the 20th century as the previous ones concerned birds collected in the late 19th century (Ebels 2002). Then in 2004 a participant in a survey of wildlife in the Antalya mountains photographed a pair at a secret location (Yöntem 2007).

With definite fish owls reported from locations around 300 km apart, we hoped that a viable population might still exist. Still, we were only half serious in spring 2009 when we asked Arnoud to go and find them. At first he was understandably reluctant. To ensure that the long road trip would be worthwhile, he and Cecilia took in several owls and other bird species along the way. Among others, they recorded Ural Owls *Strix uralensis* in Slovenia, Wallcreepers *Tichodroma muraria* in Bulgaria and Pallid Scops Owls *Otus brucei* in eastern Turkey. From there they headed west to the forests, cliffs and fast-flowing rivers of Mediterranean Turkey.

As they drove west along the south coast, they passed several interesting-looking valleys. None seemed to be quite right. They carried on to the Antalya area where Soner Bekir had suggested trying their luck. On their way to a town Soner had mentioned they crossed a river. The place looked ideal for fish owls with high, mature and dense deciduous trees standing in the clean water, and cliffs on either side. Better still, the river was full of fish and frogs, and easily accessible thanks to a good road on one side. If they could not find fish owls in this apparently ideal habitat, it would be hard to imagine finding them anywhere else. 20 June 2009 was a Saturday, and the valley was full of illegal fishermen. Almost all had left at dusk when a huge owl flew from the cliff to the river. It was only a silhouette. Arnoud could see no details of feathers, yellowish eyes or unfeathered legs, but was convinced it was not an eagle-owl. One reason was its late appearance; eagle-owls start flying a bit earlier. Another was its silence; eagle-owls seem to hoot for a few minutes before flying out most evenings, even in mid-summer.

Over the next three days, Arnoud and Cecilia searched the cliffs to look for nesting sites. At dusk they waited for the fish owl to show up, and at night they listened while camping along the river at a local fish restaurant, all in vain. However, they were encouraged by hearing the account of Ibrahim, the restaurant owner, who had lived most of his working life in Germany. About a year earlier, he had seen a huge owl sitting on a rock in the river at night. When it flew off, its wings were as long as his arms. Frustrated by the lack of further sightings, Arnoud and Cecilia decided to return in a few months, when they hoped that the owl would be hooting. On the way home they sent an email to Soner, telling him they had found a definite site but not managed to obtain photographs or sound recordings.

Soner's response was decisive. Within two weeks, on 2 July, he visited the same river with Murat Çuhadaroğlu. They had no luck at Arnoud and Cecilia's spot, but carried on upstream, searching for eyeshine reflected in the light of their torch. Most was greenish and belonged to Wild Goats *Capra aegagrus*, but some 9 km further, orange eyeshine in the top of a pine on the other side of the roaring river stopped them in their tracks. A careful look produced much excitement when they realised it was a fish owl! Soner made some excellent photographs, proving beyond doubt that at least one individual was present. The next night, Soner's friend Emin Yoğurtcuoğlu visited the same place and even saw two adults there. He also saw one closer to the location of Arnoud's 20 June sighting.

Arnoud and Cecilia went back a week later, this time by plane. Sleeping rough on the riverside near Soner's tree, they not only had excellent views of both adults but also witnessed a newly fledged juvenile jumping from the cliffs into a pine tree top. This confirmed the species' first documented nesting record in the WP. They visited this territory five times in all seasons within the next year (van den Berg et al 2009, 2010), collecting many photographs and sound recordings. Our knowledge of Turkish Fish Owl sounds grew exponentially, but the most important sound was still missing.

On Wednesday 17 March 2010, Mark and I arrived at Arnoud and Cecilia's house in the Netherlands for a meeting. As we were catching up with each other's news, Arnoud received a phone call from Soner and Emin, who we had employed to prospect for more fish owls. They had just become the first modern day birders to hear a fish owl hooting in the Western Palearctic, at a new site at a little lake in the Taurus mountains north of Adana. So no sooner had we arrived than Arnoud was preparing to leave. The next evening he arrived at Adana airport, where a car arranged for him by Soner and Emin was waiting. In the middle of the night, the site was difficult to find, and it was almost dawn when Soner finally talked him in.

By day Soner and Emin showed him little piles of crab remains and pellets under old conifers, left behind by a fish owl, something they had also found underneath the previous year's pine trees. Three friendly engineers working at the dam at one end of the lake told them that a shepherd had shot a huge owl a few years previously, which must have been the female. By the time of Arnoud's visit the male had apparently not succeeded in attracting a new one, but at time of writing he has. In the evening, the engineers prepared a picnic. Arnoud's participation came to an abrupt halt when he heard the male hooting in the distance. It carried on for much of the

Turkish Fish Owl *Bubo semenowi*, Akseki, Antalya, Turkey, 5 August 2009 (*Arnoud B van den Berg*). Walking after prey in river. Same first-year bird as in CD3-67 but silent and almost a month later.

night, never quite where Arnoud hoped that it would be. Still, for a first ever recording of Turkish Fish Owl hooting, **CD3-54** was not bad at all.

CD3-54   **Turkish Fish Owl** *Bubo semenowi* Mersin, Turkey, 19:52, 20 March 2010. Hooting of a male. Background: fast-flowing mountain streams. 100320.AB.195220.13

Oymapinar Baraji near Manavgat, east of Antalya, is a reservoir with steep banks of almost bare rock, on which by some miracle rugged woodlands of pine *Pinus*, cypress *Cupressus* and wild olive *Olea europaea* flourish. Its waters are vivid blue. For many summers, tourist boats have been taking people around the reservoir, thousands of them. One of the things the boatsmen show to their mostly Russian guests are some large owls that live near small caves in the cliffs, one pair in each of two canyons where rivers enter the lake. In June 2011, the Pilgaard family from Denmark sent photographs of the owls to a birder friend to ask what they were. The news spread quickly, and since then Oymapinar has become *the* place for anyone wanting to see Turkish Fish Owls.

Habitat of Turkish Fish Owl *Bubo semenowi*, 'Little Canyon', Oymapinar Baraji, Antalya, Turkey, 23:45, 24 July 2012 (*Dick Forsman*). From peak at right, opposite from nest from vertical cliff, CD3-55 to 56 & CD3-60 were recorded.

CD3-55   **Turkish Fish Owl** *Bubo semenowi* 'Little Canyon', Oymapinar Baraji, Antalya, Turkey, 23:45, 16 May 2012. On a snag atop a precipice, a male Turkish Fish Owl *Bubo semenowi* inflates his white throat and booms like a whale. Background: Levant Water Frog *Pelophylax bedriagae*, Eurasian Scops Owl *Otus scops* and Tawny Owl *Strix aluco*. 120516.AB.234550.11

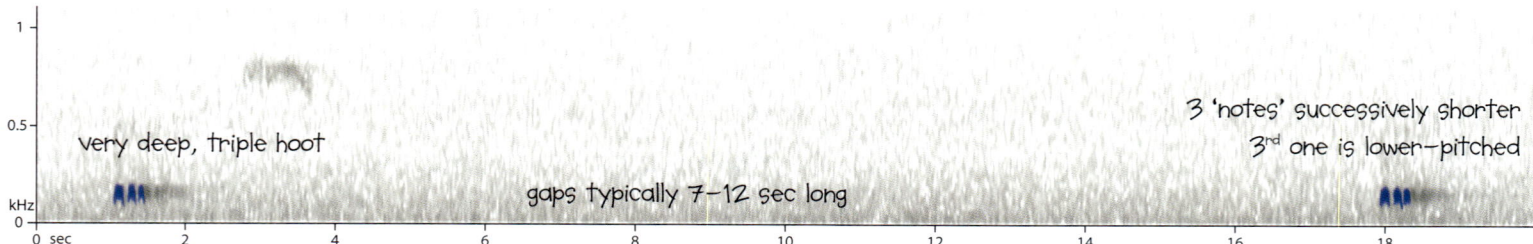

Turkish Fish Owl *Bubo semenowi*, perched near nest, 'Little Canyon', Oymapinar Baraji, Antalya, Turkey, 17 May 2012 (*Arnoud B van den Berg*). One of the adults in CD3-56 & CD1-64 but a few days later, at dawn.

Many birders have twitched the male in **CD3-55** and its mate from boats, but Arnoud recorded it at night from a hiding place on the opposite crag. To get there he explored overgrown paths, squeezed through a narrow tunnel, and climbed dangerous rocks, several nights in a row. Before any of that he had to arrange permission from two authorities. It was a privilege, but one that he had earned.

Turkish Fish Owls have a very deep voice, too deep for many small speakers to reproduce. The loudest frequency in the hoot is around 170 Hz, putting Turkish Fish Owl in the same range as a Eurasian Bittern *Botaurus stellaris*, or about an octave lower than a male Eurasian Eagle-Owl. In the Western Palearctic, only Lapland Owl *Strix lapponica* sometimes produces even lower-pitched sounds. The hoots are not especially loud, but powerful and far-carrying. The torrential streams that thunder through most territories would drown out anything less. Not here. With a surface so calm, maybe even the fish can hear them.

At the time of writing, sound recordings of only three male Turkish Fish Owls are available to me. Arnoud recorded the two that you have heard, and José Luis Copete recorded the third. A recording of a fourth by Emin was sadly lost. Emin, Murat Bozdoğan and Soner also heard a fifth and sixth male while conducting our survey (Bekir et al 2010). Hooting of all six consisted of three or four notes repeated quickly.

Amazingly, fish owl pairs often hoot in perfectly coordinated duets. In Turkey, Arnoud recorded duetting during three of the nights spent on the crag at Oymapinar Baraji, and José Luis Copete recorded an almost identical duet elsewhere. Male and female contributions are combined so smoothly and consistently, it seems hard to believe two owls could be involved. Nor is it obvious who is doing what. Listen carefully to **CD3-56**, however, and you'll hear that the first four hoots up to the slight pause are exactly the same as in solo male hooting (it's the same male as in **CD3-55**). The four higher-pitched hoots in the middle belong to the female, then the last four are from the male again. On one occasion, Arnoud recorded the complete male contribution to the duet – two sets of hoots and a gap between them – without the female (cf, **CD3-56** at 1:22).

CD3-56 **Turkish Fish Owl** *Bubo semenowi* 'Little Canyon', Oymapinar Baraji, Antalya, Turkey, 04:09, 18 May 2012. Hooting duet of male and female. Background: Eurasian Scops Owl *Otus scops*. 120518.AB.040900.12

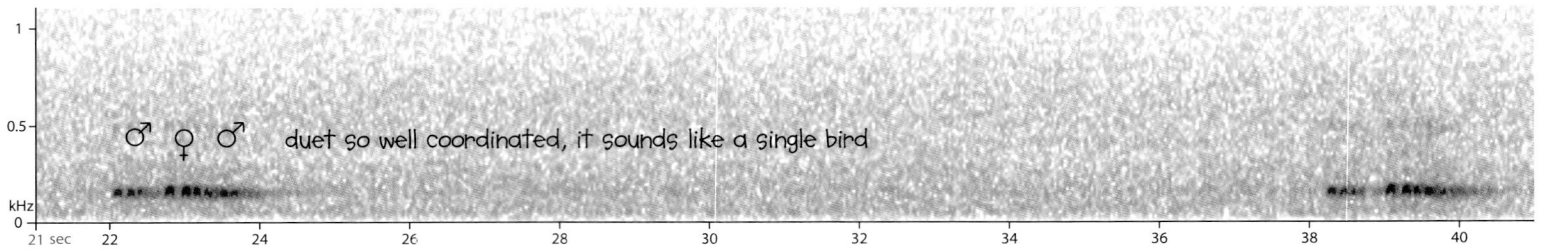

Up to now we have never been able to see a pair of Turkish Fish Owls while they were hooting. Comparing the size of the owls (females are slightly larger) and watching them inflating their pale throat 'badges' would soon confirm who did what, if only we had the opportunity. Instead, we have sexed their duets by focusing on the lower-pitched individual. Since that bird always starts the duet and is the only one we have ever heard hooting solo, we conclude that it must be the male. In Blakiston's Fish Owl *B blakistoni* too, the male is the one that starts the duet and hoots solo more often than the female. Occasionally the order is reversed in both insular nominate *blakistoni* and continental subspecies *doerriesi*, especially when agitated (Brazil & Yamamoto 1989, Jonathan Slaght pers comm).

Turkish Fish Owl once occurred all the way from Turkey to Pakistan. Pleistocene remains have also been found on the island of Crete (Weesie 1988) but the species is not known from further west (cf Louchart 2011). Away from Turkey, the only records in the past 100 years were in Israel, where it became extinct in August 1975 (Ebels 2002), and Iran, where the first pair for up to a century was found in Hormozgan province on 18 January 2004 (van Diek et al 2004). It has subsequently been recorded in two other Iranian provinces (Khaleghizadeh et al 2011). Originally *semenowi*, as Turkish is known to taxonomists, was described as a species (Zarudny 1905), based on a holotype from Khuzestan, western Iran. Subsequently, however, it has usually been considered one of four subspecies of 'Brown Fish Owl' *Bubo zeylonensis*, the others being nominate *zeylonensis* (based on a type specimen from Sri Lanka), *leschenaulti* (type specimen from Chandranagore, north-eastern India), and *orientalis* (type specimen from Dakto, modern day Vietnam).

Very few recordings of 'Brown Fish Owl' have ever been published, and the identity of some is debatable (Robb 2009, Chappuis 2010). Of the ones we trust, all are from India eastwards and all sound very different from what Arnoud has recorded in Turkey. In January 2013, Arnoud and Cecilia went to India to investigate.

In Goa, Arnoud learned about a river with at least four pairs of fish owls, along a quiet dead end road near a camp where birders can stay. Leio de Souza showed him and Cecilia large boulders with cracked crab shells, indicating where fish owls fed. They were much shier than their Turkish counterparts, and flew away immediately when humans arrived. Prolonged views like

CD3-57 **Brown Fish Owl** *Bubo zeylonensis* Bhagwan Mahaveer Wildlife Sanctuary, Goa, India, 21:07, 11 January 2013. Hooting of a male. Background: clicking sounds of frogs. 130111.AB.210700.01vv

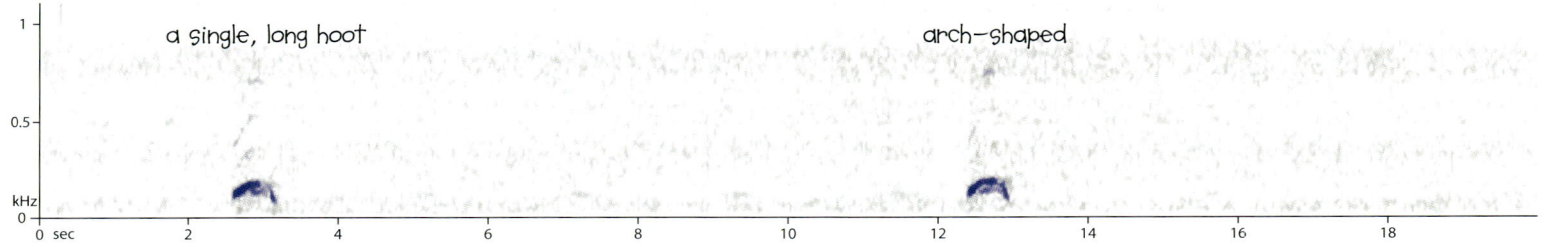

CD3-58 **Brown Fish Owl** *Bubo zeylonensis* Bhagwan Mahaveer Wildlife Sanctuary, Goa, India, 19:02, 15 January 2013. Hooting duet of a pair. 130115.AB.190204.02

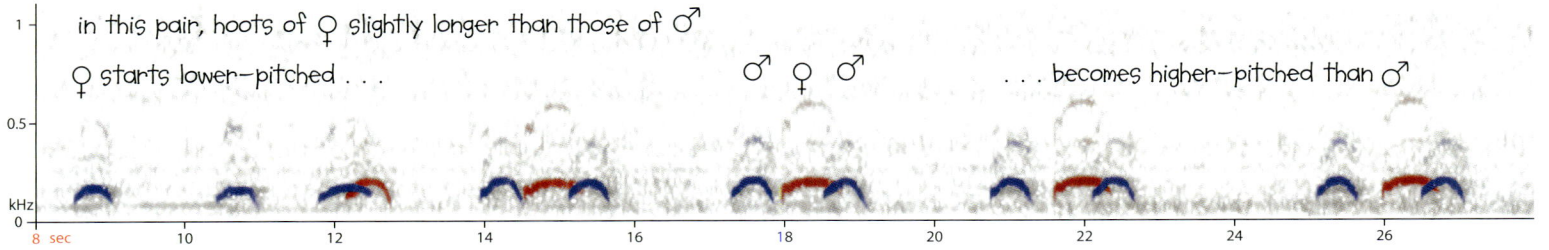

Arnoud and Cecilia had enjoyed in Turkey eluded them. Only by leaving equipment in promising spots and walking away was it possible to record the owls up close. In **CD3-57**, you can hear a male Brown Fish Owl from Goa hooting solo on a background of clicking frogs.

In **CD3-58**, a pair starts duetting after a few introductory hoots. As in Turkish Fish Owl, we believe that the male is responsible for the first and last parts, in this case single hoots, while the female produces the middle part. At first the female is lower than the male, but she gradually rises in pitch until she is almost level. Then in a second series the female is higher-pitched than

Brown Fish Owl *Bubo zeylonensis* Bhagwan Mahaveer Wildlife Sanctuary, Goa, India, 06:21, 15 January 2013. Hooting duet of male and female, separated in stereo image. The male is more distant and the female is perched closer by to its right. By the end, the female has flown to join the male. This recording shows clearly that authors such as Legge (1880) and Shashidara (1989) were wrong when they wrote that in duets, one bird gives the first and another the second and third hoots. 130115.AB.062100.11   **CD3-59**

the male, the normal state of affairs. In **CD3-59**, you can hear a duet in which the same male and female were perched some distance apart, separating the components of the duet in space.

We know of three-hoot duets like this from several places in western and central India, and from Sri Lanka. In Turkish Fish

Owl, no such three-hoot duet exists. The nearest thing we have heard was when Arnoud recorded a single strophe of a slow form of hooting. This consisted of five notes, possibly produced by just one individual (**CD3-60**). Every other time, hooting of *semenowi* sounded three to four times faster than that of *zeylonensis*.

CD3-60   **Turkish Fish Owl** *Bubo semenowi* 'Little Canyon', Oymapinar Baraji, Antalya, Turkey, 04:26, 13 May 2012. Slow hooting, probably of a male. Background: Levant Water Frog *Pelophylax bedriagae* and Eurasian Scops Owl *Otus scops*. 120513.AB.042600.02

In south-eastern Asia, 'Brown Fish Owls' sound different again. In this third vocally defined population, each strophe is a quick double hoot. When male and female duet, this gives six-note duets (**CD3-61**): two male then two higher female then two male hoots (Brazil & Yamamoto 1989). Arnoud played recordings from both of the other two 'hoot-types' to adult Turkish Fish Owls at close range several times in Turkey, and they never showed even the slightest interest. If further sound recordings confirm the differences described above, and other lines of evidence point the same way, a three-way split seems likely.

Provisionally, I suggest that *B leschenaulti* would be the correct name for the third, south-eastern species with the double hoot. Recordings attest to its presence from south-eastern Asia and as far northwest as Tangail in Bangladesh. Tangail is only 250 km east of Chandannagar, the type location of *leschenaulti*. Because of the 250 km gap, there is still some room for doubt. Sound recordings from Chandannagar might help, or alternatively genetic evidence linking the type specimen with double hooters from further east but not with single hooters from further west. Let's call this provisional south-eastern species Bengal Fish Owl in honour of the type location, and assume that *orientalis* is its darker north-eastern subspecies.

So far we know very little about the phenology of hooting in Turkish Fish Owl. All we know is that hooting has been reported in March to early April, which is the courtship period, in mid-May when there were young in the nest, and in late June when the young had already fledged. Looking to the Far East, Blakiston's Fish Owl may offer some clues about what more we might expect. Japanese *blakistoni* hoots every month of the year with a peak in late February to March, just before egg-laying, and regularly until June. It hoots much less frequently

CD3-61   **Bengal Fish Owl** *Bubo leschenaulti* Huai Kha Khaeng reserve, Uthai Thani, Thailand, April. Hooting duet of a male and female. Roland Eve.

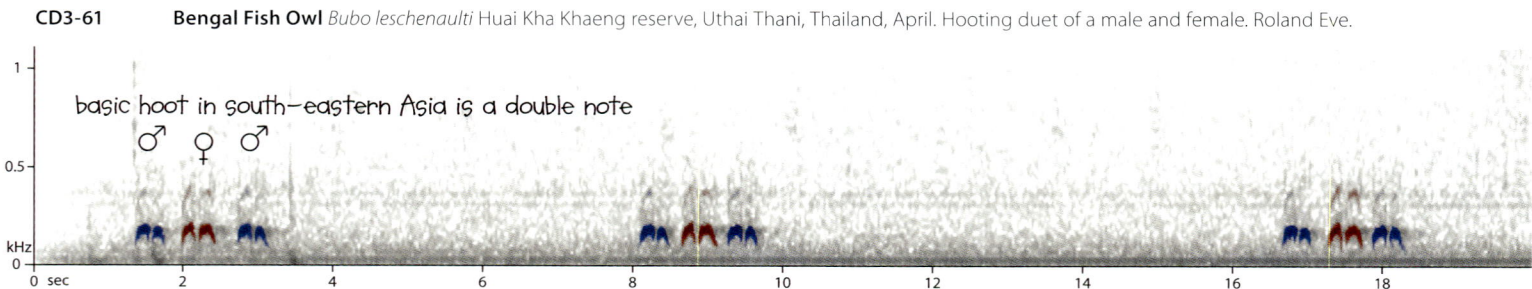

from November to early February (Brazil & Yamamoto 1989). Russian *doerriesi* duets most frequently in February and March, and continues at least until the young fledge in late May. Second calendar-year birds start hooting only in May. Their duets are weaker and less regular than those of adults, but can be heard as pair-formation takes place throughout the summer and autumn months (Pukinskiy 1974, 1993).

Arnoud and Cecilia's visit to Goa for Brown Fish Owl coincided exactly with the start of courtship. During the weeks before their visit, the staff at the Backwoods Camp had not heard the owls at all. Besides solo hooting and duets, Arnoud recorded

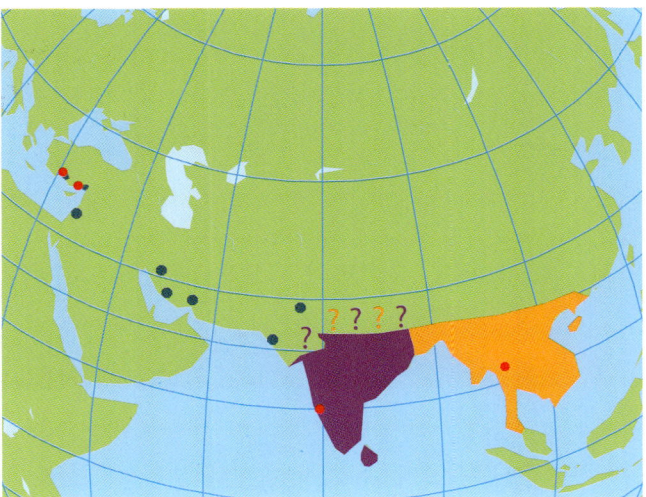

Localities of Turkish Fish Owl *Bubo semenowi* in 1915-2014 ■ and very approximate breeding distribution of Brown Fish Owl *B zeylonensis* ■ and Bengal Fish Owl *B leschenaulti* ■, based on recordings from own collection, online collections and commercially available publications. Recording locations indicated by ● dots.

Brown Fish Owl *Bubo zeylonensis* Bhagwan Mahaveer Wildlife Sanctuary, Goa, India, 03:58, 15 January 2013. Wailing call. 130115.AB.035844.11   CD3-62

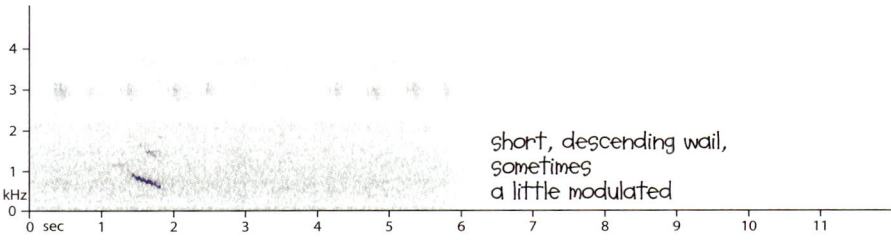

Brown Fish Owl *Bubo zeylonensis* Bhagwan Mahaveer Wildlife Sanctuary, Goa, India, 05:31, 15 January 2013. Hooting duet and wailing call. 130115.AB.053100.02   CD3-63

one other call type, a fairly short, descending wail. **CD3-62** is his best example. In **CD3-63**, the owls fly closer after one gives a wail. The same also happened on another occasion.

We have never recorded any wails of Turkish Fish Owl with certainty, but we have often heard them giving a sibilant whistle, especially the female. This seems to be a soliciting call. **CD3-64** was recorded from a boat at dawn. Two adults were sitting close

Turkish Fish Owl *Bubo semenowi* 'Little Canyon', Oymapinar Baraji, Antalya, Turkey, 06:20, 11 May 2012. Soliciting calls of two adults. Background: Great Tit *Parus major*. 120511.AB.062000.11   CD3-64

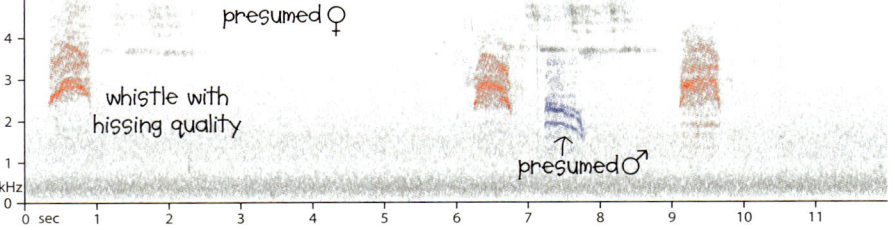

Turkish Fish Owl *Bubo semenowi*, adult, Akseki, Antalya, Turkey, 14 July 2009 (*Arnoud B van den Berg*). Bringing fish to fledgling. Same family as in CD3-65 & 66.

together in their roosting tree above a nest hole, possibly trying to reassure their nestling. The adult that calls more frequently is noticeably higher-pitched than the other. We assume that she is the female.

A call with a similar hissing timbre but inflected sharply upwards at the end featured in Arnoud's very first Turkish Fish Owl recording. Shortly before the recording started, a juvenile had flown down from the cliff to a nearby tree and was hanging

CD3-65 **Turkish Fish Owl** *Bubo semenowi* Antalya, Turkey, 21:07, 13 July 2009. Hissing call of adult with rising inflection, possibly soliciting call. Background: presumed juvenile and mountain river. 090713.AB.210726.02

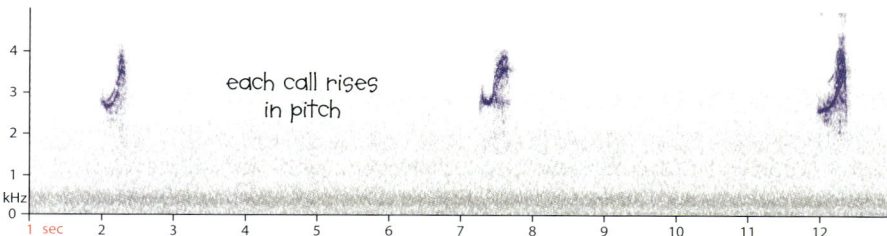

upside down in the top. This looked rather precarious, and after a while Arnoud decided to see whether he should do something about it. As soon as he started to approach, he noticed the adult perched in a tree 20 m away giving the calls in **CD3-65**, with faint contributions from the juvenile in the background.

CD3-66 **Turkish Fish Owl** *Bubo semenowi* Antalya, Turkey, 21:07, 13 July 2009. Warning 'cough' of an adult, while juvenile hangs upside down from branch. Background: mountain river. 090713.AB.210726.02

After a while the adult flew off, giving a strange sort of coughing sound (**CD3-66**). This was so different from most fish owl sounds that until I researched this chapter I was in doubt that it belonged to the owl. Then I read Pukinskiy's (1993) description of warning calls in the *doerriesi* form of Blakiston's Fish Owl: "A slight disturbance (such as a badger or dog near a nest tree) will evoke a *kkhe* sound, which sounds like the cough of someone with a cold." Jonathan Slaght sent me an example, confirming the similarity, and described situations when he had heard it. Once a juvenile *doerriesi* was calling from the nest when a group of crows flew overhead. The resident female, roosting in a tree nearby, gave the cough and the juvenile shut up immediately.

Turkish Fish Owl *Bubo semenowi*, Akseki, Antalya, Turkey, 15 July 2009 (*Arnoud B van den Berg*). Same juvenile as in CD3-67.

Another time Jonathan was sitting near a nest tree before dark with the female on the nest (not incubating yet, just preparing). When it became dark and the male arrived, the female emerged from the nest cavity. She knew Jonathan was there but the male

Two nights after its 'dangle', Arnoud and Cecilia saw the same juvenile Turkish Fish Owl perched the right way up. It had come down from the cliff and was in a large pine, where it spent the rest of the night preening and sleeping, and sometimes staring at the sky. In **CD3-67**, this juvenile was responding to Arnoud's imitation of its calls at a range of only 10-15 m. Despite the proximity, it was barely audible without the use of a parabolic microphone.

Turkish Fish Owl *Bubo semenowi* Antalya, Turkey, 21:14, 15 July 2009. Hissing calls of a juvenile with rising inflection. Background: mountain river. 090715.AB.211442.01 CD3-67

Three years later, Arnoud collected many more recordings of a juvenile, but one that was still in the nest. During long vigils on the crag opposite the 'Little Canyon' nest he recorded many begging calls (eg, **CD3-68**). These calls lack any upward inflection, and resemble the hissing whistles we heard from the roosting adults (cf, **CD3-64**), tending to go down a little towards the end. The recording starts with wingbeats of an adult arriving at the nest, and after the juvenile's loud first begging call, you can hear a few of the adult's faint calls at a faster tempo. These are probably feeding calls, as they often featured when an adult arrived with food at the nest.

In 2014, it was finally time for other members of the Sound Approach team, who had previously taken background roles, to go and experience the Turkish Fish Owls with Arnoud and Cecilia. On the morning of 13 May we chartered a boat that would take us to both nesting sites at Oymapinar Baraji. We only expected to see the owls, not hear them, so we were delighted to be able to make some recordings. At the second breeding site in the 'Grand Canyon' on the north side of the reservoir we saw an

Turkish Fish Owl *Bubo semenowi*, Akseki, Antalya, Turkey, 14 July 2009 (*Arnoud B van den Berg*). Same juvenile as in CD3-67 but quiet after dawn.

did not. She looked in his direction and gave the cough. The adult Turkish Fish Owl in Arnoud's recording had good reason to give a cough, with its young dangling upside down from a branch, and a human standing nearby.

CD3-68 Turkish Fish Owl *Bubo semenowi* 'Little Canyon', Oymapinar Baraji, Antalya, Turkey, 02:49, 14 May 2012. Begging calls of juvenile and feeding calls of adult. Background: wind in trees. 120514.AB.024900.11

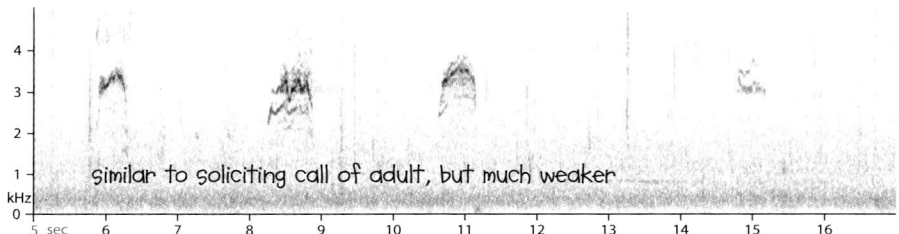

CD3-69 Turkish Fish Owl *Bubo semenowi* 'Grand Canyon', Oymapinar Baraji, Antalya, Turkey, 07:43, 13 May 2014. Chittering of a large juvenile, with feeding calls of an adult, probably female. Background: Common Chaffinch *Fringilla coelebs*. 140513.MR.074306.32

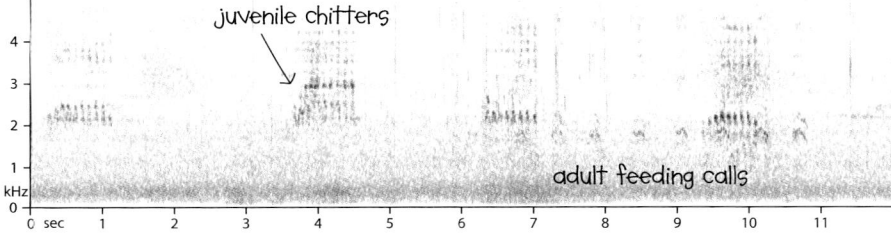

adult in the entrance to a nest. From inside, we could clearly hear chittering of a large juvenile (**CD3-69**). Superimposed on the chittering we could hear feeding calls of a second adult, probably the female.

The pair in the 'Grand Canyon' receives fewer visitors than the one in the 'Little Canyon'. In **CD3-70**, an adult of this pair bill-snaps before moving a few metres to a different perch. I suspect it was simply uneasy about the presence of our boat, and the bill-snapping was directed at us. Arnoud had once heard the sound before, when he surprised a young fish owl below its breeding cliff, but on that occasion he did not manage to record the sound.

Turkish Fish Owl *Bubo semenowi* 'Grand Canyon', Oymapinar Baraji, Antalya, Turkey, 07:53, 13 May 2014. Bill-snapping of an adult, probably male, perched outside nesting cave with juvenile and another adult inside. 140513.MR.075328.21 **CD3-70**

When we work with such a rare species at night, progress in documenting calls and especially understanding their 'meaning' can be slow. Sometimes we make a leap forward, but occasionally we have to take a step back. Four years after our first review of Turkish Fish Owl calls (van den Berg et al 2010), we now know that a high-pitched and rather Little Owl *Athene vidalii*-like *keew* call (figs 2 & 4 in van den Berg et al 2010) is in fact the excitement call of Eurasian Scops Owl *Otus scops* (cf, **CD2-23** & **CD2-24**). In retrospect we should have been more suspicious, because Arnoud heard the *keew* call for a long period high up across a river but never managed to see the caller. He never heard a scops owl hooting at this site but it was numerous in a village a few km down river.

We are still only starting to understand Turkish Fish Owl. There is so much more to find out, and adventurous birders can join the effort. Clearly we need to locate more pairs, and to understand more about their ecological requirements. In the whole world we know of only 12 occupied territories. In Turkey those include eight in Antalya province and three further east (Soner Bekir pers comm); in Iran just one pair was reported recently in Hormozgan province (van Maanen

Turkish Fish Owl *Bubo semenowi*, at nest, 'Grand Canyon', Oymapinar Baraji, Antalya, Turkey, 13 May 2014 (*Arnoud B van den Berg*). Same adult as in CD3-70.

& Cuyten 2012). Looking at outdated distribution maps for 'Brown Fish Owl' (eg, in Ali & Ripley 1981 and König et al 2008), I imagined Pakistan could be a stronghold. Roberts (1991), however, could only name four 20th century records, the last dating from 1980. Even if we were to assume that there are really five to 10 times the known number of pairs in Turkey and a similar number in Iran, Turkish Fish Owl remains a dangerously rare owl.

Turkish Fish Owl is larger than other 'Brown Fish Owls' and also much paler, especially on the head and upperparts. It inhabits more arid habitat, using cliffs rather than trees for nesting cavities. Sometimes it even nests far from permanent water. In southern Iran, the pair discovered by two Dutch birders in January 2004 was nesting in a completely arid valley, and must have been feeding among coastal mangroves 2 km away (van Diek et al 2004, Magnus Ullman pers comm). An hour after Rob Felix and Frank Willems discovered this pair, a Eurasian Eagle-Owl hooted just 100 m from their hole. The close proximity of two large owl species suggests that suitable nest sites were scarce in the area.

Arnoud brought back five feathers from Turkey and gave them to Peter de Knijff for genetic analysis. Peter sequenced a fragment of 300 base pairs for cytochrome b, compared them with sequences for Brown Fish Owl (not *semenowi*) and Buffy Fish Owl *B ketupu* in Wink et al (2008), and found three consistent differences from both, identical in all five feathers. The Turkish birds differed from both species by 2%. Unfortunately, Wink used sequences from captive 'Brown Fish Owls', and it is uncertain where they or their ancestors came from. Future comparisons will have to address this problem, and should also verify whether 'Bengal Fish Owl' is genetically distinct.

The very few Turkish Fish Owls surviving in southern Iran highlight some important gaps in our knowledge. Besides observations of pairs in Hormozgan province in 2004-2005 and 2012, local taxidermists received specimens from Fars and Bushehr provinces within the last couple of years (Khaleghizadeh 2011). Despite contacting several people that have seen fish owls in Hormozgan, I could find nobody who has ever heard them. When making taxonomic judgements based on sounds, it is always best to have examples from as many different locations as possible, so I am keen to confirm that Iranian *semenowi* sound just like those from Turkey, whenever this should prove possible.

Although we have chosen to call it Turkish Fish Owl, the species was actually described from an Iranian specimen. Nikolai Zarudny, an explorer and zoologist of Ukrainian origin who shot two in Iran, was the first to realise that these western 'brown fish owls' were different. Zarudny only knew that *semenowi* occurred in Khuzestan and the eastern slopes of the Zagros range, so perhaps he had not seen specimens already collected in Israel, Syria and Turkey in the 19th century (Ebels 2002). The scientific name *semenowi* honours Peter Petrovich Semenow, a noted explorer of Central Asia (Zarudny 1905).

Even in the 21st century, new owl species are still being discovered. Most are small species from poorly explored parts of the tropics: scops owls, pygmy owls *Glaucidium* and the like. When work started on this book, Arabian Scops Owl *O pamelae* from 1937 was the last new Western Palearctic owl. Surprisingly, one medium sized WP owl was still awaiting discovery in the genus that has Tawny Owl *Strix aluco* in its midst, the first named genus of owls, *Strix*.

Chapter 9: *Strix*

Lapland Owl

As quietly as I can, I raise my binoculars. All I can make out is a silhouette against the starlit sky, perched on the side of a spruce. With each series of hoots (**CD3-71**), the owl's whole upper body becomes swollen. Two pale marks appear just below the lower edge of the facial disk, like a silver torc on a Celtic chieftain's neck. The torc appears to bounce with each hoot, staying visible through the whole series. As the last hoot fades away it settles and virtually disappears.

A branch moves over to my right and I see the female perched on a dead tree in the open. When she hoots quietly, her timbre is strikingly different, almost growling (**CD3-72**). Soon she takes off and flies across to her mate with surprisingly audible wingbeats. The male responds with a different kind of hooting, a very deep pulse of about 3 hoots/sec at an even pitch. Shortly after joining him, the female gives two series of low-pitched chittering sounds. I suspect a nest, and with a little effort I find one.

Lapland Owl *Strix lapponica* Västmanland, Sweden, 23:30, 30 March 2006. Hooting of a female once, then wingbeats as she flies left, with pulsed hooting of male. Ends with some chittering calls of the female, by this time on the nest with the male. 06.004.MR.01745.02   CD3-72

Håkan has been listening to 'Lappugglar' *Strix lapponica* since before I was born. By the time I went to meet him in Sweden in 2012 he was in his 70s. He had been working hard on the paintings for this book, and I was looking forward to seeing them and offering some feedback. I hoped that we might also do some fieldwork, but I was not sure whether Håkan would still have much appetite for it. As it turned out he was better prepared for adventure than I. We spent three nights in the woods and only looked at his paintings on the last day.

CD3-71   **Lapland Owl** *Strix lapponica* Västmanland, Sweden, 23:30, 30 March 2006. Hooting of a male. 06.004.MR.01120.22

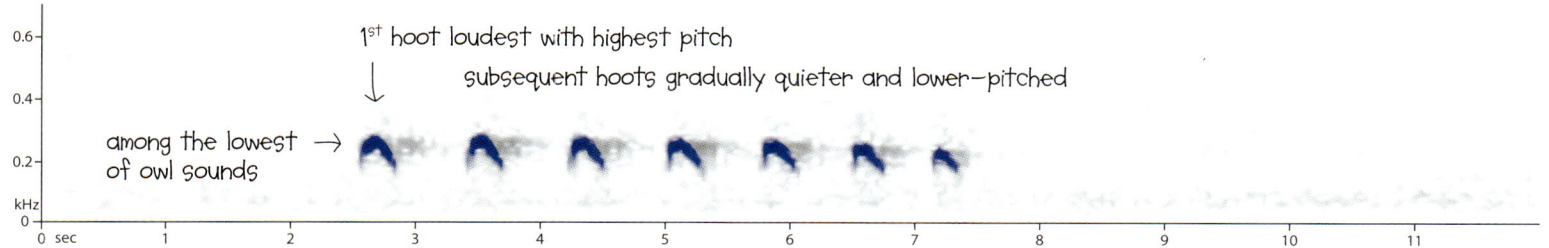

Lapland Owl *Strix lapponica*, Rovaniemi, Lapland, Finland, 5 May 2012 (*Dick Forsman*). Lapland Owl refers specifically to *lapponica*, the Eurasian version of 'Great Grey Owl', which we consider to be a different species from *S nebulosa*, the Great Gray Owl of North America.

In 2012, Lapland Owls were being seen in unusual places, often far from known breeding areas. Sometime after midwinter the vole population had taken a nosedive. In late March, Håkan had seen a minimum of 10 in one evening near Söderhamn, a coastal town 300 km north of Stockholm. By mid-April many had died and others had melted back into the forests where they were less conspicuous. We did twitch one, but sadly for me it remained silent. Breeding would be impossible with so little to eat.

Ural Owls *S uralensis* are less dependent on voles so we focussed on them instead, visiting several hotspots that Håkan knew well. When his imitations failed to draw a single response, we decided to sleep for a few hours and try again in the hours before dawn. Since we were still on location, I left my recorder working outside.

It was a treat to listen to those recordings later. The skies were full of migrating waterbirds, and several species of mammal called during the night. I am still at a loss to explain why, at the lowest point in the vole cycle while others were dying of hunger, one female Lapland Owl hooted while we slept. Later that spring, birders only found one Lapland nest in the entire country, a long way from where we had been (Stefansson 2013). Our female only hooted three times in eight minutes so just for once, I decided to shorten the gaps (**CD3-73**).

Lapland Owls hoot differently from all other *Strix* owls. Most other species have a diagnostic compound rhythm consisting of one or more introductory notes followed after a gap by a larger cluster of terminal notes (Robb et al 2013). The *hoo..... (very long gap) hu - hohohoooooooo* of Tawny Owl *S aluco* is a

classic example. With its simpler hoots, Lapland sounds closer to Short-eared Owl *Asio flammeus*. Surprisingly perhaps, it sits comfortably in the middle of the *Strix* phylogenetic tree, on a branch slightly older than that leading to Tawny and Ural Owl (eg, Wink et al 2009).

Lapland Owl's other kind of hooting is more typically *Strix*. I call it pulsed hooting (Robb et al 2013). In **CD3-71**, this was the deep, continuous throbbing by the male when the female flew towards him. There he gave 50 hoots in a row, but Wahlstedt (1969) has reported up to 100. **CD3-74** is a slightly clearer recording of this sound, but it will always be a difficult one to hear in the field. Not only is it quiet, it is also very low-pitched,

Lapland Owl *Strix lapponica*, Rovaniemi, Lapland, Finland, 5 May 2012 (*Dick Forsman*)

CD3-73   **Lapland Owl** *Strix lapponica* Möklinta, Uppland, Sweden, 02:20, 18 April 2012. Hooting of a distant female. The gaps have been shortened considerably. Background: Whooper Swan *Cygnus cygnus*, migrating Water Rail *Rallus aquaticus*, and Tawny Owl *Strix aluco*. 120418.MR.022033.33

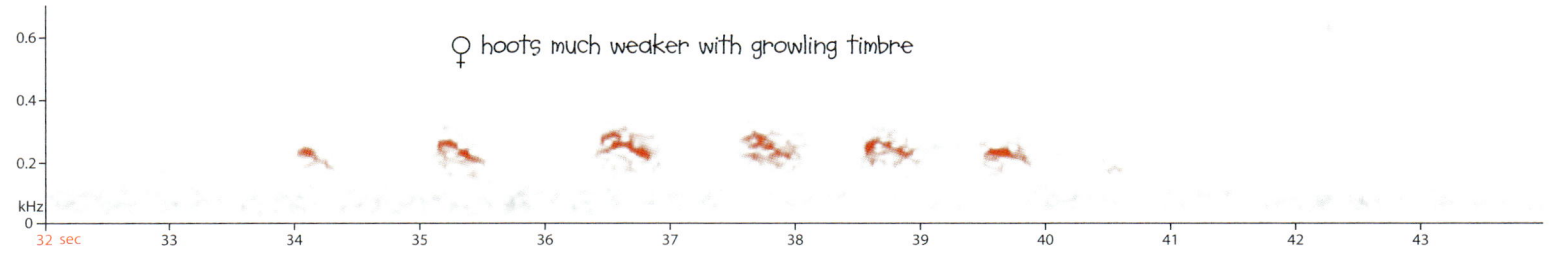

CD3-74   **Lapland Owl** *Strix lapponica* Västmanland, Sweden, 23:30, 30 March 2006. Pulsed hooting of a male and soft growls of a female. 06.004.MR.05110.21

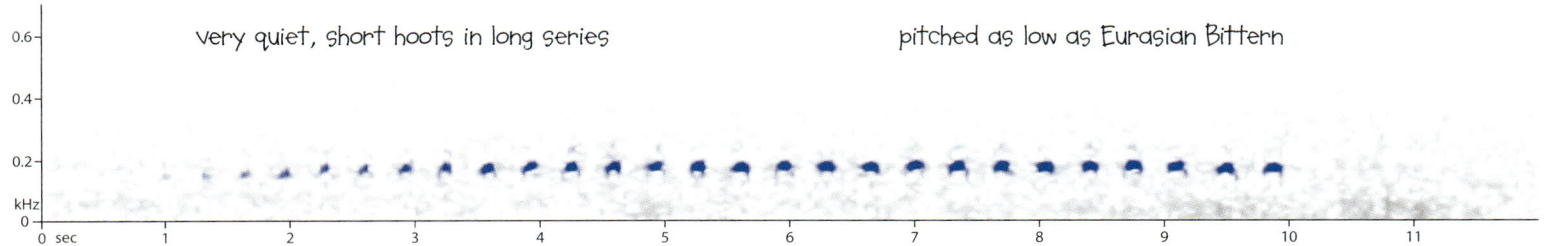

carrying about 50 m at most (Wahlstedt 1969); in the Western Palearctic only Turkish Fish Owl *Bubo semenowi* can hoot this low.

Pulsed hooting plays an important role in nest-showing. Males also use it in response to rivals (Lindblad 1967), and to stimulate females to accept food, especially if other sounds fail to elicit a response (Stefansson 1997). Sometimes male-female duets of pulsed hooting may arise. **CD3-75** starts with a female, joined a few seconds later by a male.

Great Gray Owl *S nebulosa* lives, as its spelling suggests, in North America. Darker than Lapland Owl, it has bars and not just streaks on its underparts. Nevertheless, Great Gray looks so Lapland-like that few have ever questioned their usual treatment as subspecies. Great Gray was described for science first (Forster 1772), after the Scottish naturalist Andrew Graham discovered it at Fort Severn, Ontario (Nero 1982, Mikkola & Sieradzki 2012). It was only 26 years later that Carl Peter Thunberg, an apostle of Linnaeus, published his formal description of Lapland Owl. Based on a 3.31% difference in mtDNA (Johnsen et al 2010),

CD3-75   **Lapland Owl** *Strix lapponica* Keminmaa, Lapland, Finland, 21:24, 5 June 2010. Pulsed hooting of a female, joined by a male after a few seconds. Background: Eurasian Curlew *Numenius arquatus*, Common Snipe *Gallinago gallinago*, Fieldfare *Turdus pilaris*, Song Thrush *T philomelos*, Redwing *T iliacus*, European Robin *Erithacus rubecula* and Common Rosefinch *Erythrina erythrina*. 100605.DF.212400.21

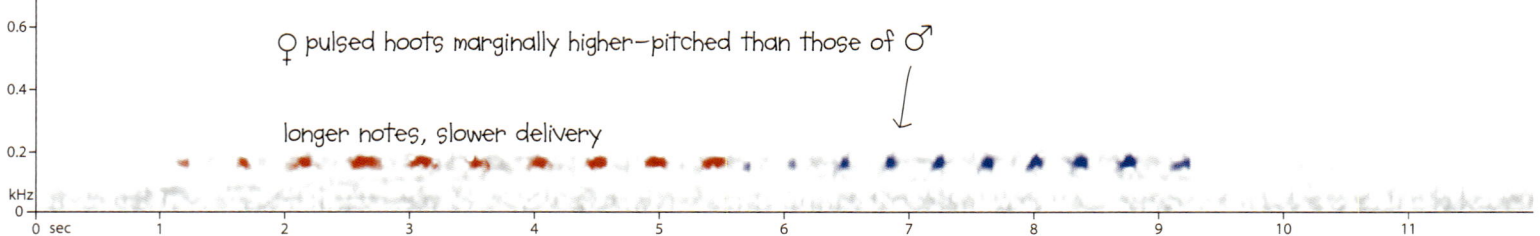

Great Gray and Lapland parted company roughly 1.7 million years ago. Even if this estimate is wrong, they have not been in touch for a long time.

Many authors assume that Great Gray Owl and Lapland Owl sound alike, and combine voice descriptions from both continents indiscriminately. CD booklets often fail to mention in which continent recordings were made. Two recent owl CDs even publish the same fake interaction between a male and female, made up of a male Great Gray and a female Lapland mixed into a single track, with poorly disguised transitions back and forth (Pelz 2008, track 56, Harvancik 2009, track 73). To draw my own conclusions, I have only used recordings of known provenance, including those from the Macaulay Library, Ithaca, New York, USA, but also from various audio publications and websites. Several friends kindly gave me access to their unpublished recordings. Joseph Medley sent me many recordings of *yosemitensis*, a new subspecies of Great Gray recently described from California, USA, on purely genetic grounds (Hull et al 2014).

Initially, I could not hear any difference between territorial hooting of Great Gray Owl and Lapland Owl. When I analysed hooting from seven male Great Gray and 16 male Lapland, some subtle differences emerged. In Great Gray, the mean number of hoots in a series was greater, at 11.4, compared to 9.7 in Lapland, but there was plenty of overlap. It was only when I stopped measuring and just listened that I noticed something more consistent. In five of the seven Great Gray, each series started with a strikingly lower-pitched hoot that was usually the weakest of the whole series. The volume was then sustained fairly evenly over the ensuing hoots before dropping again, often just slightly, at the end. In all 16 Lapland the first note was strong and the series reached full volume near the start, before tailing off gradually towards the end. The hooting in **CD3-76** belongs to a 10-month old male Great Gray.

Female Great Gray Owls completely lack the growling timbre of female Lapland Owls. Their hooting is male-like but higher-pitched with longer notes and shorter gaps in between (Beck & Winter 2000, Rognan 2007). The slightly wavering quality of

CD3-76 **Great Gray Owl** *Strix nebulosa* Fairbanks, Alaska, USA, 22:00, 8 April 1973. Hooting of a 10-month old male in captivity (picked up at two weeks of age after both parents had been shot; later released). Leonard J Peyton & The Macaulay Library at the Cornell Lab of Ornithology.

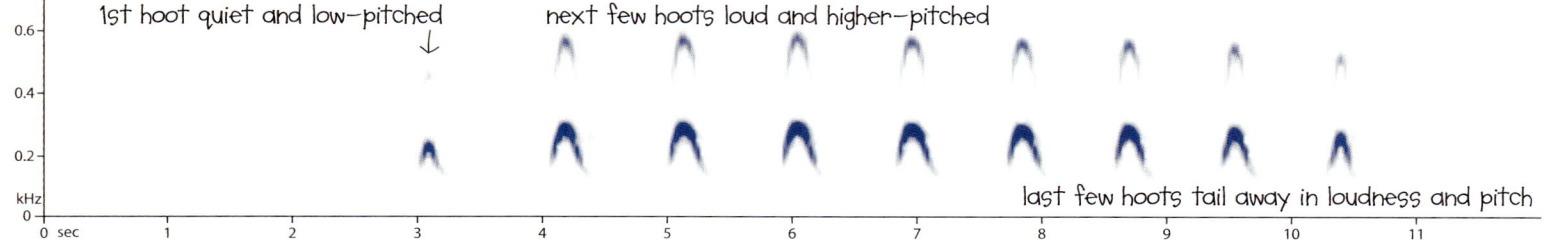

Great Gray Owl *Strix nebulosa*, Ontario, Ottawa, Canada, 31 January 2010 (*Jo T Latham*). Showing darker face and underparts than *S lapponica*, with streaking more suffused.

the female Great Gray in **CD3-77** seems to be a peculiarity of this individual.

Pulsed hooting also differs noticeably between Great Gray Owl and Lapland Owl. In Great Gray Owl it goes by the name of 'low double hoot' (eg, Beck & Winter 2000). The repeated unit is actually a single hoot, usually with an accent at either end making it sound doubled (**CD3-78**). Females have similar but higher-pitched pulsed hooting. In either sex, the accents can be less clearly articulated and the hoots may not sound doubled, as shown by the female in **CD3-79**. Based on four males of each, Great Gray's pulsed hooting is higher-pitched and slower with longer notes than Lapland's. The maximum frequency in an entire series averaged 232 Hz in Great Gray but just 181 Hz in Lapland. Great Gray averaged 1.8 hoots/sec while Lapland averaged 2.8 hoots/sec. None of these measurements showed any overlap between the two species, but my sample was very small.

The most striking vocal difference that I have noticed concerns soliciting calls and their juvenile equivalent, begging calls. Adult female soliciting calls are perhaps the commonest sound of Lapland Owl from a few days before egg-laying until the young are old enough to be heard from a distance. Stefansson (1997) describes Lapland's soliciting call as a "weak treble hoot: *Njeh, njeh, njeh*", audible from 100-300 m in forest but occasionally up to 600 m in open

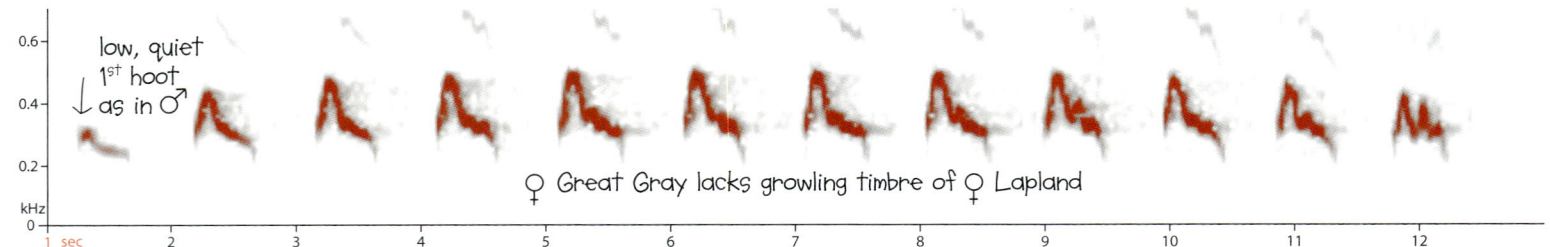

CD3-77   **Great Gray Owl** *Strix nebulosa* Union County, Oregon, USA, 20:00, 21 March 1990. Hooting of a female. David S Herr & The Macaulay Library at the Cornell Lab of Ornithology.

CD3-78 **Great Gray Owl** *Strix nebulosa* Roseaux, Minnesota, USA, 00:00, 13 May 1970. Pulsed hooting of a male. Background: frogs Anura. William W H Gunn & The Macaulay Library at the Cornell Lab of Ornithology.

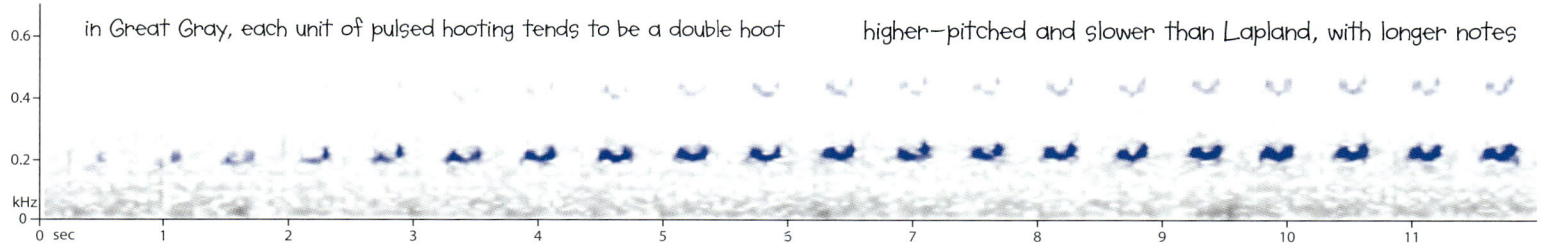

CD3-79 **Great Gray Owl** *Strix nebulosa* Union County, Oregon, USA, 20:00, 21 March 1990. Pulsed hooting of a female. David S Herr & The Macaulay Library at the Cornell Lab of Ornithology.

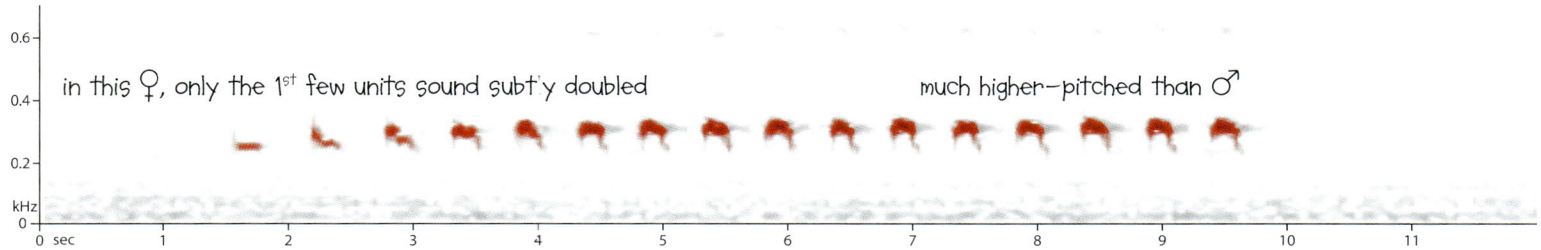

CD3-80 **Lapland Owl** *Strix lapponica* Siikajoki, Oulu, Finland, 22:55, 9 June 2003. Soliciting calls of a female. 03.010.KM.02520.32

Great Gray Owl *Strix nebulosa* Union County, Oregon, USA, 05:15, 12 May 1990. Soliciting calls of a female. Background: Black-capped Chickadee *Poecile atricapillus*, Fox Sparrow *Passarella iliaca* and Brown-headed Cowbird *Molothrus ater*. David S Herr & The Macaulay Library at the Cornell Lab of Ornithology. **CD3-81**

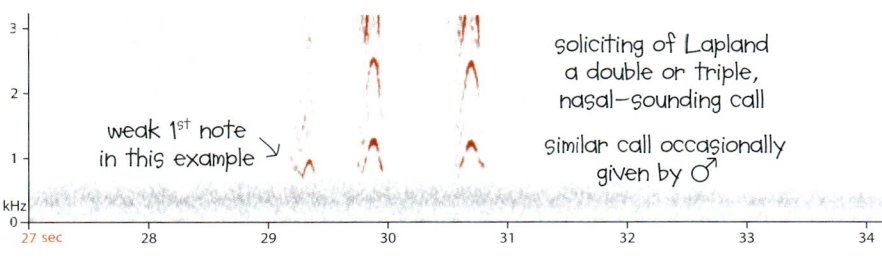
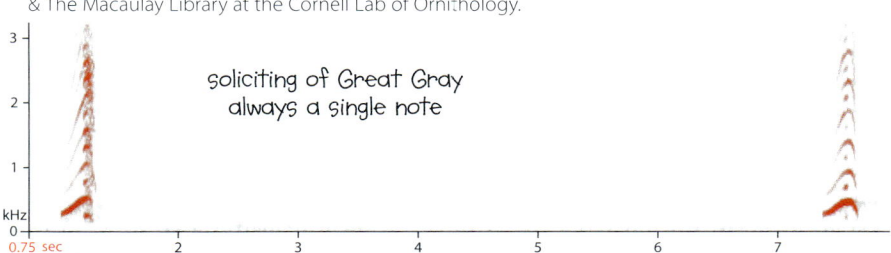

terrain." Often the call may be just doubled as in **CD3-80**, or sometimes even given four times in quick succession. Single calls may occur from time to time but are never the rule. By contrast, the soliciting call of Great Gray Owl is nearly always a single *whoop* (**CD3-81**), often preceded by a very short, high-pitched upbeat. Great Gray's *whoop* is longer than Lapland's *njeh*, and I know of only one example where the *whoop* is briefly doubled in a long sequence of single calls (Macaulay Library 47532).

When a male Lapland Owl arrives at the nest, he often gives a special 'arrival hoot' similar to his territorial hoot but without the early peak in volume and pitch; the energy is more evenly distributed through the series. Arrival hoots often have a certain roughness to them, inviting confusion with female hooting. In **CD3-82**, the female responds with a low-pitched chittering call. Both sexes may use this chittering as a 'feeding call' when offering food to small young, and the female also chitters during copulation (Mebs & Scherzinger 2004). In this recording one of the young also gives its own much higher-pitched, quieter chitter call.

CD3-82 **Lapland Owl** *Strix lapponica* Keminmaa, Lapland, Finland, 21:24, 5 June 2010. Low chittering of female, with arrival hooting of male. The higher-pitched chittering belongs to a juvenile. Background: Common Wood Pigeon *Columba palumbus*, Willow Warbler *Phylloscopus trochilus*, Song Thrush *Turdus philomelos*, Redwing *T iliacus* and European Robin *Erithacus rubecula*. 100605.DF.212400.01

The young in **CD3-83** were a couple of weeks older. Outside the nest but still unable to fly, they were at their most vulnerable. Mark was also feeling vulnerable when he

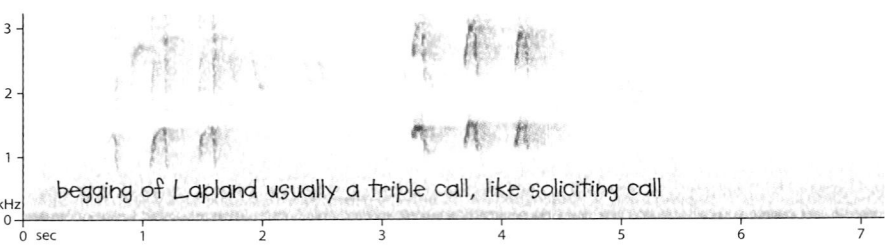

Lapland Owl *Strix lapponica* Siikajoki, Oulu, Finland, 23:00, 9 June 2003. Begging calls of two young out of the nest but still unable to fly. Background: Common Cuckoo *Cuculus canorus* and Pied Flycatcher *Ficedula hypoleuca*. 03.023.MC.04100.21   CD3-83

recorded them. While Killian changed position several times, capturing sounds of the same owlets and their mother from a variety of angles, Mark stayed put. It didn't take long for the mosquitoes to find him. At one point he asked Killian, "Are you getting bitten?" When Killian lied, "No," Mark suffered even more. The begging calls in Mark's recording are like a higher-pitched version of adult soliciting calls (cf, **CD3-80**). The repetition separates them not only from Great Gray Owl but more usefully from Ural Owl (cf, **CD4-10**), which often lives in the same habitat.

Mark was lucky that mosquitoes were the worst of his woes. Breeding Lapland Owls are highly aggressive and can cause serious injuries. Even juveniles on the forest floor, still unable to fly, can lunge at the eyes of a photographer going in close for a wide-angle shot (Stefansson 1997). When you consider how vulnerable they are in this situation, such defences are understandable.

Lapland Owl *Strix lapponica*, fledgling of c 4 weeks of age, Pyhänta, Oulu, Pohjanmaa, Finland, 11 June 2003 (*Dick Forsman*). About same age as in CD3-83.

Young Lapland Owls will generally attract attention by calling but in case they are silent, an adult distraction display may betray their presence. If necessary the adult will moan, grunt and squeak while flapping wildly and feigning injury, positioning itself in a way that should lead the intruder away from the young. If this fails to work the owl, usually a female, changes strategy to aggression.

The signs to look out for are loud bill-snapping and growling with a deep, grainy voice that Håkan likens to a grand piano being pushed across the floor. When the bill-snapping becomes faster or louder, watch out! Crouching forward, lowering her wings and raising her scapulars, the owl shifts from foot to foot on the branch, fixing you with an intense stare. If one of the young bill-snaps too, her attack is guaranteed (Stefansson 1997). Pouncing forward, gliding on rigid wings, she thrusts her legs forward at the last moment with claws open, like a White-tailed Eagle *Haliaeetus albicilla* catching a fish. The impact can actually knock a man over (Nero 1982). Attacks are at their worst when food levels are high and the young are still unable to fly.

Outside the breeding season Lapland Owls are almost indifferent to humans, so we can watch them without concerns for either our safety or theirs. Listening to a vole munching vegetation under thick grass or snow, they may not even look at us. That would mean losing their fix on the vole, which depends on the orientation of the sound-gathering facial disk. The eyes go where the disk points since, unable to move in their sockets, they are effectively locked to the owl's ears. One side of the disk is slightly higher than the other. The ears are positioned at different heights, allowing greater accuracy in the vertical plane when fixing the position of a sound.

In **CD3-84**, voles are squabbling about 2 m away underneath a thick mat of last year's grass, which has only recently emerged from a heavy blanket of snow. A Lapland Owl would hear them not only from tens of metres further away but also under half a metre of snow. After fixing the location, it

Lapland Owl *Strix lapponica*, Rovaniemi, Lapland, Finland, 6 May 2012 (*Dick Forsman*)

Although their lives revolve around voles, Lapland Owls are much less nomadic than Tengmalm's Owls, which have more difficulty in penetrating the snow. Lapland usually stay on territory from one year to the next, often despite low vole numbers. Juveniles normally disperse very short distances, and one female bred in her own birth nest the next summer (Stefansson 1997). During peak vole years Lapland Owls may call during autumn and winter (Berggren & Wahlstedt 1977), but they tend to be much quieter at that season than other *Strix* owls.

When voles become extremely scarce, Lapland Owls of any age may leave their familiar territory and go in search of food. They never come back. 390 recoveries from the Swedish ringing program have led to this and many other insights. Most are recovered less than 100 km away, and there is no clear pattern regarding direction. The data do not support the idea that Lapland Owls noticed in central and even

could punch a hole in the snow so deep that it might even disappear from view completely. This is probably the key adaptation that allowed Lapland to live further north than any other *Strix* owl.

CD3-84   **voles** Arvicolinae (probably Field Vole *Microtus agrestis* or Water Vole *Arvicola terrestris*) Västmanland, Sweden, 16:47, 18 April 2012. Voles squabbling under a thick mat of grass. Background: Common Blackbird *Turdus merula*, European Robin *Erithacus rubecula*, Great Tit *Parus major* and Common Chaffinch *Fringilla coelebs*. 120418.MR.164710.21

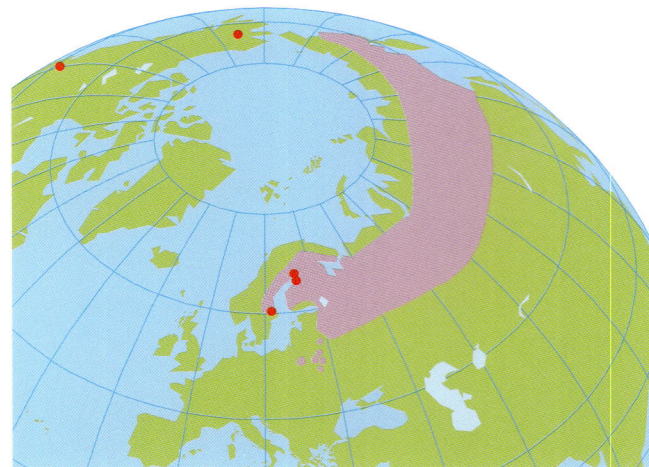

Approximate breeding distribution of Lapland Owl *Strix lapponica* ▪. Recording locations of Lapland and Great Gray Owl *S nebulosa* (in North America) indicated by ● dots.

southern Sweden during vole crashes come from the north. Stefansson (2013) believes most birds 'invading' in 2012 for example came from the same province or one adjacent to where they were found. There may be far more breeding in southern Scandinavia than birders currently realise. In recent years, the isolated population in northern Ukraine and Belarus also spread rapidly south and west, with first nests found in eastern Poland in 2010 (Ławicki et al 2013).

Periodic episodes of nomadism have kept Lapland Owl's genes well-mixed, and there is only one subspecies across the vast Palearctic taiga belt. In all but the northernmost reaches of this vast range it lives alongside a slightly smaller *Strix* owl that shows much greater variation in response to local conditions. Several of its subspecies are pale, almost angelic-looking, an appearance that could hardly be more deceptive.

Lapland Owl *Strix lapponica*, Hyvinkaa, Uusimaa, Finland, 3 January 2007 (*Dick Forsman*)

Lapland Owl *Strix lapponica*

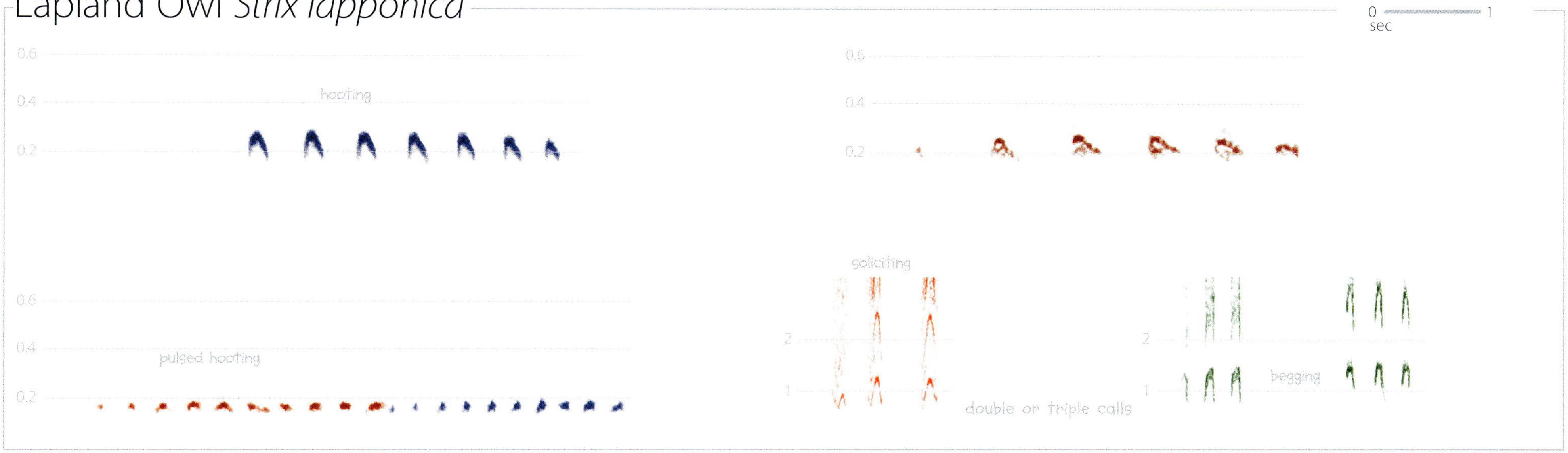
0 sec 1
hooting
pulsed hooting
soliciting
double or triple calls
begging

Ural Owl *Strix uralensis*

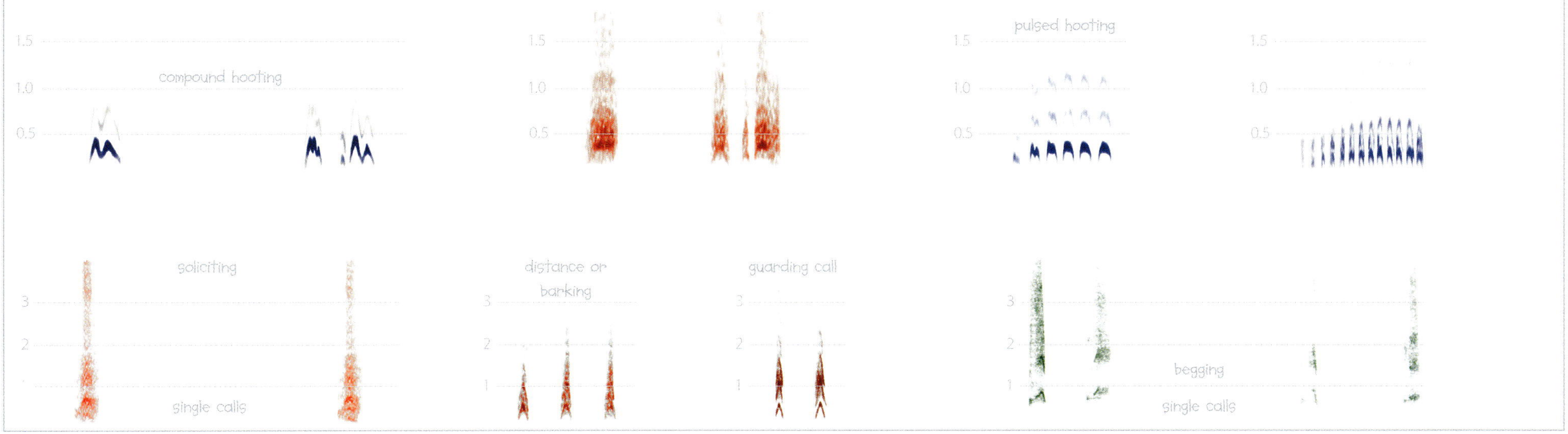
compound hooting
pulsed hooting
soliciting
single calls
distance or barking
guarding call
begging
single calls

Ural Owl

Nobody forgets a Ural Owl *Strix uralensis*. For a start they can be violent. Not in a thuggish way. Their favoured tactic is an unexpected drone strike. Burly birders walk with branches over their head anywhere near Ural Owl young, but ringers must forgo hard hats to avoid injuring their parents' talons.

For the rest of the year they channel much of this aggression towards other owls. Smaller ones do well to keep a low profile in their presence. That was what made one April night in Sweden so impressive. On a 30 km long forest track in Uppland, Per Alström and I stopped every few 100 m to listen. Besides 10 Ural Owls (one of which is in **CD4-01**), we must have heard five Tawny Owls *S aluco*, three Tengmalm's Owls *Aegolius funereus*, and at dusk even a few Eurasian Pygmy Owls *Glaucidium passerinum*. With so many smaller owls hooting in defiance one thing was certain: there was plenty of food for all.

CD4-01 **Ural Owl** *Strix uralensis* Vällen, Uppland, Sweden, 23:00, 1 April 2006. Compound hooting of a male. 06.004.MR.14030.01

Hearing so many Ural Owls was exceptional in itself. Usually they are rather taciturn, especially in spring. Even in almost ideal weather conditions, they can remain silent for hours (Holmberg 1974). The night before, Per and I had driven through a forest with the highest density of Ural Owls in Sweden. We heard not a single owl all night. A slight breeze and an overcast sky dampened any inclination to hoot. Northern Uppland has a well-known and fairly constant number of Ural Owls, and Arne Lundberg (1980) tried counting them by ear. From 1974-78 he used a standard listening method on 45 nights each spring. In three out of those five years he counted totals less than 40% of the true figure, and even in the best year he only heard 72% of known pairs. When he made short three-minute listening stops, his success rate fell as low as 5-10%.

Fortunately, there are more effective ways to tell if a territory is occupied. Experienced Scandinavian birders know how to lure Ural Owls. If you are lucky enough to be with one of these mimics then it's likely to be in snow, minus something degrees centigrade and dark. They throw out a challenge and in comes the male, sometimes with his mate for reinforcement. Håkan is a master mimic, and he is absolutely hooked on Ural Owls. I have recorded many with his help. The male in **CD4-02** came particularly close one morning as we were standing a few 100 m from a gently rumbling, ice-covered lake.

CD4-02 **Ural Owl** *Strix uralensis* Bursjön, Hälsingland, Sweden, 05:15, 24 March 2014. Hooting of a male. Background: Mistle Thrush *Turdus viscivorus*, and occasional mumbling of ice. 140324.MR.051542.11

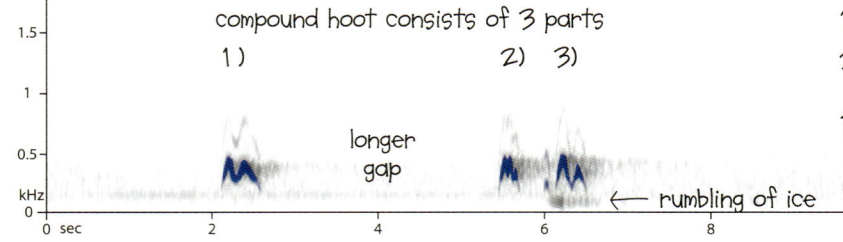

Ural Owls are residents with long-lasting pair bonds. They reaffirm their territorial borders in autumn, the time when juveniles are trying to claim real estate for themselves. By the time winter arrives, everything has usually been settled. In springtime they can devote more time to defending their young and much less to protecting their territory. Spring hooting in Ural Owls is primarily a form of negotiation between partners (Lundberg 1980). It becomes conspicuous during the preamble to breeding in early spring, but does not stop until much later.

From the courtship phase until the young leave the nest, the male always warns the larger female of his intention to bring prey. For this he uses compound hooting (cf, **CD4-01** & **CD4-02**). The female usually responds with a harsh, rising *rrrèh* that acknowledges his presence and permits him to approach (**CD4-03**). This soliciting call is similar to its equivalent in Eurasian Eagle-Owl *Bubo bubo*, but slightly shorter.

After the young hatch, more food is required. At the same time the nights become shorter and there is less time for the male to catch and deliver it. The shorter gaps between deliveries

Ural Owl *Strix uralensis* Vällen, Uppland, Sweden, 23:00, 1 April 2006. Soliciting calls of a female and compound hooting of a male. Ends with the female's wingbeats. Same pair as in CD4-01. Background: Tengmalm's Owl *Aegolius funereus* and Tawny Owl *Strix aluco*. 06.004.MR.12907.01

CD4-03

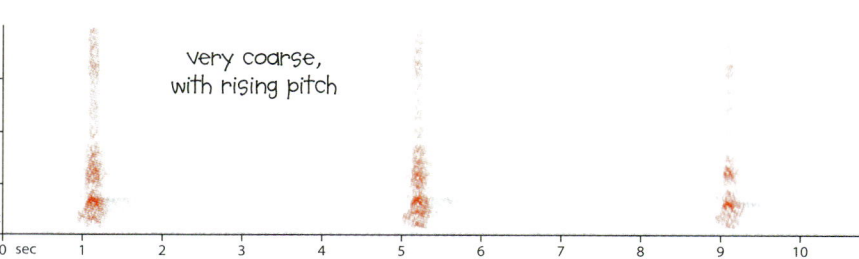

explain why hooting becomes much more noticeable in late April and May (Lundberg 1980), just before the young fledge.

In 2009, Vrezec published a paper on the Ural Owls of his native Slovenia in Dutch Birding. Arnoud was surprised by the very dark plumage of some individuals. In late May that year, he and Cecilia visited the eastern slopes of the Dinaric Alps, the ridge of mountains extending from the central European Alps into the Balkans. The Ural Owls breeding there are among the southernmost in Europe.

At the time of their visit, there was still plenty of hooting; the young were still in their nests. The male in **CD4-04** is not alone. In the distance there are at least two others. In the background, we can hear one reason why these forests support high densities of Ural Owls. The many harsh squeaks belong to Edible Dormice *Glis glis*.

Ural Owl *Strix uralensis* Veliki Rog, Carlola, Slovenia, 01:21, 27 May 2009. Hooting of three males. Background: Edible Dormouse *Glis glis*. 090527.AB.012131.11   CD4-04

Compound hooting and soliciting calls sound essentially the same in Ural Owls from Slovenia and Sweden. In **CD4-05**, both sounds feature in a food exchange between a male and a female. Carpathian/Dinaric '*macroura*' and Scandinavian '*liturata*' have long been treated as separate subspecies due to differences in plumage and proportions (eg, Cramp 1985). However, DNA studies have failed to find any evidence that they are genetically distinct populations (Hausknecht et al 2014).

In **CD4-06**, another food exchange is taking place, this time at a nestbox with small young. The female in this recording, a 10-year-old Finn, gives a continuous stream of soliciting calls. Immediately after taking the prey she disappears into the nest, presumably to hand it to the young. She goes

CD4-05 **Ural Owl** *Strix uralensis* Veliki Rog, Carlola, Slovenia, 02:07, 27 May 2009. The male announces his arrival with food by compound hooting, and the female responds with soliciting calls. The gaps between compound hoots are short, and as the male flies towards the female he shortens them even further, repeating just the first part of the compound hoot many times. When they meet, the female gives a series of high-pitched chitters. Background: Edible Dormouse *Glis glis*. 090527.AB.020745.32

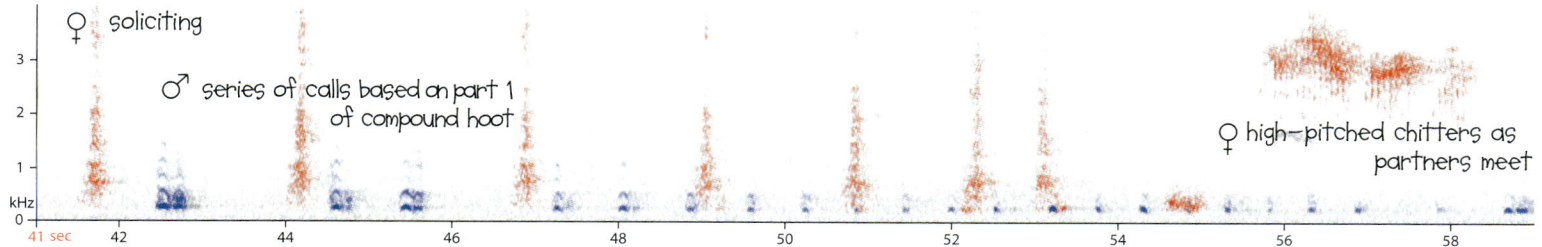

silent for a moment, then reappears and resumes calling *rrrèh* to the male. It is as if she is now saying: "Off with you! Get us some more!"

Ural Owl *Strix uralensis* Hauho, Kanta-Häme, Finland, 21:37, 1 May 2009. Compound hooting of male with very short gaps between series, which become incomplete as he approaches. Female soliciting calls almost throughout. Background: Common Wood Pigeon *Columba palumbus*, Black-throated Loon *Gavia arctica*, Common Gull *Larus canus*, European Robin *Erithacus rubecula* and Common Redstart *Phoenicurus phoenicurus*. 090501.DF.204100.11 **CD4-06**

Ural Owl *Strix uralensis*, female, Hauho, Kanta-Häme, Finland, 2 May 2009 (*Dick Forsman*)

Ural Owl *Strix uralensis*, Veliki Rog, Carlola, Slovenia, 28 June 2009 (*Arnoud B van den Berg*). At same site as CD4-04 to 05, CD4-07 & CD4-09 but a month later.

Sometimes females respond to males with their own version of compound hooting. Their hooting has a strikingly hoarse timbre, similar to that of their soliciting call. The female in CD4-07 belonged to the colour morph known only from the Carpathians and the Dinaric Alps: she appeared all-blackish with a contrasting yellow bill.

CD4-07   **Ural Owl** *Strix uralensis* Veliki Rog, Carlola, Slovenia, 19:49, 26 May 2009. Compound hooting of male and harsher female. Background: Common Cuckoo *Cuculus canorus*, Black Woodpecker *Dryocopus martius*, Eurasian Jay *Garrulus glandarius*, Common Blackbird *Turdus merula*, European Robin *Erithacus rubecula* and Common Chaffinch *Fringilla coelebs*. 090526.AB.194908.21

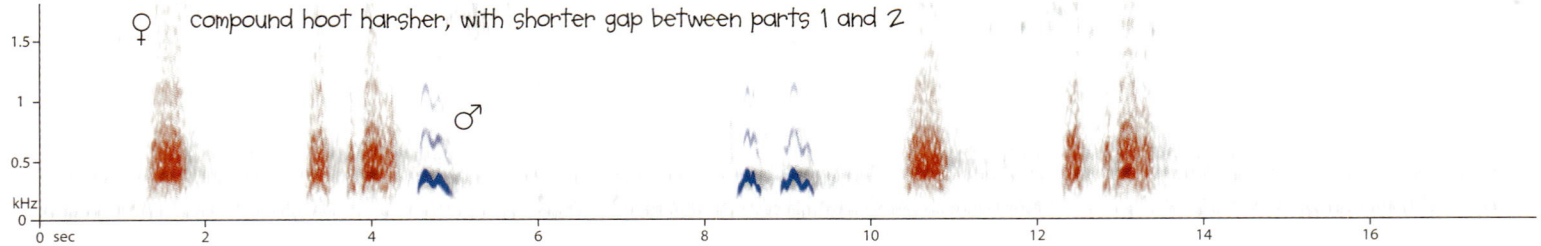

Ural Owl's pulsed hooting carries almost as far as its compound hooting. The male in **CD4-08** is the same as the one that featured in **CD4-01**. Females have a harsher version of this call. The pulses are always grouped into tidy strophes of a fairly regular length, as if they had been produced by a giant Tengmalm's Owl. Pulsed hooting features most prominently in nest-showing and in response to rivals, real or simulated. In Sweden it is often called the 'defensive call' (eg, Lindblad 1967).

Arnoud recorded pulsed hooting of several males when he and Cecilia visited Slovenia in spring 2009. There seems to be a subtle difference in pulsed hooting between northern and southern European populations of Ural Owl. When I compared seven male '*liturata*' with six male '*macroura*', the latter's hoots were delivered 16% more quickly on average, although there was plenty of overlap. The male in **CD4-09** is a typical 'southerner'.

On the whole, hooting varies remarkably little across the range of Ural Owl. Even in the smaller subspecies from Japan, both types of hooting sound basically the same as in European birds, just a little higher-pitched. In central China there is an isolated taxon that until recently was considered a subspecies

CD4-08   **Ural Owl** *Strix uralensis* Vällen, Uppland, Sweden, 23:00, 1 April 2006. Pulsed hooting of a male. Background: compound hooting of a distant male. 06.004. MR.13404.01

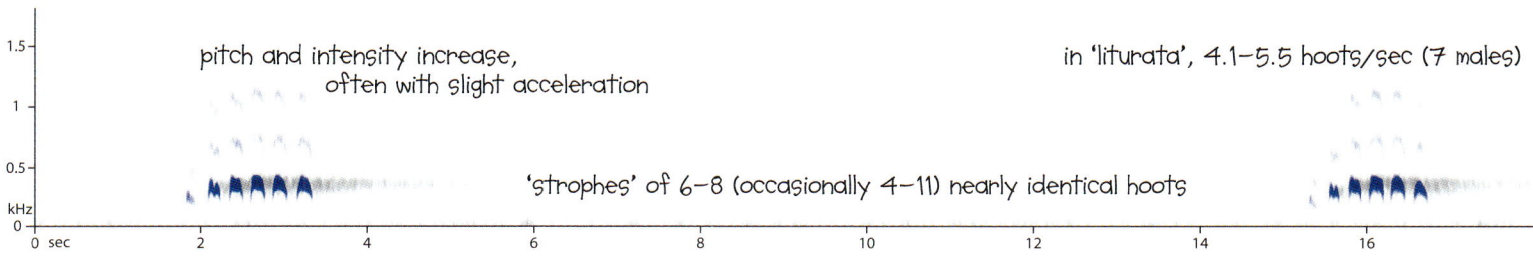

CD4-09   **Ural Owl** *Strix uralensis* Veliki Rog, Carlola, Slovenia, 01:21, 27 May 2009. Pulsed hooting of a male. Background: Edible Dormouse *Glis glis*. 090527.AB.012131.11

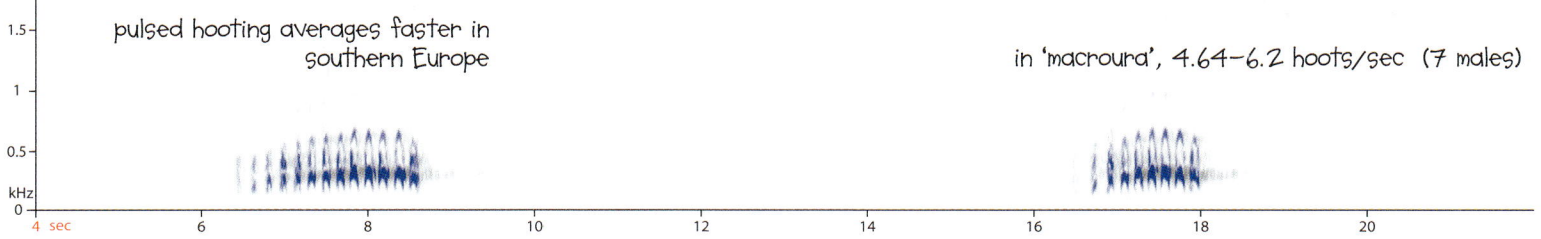

Ural Owl *Strix uralensis*, near Krakow, Poland, 2 May 2008 (*Chris van Rijswijk/birdshooting.nl*). The proportion of blackish (or greyish) morphs varies from 2.6% in Romania to 40% in the North Carpathians, but truly dark individuals like this one have never been recorded anywhere northeast of Poland. This is one reason why the Carpathian-Dinaric population has long been considered a separate subspecies, *S u 'macroura'*. Besides having many dark-morph individuals, '*macroura*' differs from other populations in having a longer tail and being slightly larger.

of Ural Owl. Sichuan Wood Owl *S davidi* is dark like most southern populations of Ural, lacking a pale morph. The only three males so far sound recorded in Gansu all had compound hooting consisting of just two parts, not three (Scherzinger 2005, Scherzinger & Fang 2006). In northern Sichuan, however, a three-part rhythmic pattern much closer to that of Ural Owl has been recorded (www.xeno-canto.org). Until recently Sichuan Wood Owl was little more than a spectre.

Talking of the supernatural, there is a goddess of birding and her name is 'the Sender'. In return for a small sacrifice - a pastry or a sweet that you really want – she can make the bird of your dreams appear. Dick is her prophet and regularly leaves offerings in exchange for a little extra luck. Once Mark and Mo, Dick and his wife Inki were working together to record young Ural Owls. After searching all weekend in vain, Dick prayed to the Sender, offering his last cigarette by piercing it on a pine needle hanging from a tree.

While waiting for an epiphany, they moved on to record Eurasian Pygmy Owls. Dick got a ladder from his car and Mo steadied it while he climbed up to a nestbox. As Dick removed the lid it slipped and knocked Mo on the head. Inki was shocked and Dick was horrified. Mark quickly recorded the young pygmy owls while Inki took Mo back to their accommodation.

"How unprofessional." Dick muttered, "I need that cigarette."
"But what if you offend the Sender?" said Mark. "You'll never get a Ural Owl."
Dick lit up, and Mark prepared for the worst.

Two days later Mark was recording the brood of four in **CD4-10**. They had been raised in a nestbox at a corner of a large 'owl meadow' between two woods, and fledged less than a week before Mark's visit. Showing him the spot, Professor Pertti Saurola had assured him that this female was "less aggressive than most of them." However, one of the young was now on the ground, right below the nestbox, and going near it would surely be asking for trouble.

Mark sat on his stool, recording from a respectful distance of about 100 m. Listening to roding Common Cuckoos *Cuculus canorus*, Eurasian Woodcocks *Scolopax rusticola*, Mistle Thrushes *Turdus viscivorus* and European Robins *Erithacus rubecula*, he began to relax. Soon he felt bold enough to take his microphones some 25 m closer. After a long recording he was making some comments when suddenly, two gruff barks behind his back stopped him in mid-sentence. Mark held the stool over his head, gathered his gear and bolted. When Dick heard the recording a few days later, he laughed out loud. "You ran away from a female Goldeneye!"

Ural Owl *Strix uralensis* Hauho, Kanta-Häme, Finland, 21:38, 25 May 2009. Begging calls of three recently fledged young. Background: Green Sandpiper *Tringa ochropus*, Eurasian Woodcock *Scolopax rusticola*, Common Cuckoo *Cuculus canorus*, Mistle Thrush *Turdus viscivorus* and European Robin *Erithacus rubecula*. 090525.MC.213800.31   CD4-10

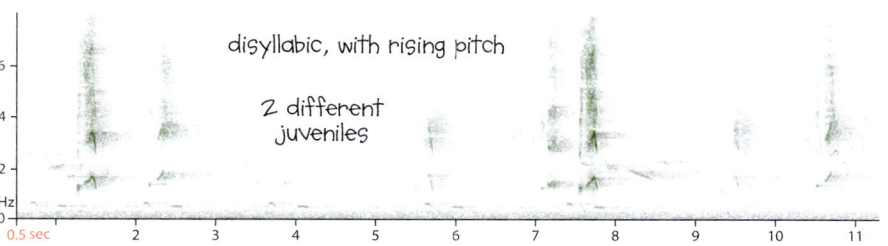

Female Ural Owls can be surprisingly docile when incubating. Their aggression only flares from the time when the young

Ural Owl *Strix uralensis*, Hauho, Kanta-Häme, Finland, 2 May 2009 (*Dick Forsman*). Female in nestbox with chicks of different ages.

Ural Owl *Strix uralensis*, Pälkäne, Pirkanmaa, Finland, 2 June 2006 (*Dick Forsman*)

CD4-11 **Ural Owl** *Strix uralensis* Hauho, Kanta-Häme, Finland, 3 May 2009. Guarding calls of a female. Background: Black-headed Gull *Chroicocephalus ridibundus*, Fieldfare *Turdus pilaris*, Song Thrush *T philomelos*, Redwing *T iliacus* and Yellowhammer *Emberiza citrinella*. 090503.DF.073000.22

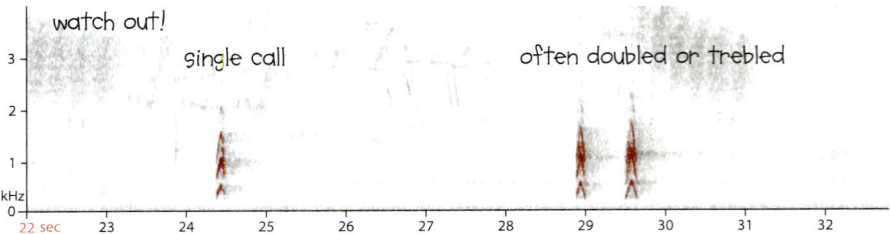

leave the nest until they are able to fly. Females usually stand guard from a hiding place in the top of a nearby tree (Mebs & Scherzinger 2004). Their first sign of nervousness is often a little compound hooting, followed by abrupt barks that I call 'guarding calls' (**CD4-11**). Males use these far less often.

To lure the intruder away, the female flies to a conspicuous perch in a direction away from the young. A drawn-out, high-pitched harsh whistle, rather unsteady in pitch and volume, serves as a distraction call. If approached, the female flies further still, repeating this until the intruder is a safe distance from the brood. Should the intruder go closer to the nest, she will start snapping her bill (**CD4-12**), even during the incubation period when she is less aggressive.

CD4-12 **Ural Owl** *Strix uralensis* Oulu, Finland, 15:30, 8 May 2002. Bill-snapping of an adult female, during nestbox inspection. Background: Common Treecreeper *Certhia familiaris*, Common Chaffinch *Fringilla coelebs* and Yellowhammer *Emberiza citrinella*. 02.006.KM.01500.32

When her attack is imminent she stares at the intruder while adopting a special posture. Shifting from foot to foot on the perch, she ruffles her plumage, droops her wings slightly and spreads her tail. In one smooth glide she strikes with sharp claws on the head and shoulders and sometimes bites hard. At 40 km/h she exerts a force equivalent to 72 kg falling from a height of 1 m (Lindblad 1967). Whenever possible she attacks from behind. The male rarely joins in.

In autumn, Ural Owls produce some of their most vicious sounds, but we no longer need to fear them. Territorial barks (**CD4-13**) are almost identical to guarding calls, but have a different meaning. Ural Owls use them most often early in the autumn and only direct them at rivals and other species of owls, not at humans. Sometimes, however, a barking Roe Deer *Capreolus capreolus* suggests a rival strongly enough to elicit a response. Territorial barking gives way to other aggressive calls during the course of the autumn, before making a brief resurgence in early spring. Male and female versions are identical, but pair members never direct these barks at one another (Scherzinger 1980).

Ural Owl *Strix uralensis*, Veliki Rog, Carlola, Slovenia, 28 June 2009 (*Arnoud B van den Berg*)

CD4-13 **Ural Owl** *Strix uralensis* Cisów-Orłowiny landscape park, Świętckrzyskie, Poland, 05:22, 6 October 2012. Territorial barks of a female in autumn, the same individual as in CD4-14. 121006.MR.052202.01

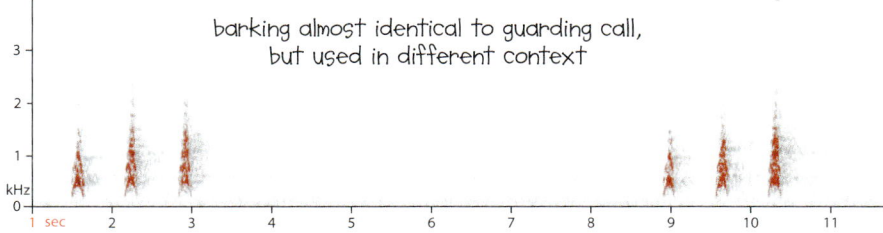

One windy night in autumn 2012, I visited the territory of a pair of Ural Owls in southern Poland. They stayed silent, so eventually I tried provoking them with imitations. I don't remember how many times I had tried when suddenly, without warning, a female gave a barrage of expletives right behind my back (**CD4-14**). My hair stood on end! I stayed around for several more hours, making a few more cautious imitations in the hope of more recordings, but she never came close again.

Ural Owl *Strix uralensis* Cisów-Orłowiny landscape park, Świętokrzyskie, Poland, 18:22, 6 October 2012. Highly aggressive response to mimicry of compound hooting. Starts with several '*koRAH* screams' leading to a '*koRAH*-series' (Scherzinger 1980). The basic unit of both is a stretched and subverted version *rrrèh* soliciting call. Harsh, rising in pitch and stressed on the second syllable, they differ from all other calls described so far in being given with the bill wide open. 121006.MR.182226.02 CD4-14

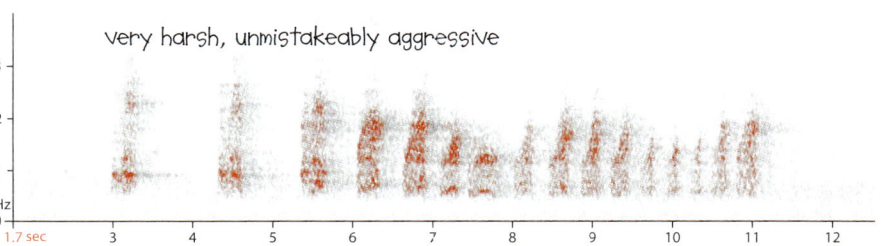

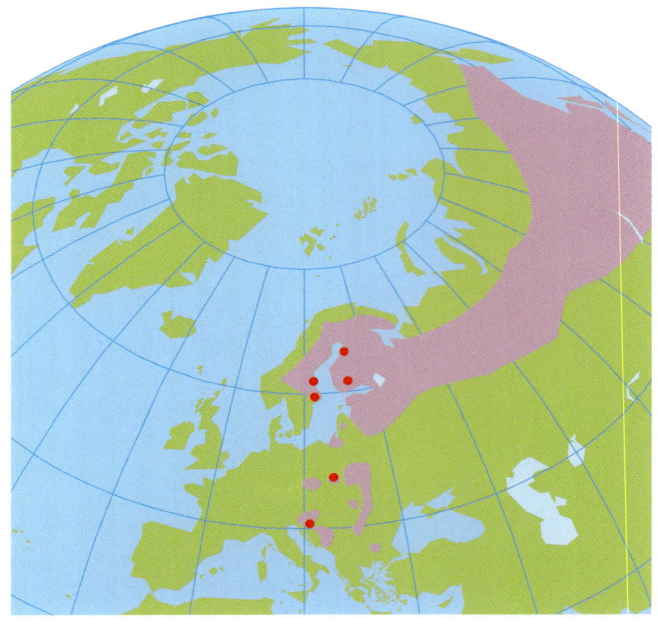

Approximate breeding distribution of Ural Owl *Strix uralensis* ■. Recording locations indicated by ● dots.

While Ural Owl has a limited distribution in Europe, another aggressive wood owl breeds across most of the continent. I once recorded an angry exchange between a pair of Tawny Owls and a male Ural (**CD4-15**). Twice, the Ural interrupted the male Tawny to show who was boss, but the Tawny was not to be silenced. There were plenty of voles for all the owls to eat so that year at least, he would be safe.

Tawny Owl may not pack quite as much punch as Ural Owl, but makes up for this in noise and numbers. Tawny is much more vocal than Ural, and over much of its range it is the commonest owl of all. For many Europeans, Tawny is the only owl they ever hear.

CD4-15   **Tawny Owl** *Strix aluco* and **Ural Owl** *S uralensis* Vällen, Uppland, Sweden, 04:00, 2 April 2006. Distance call and compound hooting of male Tawny, with soliciting calls of female. Compound hooting of male Ural. Background: wingbeats of Common Goldeneye *Bucephala clangula*. 06.004.MR.14426.12

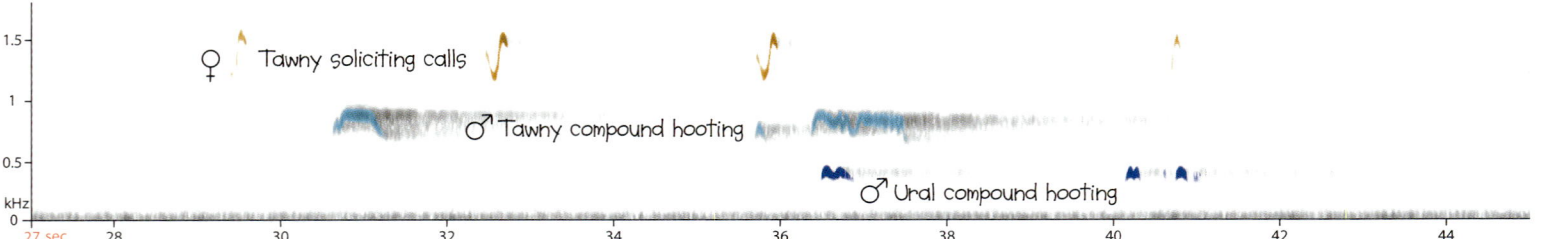

Tawny Owl

Since my childhood, sounds of Tawny Owl *Strix aluco* have been so familiar that it would be easy to take them for granted, were they not so wild and inviting. Untangling their intricacies is a challenge, but many before me have helped to clear the way. It was only when starting work on this chapter that I realised how little I knew.

In the Sound Approach team, Arnoud lives closest to Tawny Owls. Just round the corner he often sees one peeping out of the tall chimney of an old house. When he cycles past at dusk, his neighbours are switching on their lights. The curtains are open, and the folks inside are watching the news or having dinner. As he cycles on between the sports fields, he hears other Tawny Owls in the wooded North Sea dunes beyond. Arnoud finds a suitable spot and leaves his gear recording all night. **CD4-16** is a male hooting close to the microphones at 04:13 in the morning.

Familiar as these sounds seem to us, we can hardly begin to appreciate what Tawny Owls hear in them. In a few seconds they

Tawny Owl *Strix aluco*, adult roosting in chimney, Bloemendaal, Noord-Holland, Netherlands, 6 September 2010 (*Arnoud B van den Berg*)

CD4-16   **Tawny Owl** *Strix aluco* Kennemerduinen, Bloemendaal, Netherlands, 04:13, 12 May 2011. Compound hooting of a male. Measurements based on 16 solo males, four each from four Western Palearctic lineages: Balkans-northern Europe, Iberia, Italy and the Caucasus (each male's mean based on 3 compound hoots). Background: Eurasian Coot *Fulica atra*, Woodlark *Lullula arborea* and Common Nightingale *Luscinia megarhynchos*. 110512.AB.041300.01

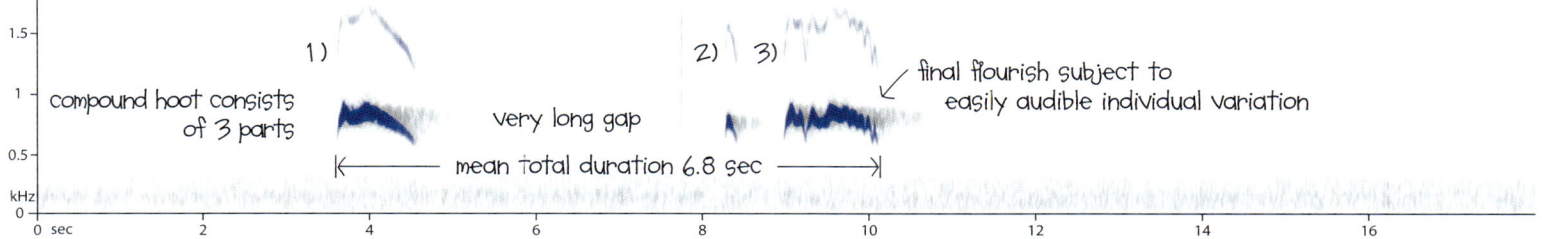

Redpath 1997, Galeotti 1998, Galeotti & Pavan 2008, Redpath et al 2000). With so many variables at play, no two neighbours sound quite the same. Even for humans, telling individuals apart by ear is often surprisingly easy.

If Tawny Owls made long distance phone calls like us, their local accents would be very noticeable to their listeners. Each habitat has its own acoustics, requiring slightly different hoots. In dense woodlands for example, lower-pitched hoots are better able to penetrate the many obstacles present. Open habitats permit higher-pitched hoots, but if conditions are windy then a lower pitch may be better. Galeotti et al (1996) found the lowest-pitched Tawny in a karst region in Italy with very dense brushwood, subject to strong east winds. The male in **CD4-17**, from a similar habitat in Portugal, is also near the lower end of Tawny's pitch range. Even the female, heard from time to time just after the male, seems unusually low-pitched.

During the last ice age, Tawny Owls in Europe retreated to three different refuges where there was still suitable habitat. From their Balkan refuge they later spread to Britain, northern Europe and eastern Europe, from Italy they went north as far as southern France, while those that had survived in Iberia made it no further than the Pyrenees (Brito 2005). There is evidence that at least two of these lineages developed slightly different hoots. Compound hoots from England have a more arched first note and a longer second note than hoots from northern Italy (Galeotti et al 1996). A fourth lineage, *S a wilkonskii* breeding in the Caucasus and south of the Caspian Sea, is more distantly related (Brito 2005). The Armenian male in **CD4-18** is one of only a handful that have ever been sound recorded.

Female Tawny Owls also hoot (**CD4-19**), although in spring they often give just one or two strophes when the male delivers prey. They

can learn a great deal about who is calling, just as we do when we answer the telephone. Based on harshness and length and the pitch and relative proportions of particular syllables, they can tell which individual it is, the sex, likely dimensions and weight, its health, level of aggression and the probable quality of its territory (Appleby &

CD4-17 **Tawny Owl** *Strix aluco* Rocha da Pena, Loulé, Portugal, 22:43, 19 March 2009. Compound hooting of a male, with occasional contributions from a female. Another male hoots in the distance. Background: Little Owl *Athene vidalii* and Eurasian Eagle-Owl *Bubo bubo*. 090319.MR.224346.01

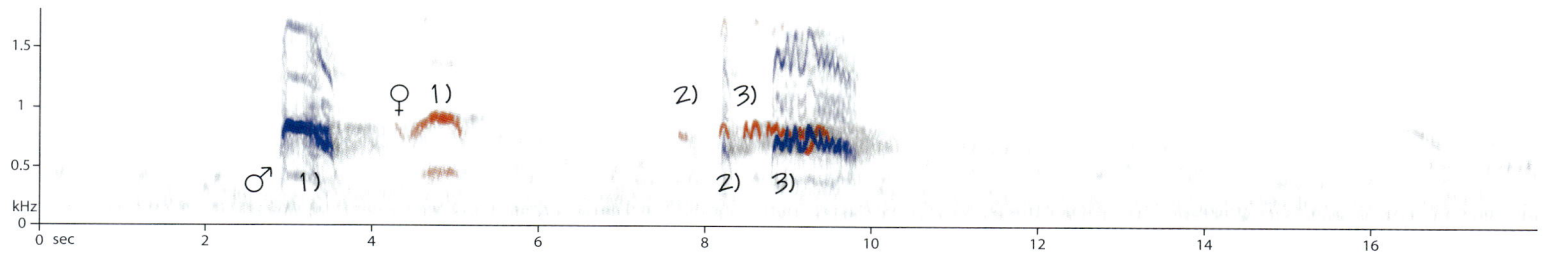

CD4-18 **Tawny Owl** *Strix aluco wilkonskii* Dilijan, Tavush, Armenia, 22:04, 2 May 2011. Hooting of a male, with another calling in the distance. 110502.MR.220456.31

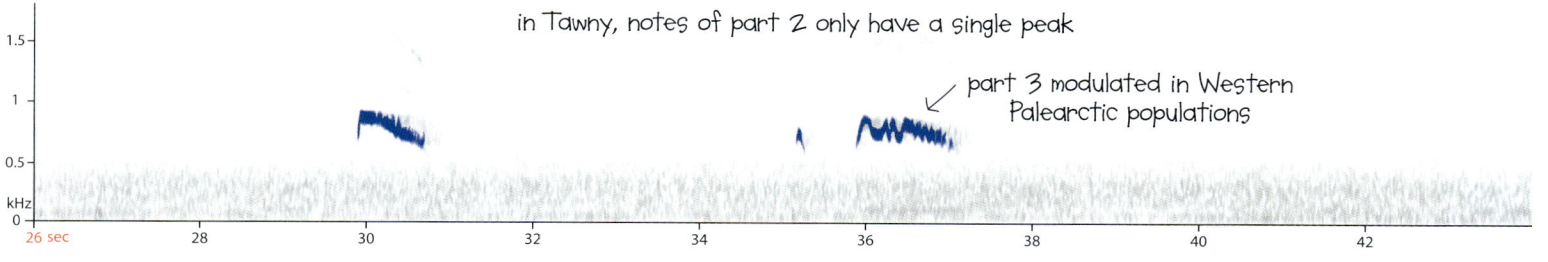

CD4-19 **Tawny Owl** *Strix aluco* Pancas, Benavente, Portugal, 21:06, 13 February 2014. Compound hooting of a female, responding to her mate in the distance. At 0:58, the male gives an excited compound hoot with more than one short note in the middle, just before copulation. This is unusual and only happens at moments of high excitement. Background: European Tree Frog *Hyla arborea* and Eurasian Stone-curlew *Burhinus oedicnemus*. 140213.MR.210640.02

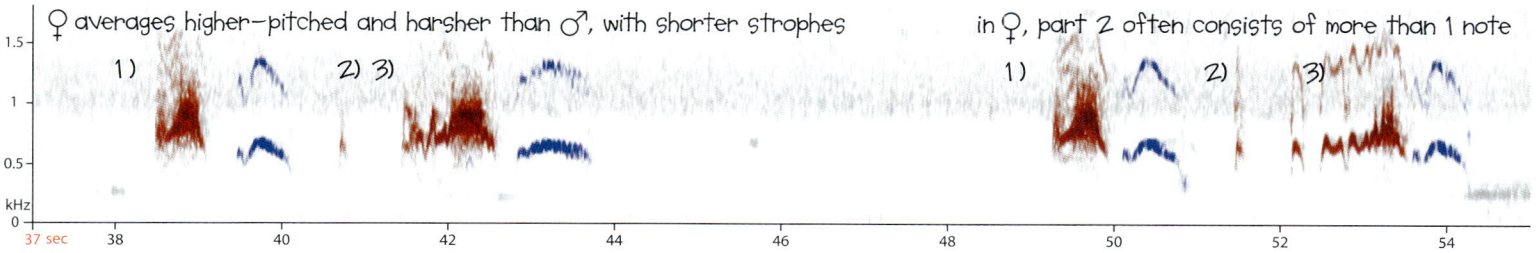

hoot much more intensively in autumn. Often females have two short, well-separated notes in the middle of a strophe instead of the male's one, but there can be anything from zero to three (Galeotti 1998, Hambling 2008). One reason why female compound hoots are so variable is because of the highly charged situations in which they occur. In fact, female compound hooting is only really equivalent to more excited variants of male compound hooting. Males also give more variable hoots when excited, but rarely have more than one middle note. In close contact with females they often shorten the gaps, both within and between strophes, and in territorial disputes their timbre may become harsh and whining. Sometimes, either sex may hoot just the first note of a compound hoot (cf, **CD4-24**).

The female's best known sound is her soliciting call. It varies from an intimate *kuWI*, barely audible at a few tens of metres, to a strident and far-carrying *kuWICK*. The timbre is slightly harsh, although this may only be evident at close range. During the breeding season, the female will often solicit for up to a minute or longer when she knows that the male is near the nest. The calls are given singly, not clustered, and this distinguishes them from the very similar 'distance call' (cf **CD4-29**). Males can go for long periods without using the soliciting call, especially during the breeding season. **CD4-20** is a male-female conversation with soliciting calls in autumn. The male's soliciting calls are marginally lower-pitched and lack the slight harshness of the female's.

Thanks to film and TV soundtracks, even people who have never heard a real Tawny Owl would be able to recognise one, at least as an owl of some kind. Their compound hooting and soliciting calls are well known, but what other sounds do they make? One of the most striking is pulsed hooting, a call type that all Western Palearctic *Strix* owls have in one form or another. In Tawny it consists of a 'bubbling' series of very short hoots, and

Tawny Owl *Strix aluco* Kennemerduinen, Bloemendaal, Netherlands, 00:11, 30 September 2011. An exchange of *kuWICK* calls between male and female. Background: distant male, and Fallow Deer *Dama dama*. 110930.AB.001103.01

CD4-20

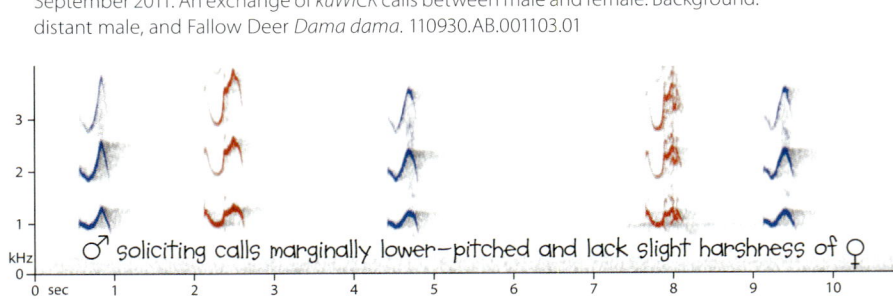

CD4-21 **Tawny Owl** *Strix aluco* Kennemerduinen, Bloemendaal/Velsen, Netherlands, 01:23, 25 September 2011. Male pulsed hooting in autumn, with soliciting calls and an incomplete compound hoot of a female. 110925.AB.012337.02

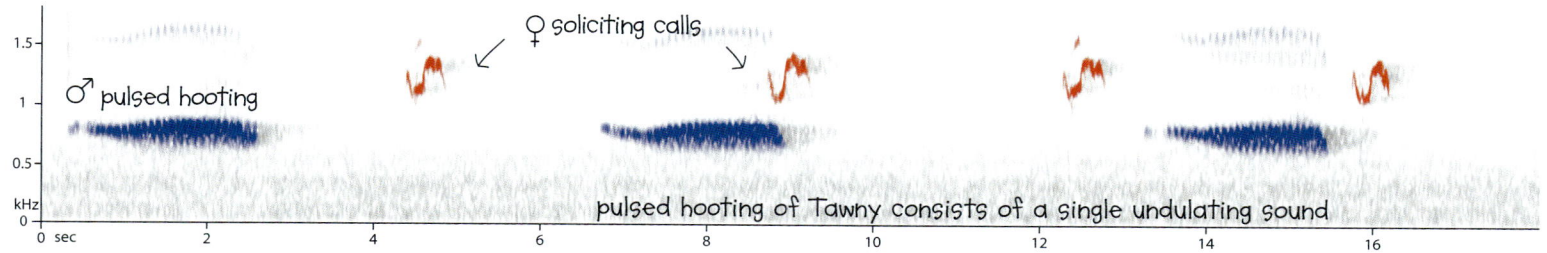

CD4-22 **Tawny Owl** *Strix aluco* Saasveld, Dinkelland, Netherlands, 20:56, 11 December 2013. Pulsed hooting of a female. Background: dripping wet trees. 131211.AB.205656.21

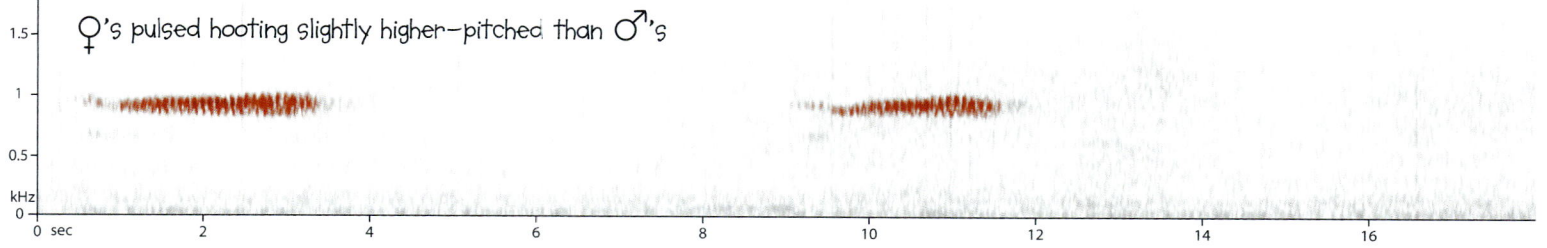

birders often compare it to Tengmalm's Owl *Aegolius funereus* or the drumming of a Common Snipe *Gallinago gallinago*. Despite being a common sound, it can easily trip up the unwary.

Autumn is the time when Tawny Owls use pulsed hooting most often and in its purest form, like the male in **CD4-21**. Arnoud recorded the female in **CD4-22** when, together with Peter Nuyten, he was following up a report of a rare autumn 'Tengmalm's Owl'. Perhaps Tawny Owl's pulsed hooting would be more familiar if autumn owling were more popular.

There is always a fine line between affection and aggression, and passions can flare easily. When a male and female Tawny Owl come close together, you never know quite what you will hear, but pulsed hooting often makes a fleeting appearance. The first note or the final note of a compound hoot can easily be extended into a pulsed hoot (**CD4-23**).

Some sounds of Tawny Owl are both infrequent and brief. While preparing this chapter I wanted to improve our examples of female hooting, and I also realised that I'd never experienced the climax of their courtship. As it was early March I thought

CD4-23   **Tawny Owl** *Strix aluco* Fårträsk, Uusimaa, Finland, 00:20, 29 April 2009. Male-female encounter at a nestbox, with *kuWICK* calls of female and mixed compound and pulsed hooting of the male. The female leaves the nest when the male arrives and it is not clear whether he feeds her or not. Background: Fieldfare *Turdus pilaris*, Song Thrush *T philomelos*, European Robin *Erithacus rubecula* and Great Tit *Parus major*. 090428.DF.232856.01

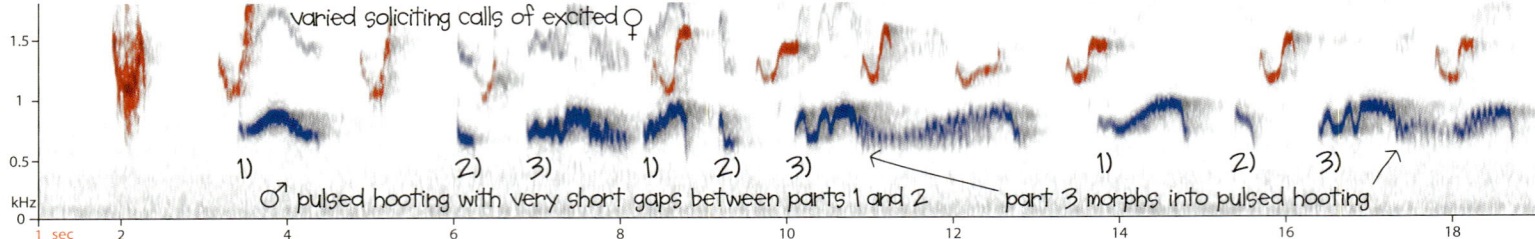

but not the time when they copulated in the tree right beside my microphones (**CD4-24**).

After the young hatch, several new sounds make their appearance. Whenever the male brings prey, the female gives faint, nasal, often slightly disyllabic feeding calls at a rate of about 3-4/sec while offering out tiny morsels to her brood (**CD4-25**, from 0:11). This is one of the first signs that they have hatched.

By the time the young become audible from below the nesting tree, their begging call is a faint, uninflected and drawn-out *seep*. From an early age, juveniles also use their chitter call. The juveniles in **CD2-26**, using both call-types, had already clambered out of the nest. As they grow older their begging calls become louder and more disyllabic (**CD4-27**), and by the time they are able to fly we can hear them from up to several hundred metres away.

As I moved closer to the juveniles in **CD4-27**, their mother started to become nervous. Her yelping *quek-quek-quek* is so

Tawny Owl *Strix aluco*, Ruissalo, Varsinais-Suomi, Finland, 15 March 2012 (*Dick Forsman*)

I might still be in with a chance, so I paid a visit to a pair that shared a barn with a pair of Common Barn Owls *Tyto alba*. I included one recording of the Tawny pair already (cf, **CD4-19**),

CD4-24 Tawny Owl *Strix aluco* Pancas, Benavente, Portugal, 22:24, 13 February 2014. Call sequence leading up to copulation. At the start, the male (left) hoots single notes and the slightly closer female (right) replies. At 0:52 the male does a complete, heavily modulated compound hoot that morphs into pulsed hooting, and flies right to the female. She does two compound hoots in quick succession and at 1:04-1:07 they copulate. Background: European Tree Frog *Hyla arborea*, Southern Tree Frog *H meridionalis* and Iberian Green Frog *Pelophylax perezi*. 140313.MR.222450.02

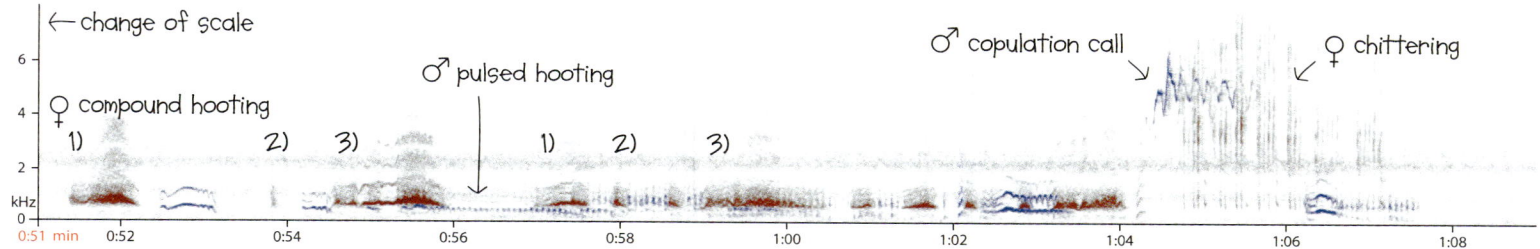

CD4-25 Tawny Owl *Strix aluco* Pancas, Benavente, Portugal, 21:57, 26 February 2013. Compound hooting of male and female, then very quiet feeding calls of female from inside the nest. Background: Mallard *Anas platyrhynchos* and Eurasian Coot *Fulica atra*. 130226.MR.215739.12

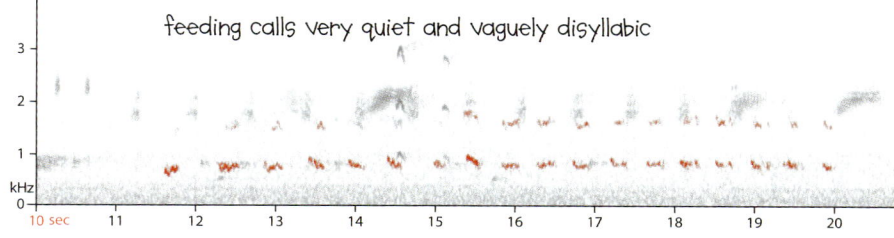

Tawny Owl *Strix aluco*, adult, Akseki, Antalya, Turkey, 21 June 2009 (*Arnoud B van den Berg*)

CD4-26 Tawny Owl *Strix aluco* Kennemerduinen, Bloemendaal, Netherlands, 00:01, 6 June 2004. Begging and chitter calls of fledglings. 04.021.AB.04332.21

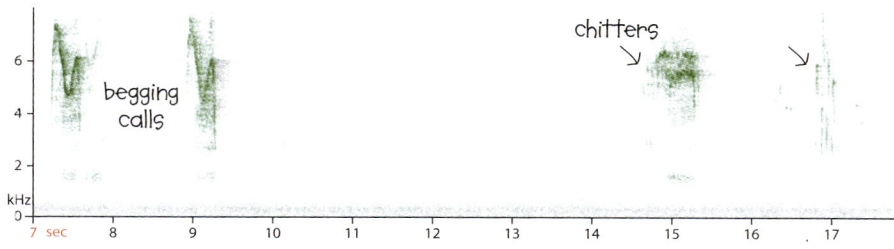

Tawny Owl *Strix aluco* Pancas, Benavente, Portugal, 22:37, 25 May 2013. Begging calls of fledged brood, with guarding calls of female and distant compound hooting of male. Background: Mallard *Anas platyrhynchos* wingbeats, and Common Barn Owl *Tyto alba*. 130525.MR.223710.11

CD4-27

Tawny Owl *Strix aluco* Pancas, Benavente, Portugal, 22:59, 25 May 2013. Guarding calls of female, with begging calls of fledglings and compound hooting of male on left. Background: Red-necked Nightjar *Caprimulgus ruficollis* and European Nightjar *C europaeus*. 130525.MR.225912.21

CD4-28

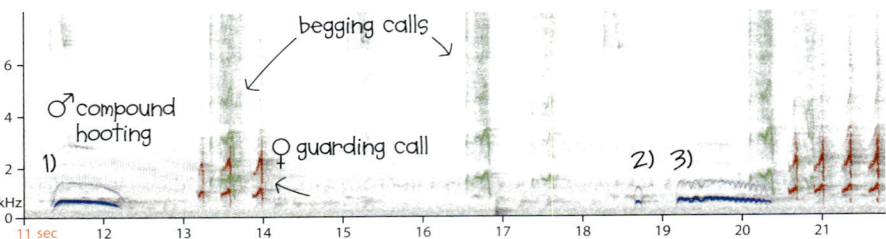

typical of such a situation that I call it her guarding call (**CD4-28**). Håkan has heard a markedly deeper version from a male. As the situation becomes more threatening, the calls become louder and sharper. The guarding call serves as a warning not only for the benefit of the brood, but also for the intruder.

Tawny Owls can be surprisingly nasty in defence of their young. Bird photography pioneer Eric Hosking lost his left eye to a Tawny, and another female attacked W A Cadman, a ringer who was inspecting a nestbox he had erected in his back garden. Determined to reprimand her, he constructed a "glorified butterfly net" and ascended the tree once again: "the Owl came almost at once, and before I could even raise the net she had struck me a glancing blow which turned my jacket right back over my shoulder. She struck me in all five times, and each time she managed to choose the exact moment when I was unable to use the net. Her most effective coup was one to the seat of my trousers!" (Cadman 1934).

While the guarding call belongs to the latter part of the breeding season, there is a slightly different call that we can

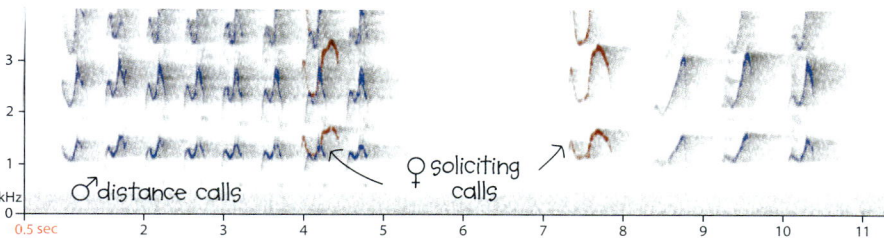

Tawny Owl *Strix aluco* Kennemerduinen, Bloemendaal/Velsen, Netherlands, 02:11, 25 September 2011. Distance calls of a male, with soliciting calls of female. 110925.AB.021132.21

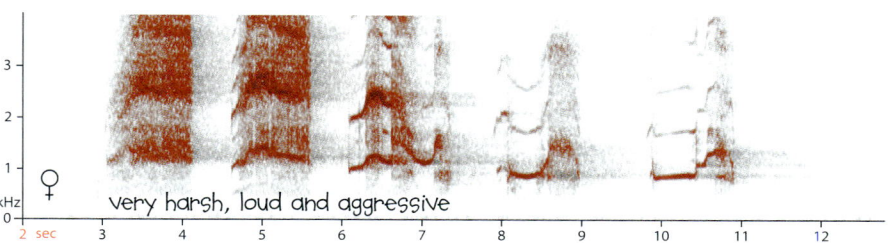

Tawny Owl *Strix aluco* Białowieża forest, Podlaskie, Poland, 18:46, 4 October 2012. Harsh screaming in response to a Tengmalm's Owl *Aegolius funereus* imitation (not included). 121004.MR.184648.01

hear all year round, especially in autumn. This 'distance call' (**CD4-29**) also consists of yelping sounds, but its delivery is slightly slower and the individual yelps are disyllabic, like a series of very fast soliciting calls. The distance call is used in long distance communication with rivals or other owl species, and never directed at the partner (Scherzinger 1980). The name refers to its role in keeping enemies at a safe distance. I have heard Tawny Owls replying to Ural Owls with this call (cf, **CD4-15**), which is a homologue to Ural's territorial barking. Often it forms the opening salvo of an aggressive interaction, to be followed up with compound hooting or other sounds. Mark once received a livid blast of distance calls after making one *kuWICK* with his trusty owl whistle. The reply was so sudden that Mo came out of the cottage to check that everything was OK.

The only time I have ever really been spooked by a Tawny Owl was during an autumn trip to Białowieża forest in Poland. I had been walking towards an area where I hoped to record Tengmalm's Owls when I heard a pair of Tawny Owls calling nearby. They stopped before I could record them but provoked a Tengmalm's into giving a *tsyuck*, so I waited. After a few minutes of silence I imitated Tengmalm's hooting. A Tawny cursed me harshly in response (**CD4-30**). According to Wendland (1963), only females use such foul language. The calls that I recorded may be a highly excited, aggressive subversion of the soliciting call, and are surely equivalent to the *koRAH* scream of Ural Owl (cf, **CD4-14**).

For me, the sound of Tawny Owls settling scores in autumn is a nocturnal highlight on a par with rutting deer and the mass migration of thrushes. In **CD4-31**, there are no thrushes, but Fallow Deer *Dama dama* are grunting in the far distance. A pair of Tawnies on the right are replying to a more distant male on the left. The males exchange compound hoots in an orderly fashion, and then the pair join forces in a duet. In their combined aggression, their voices caterwaul like fighting tomcats or foxes, and one could easily assume that these are two inexperienced young owls practicing their calls while squabbling over territory.

CD4-31   **Tawny Owl** *Strix aluco* Kennemerduinen, Bloemendaal, Netherlands, 00:11, 30 September 2011. Compound hooting of two males, and soliciting calls of a female. From 0:39, aggressive duet of nearer male and female. The breaking of branches may be part of the aggressive display. Background: acorns falling, and Fallow Deer *Dama dama*. 110930.AB.001103.01

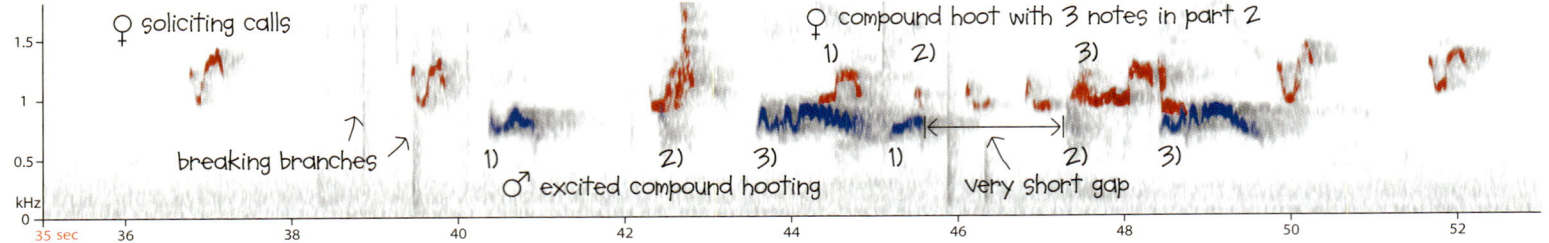

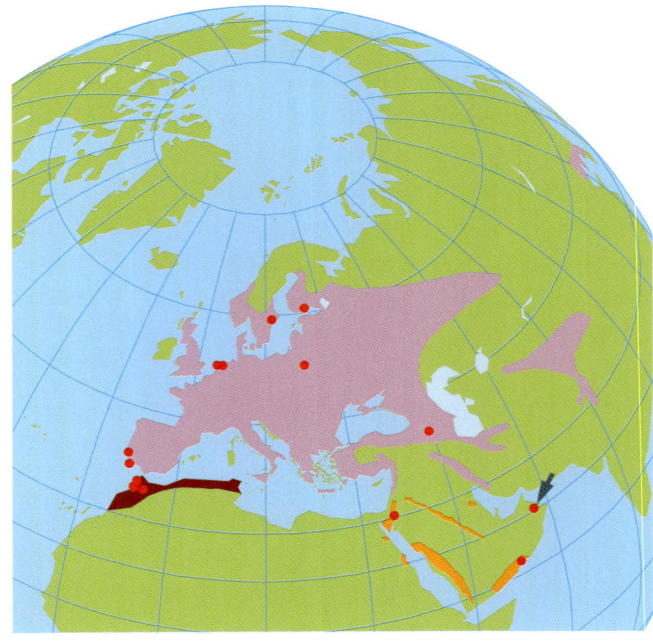

Approximate breeding distribution of Tawny Owl *Strix aluco* ■, Maghreb Wood Owl *S mauritanica* ■, Hume's Owl *S butleri* ■ and Omani Owl *S omanensis* ■ arrow. Recording locations indicated by ● dots.

However, the majority of excited close-range interactions between Tawny Owls in autumn are in fact male-female duets, very excited but nevertheless innate adult sounds. Very few seem to be male-male fights. It all comes down to levels of excitement, and in the autumn, Tawny Owls can get very excited.

It was autumn owl sounds like these that I first heard as a child, as belligerent Tawny Owls patrolled our neighbourhood in Edinburgh, Scotland. We lived not far from the Water of Leith, a small river with woodland along its banks. I recognised the owls from the traditional *tu-whit, tu-who* that my mum used to imitate them. From the security of a warm bed, I would imagine a family of owls perched on chimneypots across the road, but I rarely if ever saw them.

I still hear Tawny Owls far more often than I see them. Knowing their calls allows me to understand what they are up to in the dark. Hearing parallels in species I know less well, I can make educated guesses about them too. Compared to Tawny Owl, Maghreb Wood Owl *S mauritanica*, Hume's Owl *S butleri* and Omani Owl *S omanensis* are almost virgin species, untouched by science. Discovering them is both a pleasure and a privilege.

Tawny Owl *Strix aluco*

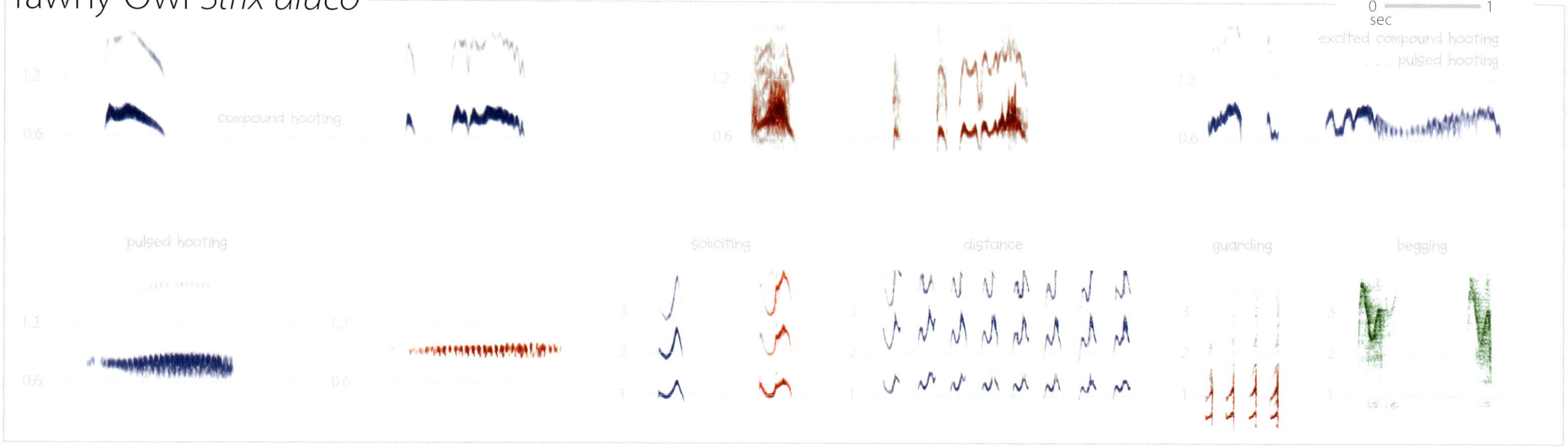
0
1
sec
excited compound hooting
. . . pulsed hooting
1.2
0.6
compound hooting
pulsed hooting
soliciting
distance
guarding
begging
3
2
1

Maghreb Wood Owl *Strix mauritanica*

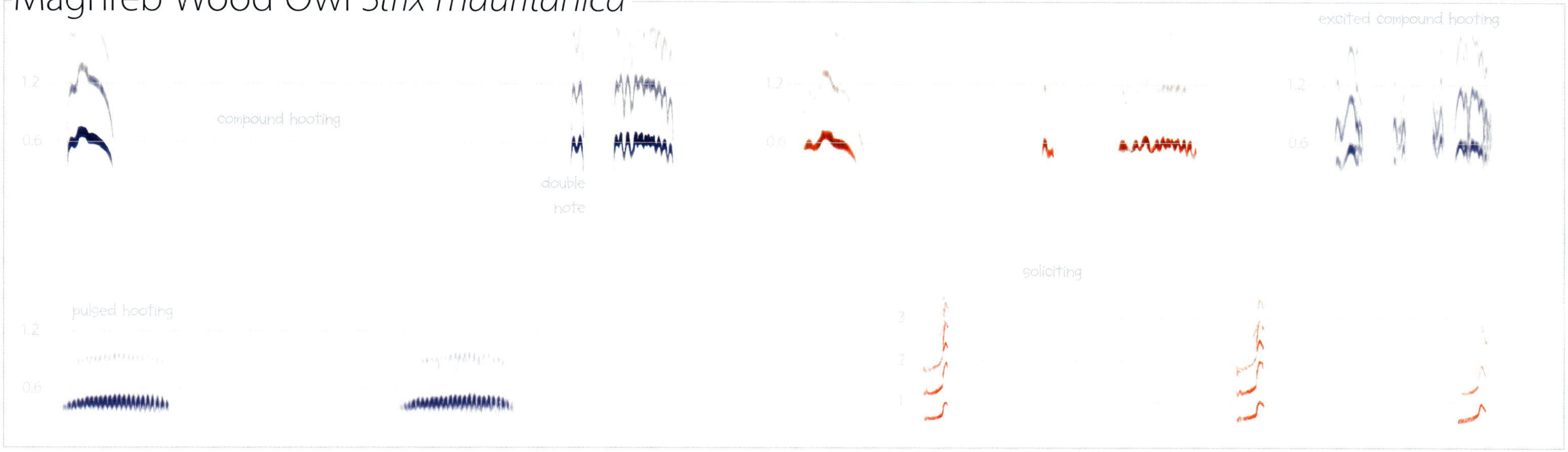
excited compound hooting
1.2
0.6
compound hooting
double
note
pulsed hooting
soliciting
3
2
1

Maghreb Wood Owl

'The Maghreb' traditionally consists of the Atlas mountains and the coastal plains from Morocco to Libya. Arnoud has recorded Maghreb Wood Owl *Strix mauritanica* in Tunisia and many sites in Morocco. One of the most beautiful was the Atlas Cedar *Cedrus atlantica* forest near Azrou in the Moyen Atlas, about 1700 m above sea level. In late June 2010, Arnoud and Cecilia stayed there for a few days. They focussed on some gravel tracks where they had previously found family groups of Barbary Ape *Macaca sylvanus* foraging in mature woodland of pine *Pinus*, cedar and oak *Quercus*.

On the evening of 23 June, there was a bright moon when Arnoud heard a male hooting high in an enormous cedar. He rolled his car slowly under the tree and pushed the microphones through the window, onto the car roof. In **CD4-32**, the male and a rival in the next territory are compound hooting.

Habitat of Maghreb Wood Owl *Strix mauritanica*, Forêt de Cèdres, Azrou, Western Middle Atlas, Morocco, 12 June 2010 (*Cecilia Bosman*). Mixed cedar wood with Barbary Apes *Macaca sylvanus*. Same site as in CD4-32.

CD4-32 **Maghreb Wood Owl** *Strix mauritanica* Forêt de Cèdres, Azrou, Western Middle Atlas, Morocco, 23:29, 23 June 2010. Compound hooting of two males, one near and one far. Background: European Nightjar *Caprimulgus europaeus*. 100623.AB.232900.11

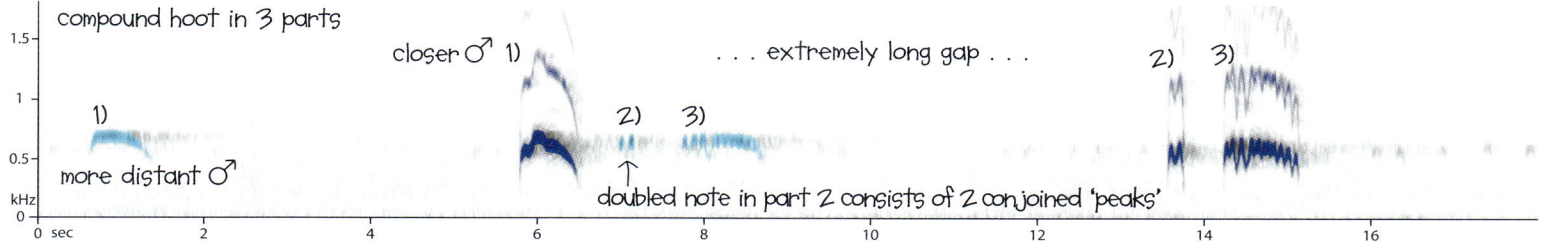

When Arnoud first played me recordings of Maghreb Wood Owls, I agreed with him that they sounded odd. At the time I was unable to say why, except that they sounded deeper than Tawny Owls *S aluco*, as if they had 'somebody else's voice'. Now having just spent three weeks listening to hundreds of recordings of Tawny, I hear another difference straight away. Listen to the second of the three parts, the double note coming after the long gap. Tawny only ever has a single note in this position, or up to three single, well-separated notes in females. Believe me, I went back and checked!

Now listen to one of those earlier recordings that Arnoud made in the same area back in 2002 (**CD4-33**). It also features two males, both doubling their second note. To me, the more interesting male is the distant one. Its first two compound hoots have total duration of 11 and 12.8 sec, respectively. This is incredibly long for a *Strix* owl, and in fact Maghreb Wood Owl's compound hoots average around 20% longer than those of Tawny Owl. They also average around 20% lower-pitched. This refers to the normal, calm version of the compound hoot. When the owls become more excited, their hoots change dramatically.

CD4-33 **Maghreb Wood Owl** *Strix mauritanica* Forêt de Cèdres, Azrou, Western Middle Atlas, Morocco, 21:17, 26 March 2002. Compound hooting of two males, one near and one far. Means based on 14 solo males from widely scattered locations in Morocco and Tunisia (each male's mean based on three compound hoots). Background: Eurasian Scops Owl *Otus scops*. 02.004.AB.11948.22

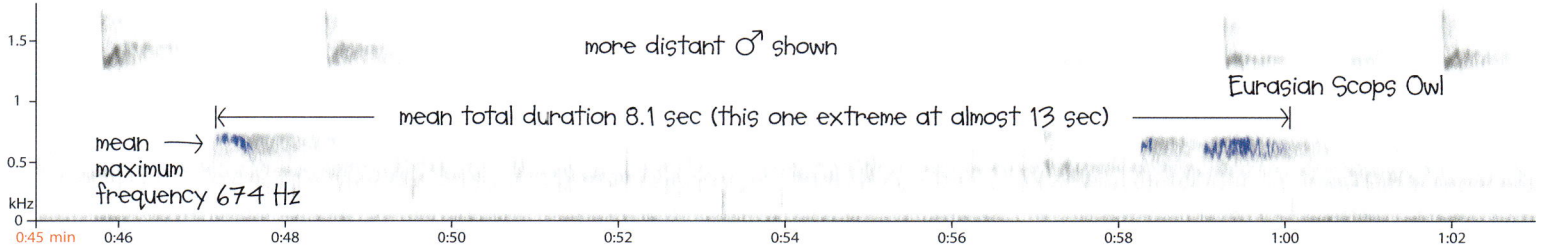

CD4-34   **Maghreb Wood Owl** *Strix mauritanica* Dar es Salam, Rabat, Zaër, Morocco, 20:34, 1 October 2009. Compound hooting of a male, and from 0:57, a female, followed by excited compound hooting of male. Background: compound hooting of a distant male. 091001.AB.203440.02

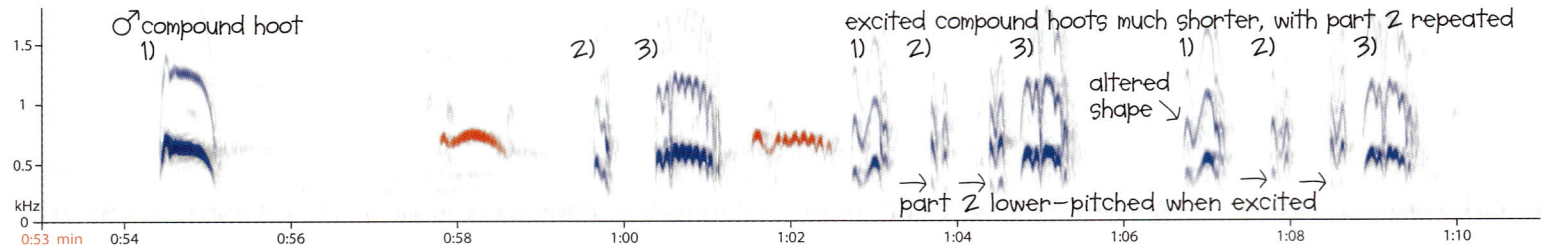

CD4-34 shows how normal compound hoots change to excited ones when a female joins a male during an autumn territorial dispute. A second male is hooting in the distance, and the female's arrival emboldens her mate's response. First he gives two compound hoots with duration of c 7.5 sec. When he starts a third, the female joins in with her own higher-pitched, shorter version. The male's subsequent, more excited compound hoots are very different and only half as long. They have not one but two sets of doubled notes in the middle, and these are much lower-pitched than in normal compound hooting. Maghreb

Maghreb Wood Owl *Strix mauritanica*, adult, Dar es Salam, Rabat, Zaër, Morocco, 1 October 2009 (*Arnoud B van den Berg*). Same bird as in CD4-34. Witherby (1905) described Maghreb Wood Owl for science thus: "Differs from typical *Syrnium aluco* [Tawny Owl's scientific name at the time] by its constantly darker coloration. The whole of the upper surface dark blackish grey, the dark colour being produced by the heavier and more pronounced transverse bars on the feathers. The feathers of the underside also much more heavily marked with transverse bars than in typical *S aluco*. Although *Syrnium aluco* is very much disposed to individual variation, the birds inhabiting Marocco [sic] and Algeria are remarkably constant in their coloration."

Maghreb Wood Owl *Strix mauritanica* Dar es Salam, Rabat, Zaër, Morocco, 05:38, 2 October 2009. Male compound hoots, becoming shorter, and female soliciting calls, becoming more urgent. From 0:32 the male switches to excited compound hooting and from 0:36 the female joins in. 091002.AB.053856.32

Maghreb Wood Owl *Strix mauritanica* Dar es Salam, Rabat, Zaër, Morocco, 21:14, 4 October 2006. Soliciting calls of female, then compound hooting of male and excited compound hooting of female. 06.013.AB.12615.32

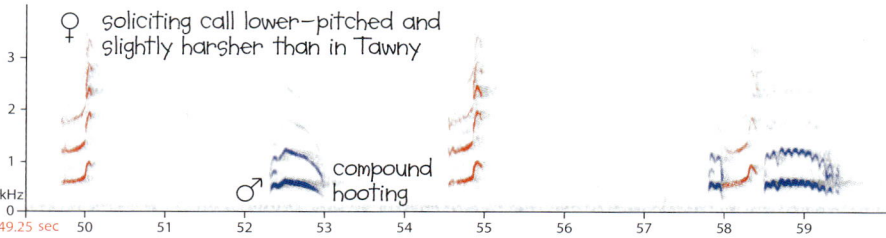

female inserts some rather eccentric, excited compound hooting of her own. It has two sets of 'middle notes': a very slow double at a high pitch and a faster double at a very low pitch. In her second compound hoot a few seconds later there are also two sets of middle notes. This time they differ in pitch, but less so in speed.

Maghreb Wood Owl may be a regional endemic, but it is much less specialised than Marsh Owl *Asio capensis tingitanus*.

Wood Owl and Tawny Owl differ much more strikingly from one another in these excited, shorter versions of the compound hoot than in the full length, more stereotyped version.

Arnoud recorded **CD4-35** at the same spot in Cork Oak *Q suber* woodlands near Rabat, early the next morning. The recording starts with the male's compound hooting and some rather prolonged soliciting calls of the female, which are lower-pitched than those of Tawny Owl. Both male and female gradually evolve towards excited compound hooting, then revert to their previous sounds.

Soliciting calls of Maghreb Wood Owl are similar to those of Tawny Owl but lower-pitched and slightly harsher in females. Arnoud has not yet recorded a male giving this call. In **CD4-36**, a female at Dar es Salam gives a series of soliciting calls, until a male answers with a compound hoot. In the long gap after his first note, the

Maghreb Wood Owl *Strix mauritanica*, hooting male, Dar es Salam, Rabat, Zaër, Morocco, 2 October 2009 (*Arnoud B van den Berg*). Same bird as in CD4-35.

Maghreb Wood Owl *Strix mauritanica*, adult, Taroudant, Souss, Morocco, 12 April 2009 (*Arnoud B van den Berg*). At night on lamppost in centre of town.

Hamdine et al (1999), studying pellets from two sites in Algeria, found that its diet consists mainly of mammals (43.6%) and birds (29.3%) but also includes a high proportion of amphibians (15.2%), reptiles (11.8%), and even invertebrates (14.7%). Maghreb Wood also lives in towns, which often support trees in areas that would not otherwise have them, such as for instance Marrakech and Taroudant.

Pulsed hooting of Maghreb Wood Owl is similar to that of Tawny Owl but much lower-pitched. Arnoud has made only one recording where it was sustained for more than a second or two, and that was from a wooded camping ground in the town of Larache (**CD4-37**). In one or two other recordings it appears only momentarily in male-female interactions. The pulse rate appears to be similar to that of Tawny, despite the difference in pitch.

Most nights in autumn, birds migrate over my house on the Portuguese coast and the majority must continue on into Morocco. The Ortolan Bunting *Emberiza hortulana* migrating overhead in **CD4-38** may have flown over as I slept, just a night or two before. The male Maghreb Wood Owl hooting beneath

Maghreb Wood Owl *Strix mauritanica* Dar es Salam, Rabat, Zaër, Morocco, 18:51, 4 October 2007. Compound hooting of a male, and presumed distance calls of another individual. Background: migrating Ortolan Bunting *Emberiza hortulana*. 071004. AB.185154.21

CD4-38

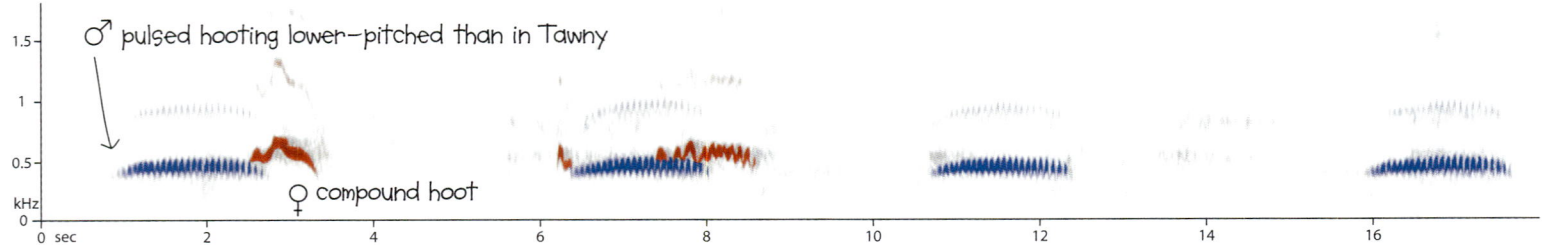

CD4-37　　**Maghreb Wood Owl** *Strix mauritanica* Larache, Rharb, Morocco, 00:14, 27 March 2006. Pulsed hooting of a presumed male and compound hooting of a presumed female. 06.002.AB.01153.11

it is another with a particularly long compound hoot: around 10 seconds long. In the background from 0:35 a second, more distant individual gives a deep *keh-keh-keh-keh…*, which is probably Maghreb Wood's equivalent to the distance call of Tawny Owl.

Maghreb Wood Owls reach their northernmost limit at the Strait of Gibraltar. The Tawny Owls of southern Iberia just to the north are much smaller, with calls and plumage similar to those found elsewhere in Europe (cf, **CD4-17**). Unlike the Moors, then, Maghreb Wood seems never to have made the 15 km crossing to Europe.

Despite their differences, calls of Maghreb Wood Owl and Tawny Owl are similar enough to suggest that they shared a common ancestor not so far back in the past. Brito (2005) estimated this to have been not more than half a million years ago. Her genetic study showed that Maghreb Wood is a completely separate entity from Tawny in Europe. Maghreb Wood's plumage is also strikingly different and only comes in a grey morph, whereas Tawny varies across a spectrum from greyish to reddish. The combination of vocal, genetic and morphological differences from Tawny suggests that Maghreb Wood is best treated as a separate species.

In the deserts of the Middle East there is a smaller *Strix* owl with orange eyes. Its shared ancestor with Maghreb Wood Owl and Tawny Owl lived sometime further back in the past. Until recently this poorly known species was sometimes lumped with Tawny, but if earlier generations had known how different it sounds, they might never have made this mistake.

Maghreb Wood Owl *Strix mauritanica*, Imouzzer, Haha, Western High Atlas, Morocco, 1 February 2013 (*Arnoud B van den Berg*)

Hume's Owl

Hewn out of pink sandstone, the ancient city of Petra, Jordan, overwhelms the ears as well as the eyes. At times it resembles an inverted tower of Babel, with all the world's languages thronging its gorges and gouged out temples. Souvenir sellers and 'air conditioned camel' touts outshout the crowd, while Pallid Swifts *Apus pallidus* scream in and out of cliffs. Birders visit Petra mainly for Sinai Rosefinch *Carpodacus synoicus*, a regional endemic. Roy Slaterus and I spent hours recording their songs in any quiet eddies we could find on the fringes of the crowd. Then we had a long

Hume's Owl *Strix butleri*, male, Dead Sea, Israel, 9 October 2009 (*Dick Forsman*)

rest in the Royal Tombs, reawakening just as a full moon was rising. As hoped, the tourists had gone. A wistful melody from a distant flute underscored the silence, but for two hours Petra's other speciality eluded us.

Just as we decided to give up, I noticed a dent in the outline of the moon. We slipped passed one Bedouin souvenir-seller who was asleep on his stall. Outside the Treasury, another was drinking tea by his tent. When we pointed to the growing lunar eclipse, he gasped, clearly even more surprised than we. A mile long cleft called the Siq is the usual entrance and exit to Petra. It is so narrow and deep that the diminishing moonlight illuminated only a narrow strip of cliff near upper rim. We walked quickly, hoping to exit in time to see the eclipse reaching totality. When we were almost there, a minor miracle took place. A distant Hume's Owl *Strix butleri* started to hoot. Reaching the entrance, we climbed up a hillside where we could listen over the plateau. The owl was not so far away. **CD4-39** is my first Hume's Owl hooting under a blood red, fully eclipsed moon.

Hume's Owl *Strix butleri*, Wadi Al Mughsayl, Dhofar, Oman, 10 February 2014 (*Dick Forsman*)

CD4-39   **Hume's Owl** *Strix butleri* Petra, Ma'an, Jordan, 23:30, 4 May 2004. Compound hooting of a male under an eclipsed moon, lured closer by a vocal imitation. 04.016. MR.12903.12

When Alan Octavian Hume described *'Asio' butleri* in 1878, he created a mystery that has deepened with the passing of time. The eponymous Butler was a British Army Officer who had sent Hume the specimen, having received it from one Mr Nash. Hume believed Nash to be living in Ormara, a port on the Mekran coast in current day Pakistan. And here is the mystery: in the 136 years since its discovery there has not been another whiff of Hume's Owl anywhere north of the Gulf of Oman, in Iran, Pakistan or anywhere else.

My second encounter with Hume's Owl took place in southern Oman, six years after Petra. By this time owls had top priority, so René and I earmarked four nights for the nocturnal specialities of the region. Mike Watson, a tour-guiding friend, gave us a tip for Hume's. In the afternoon of 15 April 2010, we made our way to the fantastically beautiful wadi complex behind the village of Mughsayl, which lies on the shores of the Indian Ocean. After driving several kilometres inland we continued on foot, wary of unexploded land-mines rumoured to be left over from the Dhofar Rebellion. It was only after this conflict ended in 1976 that Hume's was discovered in the area, the furthest east that it has been proven to occur. As we worked our way around some huge boulders that had fallen to the wadi floor, we met a large herd of camels. The thunderous echo of their groans reassured me. They probably made the same journey every day, so I relaxed about the mines.

Later in the evening two male Hume's Owls exchanged compound hoots from different directions. One was close enough for a good recording (**CD4-40**) but after a short period of activity, all became quiet. René and I waited a couple more hours in vain. I decided to stay up as long as necessary but with nothing more concrete to focus on, René said good night and set off for the car.

During the rest of the night I heard no more owls. At some point I lay down on a sandy spot and slept, oblivious to the scorpions I would find there on a later visit. At dawn I wandered back to the car, sweating profusely in the humid conditions. When I met René he had a smug grin. After leaving me he had taken a wrong turn, and so had his belly. Attending the call of nature first, he then decided to find a spot to rest and work out where he was in the morning. At this point a family of Hume's Owls, dad, mum and the kids, started calling from a nearby cliff. René's misfortune had led to the discovery of an active nest. The next night I recorded the family from dusk to dawn.

I have a confession to make. I rarely use playback, but when I returned to the spot with Killian in February 2014 I did use it. After hearing nothing for nearly an hour after dusk, I simply wanted to know whether the old nest was occupied. On hearing the recording, made at exactly that spot four years earlier, the female replied immediately. She was almost certainly incubating, and hardly left the nest during two subsequent nights. Later when I heard her mate, I thought he sounded like the same male as before, based on his compound hooting.

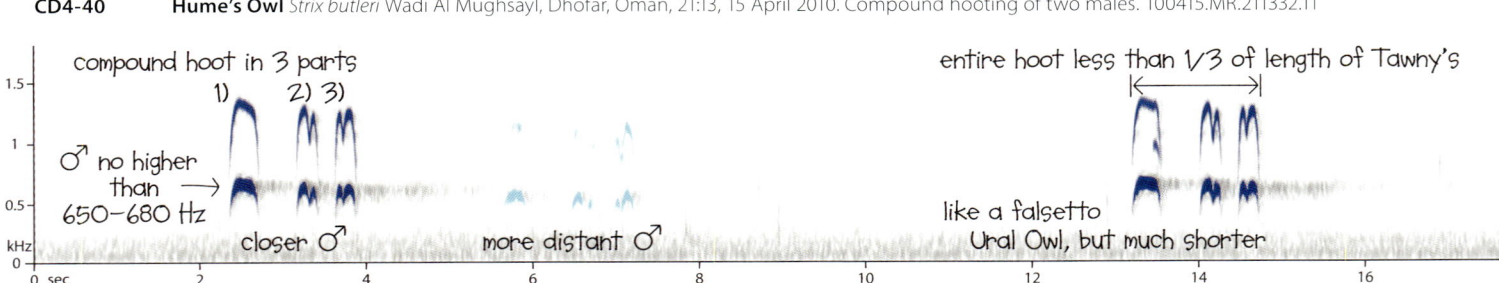

CD4-40 **Hume's Owl** *Strix butleri* Wadi Al Mughsayl, Dhofar, Oman, 21:13, 15 April 2010. Compound hooting of two males. 100415.MR.211332.11

Next morning I tried again, this time with Killian and his camera ready beside me. The male responded by hooting until well after dawn from an alcove behind an acacia some 50 m away from the nest: his roost as it turned out. Many passerines mobbed him. I recorded **CD4-41** just when the first White-spectacled Bulbul *Pycnonotus xanthopygos* dared to go in close. In later recordings the owl was almost drowned out by his detractors.

CD4-41

CD4-41 Hume's Owl *Strix butleri* Wadi Al Mughsayl, Dhofar, Oman, 07:01, 23 February 2014. Compound hooting of a male, with White-spectacled Bulbul *Pycnonotus xanthopygos* arriving and mobbing it. This is probably the same individual as the closer one in CD4-40. Background: other bulbuls and Arabian Wheatear *Oenanthe lugentoides*. 140223.MR.070142.20

The commonest call of female Hume's Owls during the breeding season is their soliciting call, a rising, whistled *queee*. On our 2010 visit I heard it for long periods during the night, much more than the male's hooting. In 2014 it was the only sound I heard from the female at all (**CD4-42**). She used it almost every time the male was close to the nest.

Hume's Owl *Strix butleri*, Wadi Al Mughsayl, Dhofar, Oman, 12 February 2014 (*Killian Mullarney*). Same male as in CD4-41 to 43, CD4-46 to 50 and CD4-56.

CD4-42 **Hume's Owl** *Strix butleri* Wadi Al Mughsayl, Dhofar, Oman, 23:57, 26 February 2014. A food exchange with soliciting calls of female and compound hooting of male. 140226.MR.235710.22

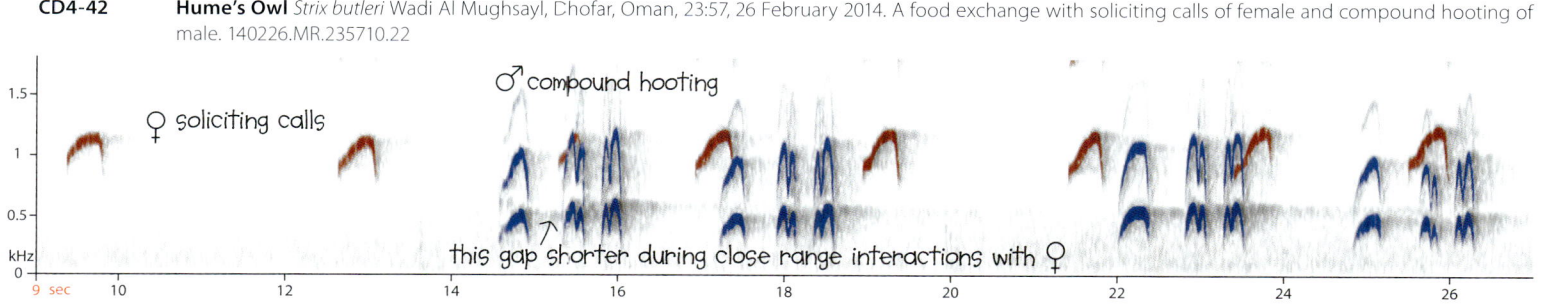

On two occasions I also heard the male using the soliciting call in exchanges with the female (eg, **CD4-43**). In both cases I now believe that he was the lower-pitched caller (contra Robb et al 2013). Female soliciting calls vary in pitch and timbre, but tend to be highest when the male is nearby and the female wants to be fed. Sometimes they become harsher, and occasionally they may be inflected downwards instead of the usual upwards.

Some Hume's have much higher-pitched compound hoots than others, up to 1 kHz or higher, but the male from René's nest was among the lowest. I am confident he was a male because in both 2010 and 2014 he hooted frequently and was highly mobile, whereas the female stayed at the nest and rarely gave anything other than soliciting calls. Although she never obliged me by proving it, I believe that high-pitched compound hooting belongs to females.

CD4-43   **Hume's Owl** *Strix butleri* Wadi Al Mughsayl, Dhofar, Oman, 00:16, 18 April 2010. Soliciting calls of both male and female. Also wingbeats of male and chittering of unidentified individual. A nestling begs in the background. 100418.MR.001602.01

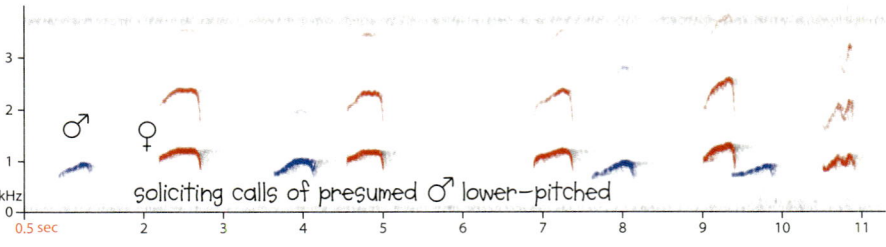

On 26 February 2014, I recorded another pair with a second set of equipment at a different spot some 600 metres from René's nest. One of them gave low-pitched compound hooting while the other gave soliciting calls. In July 2013, at exactly the same spot, Arnoud had recorded two Hume's Owls hooting, high and low-pitched. The higher-pitched one reached around 990 Hz and I conclude that it was the female (**CD4-44**).

CD4-44   **Hume's Owl** *Strix butleri* Wadi Al Mughsayl, Dhofar, Oman, 23:26, 19 July 2013. Compound hooting of a presumed female. 130719.AB.232650.22

In one dawn recording from 2010, when recording near René's nest, I picked up two Hume's Owls hooting several hundred metres away that I now believe were females (**CD4-45**). One of

CD4-45   **Hume's Owl** *Strix butleri* Wadi Al Mughsayl, Dhofar, Oman, 05:08, 18 April 2010. Compound hooting of two presumed females, one giving a six-note hoot. I have only heard this extra note from one other individual out of eight, and that was a presumed male. At close range, begging calls of a nestling and a soliciting call of a female. Background: Desert Lark *Ammomanes deserti* and Arabian Wheatear *Oenanthe lugentoides*. 100418.MR.050848.12

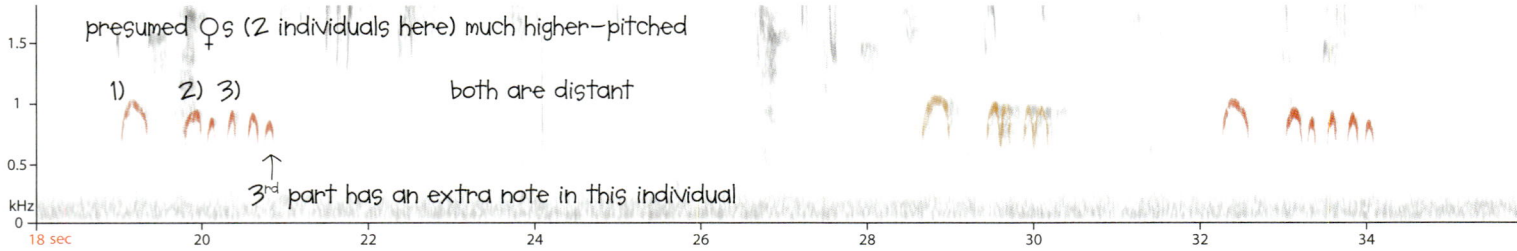

them is possibly the same as in **CD4-44**. The other, further to the right and more distant, deviates slightly from the usual rhythm.

Pulsed hooting of Hume's Owl consists of short series of pulses that usually rise in pitch and intensity. I used to think that they used pulsed hooting rarely and only for brief moments (Robb et al 2013), but in 2014 I learned otherwise. Remember the time I used a little playback? In the immediate aftermath only the female replied, but the male must have heard it too. About half an hour later I heard a sudden commotion at the border with his neighbour's territory. Two males engaged in a confrontation that lasted nearly 19 minutes.

If we listen carefully to **CD4-46**, both males are using a mixture of compound hooting and pulsed hooting but in different proportions. The slightly higher-pitched male from René's nest gives far more pulsed hoots than his lower-pitched neighbour. My interpretation is that he was probably fired up by my use of playback half an hour earlier. When he caught up with his neighbour, he delivered a fierce and totally undeserved rebuke.

Hume's Owl *Strix butleri*, Wadi Al Mughsayl, Dhofar, Oman, 25 February 2014 (*Killian Mullarney*)

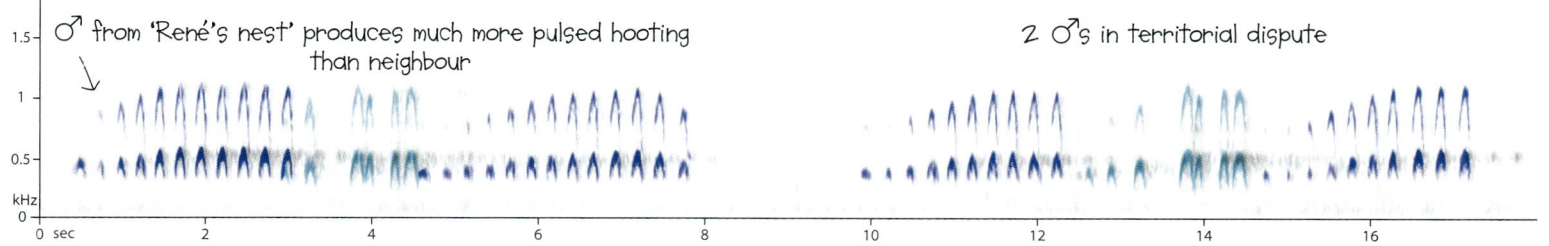

CD4-46   Hume's Owl *Strix butleri* Wadi Al Mughsayl, Dhofar, Oman, 20:05, 22 February 2014. Pulsed hooting and compound hooting in a territorial confrontation between two males. Background: bats Chiroptera. 140222.MR.200554.02

In 2010, I had recorded pulsed hooting only three times, always during brief encounters between male and female (**CD4-47**, **CD4-48** & **CD4-49**). In all three, pulsed hooting *followed* a compound hoot, whereas in the male-male confrontation I just described the pulsed hooting consistently came *first*.

CD4-47 **Hume's Owl** *Strix butleri* Wadi Al Mughsayl, Dhofar, Oman, 22:54, 17 April 2010. Male-female encounter, starting with male compound hooting. The female then flies to the hooting male while giving soliciting calls and this seems to stimulate a bout of pulsed hooting from 0:13. 100417.MR.225439.01

CD4-48 **Hume's Owl** *Strix butleri* Wadi Al Mughsayl, Dhofar, Oman, 21:46, 17 April 2010. Male-female encounter, starting with male compound hooting and soliciting calls of the female. A nestling hisses every now and then in the foreground. There is a female giving compound hoots in the distance, and the male from René's pair seems to interrupt these twice with his own. The pulsed hooting at 0:22, however, comes after his own female follows him to a more distant perch. 100417.MR.214650.01

CD4-49 **Hume's Owl** *Strix butleri* Wadi Al Mughsayl, Dhofar, Oman, 05:08, 18 April 2010. A tiny hint of pulsed hooting - just two or three notes at 0:08 - as the male delivers prey to the female then flies off. Background: Desert Lark *Ammomanes deserti*. 100418.MR.050848.01

One of the commonest calls at René's nest in April 2010 was a series of very quiet, repeated and highly variable hoots delivered in a slow, faltering rhythm. Often, the notes became tremulous and broke up into a chittering sound. The sequence sometimes ended with a compound hoot. Usually it was the male making this sound (**CD4-50**), and on more than one occasion a nestling begged intensely at the same time. I interpret the sound as a feeding call. The female allowed the male to go straight to the nest with food, so perhaps male Hume's feed their young directly. The female used this call less often, and only when the male was not around. Her version was markedly higher-pitched than his (**CD4-51**).

CD4-51 **Hume's Owl** *Strix butleri* Wadi Al Mughsayl, Dhofar, Oman, 22:54, 17 April 2010. Presumed feeding calls of female, with begging of nestling. 100417.MR.225439.01

CD4-52 **Hume's Owl** *Strix butleri* Wadi Al Mughsayl, Dhofar, Oman, 00:40, 18 April 2010. Guarding call and soliciting calls of a probable female. 100418.MR.001602.01

We could not see the young from René's nest, but there were certainly two of them and they were probably at least two weeks old. I'm sure they felt quite safe up on their cliff. I only heard what I could easily recognise as a guarding call or 'alarm call' on two occasions. In **CD4-52**, the caller was probably the female. A few minutes later a possible Gordon's Wildcat *Felis*

CD4-50 **Hume's Owl** *Strix butleri* Wadi Al Mughsayl, Dhofar, Oman, 00:30, 18 April 2010. Presumed feeding call and compound hoot of male, with soliciting calls of female. 100418.MR.001602.01

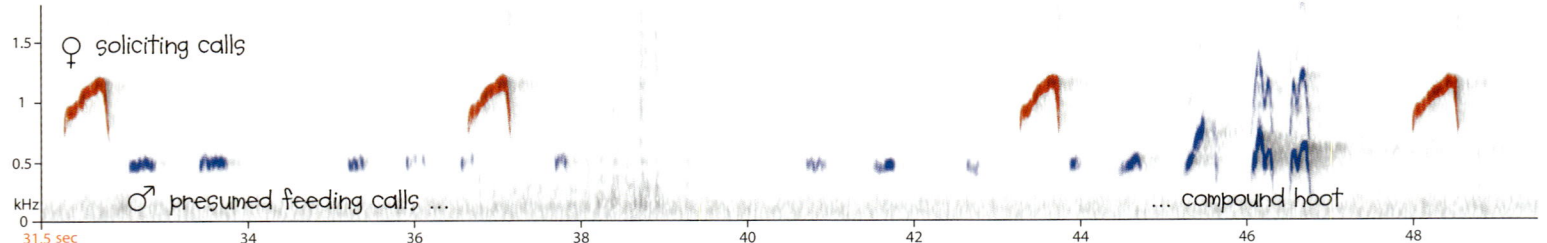

Hume's Owl *Strix butleri*, Wadi Al Mughsayl, Dhofar, Oman, 25 February 2014 (*Killian Mullarney*). In February 2014, I collected four pellets from the male's roost (the one photographed on 12 February, on p 259). In one of them I managed to identify a spiny mouse *Acomys*, thanks to skull illustrations in Aulagnier et al (2009). The other three contained at least two scorpions Buthidae and several grasshoppers of the family Acrididae. When Mendelssohn et al (1975) examined three pellets of Hume's Owl from Jericho, Israel, they found almost exactly the same combination. Elsewhere in Israel, five other small mammal species have been added to the list, as well as two reptiles and two birds (Aronson 1979). Hume's Owl is not a fussy eater.

lybica gordoni meowed once near the microphones at the base of the cliff. In **CD4-53**, the caller is certainly the female (the male was some distance away), and her first guarding call comes after I make a loud movement. Towards the end René moves too, and this elicits more calling.

Hume's Owl *Strix butleri* Wadi Al Mughsayl, Dhofar, Oman, 19:15, 17 April 2010. Guarding calls of a female and begging calls of a nestling. Background: movements by Magnus (at start) and René (near end). 100417.MR.191552.01   **CD4-53**

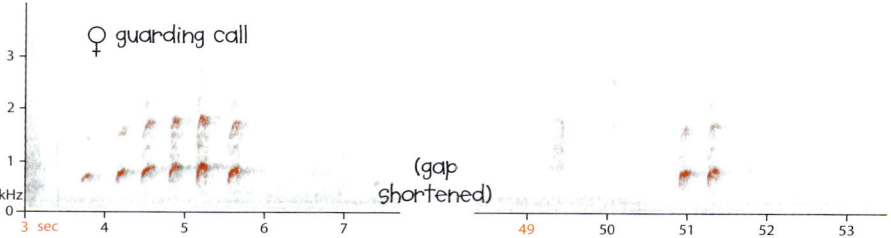

Hume's Owl *Strix butleri* Wadi Al Mughsayl, Dhofar, Oman, 19:15, 17 April 2010. Begging calls of nestlings, with soliciting calls of female and distant compound hooting of male. 100417.MR.191552.01   **CD4-54**

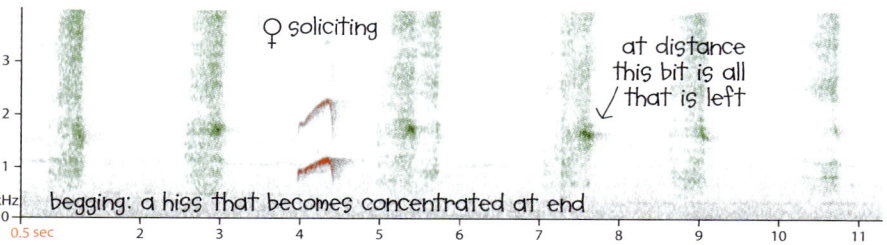

Immediately prior to this, both nestlings had been begging loudly (**CD4-54**). They had probably not been fed since the morning. The guarding calls silenced them for a moment, but soon one started calling again. Several times during the night,

I recorded feeding sequences. In **CD4-55**, you can hear the female's wingbeats as she brings prey at the start. The begging calls speed up and there are a couple of chitter calls, probably from one of the young.

CD4-55   **Hume's Owl** *Strix butleri* Wadi Al Mughsayl, Dhofar, Oman, 03:43, 18 April 2010. Begging calls of nestlings and soliciting calls of female, then chitter calls at 0:08. Background: distant compound hooting of another presumed female. 100418. MR.034342.01

Although there is some variation in the timing of breeding (Jennings 2010), most juveniles are probably independent by August. Autumn calling has been reported in September (O'Reilly 2000, Mikkola 1983) and October (Megalli et al 2011), but tour guides consider Hume's Owl notoriously difficult to hear outside the breeding season. James Smith (in litt) has heard some quiet gruff barking in November in the Dead Sea region of Israel. Perhaps this is the short, throaty cough sometimes heard between compound hoots by Leshem (1981), although he reported it from January to April. The only call I know that might fit this description was a deep *tuc-tuc*, given just once by the male when leaving René's nest (**CD4-56**).

CD4-56   **Hume's Owl** *Strix butleri* Wadi Al Mughsayl, Dhofar, Oman, 05:08, 18 April 2010. Deep *tuc-tuc* of male when leaving the nest. Background: compound hooting of a distant female, and Desert Lark *Ammomanes deserti*. 100418.MR.050848.01

The vocal repertoire of Hume's Owl still leaves plenty for adventurous birders to investigate. I wonder if they are really so quiet in autumn for example, and I'm curious to know what calls they use most during that season. Perhaps we should listen for them in August on hot nights when

field guides illustrated it with dark eyes (eg, Heinzel et al 1972). The map in Hüe & Etchécopar's monograph on birds of the Middle East (1970) showed Hume's only in Israel, Jordan and, mysteriously, southern Iran. The authors apparently did not know about specimens from central Saudi Arabia (Meinertzhagen 1930) and Sinai (Le Roi 1923). Discoveries of Hume's on the east coast of Egypt (Baha el Din & Baha el Din 2001), in Oman, southern Saudi Arabia and Yemen were all published later.

Our knowledge of Hume's Owl is gradually improving, but even in the 21st century, there is a great deal to learn. A major monograph on owls (König et al 2008) mapped Hume's in northern Oman and the United Arab Emirates, for which there was no evidence at all. In March 2013, I did stumble across a *Strix* owl in northern Oman, however, and it opened up a whole new chapter in our knowledge of this genus.

juveniles must be dispersing but very few people have ever listened. It would be odd if Hume's had no 'distance call' like Tawny Owl *S aluco*, which uses this call most often in autumn.

It may seem strange to us now, but only a couple of decades ago Hume's Owl was one of the least known birds of the Palearctic. When Arnoud first saw one in Israel in March 1977,

Omani Owl

When René and I went to northern Oman in March 2013, my modest goal was to improve our understanding of Pallid Scops Owl *Otus brucei*, and René's was to photograph them. The Al Hajar range has many Pallid Scops and most of its wadis are very quiet, so it seemed the obvious place to try. I felt certain that with enough patience we would both meet our goals.

Towards the end of our first night we found a pair of Pallid Scops Owls hooting in a deep, flat-bottomed wadi with precipitous scree slopes and enormous sheer cliffs on either side. There was very little vegetation anywhere, least of all between the rounded pebbles and boulders of the wadi floor. Only a few well-spaced, gnarled Elb Trees *Ziziphus spina-cristi* seemed capable of withstanding the flash floods that periodically wipe the wadi clean.

Habitat of Pallid Scops Owl *Otus brucei* and Omani Owl *Strix omanensis*, Al Jabal Al Akhdar, Al Hajar mountains, Oman, 20 March 2013 (*René Pop*)

Becoming intimate with Pallid Scops Owl proved to be a serious challenge. It was pointless to chase them. The noise of my feet kicking pebbles would always push them further, however quietly I walked. So every night I tried to anticipate where the pair would hoot and leave equipment recording there. Usually I was wrong. Two trees out could mean a distance of 50 m or more, too far for a usable recording. There were about 40 trees in the territory, so sooner or later I would get lucky.

By the fifth night I knew some trees the pair had visited at least twice, and put my equipment in a magnificent specimen on the border with the next territory. Then I sought out a comfortable boulder some distance away and listened. Things finally started to go my way. Not one but two male Pallid Scops Owls began to hoot in nearby trees on either side of the microphones. After they moved away I went in to check the recording. As I put on my headphones I noticed an unfamiliar owl-like hooting in the distance. Pressing 'record', I tried to ignore the large bats picking fruit in the foreground and listened for more clues (**CD4-57**).

CD4-57   **Omani Owl** *Strix omanensis* Al Jabal Al Akhdar, Al Hajar mountains, Oman, 00:19, 24 March 2013. The moment Omani Owl was discovered. A male, probably the live type specimen, is giving compound hoots on the right. Background: wingbeats of Egyptian Fruit-eating Bats *Rousettus aegyptiacus* with coughing and footsteps of goats. 130324.MR.001917.02

A few minutes later the owl, if that was what it was, changed to a pulsed kind of hooting, and there was a nasal, rising answer from the other side of the wadi. **CD4-58** starts with some four-note hoots and heavy wingbeats of a bat, then a Pallid Scops Owl hoots from 0:05. The mystery owl's pulsed hooting begins at 0:10 and the rising reply comes at 0:17. The distant bleating at 0:24 proved to be just a goat.

Omani Owl *Strix omanensis* Al Jabal Al Akhdar, Al Hajar mountains, Oman, 00:26, 24 March 2013. Continuation of the discovery. Pulsed hooting of a male on the right, and soliciting call of a presumed female on the left. Background: Pallid Scops Owl *Otus brucei*, wingbeats of Egyptian Fruit-eating Bats *Rousettus aegyptiacus*, and goats. 130324.MR.002616.12   CD4-58

I was incredibly lucky to hear three different call types of the mystery owl within a few minutes. Triangulation led me swiftly to an exciting possibility, although I hardly dared to believe it. The four-note hoot was compound hooting, the pulsed hooting was just that, and the rising call sounded like a female soliciting call. This had to be a *Strix* owl, but not Hume's *S butleri*, the only one known to occur in Arabia. Perhaps it was some Asian owl new to the peninsula, or even a species still unknown to science.

A few nights later I heard the owl again, this time with René as my witness, but it was to be a month before anyone saw it. That was when Arnoud and I returned to Oman on a mission to learn more. By now we knew that it sounded like no other owl, from Asia or anywhere else, but we still hadn't seen it. For five nights we listened at the same place but heard nothing, despite the occasional use of playback. Our luck finally improved when we lured another one at a second site a few kilometres to the south. It was recorded and we even saw something *Strix*-like in the light of a powerful torch, 40 m from where we were standing, but it flew off too quickly for a photo. By the end of the trip my frustration was almost overpowering. I felt certain that we were dealing with a new species, but still knew almost nothing about its appearance, and had learned virtually nothing new about its sounds. I prepared myself for very slow progress.

Another month on, I reluctantly stayed to work on this book while Arnoud and Cecilia went back to the wadi. We expected that by May the owls would be even more difficult to detect. To my surprise, they turned out to be much more vocal than before. Arnoud even discovered a third territory in between the other two. Failing to lure any owl down to the road with playback, he realised that he would have to go up the scree to the base of one of the cliffs. For this he chose the original March territory. Cecilia would stay down at the car and they agreed a system of laser pen signals. Two strokes of light meant, "Playback please," and more than 10 meant, "Get help I've fallen."

Steep slopes were not the only inconvenience; the temperature was 44°C when Arnoud started his climb. Anyone who has seen him in action will know how much photographic and sound recording gear he was carrying. There was traffic in the wadi for much of the evening, so his first two flashes came only around 22:00. No owl responded to Cecilia's playback. The next time, at 23:00, a male responded from a great distance. Finally, Arnoud thought of using some small speakers to play compound hooting from the April territory. The March male responded immediately, coming gradually closer. Arnoud searched for it on the cliff. At first he saw what appeared to be a black goat, but then he noticed eyes in its 'tail'. Four times it landed close to him on a rock, flying off as soon as he switched on the powerful torch that he needs for photographs.

On subsequent nights the owl gradually relaxed. Cecilia came up the slope to help with the torch, allowing Arnoud to focus his camera more easily. One of their photographs of this individual became our holotype. In the meantime, a series of close encounters allowed him to make much clearer recordings than we had managed in March or April. **CD4-59** is our closest of compound hooting to date. All of the strophes contain

Omani Owl *Strix omanensis*, male, Al Jabal Al Akhdar, Al Hajar mountains, Oman, 26 May 2013 (*Arnoud B van den Berg*). Singing from huge cliff. Same as in CD4-59, 62, 63, 69 & 70, and probably also CD4-57 & 58.

Omani Owl *Strix omanensis*, male, Al Jabal Al Akhdar, Al Hajar mountains, Oman, 24 May 2013 (*Arnoud B van den Berg*). Identical to holotype or type specimen and same bird as in CD4-59, 62, 63, 69 & 70, and probably also CD4-57 & 58.

CD4-59   **Omani Owl** *Strix omanensis* Al Jabal Al Akhdar, Al Hajar mountains, Oman, 23:32, 27 May 2013. Compound hooting of a male, almost certainly the type specimen, although Arnoud did not photograph during this particular session. 130527.AB.233200.12

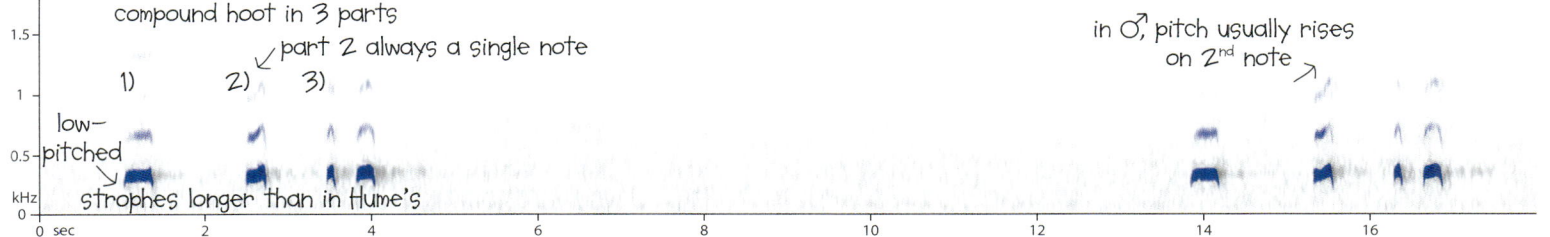

Omani Owl *Strix omanensis*, male, Al Jabal Al Akhdar, Al Hajar mountains, Oman, 26 May 2013 (*Arnoud B van den Berg*). Same as in CD4-59, 62, 63, 69 & 70, and probably also CD4-57 & 58.

four notes, and the rhythm is the same as in Richard Wagner's famous wedding march *Treulich geführt*, better known in English as *Here comes the bride*.

At the time of writing more than a year has passed since the discovery. In October 2013 we presented Omani Owl *Strix omanensis* to the ornithological community (Robb et al 2013),

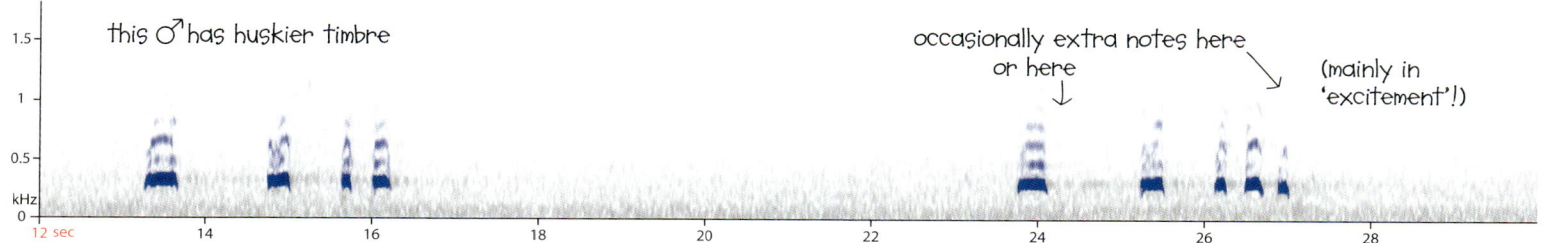

CD4-60   **Omani Owl** *Strix omanensis* Al Jabal Al Akhdar, Al Hajar mountains, Oman, 00:27, 28 April 2013. Compound hooting of a hoarse-sounding individual, which I now believe to have been a male. This was the first Omani Owl that we ever saw. It gives five-note hoots at 0:23 and 0:35. Background: domestic goat. 130428. AB.002745.42

and the news received widespread attention in the mainstream media. We have now devoted seven Sound Approach trips to the owl. A few pioneering birders have already added it to their lists, but the discovery is still very much in progress.

We have now recorded compound hooting from nine individuals and we know that its four-note rhythm varies only very slightly. In 2013 we also recorded five to seven-note hoots from two individuals in among the usual four-note hoots. One of them features in **CD4-60**, recorded during our first ever sighting. With hindsight, both were responding to playback or a human imitation, so this was an excited, more aggressive version of their compound hoot. In February 2014, we hardly provoked the owls at all, to learn as much as possible about their natural behaviour. Just one of four hooting individuals gave a five-note hoot during that trip, and that was immediately before copulation (cf, **CD4-66**).

From the moment post-migration blues set in, late in the autumn of 2013, I was itching to get back to the Al Hajar mountains. I was determined not to miss the courtship period when the owls would be more vocal and perhaps use call types we had not yet heard. We assumed that courtship would take place in the first two months of the year. Eventually Mark, Mo, Killian and I flew to Oman on 13 February. Several other people had been searching for Omani Owls in the weeks before. Most had gone to the type locality, but a few pioneers had tried to find new pairs. Immediately before our trip, John McLoughlin (aka 'Johnny Mac') had been searching by himself, while Mike Watson of Birdquest had led a specially organised Omani Owl expedition. Our friend Ian Lewis was one of the participants.

One afternoon Johnny Mac stood on the roof of a large building in the centre of a small nearby town and had a good look at the surrounding landscape. He saw one wadi with good habitat and an access road, and decided to give it a go that evening. On 4 February that was where he heard a new pair, some 20 km from the type locality. The Birdquest group followed this up, seeing a pair just before the end of the following night. At the crack of dawn three mornings later, both parties saw the male and female disappearing into separate holes in the same section of cliff. On the eve of our trip, this was excellent news.

The male of the JM ('Johnny Mac') pair turned out to be the lowest-pitched Omani Owl that we have recorded so far. Sometimes his hooting was a little hoarse; at other times it was perfectly clear. We also heard the female hooting almost every night during our February trip. In **CD4-61**, both are hooting at close range. The female's compound hooting was hoarser and much higher-pitched than the male's. The lowest note of her hoot was the second, not the first as in the male. These male-female differences were consistent for this pair, but we still need to find out whether they apply to all Omani Owls. At any rate, my previous speculation that male compound hooting was higher-pitched than that of females (Robb et al 2013) was proven wrong.

Towards the end of **CD4-61**, the male started pulsed hooting, perhaps in response to a distant rival doing the same. As in other *Strix* owls, the use of this sound changes according to context. When confronting rivals, including ones simulated with playback, males give pulsed hooting in fairly loud, well-ordered sequences. When interacting with females, however, males often just give a brief burst directly after a compound hoot.

CD4-62 is a sequence of pulsed hooting that had been stimulated by playback, and in this case the caller is the living type specimen. **CD4-63** is taken from later in the same recording. It shows how pulsed and compound hooting are sometimes mixed together in variable patterns when responding to playback or rivals. This recalls the way that the two male Hume's Owls also mixed their equivalent sounds in a territorial conflict (cf, **CD4-46**).

Both sexes give pulsed hooting, and the evidence from the JM pair is that the female's pulsed hooting is considerably higher-pitched (**CD4-64**). During our February 2014 trip she made this sound only three times. Every time, the rhythm was untidy and her strophes had an overall descending shape.

CD4-61 **Omani Owl** *Strix omanensis* 'Wadi Mac', Al Jabal Al Akhdar, Al Hajar mountains, Oman, 05:59, 17 February 2014. Compound hooting of male and female, with pulsed hooting of male towards the end. Background: pulsed hooting of a distant male Omani Owl (from 1:11), Sand Partridge *Ammoperdix heyi* and Hume's Wheatear *Oenanthe albonigra*. 140217.MR.055904.01

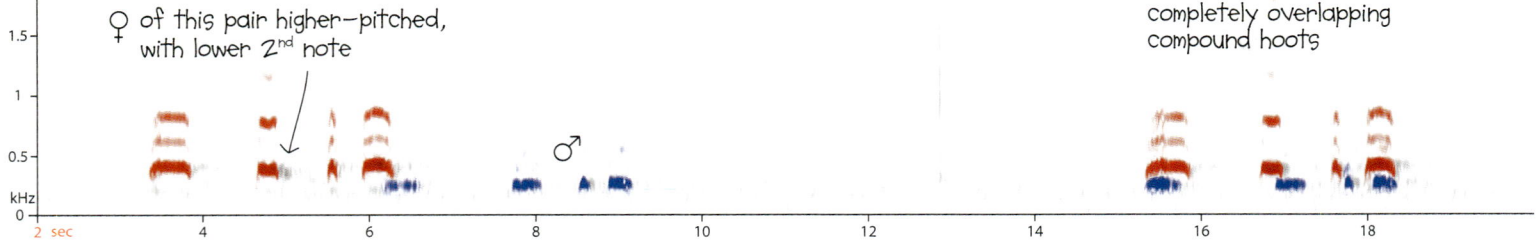

CD4-62 **Omani Owl** *Strix omanensis* Al Jabal Al Akhdar, Al Hajar mountains, Oman, 00:30, 28 May 2013. Pulsed hooting of a male, the same individual that served as a live type specimen. Background: probable begging calls of a juvenile, eg at 0:37, 0:59, 1:03, 1:13 and 1:31. 130528.AB.003000.02

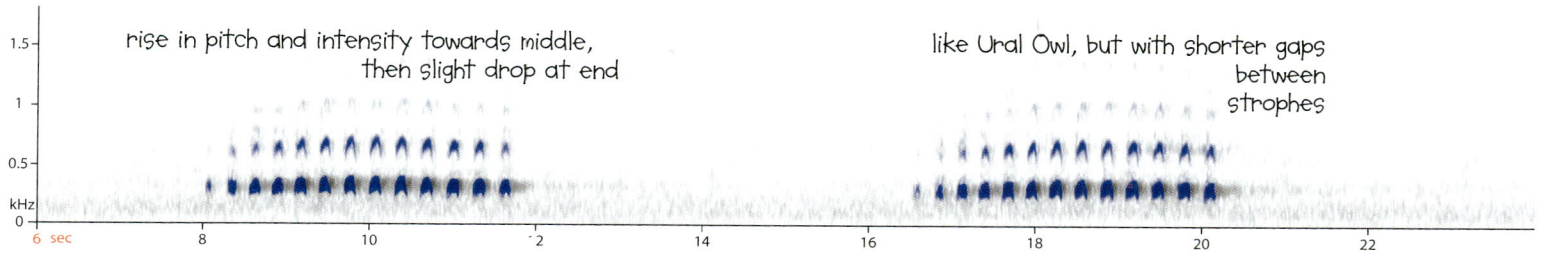

CD4-63 **Omani Owl** *Strix omanensis* Al Jabal Al Akhdar, Al Hajar mountains, Oman, after 00:30, 28 May 2013. Mixed pulsed and compound hooting of a male, the same individual that served as a living type specimen. Background: probable begging calls of a juvenile, very faint. 130528.AB.003000.02

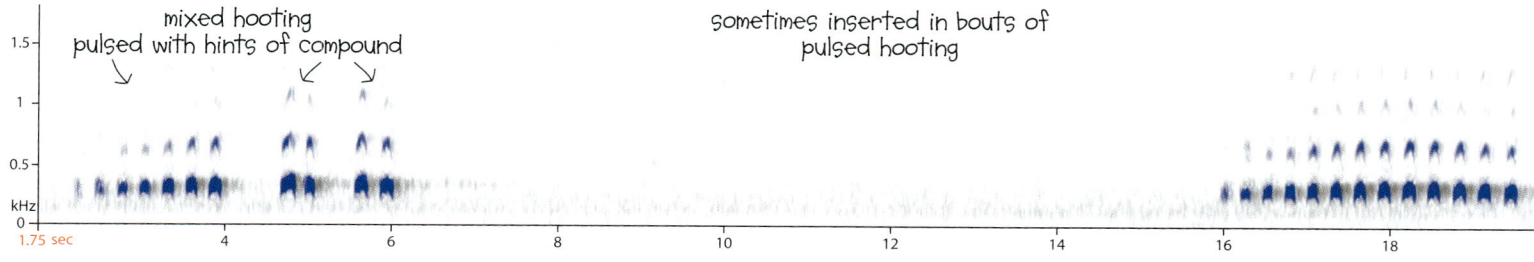

CD4-64 **Omani Owl** *Strix omanensis* 'Wadi Mac', Al Jabal Al Akhdar, Al Hajar mountains, Oman, 18:37, 15 February 2014. Pulsed hooting of a female. After the first 10 seconds, the gap to the next series has been shortened. 140215.MR.183717.22

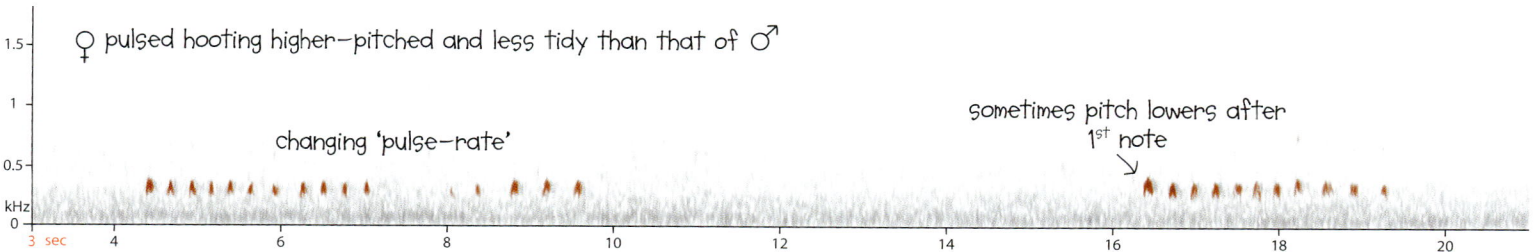

Omani Owls *Strix omanensis*, male and female, 'Wadi Mac', Al Jabal Al Akhdar, Al Hajar mountains, Oman, 17 February 2014 (*Killian Mullarney*). Same as in CD4-64 to 66. The male (left), which we only ever saw from a distance, had a more poorly defined breast band than the female but a much more striking face. His 'dark eyebrows' were even more striking than in the holotype, with a very clear outline. Their shape and position were reminiscent of the base of a ram's horns. Both individuals kept their facial disk partly folded by day.

During our six-night visit in February 2014, the JM pair were courting. We often heard and saw what appeared to be courtship feeding. A couple of compound hoots of one individual would be followed by a long series of rising, nasal calls of the other. I have no doubt that just as in other *Strix* owls, the male was announcing his arrival with compound hoots and the female was responding with soliciting calls. **CD4-65** is a typical example of such a food pass. The JM female was far less

CD4-65 **Omani Owl** *Strix omanensis* 'Wadi Mac', Al Jabal Al Akhdar, Al Hajar mountains, Oman, 06:04, 15 February 2014. Courtship feeding: female soliciting calls with male compound hooting. Background: Sand Partridge *Ammoperdix heyi* and Hume's Wheatear *Oenanthe albonigra*. 140215.MR.060430.22

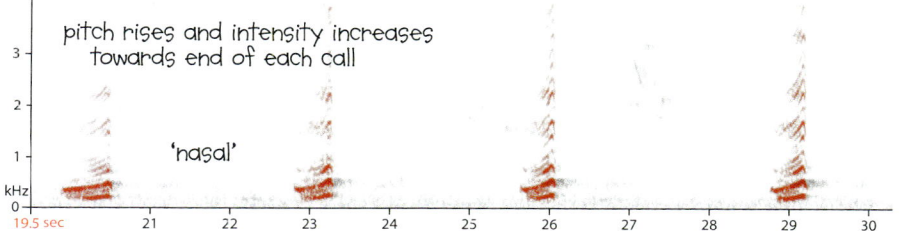

mobile than her mate, and her soliciting calls usually came from the same spot on the cliff. They were the first sound that we heard at the end of the day, and the last to cease in the morning.

Females use soliciting calls not only to demand food. At 05:59 on 14 February, the male gave one compound hoot and the female replied with soliciting calls from her roost. She continued for around 20 minutes. In the first light of dawn, I saw the male approaching the cliff. Together the pair flew to a prominent rock about 40 m from their roosts, where I could see them silhouetted against the sky. At one point they fluttered like butterflies above the edge of the cliff. They struck me as very broad-winged. When they settled on the rock again, I saw the male mount the female with flapping wings.

On another occasion I was recording when the owls moved to the same rock, this time in complete darkness. **CD4-66** starts with the female already there and the male compound hooting near the roost holes. By 0:17 he has flown left to join the female. From 0:34 the female's soliciting calls become lower-pitched and more urgent. The chittering at 0:39 suggests copulation (cf Tawny Owl *Strix aluco*: **CD4-24**).

Every night started and ended with the owls about 10-15 m apart in their respective holes on the cliff. The male's hole was sausage-shaped and angled at about 45°, with room for two in the entrance. The female's hole looked much smaller but may

CD4-66 **Omani Owl** *Strix omanensis* 'Wadi Mac', Al Jabal Al Akhdar, Al Hajar mountains, Oman, 21:19, 14 February 2014. Probable copulation, not confirmed visually. Starts with compound hooting of male on right, and soliciting calls of female on left. Male flies left to join female, continuing his compound hooting. There is a 5-note compound hoot at 0:17 (the first note is doubled). Background: wingbeats of Egyptian Fruit-eating Bat *Rousettus aegyptiacus*. 140214.MR.211905.22

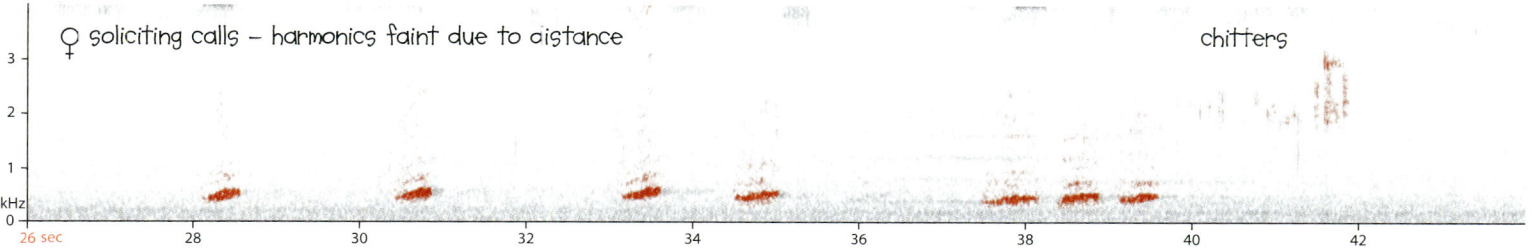

Omani Owl *Strix omanensis*, female, 'Wadi Mac', Al Jabal Al Akhdar, Al Hajar mountains, Oman, 15 February 2014 (*Killian Mullarney*). Same as in CD4-61 & CD4-64 to 66. In the shadows of a brightly lit morning, the female showed much warmer colours than the holotype Arnoud had photographed at night. We were struck by how Tawny Owl *S aluco*-like the saturated browns in her plumage made her appear. When she spread the disk, the upper part appeared darker, although she did not have such well-marked 'eyebrows' as the holotype or her mate. One feature that stood out from a distance was a darkish band on her upper breast, which we also noted during our first sighting in April 2013. The dark vertical streaks on the female's breast were every bit as strongly marked as in the holotype.

have led to a deeper chamber. Sometimes she sat with the male at his place before going to hers. One morning she seemed to stay with him for the day, but when we returned in the evening she emerged from her usual roost.

When Arnoud and Cecilia returned to Oman in late April 2014, I had little doubt that they would find the owls using one of these holes as a nest. During many nights at the spot, however, Arnoud could detect no activity at all. The JM pair remained completely silent. Had they abandoned their breeding attempt, moved elsewhere, or were they simply being incredibly secretive? I returned alone in late May, hoping that the pair had somehow evaded detection. If they had nested elsewhere on the cliff, by late May their young would surely be calling loudly enough for me to know. After a couple of nights without success, even resorting to playback, I had to conclude that Arnoud had been right: the pair had disappeared. The Pallid Scops Owls were very quiet in this wadi, so I wondered if there was a lack of food. I also worried that collectors had somehow got wind of this pair and shot them. Either way, if I was going to record any young Omani Owls, I would have to find them elsewhere.

For several nights I visited all the Omani Owl territories I knew and listened for any sound that might be from a juvenile. I assumed that their begging calls would be shaped like soliciting calls of adults, but have a much more hissing timbre. From time to time I heard calls that seemed about right, but most were foxes *Vulpes* or leaf-toed geckos *Asaccus*. I was only convinced once, after imitating male compound hooting in a territory I knew to be occupied. No owl had been calling, but immediately after my imitation I heard soliciting calls of a female and begging calls of up to two juveniles. The distance was about 600 m, so the recordings are dreadful. **CD4-67** is a juvenile on its own, while **CD4-68** is a juvenile with the female and a male Pallid Scops Owl. The begging calls continued for some time, and sometimes had a slightly descending inflection. Attempts to climb closer proved fruitless. Still, a poor recording is better than nothing. Having learned how juveniles sound, I was able to recognise them in the background of some of Arnoud's recordings from 2013 (eg, **CD4-63**, **CD4-64** & **CD4-70**).

Omani Owl *Strix omanensis* Al Jabal Al Akhdar, Al Hajar mountains, Oman, 01:11, 29 May 2014. Begging calls of a juvenile and soliciting calls of a female at 600 m distance, with continuous hooting of a male Pallid Scops Owl *Otus brucei*. The juvenile is easiest to hear at 0:00, 0:03, 0:10 and 0:13 and the female at 0:06 and 0:12. There may be a second juvenile in the background. 140529.MR.011116.32   CD4-68

I never got close enough to any juveniles for their mother to use guarding calls or 'alarm calls', although I am sure that Omani Owl will have such a call in its repertoire. Another call type that we did record is so similar to how I would expect guarding calls to sound that for a while that's what I assumed it was. However, since we only ever heard it immediately after playback or imitations of hooting, it must be territorial. **CD4-69** illustrates

CD4-67 **Omani Owl** *Strix omanensis* Al Jabal Al Akhdar, Al Hajar mountains, Oman, 01:28, 29 May 2014. Faint begging calls of a juvenile at 600 m distance. Listen for a rising, fairly high-pitched sound with a hissing timbre at 0:01, 0:04 and 0:07. A similar but lower-pitched sound at 0:05 may belong to a much closer leaf-toed gecko *Asaccus*. 140529. MR.012824.12

Omani Owl *Strix omanensis* Al Jabal Al Akhdar, Al Hajar mountains, Oman, 00:30, 28 May 2013. Distance call series in flight, then compound hooting, a reaction to playback (not included). Background: rising, nasal call of leaf-toed gecko *Asaccus* sp. 130528.AB.003000.12   CD4-69

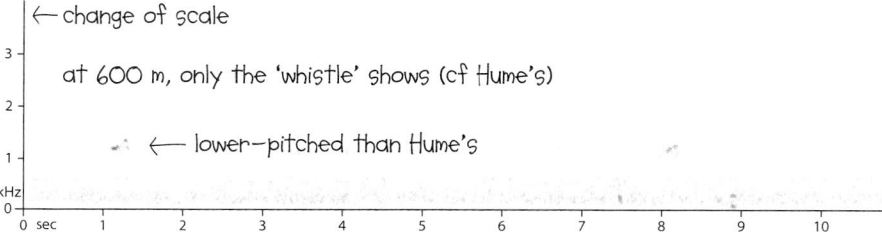

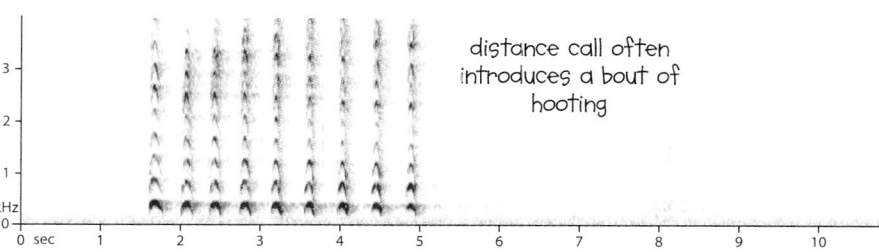

CD4-70   **Omani Owl** *Strix omanensis* Al Jabal Al Akhdar, Al Hajar mountains, Oman, 00:55, 28 May 2013. Three series of distance calls after playback (not included). Background: presumed juvenile begging calls, best from 0:55, and Dhofar Toad *Bufo dhufarensis*. 130528.AB.005500.12

this 'distance call' in flight, and in **CD4-70** the individual barks are grouped into much shorter strophes.

On an owling trip like ours in February 2014, it can be difficult to find a sensible daily rhythm. Exhaustion threatens to strike but adrenaline keeps it at bay. Sometimes we stayed out all night. Other nights we returned to the hotel for a few hours of sleep, with varying success. One time we returned mid-evening and agreed to go out at again 04:00. I managed to sleep but Killian stayed awake. When he returned from photographing a Pallid Scops Owl just outside our room at 00:30, I woke up. My thoughts turned to the owls and soon I was driving to the wadi. I decided to leave recording equipment at three different places to find out whether the JM pair had any neighbours. Having done so, I was heading back through the wadi to go and fetch the others when an Omani Owl flew across the track right in front of me.

Omani Owl *Strix omanensis*, male, Al Jabal Al Akhdar, Al Hajar mountains, Oman, 26 May 2013 (*Arnoud B van den Berg*). Same as in CD4-59, 62, 63, 69 & 70, and probably also CD4-57 & 58.

With my torch I found it only about 10 m from the car, perched on a large rock just left of the track with its back towards me. I noticed two broad tail bars and when it looked over its shoulder I saw its orange eyes. The facial disk was fully open and it had prominent dark 'eyebrows'. When it turned sideways, I noticed the marbled pattern on the side of its head. After about 20 sec it flew off up the slope and landed on a cliff near another individual, its mate. Both were standing sideways on the steeply angled rock face, one leg fully stretched and the other one held short due to the height difference. Their attention was focused on the rock just in front of them, and they pounced every now and then. I could not see what they were hunting, but it must have been tiny. When one of them flew, my torch lit up its underside. The dark wingtip and broad trailing edge contrasted strongly with the whitish interior of the underwing.

Habitat of Omani Owl *Strix omanensis*, Al Jabal Al Akhdar, Al Hajar mountains, Oman, 23 April 2014 (*Arnoud B van den Berg*)

For the meantime, the known population of Omani Owl numbers only around 15 individuals. The total number of territories detected in 2013-14 stands at seven, located in the two wadis we have worked in, some 20 km apart. There is also a third wadi, where Pieter van Eijk heard an unexplained owl sound while camping in February 2008. At the time he thought it must be a Hume's Owl, until he heard recordings of that species and learned that in Oman it only breeds in the

Omani Owl *Strix omanensis*, male, Al Jabal Al Akhdar, Al Hajar mountains, Oman, 26 May 2013 (*Arnoud B van den Berg*)

south. Five years later when Pieter heard recordings of Omani Owl, the mystery was finally solved (van Eijk 2013). His campsite was some 33 km from the discovery site, and all three wadis are within 54 km of one another.

Now that we have a better idea of Omani Owl breeding phenology, BirdLife International is seeking Omani collaboration for a wider survey. Does it occupy the whole of the Al Hajar range, or is it restricted to the central part where we have observed it? Does it go all the way to the highest peaks, up to 2980 m, or is it just in the 380-700 m range where we have heard it? Our experience suggest that February would be the best time to find out, with the owls calling every dusk and dawn at the very least.

I wonder if there are still important *Strix* populations in the wider region waiting to be discovered. Might there be *butleri* in Iran or Pakistan after all, or an undiscovered owl in some remote mountain range in the Sahara? Rumours of a *Strix* owl on the island of Socotra about 380 km south of Yemen have circulated for over a century (Jennings 2010), but the task of confirming them is still up for grabs.

When I started work on this book, I hoped to discover which owls could be identified according to their sounds, regardless of their official taxonomic rank. I also hoped to learn new ways to sex and age owls by their sounds, and to understand more of what they were up to in the dark. Then in 2009, Arnoud rediscovered fish owls in Turkey and recorded sounds that showed they were a separate species. Enough reasons to come up with a title like *Undiscovered owls*, which first appeared in my notebook a year before my first encounter with Omani Owl.

The title takes its inspiration from Carl Jung's *The Undiscovered Self* (1957). Mankind can only be saved from collective madness, writes Jung, if each of us discovers our true self. Owls help me to find mine. To listen to them, I step outside my routine and look for wild places where the world feels more authentic. Escaping from noise allows quiet thoughts and intuitions to be heard. Being in the dark liberates my mind from visual-only reality. When I am owling, anything seems possible.

On 24 March 2013, serendipity was on my side. Having studied the sounds of all the other owls of the Western Palearctic, I quickly recognised Omani Owl as something new. I may never have such good luck again, but the experience taught me that anything *is* possible.

What else might we discover lurking just beyond the horizon that separates mind from silence, if only we learn to listen more like owls?

Hume's Owl *Strix butleri*

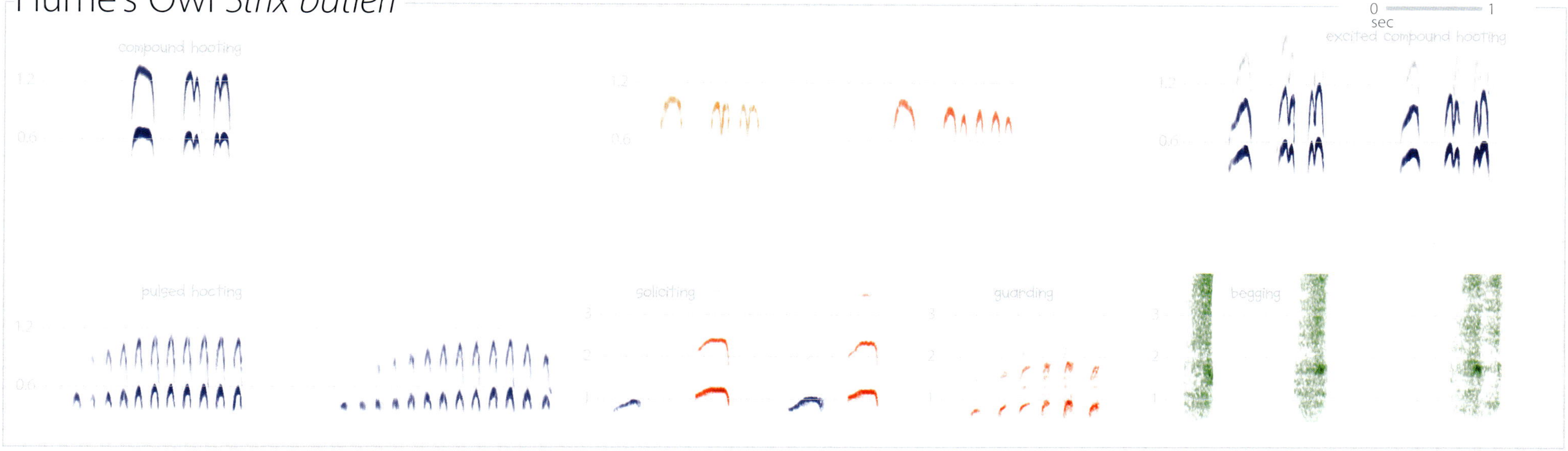

Omani Owl *Strix omanensis*

longer duration & lower pitch than Hume's

2nd part always single note

... and finally

In the 1980s many birders experienced their first Hume's Owl *Strix butleri* in Israel alongside Hadoram Shirihai. Hadoram's exclusive site was guarded by a member of the Israeli military, who kindly let birders look at the owls through a night vision scope.

Hadoram had appeared dramatically on the birding scene selling what became known as 'the Hadoram experience'. At the time, Peter Grant and Killian Mullarney were running Sunbirder trips to Eilat, a concept where a group of 60 or more birders stayed in the same place and could choose either to go birding independently or to take organised daily tours. At night everyone attended a log call. The Hadoram experience involved two or three exhilarating days driving madly through the Negev desert, finding birds like MacQueen's Bustard *Chlamydotis macqueenii* and Saker Falcon *Falco cherrug*.

One evening Hadoram arrived at the log with his latest crew of wild-eyed companions, just as Peter was starting the log. Hadoram strode up the central aisle carrying a cloth bag. He reached inside and pulled out a squawking black gamebird, demanding that Peter identify it. As half the room ticked Black Francolin *Francolinus francolinus*, Peter laughed and identified it as a chicken. Evidently, Hadoram had 'borrowed it' from the pets' corner of a local kibbutz and tethered it in an attempt to lure a Saker for his group.

In the intervening 30 years, Hadoram wrote the scholarly *Birds of Israel* (Shirihai et al 1996) and became better known for photographing the world's rarest petrels. A few years ago, he became the first person to discover where the legendary Zino's Petrel *Pterodroma madeira* could be observed regularly at sea. Hadoram sometimes visits Britain in order to examine bird skins held in The Natural History Museum at Tring. In excitement over one collection of albatross remains, he and a member of staff nearly pushed the cabinet through a wall, to the amazement of other researchers who could hear the noise in adjacent rooms.

Coming right up to date, a group of Hadoram's colleagues have been rocking the cabinets again. Stimulated by our discovery of the Omani Owl *S omanensis*, they re-examined the shabby old type specimen of *Strix butleri* from Ormara in southern Pakistan (Hume 1878). When they compared its DNA with that of other Hume's Owls, they found a surprisingly large difference. They went on to describe more subtle differences in morphology. Kirwan et al (2015) believe that all Hume's Owls other than the Pakistani type specimen may be assigned to a 'new' species. The name they propose for this, the bird everyone has been identifying as Hume's, is *Strix hadorami*.

The oldest specimen of Hume's Owl dates from 1864, when Claude Wilmott Wyatt shot an unidentified owl in Wadi Feiran, Sinai. Wyatt was a "very shy, reserved, and silent man" (Ibis 43: 347-348, 1901), and perhaps this is why he never named his owl. Fifteen years later, Tristram (1879) identified Wyatt's specimen as Hume's newly described *butleri*. For well over a century nobody questioned the link.

Kirwan et al's conclusions will have surprised many, but how solid are they? The DNA part of their paper is based on a sequence of just 218 base pairs, the most important branches in their phylogenetic tree have no support, and DNA of Omani

Owl has yet to be sequenced. The mystery of Hume's type specimen is still unsolved, and sadly it no longer hoots. Pending further research, we use the names Hume's Owl and *Strix butleri* according to their December 2014 meaning.

In the meantime, Hume's original *Strix butleri* presents an opportunity. The number of skilled observers in Pakistan and especially Iran is growing fast, but there must be vast areas of habitat suitable for a cliff-dwelling owl that have yet to be explored. Night birding in particular could bring rich rewards. Beaman (1994) chose the headland just south of Ormara as the point where the Palearctic meets the Oriental region. The owl that Hume described in 1878 could still be lurking near this desert frontier, or elsewhere in south-western Asia, just waiting to be rediscovered. If it is, we're itching to know how it sounds.

Names always keep people talking, and the ones we have used in this book will no doubt also provide fuel for the fire. In the end, though, what we choose to call our owls is far less interesting than the owls themselves. What matters most to us is how they call, and especially whether anyone is willing to listen.

The Sound Approach, 20 January 2015

Håkan Delin's artwork

page		
	16	dark *guttata* form of Common Barn Owl
	22	white Common Barn Owl hunting in broad daylight - an English sight (hunting by day is seen mostly in Britain, probably because Northern Goshawk is rare there)
	30	Madeira Barn Owl trying to catch a Madeiran Storm Petrel on a moon-lit night on Bugio
	42	Tengmalm's Owl in nest hole in old aspen with lichens
	43	Tengmalm's Owl attended by Crested Tit
	47	'murderous intent': a Ural Owl gliding in towards a Tengmalm's Owl
	47	Tengmalm's Owl almost caught by a Ural Owl
	53	Little Owl in Las Serenas, Extremadura, with Great Bustards
	57	Little Owl may look like an 'angry little ballerina'
	67	pale *lilith* subspecies of Cucumiau in Israel (a 'mean female desert ghost')
	72	Northern Hawk-Owl very fluffed up at minus 17°C
	73	male Northern Hawk-Owl giving the fast, shivering territorial call: neck stretched, body trembling
	73	this Northern Hawk-Owl's had to raise its tail as there was little room in its nest: with too much space the eggs would get cold (Ural Owl does the same on eggs)
	75	Northern Hawk-Owl hates big raptors: attacking Ural Owl; its aggressive call *kirrirrritt* almost reminds of a giant Crested Tit
	78	Northern Hawk-Owl, an expert in taking 'elevator-flight' to perch
	79	Northern Hawk-Owl from behind
	84	Eurasian Pygmy Owl standing on a Mealy Redpoll it has killed
	85	Eurasian Pygmy Owl at dusk: passing overhead like a little arrowhead when challenged by imitation of its territory call
	89	Eurasian Pygmy Owl is unpopular: attended by two curious and rather hostile Siberian Jays
	94	Eurasian Scops Owl in plane tree in morning light; looking curious, with tufts lowered
	98	Eurasian Scops Owl at day roost in ivy, in camouflage posture with tufts right up and eyes shut
	100	Eurasian Scops Owl swooping down on pavement for cricket, at midnight
	123	Pallid Scops Owl in olive tree, tufts down
	124	Pallid Scops Owl at day roost
	134	adult Long-eared Owl hunting in morning mist in summer; when relaxed, tufts are lowered and at dawn pupils are still dilated, becoming more like Tawny Owl
	142	Long-eared Owl at day roost in autumn; has taken camouflage posture
	143	Long-eared Owl at day roost in winter; fluffed up, eyes closed
	147	Short-eared Owl on stump of birch
	148	applause: Short-eared Owl wing clapping during display flight, interspersed by volleys of hooting

page	149	Short-eared Owl hunting at dusk
	155	this Short-eared Owl has just landed on a beach after a long flight over sea in autumn
	158	Marsh Owl perched
	159	Marsh Owl hunting at dusk; in Morocco darker on underparts than in southern Africa
	173	Pharaoh Eagle-Owl's day roost
	178	female Eurasian Eagle-Owl on nest, safe in her castle, on cliff ledge of granite
	179	Eurasian Eagle-Owl ready to hunt
	181	male Eurasian Eagle-Owl hooting at dusk: tufts right up, tail raised, throat bulging and showing much white
	183	Eurasian Eagle Owl giving alarm, diabolic cackling: tufts lowered, beak wide open; telling young to keep motionless
	186	two young Eurasian Eagle-Owls, still in the nest, one trying to decide whether to hide or not, the other powering up, knowing it has been discovered
	187	Eurasian Eagle-Owl, 'Lord of the night'
	190	male hooting Snowy Owl on the banks of the Lena river; it has a relatively small head, hunting by eyesight rather than by ear
	192	male Snowy Owl hovering, looking for voles
	193	female Snowy Owl on snowy field; this owl has a very special profile.
	194	male Snowy Owl scolding at nest with mouth wide open, looking like a black hole in his head; sounds like female Mallard
	198	female Snowy Owl on snowy field late at dusk
	216	Lapland Owl in old spruce in poor light, gleaming white crescents below face
	218	Lapland Owl on top of young spruce
	224	asymmetry of facial discs is most obvious in Lapland Owl when it is looking down, listening for scraping sound made by vole; it is big but mostly just consists of feathers: thin birch twigs suffice as a perch
	225	Lapland Owl on roof of a tiny haybarn, typical for farmland around the Gulf of Bothnia, far north
	229	adult Ural Owl on nest stump ('chimney') of big pine, with Water Vole in its mouth; ready to jump down to young
	230	young Ural Owls will easily climb a vertical trunk to avoid danger
	236	fluffed-up and crouched female Ural Owl: barking, bill-snapping, wing-rapping and trotting on branch of pine, ready to attack intruder
	240	Tawny Owl occupying a nest hole in an oak, half of head in shadow
	242	male Tawny Owl in hooting posture
	246	two young Tawny Owls; one realizes it is being seen, has given up, the other one still tries to avoid being discovered, taking 'stump posture' with eyes closed
	264	Hume's Owl's day roost in desert cliff
	265	headlights on Hume's Owl with a gerbil in its claws; orange iris retracted, black pupil dilated

Species guide to the accompanying CDs

See the main text for details such as location, date, age, sex, background species and catalogue number

Common Barn Owl *Tyto alba*	CD1-01/05 & 07/12
American Barn Owl *Tyto furcata*	CD1-06
Slender-billed Barn Owl *Tyto gracilirostris*	CD1-13/15
Madeira Barn Owl *Tyto schmitzi*	CD1-16/21
Cape Verde Barn Owl *Tyto detorta*	CD1-22/28
Tengmalm's Owl *Aegolius funereus*	CD1-29/31 & 33/42
Boreal Owl *Aegolius richardsoni*	CD1-32
Little Owl *Athene vidalii*	CD1-43/57
Cucumiau *Athene noctua*	CD1-58/72
Northern Hawk-Owl *Surnia ulula*	CD1-73/74 & 76/82
American Hawk-Owl *Surnia ulula caparoch*	CD1-75
Parrot Crossbill *Loxia pytyopsittacus*	CD1-83
Eurasian Pygmy Owl *Glaucidium passerinum*	CD2-01/11
Eurasian Scops Owl *Otus scops*	CD2-12/13 & 16/24
Common Midwife Toad *Alytes obstetricans*	CD2-14
Iberian Midwife Toad *Alytes cisternasii*	CD2-15
Cyprus Scops Owl *Otus cyprius*	CD2-25/26 & 28/36
Oriental Scops Owl *Otus sunia rufipennis*	CD2-27
Pallid Scops Owl *Otus brucei*	CD2-37/48
Arabian Scops Owl *Otus pamelae*	CD2-49/50 & 52/56
African Scops Owl *Otus senegalensis*	CD2-51
Long-eared Owl *Asio otus otus*	CD2-57/62 & 65/76
Canarian Long-eared Owl *Asio otus canariensis*	CD2-63
Wilson's Owl *Asio wilsonianus tuftsi*	CD2-64
Short-eared Owl *Asio flammeus*	CD2-77/84 & 86/89
Field Owl *Asio domingensis sanfordi*	CD2-85 & 90

Marsh Owl *Asio capensis*	CD3-01/11
Arabian Eagle-Owl *Bubo milesi*	CD3-12/13 & 16/18
Spotted Eagle-Owl *Bubo africanus*	CD3-14
Greyish Eagle-Owl *Bubo cinerascens*	CD3-15
Pharaoh Eagle-Owl *Bubo ascalaphus*	CD3-19/26
Eurasian Eagle-Owl *Bubo bubo*	CD3-27/44
'Byzantine Eagle-Owl' *Bubo bubo interpositus*	CD3-45/46
Snowy Owl *Bubo scandiacus*	CD3-47/53
Turkish Fish Owl *Bubo semenowi*	CD3-54/56 & 60 & 62/70
Brown Fish Owl *Bubo zeylonensis*	CD3-57/59
Bengal Fish Owl *Bubo leschenaulti*	CD3-61
Lapland Owl *Strix lapponica*	CD3-71/75 & 80 & 82/83
Great Gray Owl *Strix nebulosa*	CD3-76/79 & 81
voles *Arvicolinae*	CD3-84
Ural Owl *Strix uralensis*	CD4-01/15
Tawny Owl *Strix aluco*	CD4-15/31
Maghreb Wood Owl *Strix mauritanica*	CD4-32/38
Hume's Owl *Strix butleri*	CD4-39/56
Omani Owl *Strix omanensis*	CD4-57/70

References

Alcover, J A & Florit, X 1989. Els ocells del jaciment arqueològic de la Aldea, Gran Canària, Butlletí de la Institució Catalana d'Història Natural 56 (Secció de Geologia, 5): 47-55.
Alegre, J, Hernández, A, Purroy, F J & Sánchez, A J 1989. Distribución altitudinal y patrones de afinidad trófica geográfica de la Lechuza Común (*Tyto alba*) en León. Ardeola 36: 41-54.
Alexander, W B 1935. Minutes of the 377th meeting, December 12, 1934. Bulletin of the British Ornithologists' Club 55: 60.
Ali, S & Ripley, S D 1981. Handbook of the Birds of India and Pakistan 3. Second edition. Delhi.
Aliabadian, M, Alaee, K, N & Darvish, J 2012. Phylogenetic systematics of Barn Owl (*Tyto alba* (Scopoli, 1769)) complex inferred from mitochondrial rDNA (16S RRNA) taxonomic implication. Journal of Taxonomy and Biosystematics 4: 1-12.
Antoniazza, S, Burri, R, Fumagalli, L, Goudet, J & Roulin, A 2011. Local adaptation maintains clinal variation in melanin-based coloration of European barn owls (*Tyto alba*). Evolution 64: 1944-1954.
Appleby, B M & Redpath, S M 1997. Indicators of male quality in the hoots of Tawny Owls (*Strix aluco*). Journal of Raptor Research 31: 65-70.
Aronson, L 1979. Hume's Tawny Owl *Strix butleri* in Israel. Dutch Birding 1: 18-19.
Aulagnier, S, Haffner, P, Mitchell-Jones, A J, Moutou, F & Zima, J 2009. Mammals of Europe, North Africa and the Middle East. London.
Baha el Din, S & Baha el Din, M 2001. Status and distribution of Hume's (Tawny) Owl *Strix butleri* in the Eastern Desert of Egypt. Bulletin of the African Bird Club 8: 18-20.
Bakker, D 1957. De Velduil in de Noordoostpolder. De Levende Natuur 60: 104-108.
Ballman, P 1973. Fossile Vögel aus dem Neogen der Halbinsel Gargano (Italien). Scripta Geologica 17: 1-75.
Bannerman, D A 1963. Birds of the Atlantic Islands 1: a history of the birds of the Canary Islands and the Salvages. Edinburgh.
Bannerman, D A 1965. Birds of the Atlantic Islands 2: a history of the birds of Madeira, the Desertas, and the Porto Santo Islands. Edinburgh.
Bannerman, D A & Bannerman, W M 1958. Birds of Cyprus. Edinburgh.
Bannerman, D A & Bannerman, W M 1966. Birds of the Atlantic Islands 3: a history of the birds of the Azores. Edinburgh.
Barn Owl Trust 2012. Barn Owl Conservation Handbook. A comprehensive guide for ecologists, surveyors, land managers and ornithologists. Exeter.
Bates, G L 1937a. On interesting Birds recently sent to the British Museum from Arabia by Mr. N. St. J. B. Philby. Bulletin of the British Ornithologists' Club 57: 17-21.
Bates, G L 1937b. Descriptions of two new races of Arabian birds: *Otus senegalensis pamelae* and *Chrysococcyx klaasi arabicus*. Bulletin of the British Ornithologists' Club 57: 150-151.
Beaman, M 1994. Palearctic birds. A checklist of the birds of Europe, North Africa and Asia north of the foothills of the Himalayas. Stonyhurst.
Beck, T W & Winter, J 2000. Survey protocol for the Great Gray Owl in the Sierra Nevada of California. Prepared for the US Department of Agriculture Forest Service, Pacific Southwest Region, Vallejo, California, USA.
Bekir, S, Yoğurtçuoğlu, E & Bozdoğan, M 2010. Balık Baykuşu (*Bubo zeylonensis*) Araştırma Raporu 2010. [Brown Fish Owl (*Bubo zeylonensis*) Research Report 2010.] (In Turkish.)
van den Berg, A B 1974. Merkwaardig gedrag van Velduilen op Schiermonnikoog. Het Vogeljaar 22: 830.
van den Berg, A B, Bekir, S, de Knijff, P & The Sound Approach 2010. Rediscovery, biology, vocalisations and taxonomy of fish owls in Turkey. Dutch Birding 32: 287-298.
van den Berg, A B, Bekir, S & The Sound Approach 2009. DBActueel: Brown Fish Owl in Turkey and first breeding record for WP. Dutch Birding 32: 268-270.
van den Berg, A B, Bison, P & Kasparek, M 1988. Striated Scops Owl in Turkey. Dutch Birding 10: 161-166.
van den Berg, A B & Haas, M 2005. WP reports. Dutch Birding 27: 403-425
Berggren, V & Wahlstedt, J 1977. Lappugglans *Strix nebulosa* läten. Vår Fågelvärld 36: 243-249.

Bergier, P & Thévenot, M 1991. Statut et écologie du Hibou du Cap Nord-Africain *Asio capensis tingitanus*. Alauda 59: 206-224.
Bondrup-Nielsen, S 1984. Vocalizations of the Boreal Owl, *Aegolius funereus richardsoni* in North America. Canadian Field Naturalist 98: 191-197.
Boukhamza, M, Hamdine, W & Thévenot, M 1994. Données sur le régime alimentaire du Grand-Duc Ascalaphe (*Bubo bubo ascalaphus*) en milieu steppique (Aïn Ouessera, Algérie). Alauda 62: 150-152.
Brazil, M A & Yamamoto, S 1989. The behavioural ecology of Blakiston's Fish Owl *Ketupa blakistoni* in Japan: calling behaviour. P 403-410 in: Meyburg, B-U & Chancellor, R D (editors), Raptors in the modern world: proceedings of the III world conference on birds of prey and owls. World Working Group on Birds of Prey and Owls, Berlin.
Brito, P H 2005. The influence of Pleistocene glacial refugia on tawny owl genetic diversity and phylogeography in western Europe. Molecular Ecology 14: 3077-3094.
Broekhuizen, S, Hoekstra, B, van Laar, V, Smeenk, C & Thissen, J M B 1992. Atlas van de Nederlandse zoogdieren. Third edition. Utrecht.
Broggi, J, Copete, J L, Kvist, L & Mariné, R 2013. Is there genetic differentiation in the Pyrenean population of Tengmalm's Owl (*Aegolius funereus*). Ardeola 60: 123-132.
Bühler, P & Epple, W 1980. De Lautäußerungen der Schleiereule (*Tyto alba*). Journal für Ornithologie 121: 36-70.
Bunn, D S, Warburton, A B & Wilson, R D S 1982. The Barn Owl. Calton.
Byrjedal, I & Langhelle, G 1986. Sex and age biased mobility in Hawk Owls *Surnia ulula*. Ornis Scandinavica 17: 306-308.
Cadman, W A 1934. An attacking Tawny Owl. British Birds 28: 130-132.
Canário, F, Leitão, A H & Tomé, R 2012. Predation attempts by Short-eared and Long-eared Owls on migrating songbirds attracted to artificial lights. Journal of Raptor Research 46: 232-234.
Carlyon, J 2011. Nocturnal birds of Southern Africa. Pietermaritzburg.
Catchpole, C K & Slater, P J B 2008. Bird song. Biological Themes and Variations. Second edition. Cambridge, UK.
Catry, P, Costa, H, Elias, G & Matias, R 2010. Aves de Portugal. Ornitologia do território continental. Lisbon.
Chappuis, C 2000. Oiseaux d'Afrique 1. Sahara, Maghreb, Madère, Canaries & Îles du Cap-Vert. 4 CDs and booklet. Paris.
Chappuis, C 2010. Review of Indian bird sounds. Dutch Birding 32: 132-133.
Chappuis, C, Deroussen, D & Warakagoda, D 2008. Indian bird sounds – The Indian Peninsula. 5 CDs and booklet. Hyderabad.
Charter, M, Peleg, O, Leshem, Y & Roulin, A 2012. Similar patterns of local barn owl adaptation in the Middle East and Europe with respect to melanic coloration. Biological Journal of the Linnean Society 106: 447-454.
Clark, R J 1975. A field study of the Short-eared Owl, *Asio flammeus* (Pontoppidan), in North America. Wildlife Monographs 47: 3-67.
Clottes, J 2002. Paleolithic cave art in France. Adorant magazine, published online at www.bradshawfoundation.com
Constantine, M, Hopper, N & The Sound Approach 2012. Catching the bug. Poole.
Cramp, S (editor) 1985. The birds of the Western Palearctic 4. Oxford.
Delgado, M del M, Caferri, E, Méndez, M, Godoy, J A, Campioni, L & Penteriani, V 2013. Population characteristics may reduce the levels of individual call identity. PLoS ONE 8: e77557.
Delgado, M del M & Penteriani, V 2006. Vocal behaviour and neighbour spatial arrangement during vocal displays in eagle owls (*Bubo bubo*). Journal of Zoology 271: 3-10.
Deroussen, F & Millancourt, H 2003. Chouettes et hiboux de France et d'Europe. CD and booklet. Charenton.
Desfayes, M & Géroudet, P 1949. Notes sur le Grand-Duc. Nos Oiseaux 20: 49-60.
van Diek, H, Felix, R, Hornman, M, Meininger, P L, Willems, F & Zekhuis, M 2004. Bird counting in Iran in January 2004. Dutch Birding 26: 287-296.
Dorogov, I 1987. [Ecology of the rodent-eating predators of Wrangel Island and their role in lemming dynamics.] Academy of Sciences of the USSR. Vladivostok. (In Russian.)
Dragonetti, M 2007. Individuality in scops owl *Otus scops* vocalisations. Bioacoustics 16: 147-172.
Dreiss, A N, Antoniazza, S, Burri, R, Fumagalli, L, Sonnay, C, Frey, C, Goudet, J & Roulin, A 2011. Local adaptation and matching habitat choice in female barn owls with respect to melanic coloration. Journal of Evolutionary Biology 25: 103-114.
Eastham, A 1968. The avifauna of Gorham's Cave. Gibraltar. Bulletin of the Institute of Archeology 7: 37-42.

Eastham, A 2012. The Magdalenians and Snowy Owls. P 238-243 in: Potapov, E & Sale, R, The Snowy Owl. London.
Ebels, E B 2002. Brown Fish Owl in the Western Palearctic. Dutch Birding 24: 157-161.
van Eijk, P 2013. Presumed second locality for Omani Owl. Dutch Birding 35: 387-388.
Eken, G 1997. Regular wintering by Scops Owls *Otus scops* in Turkey, at Havran Delta. Sandgrouse 19: 147.
Escarguel, G, Marandat, B & Legendre, S 1997. Sur l'âge numérique des faunes de mammifères du Paléogène d'Europe occidentale, en particulier celles de l'Eocène inférieur et moyen. P 443-460 in: Aguilar, J-P, Legendre, S & Michaux, J (editors), Actes du Congrès Biochrom '97. Montpellier.
Evans, D L 1980. Vocalizations and territorial behavior of wintering Snowy Owls. American Birds 34: 748-749.
Exo, K-M 1984. Die akustische Unterscheidung von Steinkauzmännchen und –weibchen (*Athene noctua*). Journal für Ornithologie 125: 94-97.
Exo, K-M & Scherzinger, W 1989. Stimme und Lautrepertoire des Steinkauzes (*Athene noctua*): Beschreibung, Kontext und Lebensraumanpassung. Ökologie der Vögel 11: 149-187.
Flint, P & Stewart, P 1992. The birds of Cyprus. British Ornithologists' Union check-list 6. Tring.
Florit, X & Alcover, J A 1987. Els ocells del Pleistocè Superior de la Cova Nova (Capdepera, Mallorca). II fauna associada i discussió. Bolletí de la Societat d'Història Natural de les Balears 31: 33-44.
Forster, J R 1772. Descriptiones Avium Rariorum e Sinu Hudsonis. Philosophical Transactions of the Royal Society 62: 423-433..
Frey, H 1973. Zur Ökologie Nieder-Österreichischer Uhupopulationen. Diss Tierärztl Hochsch. Wien.
Fry, C H, Keith, S & Urban, E K 1988. Handbook of the birds of Africa 3. London.
Fuchs, J, Pons, J-M, Goodman, S M, Bretagnolle, V, Melo, M, Bowie, R C K, Currie, D, Safford, R, Virani, M Z, Thomsett, S, Hija, A, Cruaud, C & Pasquet, E 2008. Tracing the colonization history of the Indian Ocean scops-owls (Strigiformes: *Otus*) with further insight into the spatio-temporal origin of the Malagasy avifauna. BMC Evolutionary Biology 8: 197.
Galeotti, P 1998. Correlates of hoot rate and structure in male Tawny Owls *Strix aluco*: Implications for male rivalry and female mate choice. Journal of Avian Biology 29: 25-32.
Galeotti, P R, Appleby, B M & Redpath, S M 1996. Macro and microgeographical variations in the 'hoot' of Italian and English tawny owls (*Strix aluco*). Italian Journal of Zoology 63: 57-64.
Galeotti, P & Pavan, G 2008. Differential responses of territorial Tawny Owls *Strix aluco* to the hooting of neighbours and strangers. Ibis 135: 300-304.
Galeotti, P & Rubolini, D 2007. Head ornaments in owls: what are their functions? Journal of Avian Biology 38: 731-736.
Galeotti, P & Sacchi, R 2001. Turnover of territorial Scops Owl *Otus scops* as estimated by spectrographic analyses of male hoots. Journal of Avian Biology 32: 256-262.
Geniez, P & López-Jurado, L F 1998. Nouvelles observations ornithologiques aux Îles du Cap-Vert. Alauda 66: 307-311.
Glue, D E 2002. Little Owl *Athene noctua*. In: Wernham, C V, Toms, M P, Clark, G M et al (editors), The Migration Atlas: Movements of the birds of Britain and Ireland. London.
Glutz von Blotzheim, U N & Bauer, K M 1980 Handbuch der Vögel Mitteleuropas 9. Wiesbaden.
Guérin-Méneville, F E 1843. Oiseaux nouveaux découverts par MM. Ferret et Galinier pendant leur voyage en Abyssinie. *Bubo cinerascens*. Revue Zoologique par la Société Cuvierienne 6: 321.
Guerra, C, Bover, P & Alcover, J A 2012. A new species of extinct little owl from the Pleistocene of Mallorca (Balearic Islands). Journal of Ornithology 153: 347-354.
Hagemeijer, W J M & & Blair, M J 1997. The EBCC Atlas of European breeding birds. London.
Halder, R 2004. A sound guide to the birds of Bangladesh. CD and booklet.
Hambling, R 2008. Tawny owl calls and vocalizations. www.godsownclay.com/TawnyOwls/Calls/tawnyowlcalls1.html. Accessed on 10 April 2014.
Hamdine, W, Bouzhemza, M, Doumandji, S-E, Poitevin, F & Thévenot, M 1999. Premières données sur le régime alimentaire de la Chouette hulotte (*Strix aluco mauritanica*) en Algérie. Ecologia Mediterranea 25: 111-123.

Hansson, L & Henttonen, H 1985. Gradients in density variations of small rodents: the importance of latitude and snow cover. Oecologia 67: 394-402.
Hardouin, L A, Reby, D, Bavoux, C, Burneleau, G & Bretagnolle, V 2007. Communication of male quality in owl hoots. The American Naturalist 169: 552-562.
Hardouin, L A, Bretagnolle, V, Tabel, P, Bavoux, C, Burneleau, G & Reby, D 2009. Acoustic cues to reproductive success in male owl hoots. Animal Behaviour 78: 907-913.
Harrop, A H J 2010. Records of Hawk Owls in Britain. British Birds 103: 276-283.
Harvancik, S 2009. Owls of Slovakia in pictures. CD and book. Zvolen.
Hausknecht, R, Jacobs, S, Müller, J, Zink, R, Frey, H, Solheim, R, Vrezec, A, Kristin, A, Mihok, J, Kergalve, I, Saurola, P & Kuehn, R 2014. Phylogeographic analysis and genetic cluster recogition for the conservation of Ural Owls (*Strix uralensis*) in Europe. Journal of Ornithology 155: 121-134.
Hawley, R G 1966. Observations on the Long-eared Owl. Sorby Record 2: 95-114.
Haynes, S, Jaarola, M & Searle, J B 2003. Phylogeography of the Common Vole (*Microtus arvalis*) with particular emphasis on the colonisation of the Orkney archipelago. Molecular Ecology 12: 951-956.
Hazevoet, C J 1995. The birds of the Cape Verde Islands. British Ornithologists' Union check-list 13. Tring.
Heim de Balsac, H & Mayaud, N 1962. Les oiseaux du nord-ouest de l'Afrique. Paris.
Heinzel, H, Fitter, R & Parslow, J 1972. The birds of Britain and Europe with North Africa and the Middle East. London.
Hipkiss, T, Hörnfeldt, B, Lundmark, A & Norbäck, M 2002. Sex ratio and age structure of nomadic Tengmalm's owls: a molecular approach. Journal of Avian Biology 33: 107-110.
Holmberg, T 1974. En studie av slagugglans *Strix uralensis* läten. Vår Vågelvärld 33: 140-146.
del Hoyo, J, Elliott, A & Sargatal, J (editors) 1999. Handbook of the birds of the world 5. Barcelona.
del Hoyo, J & Collar, N J 2014. Illustrated checklist of the birds of the world 1: non-passeriformes. Barcelona.
Horner, K O & Hubbard, J P 1982. An analysis of birds limed in spring at Paralimni, Cyprus. Cyprus Ornithological Society (1970) report 7: 54-104.
Hüe, F & Etchécopar, R D 1970. Les oiseaux du Proche et du Moyen Orient. Paris.
Huguet, P & Chappuis, C 2002. Bird sounds of Madagascar, Mayotte, Comoros, Seychelles, Réunion and Mauritius. 4 CDs and booklet.
Hull, J M, Englis, A, Medley, J R, Jepsen, E P, Duncan, J R, Ernest, H B & Keane, J J 2014. A new subspecies of Great Gray Owl (*Strix nebulosa*) in the Sierra Nevada of California. Journal of Raptor Research 48: 68-77.
Hume, A 1878. *Asio butleri*, Sp. Nov.? Stray Feathers 7: 316-318.
Hüni, M 1982. Exkursion der Ala in die Sudosttürkei, 3-17. April 1982. Ornithologische Beobachter 79 : 221-223.
Irby, L H 1895. The ornithology of the Strait of Gibraltar. Second edition. London.
Isenmann, P & Moali, A 2000. Birds of Algeria. Paris.
Jaume, D, McMinn, M & Alcover, J A 1993. Fossil birds from the Bujero del Silo, La Gomera (Canary Islands), with a description of a new species of quail (Galliformes: Phasianidae). Boletim do Museu Municipal do Funchal, Sup 2: 147-165.
Jennings, M C 2010. Atlas of the breeding birds of Arabia. Fauna of Arabia 25: 1-772.
Johnsen, A, Rindal, E, Ericson, P G P, Zuccon, D, Kerr, K C R, Stoeckle, M Y & Lifjeld, J T 2010. DNA barcoding of Scandinavian birds reveals divergent lineages in trans-Atlantic species. Journal of Ornithology 151: 565-578.
Jolly, D, Prentice, I C, Bonnefille, R, Ballouche, A, Bengo, M, Brenac, P, Buchet, G, Burney, D, Cazet, J-P, Cheddadi, R, Edorh, T, Elenga, H, Elmoutaki, S, Guiot, J, Laarif, F, Lamb, H, Lezine, A-M, Malet, J, Mbenza, M, Peyron, O, Reille, M, Reynaud-Farrera, I, Riollet, G, Ritchie, C, Roche, E, Scott, L, Ssemmanda, I, Straka, H, Umer, M, Van Campo, E, Vilimumbalo, S, Vincens, A & Waller, M 1998. Biome reconstruction from pollen and plant macrofossil data for Africa and the Arabian peninsula at 0 and 6000 years. Journal of Biogeography 25: 1007-1027.
Joubert, H J 1943. Nest and eggs of the S. African Marsh Owl. Ostrich 14:42-44.
Keijl, G O & Sandee, H 1996. On occurrence and diet of the Marsh Owl *Asio capensis* in the Merja Zerga, northwest Morocco. Alauda 64: 451-453.

Kellomäki, E 1977. Food of the Pygmy Owl *Glaucidium passerinum* in the breeding season. Ornis Fennica 54: 1-29.
Kemp, A 1987. Owls of Southern Africa. Cape Town.
Kemp, J 1981. Breeding Long-eared Owls in West Norfolk. Norfolk Bird & Mammal Report 1980. Transactions of the Norfolk & Norwich Naturalists' Society 25: 234-286.
Khaleghizadeh A, Scott, D A, Tohidifar, M, Musavi S B, Ghasemi M, Sehhatisabet M E, Ashoori A, Khani A, Bakhtiari P, Amini H, Roselaar C, Ayé R, Ullman M, Nezami B & Eskandari F 2011. Rare Birds in Iran in 1980–2010. Podoces 6: 1-48.
Kirwan, G M, Schweizer, M & Copete, J L 2015. Multiple lines of evidence confirm that Hume's Owl *Strix butleri* (A. O. Hume, 1878) is two species, with description of an unnamed species (Aves: Non-Passeriformes: Strigidae). Zootaxa 3904: 28–50.
König, C 1968. Lautäußerungen von Rauhfußkauz (*Aegolius funereus*) und Sperlingskauz (*Glaucidium passerinum*). Vogelwelt, Beiheft 1: 115-138.
König, C 1970. Herbstbalz der Zwergohreule (*Otus scops*). Ornithologische Mitteilungen 22: 44-45.
König, L 1973. Das Aktionssystem der Zwergohreule *Otus scops scops* (Linné 1758). Journal of Comparative Ethology, Supplement 13: 1-124.
König, C, Weick, F & Becking, J-H 2008. Owls of the world. Second edition. London.
Konishi, M 1973. How the owl tracks its prey: experiments with trained barn owls reveal how their acute sense of hearing enables them to catch prey in the dark. American Scientist 61: 414-424.
Koopman, M E, McDonald, D B, Hayward, G D, Eldegard, K, Sonerud, G A & Sermach, S G 2005. Genetic similarity among Eurasian subspecies of boreal owls *Aegolius funereus*. Journal of Avian Biology 36: 179-183.
Korpimäki & Hakkarainen 2012. The Boreal Owl – ecology, behaviour and conservation of a forest-dwelling predator. Cambridge, UK.
Kuhk, R 1953. Lautäußerungen und jahreszeitliche Gesangstätigkeit des Rauhfußkauzes, *Aegolius funereus* (L.). Journal für Ornithologie 94: 83-93.
Kullberg, C 1995. Strategy of the Pygmy Owls while hunting avian and mammalian prey. Ornis Fennica 72: 72-78.
Laidler, D 2010. Spotted Eagle Owl growing up. Video uploaded on 20 November 2010. www.youtube.com/watch?v=2KPeM1uqSKk
Ławicki, Ł, Abramčuk, A V, Domashevsky, S V, Paal, U, Solheim, R, Chodkiewicz T & Woźniak, B 2013. Range extension of Great Grey Owl in Europe. Dutch Birding 35: 145-154.
Legge, W V 1880. A history of the birds of Ceylon. London.
Lerman, S B, Smith, J P & Atwood, J A 2006. Factors affecting the winter distribution of Striated Scops-Owl, (*Otus brucei*), in southern Israel. IV North American Ornithological Conference, Veracruz, Mexico. Poster.
Leshem, J 1981. The occurrence of Hume's Tawny Owl in Israel and Sinai. Sandgrouse 2: 100-102.
Lindblad, J 1967. I ugglemarker. Book and gramophone record. Stockholm.
Lindén, A 2013. Identifying the songs of Eurasian Scops Owl and Eurasian Pygmy Owl. Caluta 4: 12-20.
Löfgren, O, Hörnfeldt, B & Carlsson, B-G 1986. Site tenacity and nomadism in Tengmalm's Owl (*Aegolius funereus* (L.)) in relation to cyclic food production. Oecologia 69: 321-326.
López-Darias, M, Hernández, A & Hernández, J 2006. Búho Chico *Asio otus* in: Noticiario Ornitológico. Ardeola 53: 206.
Louchart, A 2011. Paleornithology, *Bubo insularis* and deletion of putative records of Brown Fish Owl in the western Mediterranean. Dutch Birding 33: 251-252.
Lundberg, A 1980. Vocalizations and courtship feeding of the Ural Owl *Strix uralensis*. Ornis Scandinavica 11: 65-70.
van Maanen, E & Cuyten, K 2012. In search of Carnivores at the "end of the world". Report of a trip to Iran 7-16 April 2012. The Anatolian Leopard Foundation/Plan for the Land.
Magnin, G 1991. A record of the Brown Fish Owl *Ketupa zeylonensis* from Turkey. Sandgrouse 13: 42-44.
Marti, C D, Poole, A F & Bevier, L R 2005. Barn Owl (*Tyto alba*). The birds of North America online (bna.birds.cornell.edu/bna/species/001). Ithaca.
Martins, R P & Hirschfeld, E 1998. Comments on the limits of the Western Palearctic in Iran and the Arabian Peninsula. Sandgrouse 20: 108-34.
Mebs, T & Scherzinger, W 2004. Uilen van Europa. Baarn.
Megalli, M, Moldovan, S & Gilbert, H 2011. Trip report: Sinai, Red Sea, Oases, North Coast Oct. 4-19, 2011. Downloaded from: www.birdinginegypt.com.

Meinertzhagen, R 1930. Nicoll's Birds of Egypt. London.
Mendelsson, H, Yom-Tov, Y & Safriel, U 1975. Hume's Tawny Owl *Strix butleri in* the Judean, Negev and Sinai Deserts. Ibis 117: 110-111.
Mikkola, H 1983. Owls of Europe. Calton.
Mikkola, H 2012. Owls of the world, a photographic guide. London.
Mikkola, H & Sieradzki, A 2012. Early history of the Great Gray Owl in the New and Old World. Ontario Birds 30: 26-29.
Miller, A H 1934. The vocal apparatus of some North American owls. Condor 36: 204-213.
Milza, J-C 1997. *Athene angelis* n. sp. (Aves, Strigiformes), nouvelle espèce endémique insulaire éteinte du Pléistocène moyen et supérieur de Corse (France). Comptes Rendus de l'Academie des Sciences de Paris, série IIa 324: 677-684.
Moreau, R E 1972. The Palearctic-African bird migration systems. London.
Moreno, J M 2000. Cantos y reclamos de las aves de Canarias. 2 CDs and book. Santa Cruz de Tenerife.
Mori, E, Menchetti, M & Ferretti, F 2014. Seasonal and environmental influences on the calling behaviour of Eurasian Scops Owls. Bird Study 61: 277-281.
Mourer-Chauviré, C 1975. Les oiseaux du Pléistocène moyen et supérieur de France. Documents du Laboratoire de Géologie de la Faculté de Sciences de Lyon 64: 1-624.
Mourer-Chauviré, C 1987. Les Strigiformes (Aves) des Phosphorites du Quercy (France): Systématique, biostratigraphie et paléobiogéographie. In: Mourer-Chauviré, C (editor), L'évolution des Oiseaux d'après le Témoignage des Fossiles. Documents des Laboratoires de Géologie de Lyon 99: 89-135.
Mourer-Chauviré, C, Alcover, J A, Moya, S & Pons, J 1980. Une nouvelle forme insulaire d'effraie géante, *Tyto balearica* n. sp., (Aves, Strigiformes), du Plio-Pléistocène des Baleares. Géobios 13: 803-811.
Mourer-Chauviré, C & Geraads, D 2010. The Upper Pliocene Avifauna of Ahl al Oughlam, Morocco. Systematics and Biogeography. Records of the Australian Museum 62: 157-184.
Mourer-Chauviré, C, Salotti, M, Pereira, É, Quinif, Y, Courtois, J-Y, Dubois, J-N & La Milza, J C. *Athene angelis* n. sp. (Aves, Strigiformes), nouvelle espèce endémique insulaire éteinte du Pléistocène moyen et supérieur de Corse (France). Comptes rendus de l'Académie des sciences. Série 2, Sciences de la terre et des planètes, Paris, v 324, no 8, 1997, p 677-684.
Mourer-Chauviré, C & Sanchez Marco, A 1988. Présence de *Tyto balearica* (Aves, Strigiformes) dans des gisements continentaux du Pliocène de France et d'Espagne. Géobios 21: 639-644.
Mundkur, T 1986. Occurrence of the Pallid Scops Owl *Otus brucei* (Hume) in Rajkot, Gujarat. Newsletter for Birdwatchers 26: 10-11.
de Naurois, R 1982. Le statut de l'Effraie de l'archipel du Cap Vert *Tyto alba detorta*. Rivista Italiana di Ornitologia 52: 154-166.
Nero, R W 1982. The Great Gray Owl, phantom of the Northern Forest. Washington.
van Nieuwenhuyse, D, Génot, J-C & Johnson, D H 2008. The Little Owl. Conservation, Ecology and Behavior of *Athene noctua*. Cambridge, UK.
Nijman, V & Aliabadian, M 2013. DNA Barcoding as a tool for elucidating species delineation in wide-ranging species as illustrated by owls (Tytonidae and Strigidae). Zoological Science 30: 1005-1009.
Nybo, J O & Sonerud, G A 1990. Seasonal changes in the diet of Hawk Owls *Surnia ulula*: the importance of snow cover. Ornis Fennica 67: 45-51.
O'Reilly, R 2000. Trip report: Oman – 22 September to 5 October 2000. www.osme.org.
Olson, S L 2012. A new species of small owl of the genus *Aegolius* (Aves: Strigidae) from Quaternary deposits on Bermuda. Proceedings of the Biological Society of Washington 125: 97-105.
Olsson, V 1979. Studies on a population of Eagle Owls *Bubo bubo* (L.) in southeast Sweden. Viltrevy 11: 1-99.
Omote, K, Nishida, C, Dick, M H & Masuda, R 2013. Limited phylogenetic distribution of a long tandem-repeat cluster in the mitochondrial control region in *Bubo* (Aves, Strigidae) and cluster variation in Blakiston's fish owl (*Bubo blakistoni*). Molecular Phylogenetics and Evolution 66: 889-897.
Ottens, G & Jonker, M 2010. Ruigpootuilen in Drenthe in 2008-2010: terug van weggeweest? Uilen 1: 80-89.
Parmalee, P W & Klippel, W E 1982. Evidence of a Boreal Avifauna in Middle Tennessee during the Late Pleistocene. Auk 99: 365-368.

Pavia, M 2004. A new large barn owl (Aves, Strigiformes, Tytonidae) from the Middle Pleistocene of Sicily, Italy, and its taphonomical significance. Geobios 37: 631-641.

Pavia, M 2008. The evolution dynamics of the Strigiformes in the Mediterranean islands with the description of *Aegolius martae* n. sp. (Aves, Strigidae). Quaternary International 182: 80-89.

Pavia, M & Mourer-Chauviré, C 2002. An overview of the genus *Athene* in the Pleistocene of the Mediterranean islands, with the description of *Athene trinacriae* n. sp. (Aves: Strigidae). Proceedings of the 5th Symposium of the Society of Paleontology and Evolution 13-27.

Payne, R S & Drury, W H 1958. Marksman of the darkness. Natural History 67: 316-323.

Pellegrino, I, Negri, A, Cucco, M, Mucci, N, Pavia, M, Sálek, M, Boano, G & Randi, E 2014. Phylogeography and Pleistocene refugia of the Little Owl *Athene noctua* inferred from mtDNA sequencing. Ibis 156: 639-657.

Pelz, P 2008. Europas Ugglor / Owls of Europe. CD and booklet.

Penteriani, V 2002. Variation in the function of Eagle Owl vocal behaviour: territorial defence and intra-pair communication? Ethology, Ecology & Evolution 14: 275-281.

Penteriani, V, Alonso-Alvarez, C, Delgado, M del M, Sergio, F & Ferrer, M 2006. Brightness variability in the white badge of the eagle owl *Bubo bubo*. Journal of Avian Biology 37: 110-116.

Penteriani, V, Delgado, M del M, Alonso-Alvarez, C & Sergio, F 2007. The importance of visual cues for nocturnal species: eagle owls signal by badge brightness. Behavioral Ecology 18: 143-147.

Penteriani, V, Delgado, M del M, Campioni, L & Lourenço, R 2010. Moonlight makes owls more chatty. PLoS One 5: 1-5.

Penteriani, V & Delgado, M del M 2009. The dusk chorus from an owl perspective: Eagle Owls vocalize when their white throat badge contrasts most. PLoS ONE 4: 1-4.

Penteriani, V, Delgado, M del M, Stigliano, R, Campioni, L & Sánchez Medina, M 2014. Owl dusk chorus is related to individual and nest site quality. Ibis 156: 892-895.

Polakowski, M, Broniszewska, M & Skierczyński, M 2008. Sex and age composition during autumn migration of Pygmy Owl *Glaucidium passerinum* in Central Sweden in 2005. Ornis Svecica 18: 82-86.

Pons, J-M, Kirwan, G M, Porter, R F & Fuchs, J 2013. A reappraisal of the systematic affinities of Socotran, Arabian and East African scops owls (*Otus*, Strigidae) using a combination of molecular, biometric and acoustic data. Ibis 155: 518-533.

Potapov, E & Sale, R 2012. The Snowy Owl. London.

Pozdnyakov, V I & Sofronov, Y N 2005. [Snowy Owl in the Lena Delta.] P 36-40 in: Volkov, S, Mozorov, V & Sharikov, A (editors), [Owls of Northern Eurasia]. Moscow. (In Russian with English summary.)

Pukinskiy, Y B 1974. Blakiston's Fish Owl vocal reactions. Vestnik Leningradskogo Universityrsiteta 3: 35-39. (In Russian with English summary.)

Pukinskiy, Y B 1993. Blakiston's Fish Owl *Ketupa blakistoni*. P 290-302 in V D Ilichev (editor), Birds of Russia and adjacent regions. Moscow. (In Russian.)

Rando, J C, Alcover, J A, Michaux, J, Hutterer, R & Navarro, J F 2011. Late-Holocene asynchronous extinction of endemic mammals on the eastern Canary Islands. The Holocene 22: 801-808.

Rando, J C, Alcover, J A, Navarro, J F, Michaux, J & Hutterer, R 2011. Poniendo fechas a una catástrofe: 14C, cronologías y causas de la extinción de vertebrados en Canarias. El Indiferente 21: 6-15.

Rando, J C, Alcover, J A, Olson, S L & Pieper, H 2013. A new species of extinct scops owl (Aves: Strigiformes: Strigidae: *Otus*) from São Miguel Island (Azores Archipelago, North Atlantic Ocean). Zootaxa 3647: 343-357.

Rando, J C, Pieper, H, Alcover, J A & Olson S L 2012. A new species of extinct fossil scops owl (Aves: Strigiformes: Strigidae: *Otus*) from the Archipelago of Madeira. Zootaxa 3182: 29-42.

Rasmussen, P C & Anderton, J C 2005. Birds of South Asia: the Ripley guide 1 & 2. Barcelona.

Redpath, S M, Appleby, B M & Petty, S J 2000. Do male hoots betray parasite loads in Tawny Owls? Journal of Avian Biology 31: 457-462.

Rifai, L B, Al-Melhim, W N, Gharaibeh, B M & Amr, Z S 2000. The diet of the Desert Eagle Owl, *Bubo bubo ascalaphus*, in the Eastern Desert of Jordan. Journal of Arid Environments 44 369–372.

Robb, M 2009. Review: Indian bird sounds by C Chappuis, F Deroussen & D Warakagoda 2008. Dutch Birding 31: 368-369.

Robb, M R, van den Berg, A B & Constantine, M 2013. A new species of *Strix* owl from Oman. Dutch Birding 35: 275-310.
Roberts, T J 1991. The birds of Pakistan 1. Non-Passeriformes. Karachi.
Roberts, T J & King, B 1986. Vocalizations of the Owls of the Genus *Otus* in Pakistan. Ornis Scandinavica 17: 299-305.
Robertson, G & Gilchrist, H 2003. Wintering Snowy Owls feed on sea ducks in the Belcher Islands, Nunavut, Canada. Journal of Raptor Research 37: 164-166.
Rognan, C B 2007. Bioacoustic techniques to monitor Great Gray Owls (*Strix nebulosa*) in the Sierra Nevada. MA thesis, Humboldt State University.
Rohner, C, Smith, J N M, Stroman, J & Joyce, M, Doyle, F I & Boonstra, R 1995. Northern Hawk-Owls in the Nearctic boreal forest: prey selection and population consequences of multiple prey cycles. The Condor 97: 208-220.
Le Roi, O 1923. Die Ornis der Sinai-Halbinsel. Journal für Ornithologie 71: 28-95.
Rosmay, C D & Roselaar, C S 2013. American Hawk-Owl caught off Las Palmas, Gran Canaria, Canary Islands, in October 1924. Dutch Birding 35: 1-6.
Roselaar, C S 2006. The boundaries of the Palearctic region. British Birds 99: 602-618.
Rothschild, W & Hartert, E 1910. *Bubo bubo interpositus* subspec. nov. Novitates Zoologicae 17: 111.
Roulin, A 2004. Covariation between plumage colour polymorphism and diet in the Barn Owl *Tyto alba*. Ibis 146: 509-517.
Roulin, A, Kölliker, M & Richner, H 2000. Barn owl (*Tyto alba*) siblings vocally negotiate resources. Proceedings of the Royal Society B: Biological Sciences 267: 459-463.
Saint-Girons, M C, Thévenot, M & Thouy, P 1974. Le regime alimentaire de la Chouette Effraie (*Tyto alba*) et du Grand-Duc Ascalaphe (*Bubo bubo ascalaphus*) dans quelques localités marocains. C.N.R.S. II, Travaux R C P 249: 257-265.
Sándor, A D & Orbán, Z 2008. Food of the Desert Eagle Owl, *Bubo ascalaphus*, in Siwa Oasis, Western Desert, Egypt. Zoology in the Middle East 43: 5-7.
Sánchez Marco, A 2004. Avian zoogeographical patterns during the Quaternary in the Mediterranean region and paleoclimatic interpretation. Ardeola 51: 91-132.
Sangster, G 2013. Integrative taxonomy of birds: Studies into the nature, origin and delimitation of species. Doctoral thesis, Stockholm University.
Sangster, G, King, B F, Verbelen, P & Trainor, C R 2013. A new species of the genus *Otus* (Aves: Strigidae) from Lombok, Indonesia. PLOS one 8: 1-13.
Sargeant, D E, Eriksen, H & Eriksen, J 2008. Birdwatching guide to Oman. Second edition. Muscat.
Saurola, P 1995. Suomen Pöllöt. CD and book. Helsinki.
Saurola, P 2002. Natal dispersal distances of Finnish owls: results from ringing. In: Newton, I, Kavanagh, R, Olsen, J & Taylor, I (editors), Ecology and Conservation of Owls. Collingwood.
Savigny, N J C L 1809. Description d'Égypte 23: 295. Paris.
sccontaindergarden 2012. Walks With Birds – Desert Eagle Owl. Online video, accessed on 16 October 2013. www.youtube.com/watch?v=BTcsZLIo3mQ
Schaanning, H T L 1907. Østfinmarkens fuglefauna. Bergens Museum Aarbog 8: 1-98.
Scherzinger, W 1970. Zum Aktionssystem des Sperlingkauzes (*Glaucidium passerinum*, L.). Zoologica 118: 1-120.
Scherzinger, W 1974a. Die Jugendentwicklung des Uhus (*Bubo bubo*) mit Vergleichen zu der von Schneeeule (*Nyctea scandiaca*) und Sumpfohreule (*Asio flammeus*). Bonner Zoologische Beiträge 25: 123-147.
Scherzinger, W 1974b. Zur Ethologie und Jugendentwicklung der Schnee-Eule (*Nyctea scandiaca*) nach Beobachtungen in Gefangenschaft. Journal für Ornithologie 115: 8-49.
Scherzinger, W 1980. Zur Ethologie der Fortpflanzung und Jugendentwicklung des Habichtskauzes (*Strix uralensis*) mit vergleich zum Waldkauz (*Strix aluco*). Bonner Zoologische Monographien 15.
Scherzinger, W 2005. Remarks on Sichaun Wood Owl *Strix uralensis davidi* from observations in south-west China. Bulletin of the British Ornithologists' Club 125: 275-286.
Scherzinger, W & Fang, Y 2006. Field Observations of the Sichuan Wood Owl *Strix uralensis davidi* in western China. Acrocephalus 27: 3-12.

Schnurre, O 1936. Zur Biologie des deutschen Uhus. Beiträge zur Fortpflanzungsbiologie der Vögel 12: 1-12, 54-69.
Schwerdtfeger, O 1991. Altersstruktur und Populationsdynamik beim Rauhfußkauz (*Aegolius funereus*). Populationsoekologie Greifvogel- und Eulenarten 2. Wissenschaftliche Beitraege Universitaet Halle: 493-505.
Scott, D 1997. The Long-eared Owl. London.
Sharpe, R B 1886. *Bubo milesi* sp. n. Ibis 28: 163-164.
Shashidara, M 1989. Comment on Brown Fish Owls. Newsletter for Birdwatchers 29: 10.
Shehab, A H & Ciach, M 2008. Diet Composition of the Pharaoh Eagle Owl, *Bubo ascalaphus*, in Azraq Nature Reserve, Jordan. Turkish Journal of Zoology 32: 65-69.
Shenbrot, G, Krasnov, B & Burdelov, S 2010. Long-term study of population dynamics and habitat selection of rodents in the Negev Desert. Journal of Mammalogy 91: 776-786.
Shepard, P 1978. Thinking animals. New York.
Shirihai, H, Dovrat, E, Christie, D A, Harris, A & Cottridge, D 1996. The birds of Israel. London.
Siverio, F 2008. Lechuza común *Tyto alba*. In: Lorenzo, J A (editor), Atlas de las aves nidificantes en el Archipiélago Canario (1997-2003). Madrid.
Siverio, F, Barone, R, Siverio, M, Trujillo, D & Ramos, J J 1999. Response to conspecific calls, distribution and habitat of *Tyto alba* (Aves: Tytonidae) on La Gomera, Canary Islands. Revista de la Academia Canaria de Ciencias 11: 213-222.
Siverio, F, Trujillo, D & Ramos, J J 2001. Notes on the distribution of the Madeiran Barn Owl *Tyto alba schmitzi* (Aves: Tytonidae). Revista de la Academia Canaria de Ciencias 13: 199-205.
Siverio, F, Mateo, J A & López-Jurado L F 2007. On the presence and biology of the Barn Owl *Tyto alba detorta* on Santa Luzia, Cape Verde Islands. Alauda 75: 91-93.
Smith, N, Bates, K & Fuller, M 2012. Wintering Snowy Owls at Logan International Airport. P 208-210 in: Potapov, E & Sale, R 2012, The Snowy Owl. London.
Smith, V W & Killick-Kendrick, R 1964. Notes on the breeding of the Marsh Owl *Asio capensis* in Northern Nigeria. Ibis 106: 119-123.
Snow, D W & Perrins, C M 1998. The birds of the Western Palearctic. Concise edition. Vol 1. Non-passerines. Oxford.
Solheim, R, Jacobsen, K O & Øien, I 2008. Snøuglenes vandringer: Ett år, tre ugler og ny kunnskap. Vår Fuglefauna 31: 102-109.
Solheim, R, Jacobsen, K O, Øien, I & Aarvak, T 2009. Snøuglenes vandringer fortsetter. Vår Fuglefauna 32: 172-176.
Sonerud, G A 1994. Haukugle *Surnia ulula*.
Sonerud, G A 1997. Hawk Owls in Fennoscandia: population fluctuations, effects of modern forestry, and recommendations on improving foraging habitats. Journal of Raptor Research 31: 167-174.
Sorace, A 1987. Note sul canto territoriale del Barbagianni, *Tyto alba*. Rivista Italiana di Ornitologia 57: 144-145.
Sorbi, S 2013. Découverte de la Chevêchette d'Europe *Glaucidium passerinum* en Belgique et suivi d'une tentative de nidification. Aves 50: 2-8.
Stefansson, O 1997. Nordanskogans vagabond. Lappugglan (*Strix nebulosa lapponica*). Boden.
Stefansson, O 2013. Nordanskogans vagabond. Lappugglan (*Strix nebulosa lapponica*). Supplement nr 4. Boden.
Streseman, E 1943. Ueberblick über die Vögel Kretas und den Vogelzug in der Aegaeis. Journal für Ornithologie 91: 448-514.
Sutton, G M 1932. The birds of Southampton Island. Memoirs of the Carnegie Museum 12 (part 11, sec 2): 3-267.
Svensson, L, Grant, P J, Mullarney, K & Zetterström, D 2009. Collins bird guide. Second edition. London.
Taylor, I 1994. Barn owls. Predator-prey relationships and conservation. Cambridge, UK.
Temminck, C J 1821, *Strix africana*. In: Temminck, C J & Laugier de Chartrouse, M, Nouveau recueil de planches coloriées d'oiseaux, livr 9, pl 50. Paris.
Thévenot, M 2006. Aperçu du régime alimentaire du Grand-duc d'Afrique du Nord *Bubo ascalaphus* à Tata, Moyen Draa. Go-South Bulletin 3: 28-30.
Thorstrom, R, Hart, J & Watson, R T 2007. New record, ranging behaviour, vocalization and food of the Madagascar Red Owl *Tyto soumagnei*. Ibis 139: 477-481.
Tristram, H B 1879. Letter to the editor: *Asio butleri* and *Caprimulgus tamaricis*. Stray feathers 8: 416-417.
Tulloch, R J 1968. Snowy Owls breeding in Shetland in 1967. British Birds 61: 119-132.
Tyrberg, T 1998. Pleistocene birds of the Palearctic: a catalogue. Cambridge, Massachusetts.

Tyrberg, T 2008. Pleistocene birds of the Palearctic, online supplement. web.telia.com/~u11502098/pleistocene.html. Accessed on 8 February 2013.
Vaurie, C 1960. Systematic Notes on Palearctic Birds, no 41 Strigidae: The genus *Bubo*. American Museum Novitates 2000: 1-31.
Vein, D & Thévenot, M 1978. Etude sur le Hibou grand-duc *Bubo bubo ascalaphus* dans le Moyen-Atlas marocain. Nos Oiseaux 34: 347-351.
Voous, K H 1950. On the distributional and genetical origin of the intermediate populations of the Barn owl (*Tyto alba*) in Europe. In: Jordans, A & Peus, F, Syllegomena Biologica, Festschrift zum 80. Geburtstage von Herrn Pastor Dr Med H C Otto Kleinschmidt. Wittenburg.
Voous, K H 1988. Owls of the Northern Hemisphere. London.
Vrezec, A 2009. Melanism and plumage variation in *macroura* Ural Owl. Dutch Birding 31: 159-170.
Vyn, G 2006. Voices of North American owls. 2 CDs and booklet. Ithaca.
Wahlstedt, J 1969. Jakt, matning och läten hos lappuggla *Strix nebulosa*. Vår Fågelvärld 28: 89-101.
Warakagoda, D 1997. The birds sounds of Sri Lanka. An identification guide. 2 CDs and booklet. Nugegoda.
Watson, A 1957. The behaviour, breeding and food-ecology of the Snowy Owl *Nyctea scandiaca*. Ibis 99: 419–462.
Weesie, P D M 1982. A Pleistocene endemic island form within the genus *Athene*: *Athene cretensis* n. sp. (Aves, Strigiformes) from Crete. Proceedings of the Koninklijke Nederlandse Akademie Wetenschappen, Series B 85: 323-336.
Weesie, P D M 1988. The Quaternary avifauna of Crete, Greece. Palaeovertebrata 18: 1-94.
Weick, F 2006. Owls (Strigiformes). Annotated and Illustrated Checklist. Berlin.
Weir, J T & Schluter, D 2008. Calibrating the avian molecular clock. Molecular Ecology 17: 2321-2328.
Wendland, V 1957. Aufziechnungen über Brutbiologie und Verhalten der Waldohreule (*Asio otus*). Journal für Ornithologie 98: 241-261.
Wendland, V 1963. Fünfjährige Beobachtungen an einer Population des Waldkauzes (*Strix aluco*) im Berliner Grunewald. Journal für Ornithologie 104: 23-57.
Whaley, D 1991. Scops Owl. Cyprus Ornithological Society 1957. Newsletter 2/91: 3.
Wiesner, J 1992. Dismigration und Verbreitung des Sperlingskauzes (*Glaucidium passerinum* L.) in Thüringen. Naturschutzreport/Jena 4: 62-66.
de Wijs, R 2009. De meerkoetroep van de...... www.home.zonnet.nl/myotis/uilkoet.htm
Wink, M 2008. Phylogenetic and phylogeographic relationships. In: van Nieuwenhuyse, D, Génot, J-C & Johnson, D H, The Little Owl. Conservation, Ecology and Behavior of *Athene noctua*. Cambridge.
Wink, M, El-Sayed, A-A, Sauer-Gürth, H & Gonzalez, J 2009. Molecular phylogeny of owls (Strigiformes) inferred from DNA sequences of the mitochondrial cytochrome *b* and the nuclear RAG-1 gene. In: Johnson, D H, Nieuwenhuyse, D & Duncan, J R (editors), Proceedings of the Fourth World Owl Conference October-November 2007, Groningen, The Netherlands. Ardea 97: 581-591.
Wink, M & Heidrich, P 1999. Molecular phylogeny and systematics of owls (Strigiformes). In: König, C, Weick, F & Becking, J-H, Owls of the world. Robertsbridge.
Wink, M, Heidrich, P, Sauer-Gürth, H, Elsayed, A-A & Gonzalez, J 2008. Molecular phylogeny and systematics of owls (Strigiformes). In: König, C, Weick, F & Becking, J-H (editors), Owls of the world, second edition. London.
Witherby, H F 1905. *Surnium aluco mauritanicum*, n. subsp. Bulletin of the British Ornithologists' Club 15: 36-37.
Woods, R W & Woods, A 1997. Atlas of breeding birds of the Falkland Islands. Oswestry.
Yalden, D 1999. The history of British mammals. London.
Yalden, D W & Albarella, U 2009. The history of British birds. Oxford.
Yöntem, O 2007. An observation of Brown Fish Owl *Ketupa zeylonensis* in Turkey. Sandgrouse 29: 94-95.
Zarudny, N A 1905. Zwei ornithologische Neuheiten aus West-Persien. Ornithologisches Jahrbuch 16: 141–142.

Index

Page numbers in **bold**: sound recordings; in *italic*: photograph or illustration (background species of sonagram captions not listed)

Accipiter gentilis   46, 91, 284
Acrocephalus schoenobaenus   15, 147, 148
Aegolius funereus   9, *38*, 39-49 (**39-40**, *42-47*, **42-49**), 60, 79, 84, 85, 90, 225, 228, 229, 233, 243, 247, 284
  - *funereus caucasicus*   41, 42
  - *martae*   41
  - *richardsoni*   **40**, 41
alarm call   54, 56, 57, 59, 69, 111, 153, 194, 262, 277
Alaska   16, 74, 153, 219
Alauda arvensis   91, 148, 149, 151-153
Aldeia da Luz   179
Alectoris whitakeri   62, 99
Algarve   93, 94
Algeria   176, 252, 254
Al Hajar range   2, 121, 266-280
Alps   22, 41, 67, 230, 232
Alqueva reservoir   179, 180
Alström, Per   6, 228
Alytes cisternasii   **95**, 183
  - *obstetricans*   **95**
Ameland   149, 150
Antalya mountains   200-212, 245
Anthus berthelotii   28
  - *cervinus*   189
  - *campestris*   28
  - *richardi*   163
  - *rubescens japonicus*   110
Ape, Barbary   *250*
Apodemus flavicollis   47, 48
  - *sylvaticus*   22, 101
Apus apus   85
  - *pallidus*   256
Arabia   15, 17, 122, 124, 125, 130, 167, 169, 171, 267
Arava valley   123
Arvicola terrestris   **225,** *229*, 285
Asio capensis   156-163 (**145**, *157-159*, **157-163**, *161-163*), 253, 285

  - *capensis tingitanus*   156-163 (**145**, *157-159*, **157-163**, *161-163*), 253, 285
  - *domingensis*   151, 152, 154, **155**
  - *domingensis bogotensis*   152
  - *domingensis domingensis*   152
  - *domingensis galapagoensis*   152
  - *domingensis pallidicaudatus*   152
  - *domingensis portoricensis*   152
  - *domingensis sanfordi*   151, 152, 154, **155**
  - *domingensis suinda*   152
  - *flammeus*   2, 6, 144-156 (**145**, *146-149*, **147-155**, *153-155*), 158-161, 197, 217, 285
  - *flammeus flammeus*   151
  - *flammeus ponapensis*   152
  - *flammeus sandwichensis*   152
  - *otus*   21, 48, 132-145 (*132-134*, **133**, **135-143**, *137-138*, *140*, *142-144*, **145**), 184, 284-285
  - *otus canariensis*   137
  - *wilsonianus*   136-**138**
  - *wilsonianus tuftsi*   137-**138**
  - *wilsonianus wilsonianus*   137
Askalaphos   176
Athenaeum club   125
Athene angelis   60
  - *cretensis*   60
  - *noctua*   2, 23, 51, 60-69 (**61-69**, *62*, *64-65*, *67-69*), 99, 103, 161, 163, 284
  - *noctua glaux*   **61**, 62, **63**, 64, **66**, **68**, 161, 163
  - *noctua indigena*   67, 68
  - *noctua lilith*   **61**, 62, **63**-68 (*64*, *65*, **66**, *67*), 284
  - *noctua noctua*   **61**, *62*, **63**
  - *noctua plumipes*   68
  - *noctua saharae*   62, **64**, *64*, **66**
  - *noctua sarda*   **67**
  - *trinacriae*   60
  - *vallgomerensis*   60
  - *vidalii*   13, 14, 19, 20, 45, 50-61 (*50*, *51*, **52**, *53*, **54-59**, *55*, *57*, *59*, *60*, **61**), 65, 66, 103, 135, 211, 241, 284
Atlas mountains   64, 124, 176, 250, 251, 255

autumn calling   11, 15, 49, 56, 89, 90, 95, 104, 142, 143, 149, 156, 180, 183, 225, 229, 237, 242, 243, 247, 248, 252, 254, 264, 265
Azores   114, 137, 155
Azrou   18, 250, 251
Backwoods Camp   207
badges   180, 181, 204
Baffin Island   191
Baikal, Lake   94
Balearic Islands   24
Balkan mountains   22
Baltic states   22, 89
Bangladesh   206
barking call   141, 143, 156, 237, 247
Barrow   197
Bat, Egyptian Fruit-eating   115, 267, 275
Bates, George Latimer   125, 127, 130
Bear, Brown   41, 73
beckoning call   54, 55, 57, 58, 87, 88
begging call   10, 20, 21, 36, 37, 46, 49, 56, 59, 61, 68, 69, 75, 77, 78, 81, 86, 88, 89, 101, 102, 104, 110, 112, 122, 123, 131, 140, 141, 145, 154, 155, 160, 161, 169, 174, 177, 186, 195, 196, 199, 210, 211, 220, 222, 227, 235, 244-246, 249, 260, 262, 263, 264, 273, 277, 278, 281
begging-snoring   58
Bekir, Soner   6, 200, 211
Belarus   226
Belgium   43, 91
Berlenga   156
Bermuda   41
Białowieża forest   47, 48, 90, 91, 247
bill-snapping   17, 139, 140, 142, 152, 153, 160, 163, 185, 186, 187, 211, 224, 236
Birecık   118-120
Bittern, Eurasian   87, 203, 217
Black Sea   22, 94, 180
Bloem, Karla   8, 187
boid   48, 196, 197
Botaurus stellaris   87, 203, 217
Bothnia, Gulf of   47, 285
Bouches-du-Rhône   197
Bozdoğan, Murat   203
Bragança, Dom Carlos de   161
Branco   36
Britain   22, 41, 51, 89, 105, 144, 240, 282, 284
Bubo africanus   165, **166**, *167*, 169, 193
- *ascalaphus*   *7*, 169-177 (*170-171*, **171-174**, *173-176*, **177**), 188, 193, 285
- *ascalaphus 'desertorum'*   171
- *bengalensis*   193
- *blakistoni*   204, 206-209
- *blakistoni doerriesi*   204, 207, 209
- *bubo*   13, 24, 93, 103, 104, 168, 169, 172, 173, 176-188 (**177**, *178-179*, **179-186**, *181*, *183-187*, **188**), 194, 203, 213, 229, 241, 285
- *bubo interpositus*   **177**, **188**
- *bubo kiautschensis*   **180**
- *bubo sibiricus*   188
- *capensis*   167, 176, 193
- *cinerascens*   165, **166**, *167*, 193
- *ketupu*   213
- *leschenaulti*   204, **206**, 207, 213
- *leschenaulti orientalis*   204, 206
- *milesi*   15, 130, 164-169 (*164*, **165-166**, *167-169*, **168-169**), **177**, 193
- *scandiacus*   9, 133, 188-199 (*189-190*, **190-192,** *192-195*, **194-195**, *197*, **199**)
- *semenowi*   2, 6, 133, 199-213 (**199**, *201*, **202**, *202-203*, **204-207**, *208-210*, **209-211**, *212*), 218, 280, 285
- *virginianus*   40, 187, 193, 198
- *zeylonensis*   200, 204, **205**, 206, **207**, 212-213
Bufo calamita   52, 100
- *dhufarensis*   127, *164*, 165, 168, 278
Bugio   29-31, 284
Bulbul, White-spectacled   259
Bulgaria   62-64, 180, 200
Bunting, Ortolan   254
Bushehr   213
Bustard, Great   *53*, 284
- MacQueen's   282
Buteo buteo   184
- *rufinus*   170
Buzzard, Common   184
- Long-legged   170
cackling   54, 57, 61, 68, 69, 191, 194, 195, 285
Cádiz   161
Cadman, W A   246
Calidris alpina   163, 190, 191
- *falcinellus*   73
- *ferruginea*   189, 190
- *melanotos*   189, 191, 192, 195

California   219
Calliope calliope   85, 141
Calonectris borealis   26, 29, 30
 - *edwardsii*   33
Canada   40, 74, 154, 195-197, 220
Canary Islands   17, 25-28, 79, 105, 137
Canis lupus arabs   15
Cape Verde Islands   17, 33-36
Capra aegagrus   201
Capreolus capreolus   237
Caroline Islands   152
Carpodacus synoicus   256
Caspian Sea   240
Catalonia   104, 143
Catania   62, 99
Caucasus   41, 239, 240
cave art   197
Certhia brachydactyla dorotheae   106, 108
Cervus elaphus   95, 183
Chandranagore   204
Chappuis, Claude   191
Cherchi, Fabio   6, 67
chimpanzee   76, 182
China   124, 233
chirrup call   20, 21
chitter call   45, 77, 84, 87, 91, 160, 182, 186, 194, 195, 199, 211, 215, 222, 231, 244, 245, 260, 262, 264, 275
Chlamydotis macqueenii   282
Chrysococcyx caprius   125
chugging call   58, 65
Cicada orni   93
Cinclus cinclus   85
Circus cyaneus   147, 148
Clark, Richard   6, 154
Columba oenas   118
Constantine, Mo   6, 234
contact call   18, 45, 48, 54, 139
Coot, Eurasian   66, 144, 239, 245
Copete, José Luis   7, 203
copulation call   10, 19, 20, 21, 58, 76, 86, 100, 101, 121, 122, 128, 129, 139, 140, 182, 241, 245, 275
Cornwall   79
Corsica   17, 23, 24, 60, 67
Corso, Andrea   7, 62, 65, 105

Corvus corax tingitanus   137
 - *cornix*   73, 79, 149
Coturnix coturnix   68, 163
courtship   9, 10, 13-15, 17-19, 27, 28, 31, 32, 35-37, 45, 58, 74, 97, 136, 139, 148, 149, 159, 173, 180-182, 191, 206, 207, 229, 243, 271, 274, 275
courtship feeding   9, 58, 274, 275
Crete   41, 60, 104, 204
crickets   14, 29, 32, 93, 94, 102
croaking   52, 100, 101, 110, 122, 128
Crocidura   22
Crossbill, Cyprus   106
 - Parrot   78
Crow, Hooded   73, 79, 149
Cuckoo, Common   72, 141, 183, 222, 232, 235
 - Diederik   125
Cuculus canorus   72, 141, 183, 222, 232, 235
Cucumiau   2, 23, 51, 60-69 (**61**-**69**, *62*, *64-65*, *67-69*), 99, 103, 161, 163, 284
Çuhadaroğlu, Murat   200
Curlew, Eurasian   141, 147-154, 218
 - Slender-billed   157
Cyanopica cooki   103, 181
Cyprus   67, 68, 94, 105-114
Dakto   204
Dama dama   242, 247, 248
Danube   22
Dead Sea   256, 264
Deer, Fallow   242, 247, 248
 - Red   95, 183
 - Roe   237
Delin, Håkan   6, *7*, 9, 46, 47, 75, 78, 79, 84, 173, 176, 179, 180, 184, 194, 196, 215, 216, 224, 228, 246, 284
departure call   87, 88, 141
descending growl   145, 160
Deserta Grande   30
Desertas   17, 29, 30
devil's cackle   173, 177, 183, 184, 194, 195, 199
Dhofar   15, 125-130, 165-169, 257-264, 278
Dhofar Rebellion   258
Dicrostonyx   197
Didner, Eric   8, 35
Dinaric Alps   230, 232, 234
Dipper, Black-bellied   85

dispersal   60
display flight   13, 147-151, 158, 285
distance call   238, 242, 247, 254, 255, 265, 277, 278
distraction display   141, 152, 154, 162, 163, 184, 193, 223
dormouse   24, 230, 231, 233
 - Edible   230, 231, 233
Dove, Stock   118
Dryocopus martius   44, 45, 73, 232
duetting   54, 55, 75, 88, 106-108, 116, 117, 128, 129, 139, 141, 156, 166, 168, 180, 199, 203-207, 218, 247, 248
Duluth-Superior harbour area   196
Dunlin   163, 190, 191
Eagle, White-tailed   224
Ebro Delta   104, 142
'ear tufts' – see pinna
eclipse, lunar   116, 257
Edinburgh   248
egg-laying   13, 20, 58, 101, 113, 159, 168, 206, 220
Egypt   161, 175, 176, 265
Eijk, Pieter van   279, 280
Elb Tree   115, 116, 266
elephant, dwarf   24, 60
Elephas falconeri   24, 60
Emberiza hortulana   254
English Channel   91
Eocene   16
Erithacus rubecula   84, 87, 88, 90, 143, 181, 183, 218, 222, 225, 231, 232, 235, 244
Eritrea   125, 176
Ethiopia   166, 167, 176
Etna, Mt   62, 98, 99
Euphrates river   118
Eve, Roland   6, 206
eventual variation   97
excitement call   10, 52, 54, 55, 57, 61, 65-67, 77, 78, 89, 103, 111, 112, 122, 129, 130, 131, 145, 151, 154, 155, 183, 194, 211
extinct species   16, 26, 34, 41, 114, 157,
Extremadura   178, 179, 182, 284
Falco biarmicus   62, 170
 - *cherrug*   282
 - *peregrinus*   149, 152, 153
Falcon, Lanner   62, 170
 - Peregrine   149, 152, 153
 - Saker   282
Falkland Islands   151, 152, 155

Fars   213
feeding call   10, 45, 58, 59, 87, 88, 101, 102, 152, 160, 210, 211, 222, 244, 245, 262
Felis lybica gordoni   263
Felix, Rob   8, 213
Fennoscandia   43
Finland   39, 43-46, 48, 71, 72, 75-78, 80, 83, 85-89, 133, 138, 140, 154, 183-186, 215, 217, 218, 221-223, 225, 226, 231, 235, 236, 244
Flint, Peter   7, 106, 109, 113
floating males   178
Flycatcher, African Paradise   125
Fontainhas   33-36
Forsman, Dick   6, 19, 39, 44-46, 60, 71, 72, 76-78, 80, 83, 87, 88, 128, 133, 138, 140, 152, 154, 162, 167, 169, 170, 176, 183-185, 202, 215, 217, 223, 225, 226, 231, 234, 235, 244, 256, 257
 - Inki   6, 234
Fort Severn   218
forward-threat posture   185
fossils   26, 114, 173, 174, 198
Fox, Red   139, 184
France   22, 67, 105, 197, 240
Francolin, Black   282
Francolinus francolinus   282
Franke, Patrick   6, 184
Frog, Common   100
 - European Tree   14, 135, 241, 245
 - Southern Tree   14, 18, 54, 55, 93, 94, 134, 135, 245
Fuerteventura   25-28, 105, 137
Fulica atra   66, 144, 239, 245
Galapagos Islands   152
Gallinago gallinago   15, 76, 78, 141, 148, 150, 151, 218, 243
Gallinula chloropus   144
Gansu   234
Gargano   23, 24
Garganoaetus   24
gecko, giant   34
Genet, Common   101
Genetta genetta   101
genus   10, 16, 60, 91, 165, 192, 193, 197, 198, 213, 265
Georgia   188
gerbil   172, 285
Gerbillus   172
Germany   39, 83, 84, 86, 184, 200
Geronticus eremita   119
Ghana   128

Gibraltar   157, 197, 255
Glaucidium passerinum   46, **81**, 82-91 (*82*, **83**-**88**, *84-85*, *87-90*, 90-**91**), 93, 184, 228, 234
 - *siju*   91
Glis glis   230, 231, 233
Goa   109, 204, 205, 207
Goat, Wild   201
Goldcrest   45, 85, 86
Gomera, La   25
Gordon, Jeff   106, 108
Goshawk, Northern   46, 91, 284
Goulimine   170,
Graham, Andrew   218
Gran Canaria   25, 137
Grant, Peter   282
Great Lakes   196
Greater Antilles   152
Grebe, Little   144
Greece   67, 68, 104
Grouse, Caucasian Black   41
 - Hazel   45
 - Red   148
 - Willow   189, 191, 192, 195, 196
Guadiana River   179
Guanche   26
guarding call   141, 227, 236, 237, 245, 246, 249, 262, 263, 277, 281
Gull, Ross's   190
Gunn, William (Bill)   6, 40, 221
Gutiérrez, Ricard   8, 142
Gyps fulvus   178
Hades   176
Halcyon leucocephala   35, 36, 125
Haliaeetus albicilla   224
Halichoerus grypus   147
Hammouradia, Hamida   6, 160, 162
hamster   24
Hare, Brown   184
 - Snowshoe   74
Harrier, Hen   147, 148
Hawaii   152, 155
hearing ability   21, 143
hedgehog   24
Herr, David   6, 138, 220, 221
home range   15,
Honold, Johannes   6, 110-112

hooting   9, 10, 39, 40, 42-44, 49, 52-54, 57, 61-67, 71-75, 81, 83-87, 91, 93-101, 105, 106, 108-110, 115-117, 119-122, 125, 127-129, 131, 133, 135, 137-139, 142, 143, 145, 147, 148, 150, 158, 165, 166, 168, 170-173, 177, 179-183, 186-188, 190-192, 194, 195, 199-207, 211, 215, 217-222, 227-234, 236-239, 241-254, 257-264, 266-269, 271-273, 275, 277, 281
 - compound   227-234, 236-239, 241, 242, 245-254, 257-264, 267-269, 271-273, 275, 277, 281
 - engagement   43, 44
 - excited   81, 83-85
 - excited compound   249, 252, 253, 281
 - frustration   81, 85, 86
 - pulsed   215, 217, 218, 220, 221, 227, 233, 242-245, 249, 254, 261, 262, 267, 272, 273, 281
Hormozgan   204, 211, 213
Hosking, Eric   246
Hume, Alan Octavian   257, 283
Hydrobates pelagicus   60
Hyla arborea   14, 135, 241, 245
 - *meridionalis*   14, 18, 54, 55, 93, 94, 134, 135, 245
Iberian peninsula   22
Ibis, Northern Bald   119
ice age (see Pleistocene)   22, 197, 240
Ilhéu Grande   36
imitating owls   44, 277
immediate variation   97
incubation   9, 58, 101, 113, 170, 191, 236
India   109, 204, 205, 207
individual variation   40, 97, 150, 157, 239, 252
interference   134
International Owl Center   187
Inuit   197
Iran   204, 211, 213, 257, 265, 280, 283
Ireland   22, 60, 105
Israel   22, 68, 113, 123, 176, 188, 204, 213, 256, 263-265, 282, 284
Italy   23, 41, 62, 65, 67, 68, 104, 239, 240
Jabal Samhan range   14
Jaculus   172
Jännes, Hannu   6, 48
Japan   124, 206, 233
Jay, Siberian   *89*, 284
jerboa   172
jird   172
Jordan   171, 256, 257, 265
Jung, Carl   280

301

Kazakhstan   69, 94, 96, 148
Kemi region   47
Ketupa   193
Khuzestan   204, 213
Kikinda   143
Kingfisher, Grey-headed   35, 36, 125
Knijff, Peter de   8, 213
Kokkola   85
koRAH scream   237, 247
Krain   67
Lagopus lagopus   189, 191, 192, 195, 196
 - *mutus*   196
 - *scotica*   148
Lameiros   30
Lanzarote   25, 26
Lapland   39, 71, 76-78, 152, 154, 190, 191, 194, 215, 217, 218, 222, 225
Larache   161, 254
Latham, Jo   8, 220
laurisilva   114
Lehto, Harry   8, 72
Leith, Water of   248
lemming   190, 195-198
 - collared   197, 198
 - Siberian Brown   190
Lemmus sibiricus   190
Lena delta   189-192, 194, 195
Lena-Nordenskjöld International Biological Station   189, 195
Lepus americanus   74
 - *europaeus*   184
Lewis, Ian   8, 271
Libya   250
Lidster, James   8, 157
Lindholm, Antero   8, 89
Linnaeus, Carl   192, 218
location roll   44, 45
Logan Airport   196
Lophophanes cristatus   43, 75, 85, 284
Lovibond, Pamela   125
Lower Kolyma   196
Loxia curvirostris guillemardi   106
 - *pytyopsittacus*   **78**
Lundberg, Arne   228
Lymnocryptes minimus   73
Macaca sylvanus   250

Macaronesia   24, 28, 33
Macaulay Library   6, 17, 40, 74, 138, 154, 166, 195, 219-222
Macroscincus coctei   34
Mactavish, Bruce   8, 196, 197
Madeira   6, 17, 29-32, 114, 156
Magdalenians   197
Maghreb   250
Magpie, Azure-winged   103, 181
Mallorca   24, 60
Malpaisomys insularis   26, 28
Malvagna   62
Mammoth, Woolly   189
Mammuthus primigenius   189
Marrakech   254
Marten, Beech   45
 - Pine   45
Martes foina   45
 - *martes*   45
McAdams, Dave   6, 84, 85
McLoughlin, John (aka 'Johnny Mac')   6, 271, 272
Medley, Joseph   8, 219
Meek, Eric   8, 146
Megascops asio   74
Menorca   24
Meriones   172
Merja Zerga   157-163
mesoptile plumage   195
Micromys   22
Micronesia   152
Microtus agrestis   79, 150, **225**
 - *arvalis*   22, 147
 - *oeconomus*   79
migration   15, 56, 104, 105, 113, 156, 183, 247, 271
Miles, Colonel S B   167
Miocene   23
mobbing   21, 32, 37, 46, 78, 85, 156, 259
monsoon, Indian Ocean   15
 - Southwest   36, 125, 126, 165, 168
Mongolia   68
Monteiro, Paolo   8, 102, 103
Moorhen, Common   144
Moors   255
Morocco   7, 18, 62-64, 66, 68, 94, 157-163, 169-175, 250-255
Motacilla alba   178
mouse, harvest   22

- house   22, 26, 34, 156
- Lava   26, 28
- Wood   22, 101
- Yellow-necked   47, 48

Moyer, David   6, 166
mtDNA   40, 108, 114, 130, 137, 176, 188, 218
Mughsayl   257-264
Mullarney, Killian   6, 71, 77, 141, 173, 222, 258, 259, 261, 263, 271, 274, 276, 278, 282
Mus musculus   26, 34
Muscat   8, 167
Mustela erminea   150, 190
Myodes glareolus   48, 79
Napoleon   175
Necrobyas rossignoli   16
Neomys   22
nest-showing call   10, 138, 139, 182, 218, 233
nestbox   44, 45, 76-78, 85, 87, 88, 230, 234-236, 244, 246
nestling   45, 58, 59, 77, 87, 88, 102, 110, 147, 152, 153, 160, 162, 182, 185, 186, 191, 194, 195, 208, 260, 262-264
Netherlands   15, 44, 48, 136, 139, 141-144, 150, 156, 160, 201, 239, 242, 243, 245, 247, 248
New Guinea   16
Niedersachsen   39, 83, 84, 86
Nizhny Bobrowski   190
nocturnal migration   15, 156
nomadism   226
Norway   79
Novaya Zemlya   191, 197
Numenius arquata   141, 147-154, 218
 - *tenuirostris*   157
Nunes, João   6, 30-32
Nuyten, Peter   6, 44, 149, 150, 243
Nyctea   192, 193
Oceanodroma castro   29, *30*, 284
 - *jabejabe*   33
Oenanthe cypriaca   106
Oliveira, Artur Vaz   8, 13
Oman   14, 15, 68, 69, 115-119, 121-123, 125-130, 165-169, 257-280
Orkney   146-153
Ormara   257, 282, 283
ornaments   144
Oryctolagus cuniculus   181
Osprey   176
otter   23

Otus brucei   105, 114-124 (*115*, **115-118**, **117**, *119-121*, **120-123**, *123-124*), 126, **131**, 200, *266*, 267, 277, 278, 284
 - *cyprius*   91, 94, 96, 105-114 (**106**, *107*, **108-112**, *111-114*), **131**
 - *frutuosoi*   114
 - *jolandae*   91
 - *mauli*   114
 - *pamelae*   15, 105, 125-131 (**125**, *126-128*, **127**, **129-131**, *130*), 166-169, 213
 - *scops*   62, 91, 92-105 (*92, 94*, **94-95**, *96*, **97**, *98*, **99-103**, *100, 102-104*), 106, 108, 110-114, 117, 121-122, 126, 128-129, 130, **131**, 155, 202, 204, 206, 211, 284, 251
 - scops cyclades   94
 - scops mallorcae   94
 - scops pulchellus   94
 - scops scops   94
 - scops turanicus   94
 - senegalensis   104, 105, 125, **127**, 130
 - socotranus   96, 108
 - sunia   96, 105, 108, **109**
 - sunia japonicus   108
 - sunia rufipennis   **109**
 - sunia stictonotus   108
Ouacha, Lahcen   6, 174
Oued Loukkos   160, 161
Oued Massa   64, 66, 170
Owl, African Barn   33
 - African Grass   17, 158
 - African Scops   104, 105, 125, **127**, 130
 - American Barn   16, **17**
 - American Hawk-   **74**, 79
 - Arabian Eagle-   15, 130, 164-169 (*164*, **165-166**, *167-169*, **168-169**), **177**, 193
 - Arabian Scops   15, 105, 125-131 (**125**, *126-128*, **127**, **129-131**, *130*), 166-169, 213
 - Ashy-faced   16
 - Australian Masked   17
 - Bengal Fish   204, **206**, 207, 213
 - Blakiston's Fish   204, 206-209
 - Boreal   **40**, 41
 - Brown Fish   200, 204, **205**, 206, **207**, 212-213
 - Buffy Fish   213
 - Byzantine Eagle-   177
 - Canarian Long-eared   **137**, *137*
 - Cape Eagle-   167, 176, 193
 - Cape Verde Barn   17, 24, 32-**37**(**33,** *34-36*, **35-36**)

- Common Barn   11, *12*, 13-21 (**13-15**, *16*, **18-21**), *19*, *22*, *23*, 24-28, 30-33, 35-**37**, 39, 55, 57, 59, 76, 111, 133, 139, 169, 244, 245, 284
- Cuban Pygmy   91
- Cyprus Scops   91, 94, 96, 105-114 (**106**, *107*, **108-112**, *111-114*), **131**
- Eastern Barn   16
- Eastern Grass   17
- Eastern Screech   74
- Eurasian Eagle-   13, 24, 93, 103, 104, 168, 169, 172, 173, 176-188 (**177**, *178-179*, **179-186**, *181*, *183-187*, **188**), 194, 203, 213, 229, 241, 285
- Eurasian Pygmy   46, 47, **81**, 82-91 (*82*, **83-88**, *84-85*, *87-90*, 90-**91**), 93, 184, 228, 234, 248
- Eurasian Scops   62, 91, 92-105 (*92*, *94*, **94-95**, *96*, **97**, *98*, **99-103**, *100*, *102-104*), 106, 108, 110-114, 117, 121-122, 126, 128-129, 130, **131**, 155, 202, 204, 206, 211, 248, 251
- Field   151, 152, 154, **155**
- giant   *23*, 24, 60
- Great Gray   215, 218-222 (**219-221**, *220*), 226
- Great Horned   40, 187, 193, 198
- Greyish Eagle-   165, **166**, *167*, 193
- Hume's   41, 248, 256-265 (*256-257*, **257-264**, *259*, *261*, *263-265*), 267, 269, 272, 277, 279, **281**, 281-283, 285
- Indian Eagle-   193
- Lapland   203, 214-227 (*214*, **215**, *216-218*, **217-218**, **221-222**, *223-226*, **225**, **227**), 285
- Little   13, 14, 19, 20, 45, 50-61 (*50*, *51*, **52**, *53*, **54-59**, *55*, *57*, *59*, *60*, **61**), 65, 66, 103, 135, 211, 241, 284
- Long-eared   21, 48, 132-145 (*132-134*, **133**, **135-143**, *137-138*, *140*, *142-144*, **145**), 184, 284-285
- Madagascar Red   32
- Madeira Barn   17, 24, 29-33 (*29-30*, **30-32**, *32*), **37**, 284
- Madeira Scops   114
- Maghreb Wood   248-255 (**249**, *250*, **251-254**, *252-255*)
- Marsh   145, 156-163, 253
- Northern Hawk-   48, 70-81 (*70*, **71-72**, *72-73*, **74-78**, *75-80*, **81**)
- Omani   2, 6, **115**, 248, 266-283 (*266*, **267**, *268-270*, **269**, **271-273**, *274*, **275**, *276*, **277-278**, *278-280*, **281**), 284
- Oriental Scops   96, 105, 108, **109**
- Pallid Scops   105, 114-124 (*115*, **115-118**, **117**, *119-121*, **120-123**, *123-124*), 126, **131**, 200, 248, 266, 267, 277, 278
- Pharaoh Eagle-   *7*, 169-177 (*170-171*, **171-174**, *173-176*, **177**), 188, 193, 285
- Rinjani Scops   91
- São Miguel Scops   114
- São Tomé Barn   36
- Short-eared   2, 6, 144-156 (**145**, *146-149*, **147-155**, *153-155*), 158-161, 197, 217, 285
- Sichuan Wood   234
- Sicilian Barn   24, 41
- Slender-billed Barn   17, 18, 24-28 (*25*, **26-28**, *27*), 31, 34, **37**
- Snowy   9, 133, 188-199 (*189-190*, **190-192**, *192-195*, **194-195**, *197*, **199**), 285
- Socotra Scops   96, 108
- Spotted Eagle-   165, **166**, *167*, 169, 193
- Tawny   **10**, 20, 48, 83, 93, 95, 105, 133-136, 139, 141, 202, 213, 216, 217, 228, 229, 238-249 (**238-239**, *239-240*, **241-249**, *242-246*), 251-255, 258, 265, 275, 276, 284-285
- Tengmalm's   9, *38*, 39-49 (**39-40**, *42-47*, **42-49**), 60, 79, 84, 85, 90, 225, 228, 229, 233, 243, 247
- Turkish Fish   2, 6, 133, 199-213 (**199**, *201*, **202**, *202-203*, **204-207**, *208-210*, **209-211**, *212*), 218, 280
- Ural   46-47, *47*, *75*, 84, 200, 216, 217, 222, 227-238 (**227-233**, *229-232*, *234-237*, **235-238**), 247, 258, 273, 284-285
- Wilson's   136-**138**

Oymapinar Baraji   202-204, 206, 207, 210-212
Pakistan   96, 204, 212, 257, 280, 282, 283
palaeontology   26
Palmas, Las   79
Pancas   13, 14, 20, 133, 135, 136, 139, 161, 162, 241, 245, 246
Pandion haliaetus   176
pant-hooting   76, 81
Paralimni   113
Partridge, Sicilian   62, 99
Patti, Nino   6, 62
pellets   11, 26, 34, 172, 190, 201, 254, 263
Peloritani range   62
Penteriani, Vincenzo   6, 180
Periparus ater   85, 106, 108
  - *ater cypriotes*   106, 108
Persephone   176
Petra   256, 257
Petrel, British Storm   60
  - Cape Verde Storm   33
  - Desertas   29, 30
  - Fea's   35
  - Grant's Storm   156
  - Madeiran Storm   29, *30*, 284
  - Zino's   26, 32, 282
Peyton, Leonard   6, 74, 219

Philby, Harry St John   125, 127
- Kim   125
Phylloscopus inornatus   142
Pigeon, Bruce's Green   125
pika   24
Pilgaard family   202
pinna (ear tufts)   143, 144, 284, 285
Pipit, Asian Buff-bellied   110
  - Berthelot's   28
  - Red-throated   189
  - Richard's   163
  - Tawny   28
playback   74, 83, 97, 101, 104, 123, 258, 261, 267, 268, 271, 272, 276-278
Pleistocene   23, 24, 25, 41, 74, 89, 197, 198, 204
Plover, European Golden   163
  - Pacific Golden   189
Pluvialis apricaria   163
  - *fulva*   189
Poecile montanus   85
Poelstra, Jelmer   6, 166
Poland   47, 48, 89-91, 226, 234, 237, 247
Pontic Alps   41
Pop, René   6, 26-28, 33, 34, 51, 55, 59, 62, 68, 69, 104, 107, 111-116, 122, 137, 153, 168, 257, 258-264, 266, 267
Portel, La   197
Porto Santo   17, 29, 32, 156
Portugal   11, 13-15, 18-22, 28, 51, 52, 54-59, 93-97, 100-105, 112, 113, 133-136, 139-142, 156, 161, 173, 179, 180, 183, 240, 241, 245, 246
Potter, Harry   133
Pozdnyakov, Vladimir   6, 189, 190, 195
Praedicrostonyx hopkinsi   198
predation   23, 84
Pretorius, Matt   8, 158, 163
Pröhl, Kathrin   170
  - Torsten   6, 170
projection   134
Ptarmigan, Rock   196
Pterodroma deserta   29, 30
  - *feae*   35
  - *madeira*   26, 32, 282
Puffinus boydi   33
  - *olsoni*   26
purring   18-21, 36, 37, 166
Pycnonotus xanthopygos   259

Pyrenees   43, 240
Quail, Common   68, 163
Rabat   252-254
Rabbit, European   181
Rail, Water   134, 135, 163, 217
Rallus aquaticus   134, 135, 163, 217
Ramadan   126, 163, 168
Rana temporaria   100
Randazzo   62
Rat, Black   26, 156
  - Brown   184, 196
Rattus norvegicus   184, 196
  - *rattus*   26, 156
Raven, African Northern   137
Red Sea   125
redness   16, 22, 23
Redpoll, Mealy   85, 284
Redshank, Common   151, 163
  - Spotted   73
Regulus regulus   45, 85, 86
Reich, Steve   108
Rhodostethia rosea   190
Rift Valley   176
Rijswijk, Chris van   8, 234
Rissani   7, 171, 173-175
Robin, European   84, 87, 88, 90, 143, 181, 183, 218, 222, 225, 231, 232, 235, 244
roll, flight   45
  - location   44, 45
roosting   93, 119, 123, 143, 158, 178, 208-210, 239
Rosa, Davide De   6, 67
Rosefinch, Sinai   256
Rosmaninhal   13, 14, 19-21, 51, 52, 54-57, 59, 93, 95-97, 100-103, 140-142
Rousettus aegyptiacus   115, 267, 275
Rubythroat, Siberian   85, 141
Russia   94, 105, 141, 188-192, 194, 195
Sagres   104, 156
Sandpiper, Broad-billed   73
  - Curlew   189, 190
  - Pectoral   189, 191, 192, 195
Santa Luzia   34
Santiago   35, 36
Santo Antão   33-36
São Domingos mines   13, 18,

São Nicolau   35
Sardinia   17, 23, 24, 60, 67
Saudi Arabia   125, 126, 167, 169, 265
Saurola, Pertti   6 234
scale   89-91
Scandinavia   89, 197, 226, 228, 230
Schiphol airport   143
Schreier, Georg   6, 104
Scolopax rusticola   45, 84, 87, 183, 235
Scotopelia   193
scream, mobbing   21, 32, 37
  - rivalry   18, 27, 28, 36, 37
screech, courtship   13-15, 17, 19, 27, 28, 31, 32, 35, 36, 37
  - perennial   13-15, 17-19, 26, 28, 30, 31, 33, 35, 37, 76
Seal, Grey   147
Selvagens   155
Semenow, Peter Petrovich   213
Sender, the   234
Serbia   143
serendipity   280
Seville   180
Sharpe, Richard Bowdler   167
Shearwater, Boyd's   33
  - Cape Verde   33
  - Cory's   26, 29, 30
  - Lava   26, 28
Shetland Islands   91
shrew, long-tailed   22
  - water   22
  - white-toothed   22
Shirihai, Hadoram   282
Siberia   43, 189, 193
Sichuan   234
Sicily   23, 24, 41, 60, 62, 67, 68, 98, 99
Sierra Norte   180, 181, 183, 184
Sinai   265, 282
Sintra   15, 58, 59
Siverio, Felipe   25, 26
Sivrikaya   41, 42
skink, giant   34
Skokholm   60
Skomer   60
Skylark, Eurasian   91, 148, 149, 151-153
Slaght, Jonathan   8, 204, 209
Slaterus, Roy   6, 41, 188, 256

Slovenia   67, 200, 230-233, 237
Smith, James   8, 123, 264
Snipe, Common   15, 76, 78, 141, 148, 150, 151, 218, 243
  - Jack   73
Socotra   280
Söderhamn   216
Sofronov, Yuri   6, 189
Somalia   125
song, aggressive   54-57, 61, 65-67
song croak   157-160, 163
Sorex   22
sound,
  - reflections of   94
  - perceptibility of   9
sound tail   47
South Africa   158, 167, 176
South Korea   180
Souza, Jennifer de   6
  - Leio de   6, 204
Spain   22, 41, 60, 104, 142, 143, 161, 178-184
species limits   11
species properties   11
Sri Lanka   204, 205
Star Wars   84
Starling, Common   93
  - Spotless   101
Stefansson, Ove   6, 76
Stoat   150, 190
Stockholm   216
Strait of Gibraltar   157, 255
Strange, Ian   6, 151, 155
Strigidae   10, 16, 39
Strix aluco   **10**, 20, 48, 83, 93, 95, 105, 133-136, 139, 141, 202, 213, 216, 217, 228, 229, 238-249 (**238-239**, *239-240*, **241-249**, *242-246*), 251-255, 258, 265, 275, 276, 284-285
  - *aluco wilkonskii*   240, **241**
  - *butleri*   41, 248, 256-265 (*256-257*, **257-264**, *259*, *261*, *263-265*), 267, 269, 272, 277, 279, **281**, 281-283, 285
  - *davidi*   234
  - *hadorami*   282
  - *lapponica*   203, 214-227 (*214*, **215**, *216-218*, **217-218**, **221-222**, *223-226*, **225**, **227**), 285
  - *mauritanica*   248-255 (**249**, *250*, **251-254**, *252-255*)
  - *nebulosa*   215, 218-222 (**219-221**, *220*), 226
  - *nebulosa yosemitensis*   219

- *omanensis*   2, 6, **115**, 248, 266-283 (*266*, **267**, *268-270*, **269**, **271-273**, *274*, **275**, *276*, **277-278**, *278-280*, **281**)
- *uralensis*   46-47, *47*, *75*, 84, 200, 216, 217, 222, 227-238 (**227-233**, *229-232*, *234-237*, **235-238**), 247, 258, 273, 284-285
- *uralensis liturata*   230, 233
- *uralensis macroura*   230, 233-234

Sturnus unicolor   101
- *vulgaris*   93

Suarez, Pedro Lopez   36
subfossil   114
Suopajärvi, Matti   6, 47
Surnia ulula   48, 70-81 (*70*, **71-72**, *72-73*, **74-78**, *75-80*, **81**), 284
- *ulula caparoch*   **74**, 79
- *ulula ulula*   48, 70-81 (*70*, **71-72**, *72-73*, **74-78**, *75-80*, **81**), 284

Sweden   9, 39, 40, 46, 48, 76, 78, 85, 179, 192, 196, 215, 217, 225, 226, 228-230, 233, 238
Swift, Common   85
- Pallid   256

Sylvia melanothorax   106
Syria   65, 213
Tachybaptus ruficollis   144
Taïf   169
Taimyr peninsula   197
Tangail   206
Tangier   161
Tarantola caboverdiana   34
- *gigas*   34

Taurus mountains   201
Taylor, Philip   6, 195
taxonomy   11, 68, 187, 192
- integrative   11

Tchagra, Black-crowned   125
Tchagra senegala   125
Tenerife   137
Tennessee   74
Terpsiphone viridis   125
territorial barking   237, 247
territory   22, 42, 43, 48, 54, 56, 58, 60, 76, 79, 83, 89, 97, 116, 149, 154, 158, 159, 170-172, 174, 181, 184, 189, 196, 201, 203, 211, 225, 228, 229, 237, 240, 247, 250, 261, 267, 268, 277, 279, 284
- winter   79, 89, 196

Terschelling   150
Tetrao mlokosiewiczi   41
Tetrastes bonasia   45
Texel   146, 150

Thrush, Mistle   85, 228, 235
- Song   47, 49, 72, 78, 86, 88, 156, 181, 183, 186, 218, 222, 236, 244

Thunberg, Carl Peter   218
Tichodroma muraria   200
Tiksi   189
Tit, Coal   85, 106, 108
- Crested   *43*, 75, 85, 284
- Cyprus Coal   106, 108
- Willow   85

Toad, Common Midwife   **95**
- Dhofar   127, *164*, 165, 168, 278
- Iberian Midwife   **95**, 183
- Natterjack   52, 100

Tomé, Ricardo   8, 104
Treecreeper, Cyprus Short-toed   106, 108
Treron waalia   125
trill calls   83, 86-88
Tringa erythropus   73
- *totanus*   151, 163

Trois Frères   197
Troodos mountains   106, 108
Trujillo, Domingo   8, 25, 32
Turdus philomelos   47, 49, 72, 78, 86, 88, 156, 181, 183, 186, 218, 222, 236, 244
- *viscivorus*   85, 228, 235

Turkey   41, 42, 62-66, 68, 113, 118, 120, 122, 188, 200-213, 245, 280
twilight   72, 181
Tyto alba   11, *12*, 13-21 (**13-15**, *16*, **18-21**), *19*, *22*, *23*, 24-28, 30-33, 35-**37**, 39, 55, 57, 59, 76, 111, 133, 139, 169, 244, 245, 284
- *alba affinis*   17, 33
- *alba alba*   17, *22*
- *alba erlangeri*   14, **15**, 17, 23
- *alba ernesti*   17, 23
- *alba guttata*   **15**, *16*, 17, 21-23, 33, 284
- *balearica*   23, 24
- *balearica cyrneichnusae*   23, 23
- *capensis*   17, 158
- *delicatula*   16
- *detorta*   17, 24, 32-**37**(**33,** *34-36*, **35-36**)
- *furcata*   16, **17**
- *gigantea*   23, 24
- *glaucops*   16
- *gracilirostris*   17, 18, 24-28 (*25*, **26-28**, *27*), 31, 34, **37**
- *longimembris*   17
- *mourerchauvineae*   24

- *novaehollandiae* 17
- *robusta* 23, 24
- *schmitzi* 17, 24, 29-33 (*29-30*, **30**-**32**, *32*), **37**, 284
- *soumagnei* 32
- *thomensis* 36
Tytonidae 9, 16
Ukraine 226
United Arab Emirates 171, 265
Uppland 217, 228, 229, 233, 238
Uppsala 192
Ural River 124
Urals 79, 188
Ursus arctos 73
USA 17, 74, 138, 153, 196, 219-221
vagrancy 80, 91, 93, 105, 156
Vietnam 204
vocal development 187
vole 22, 42, 43, 47, 48, 71, 73, 74, 79, 89, 143, 144, 147, 150, 152, 184, 216, 224-226 (**225**), 238, 285
- Bank 48, 79
- Common 22, 147, 150
- cycles 42
- Field 79, 150, **225**
- Root 79
- Water **225,** *229*, 285
Voous, K H 8, 22, 167
Vulpes vulpes 139, 184
Vulture, Griffon 178, 182
Vyn, Gerrit 6, 17
Wadi Bisha 125
Wadi Dana 171
Wadi Darbat 15, 125-130, 165-169
Wagner, Richard 270
Wagtail, White 178
Wallcreeper 200
Warbler, Cyprus 106
- Sedge 15, 147, 148
- Yellow-browed 142
Watson, Mike 8, 121, 127, 257, 271
weight 85, 97, 184, 240
Western Sahara 172
Whaley, David 106
Wheatear, Cyprus 106
Wildcat, Gordon's 262
Willems, Frank 8, 213

wing-clapping 138, 139, 148-150, 158, 163, 285
Wolf, Arabian 15
Woodcock, Eurasian 45, 84, 87, 183, 235
Woodpecker, Black 44, 45, 73, 232
Wyatt, Claude Wilmott 282
yelping call 58
Yemen 125, 126, 167, 265, 280
Yläne 71
Yoğurtcuoğlu, Emin 6, 201, 203
Zagros range 213
Zambia 127
Zarudny, Nikolai 213
Ziziphus spina-cristi 115, 116, 266